Directors' Liability and Indemnification

A Global Guide

Consulting Editor **Edward Smerdon**

Consulting editor
Edward Smerdon

Publisher
Sian O'Neill

Editor
Carolyn Boyle

Marketing manager
Alan Mowat

Production
John Meikle, Russell Anderson

Publishing directors
Guy Davis, Tony Harriss, Mark Lamb

Directors' Liability and Indemnification: A Global Guide
is published by
Globe Law and Business
Globe Business Publishing Ltd
New Hibernia House
Winchester Walk
London Bridge
London SE1 9AG
United Kingdom
Tel +44 20 7234 0606
Fax +44 20 7234 0808
Web www.gbplawbooks.com

Printed by Antony Rowe Ltd

ISBN 1-905783-06-X/978-1-905783-06-9

Table of contents

Preface

Edward Smerdon
Reynolds Porter Chamberlain LLP

It was once the case that directors' conduct came under very little scrutiny. In recent years, however, the liabilities and duties of directors have grown in prominence both inside and outside the boardroom.

Much of the heightened interest has been fuelled by high-profile corporate scandals in Europe and the United States, such as Equitable Life, Enron and Worldcom. In accordance with a developing 'blame culture', directors appear to be an ever more popular litigation target, particularly for shareholders following corporate insolvency.

At the same time, many jurisdictions are introducing legislation that increases the responsibilities of directors, tightens the regulation of their conduct and makes it easier to bring claims against them. This has been through a combination of new official penalties and increased private rights of shareholders - whether individually or collectively - and companies themselves to bring civil claims.

With such developing exposure, the extent to which indemnification rights and insurance protection are available to directors has become increasingly significant. Without measures such as these to provide comfort, there is a risk that directors may be deterred from taking positions of responsibility.

Many companies are moving from operating on a purely national basis to exploring markets globally. Assumptions and misconceptions frequently arise regarding the true nature of the exposures faced by directors in any given place. The purpose of this book is to provide an accessible and comprehensive guide to the important features of liability and protection in 24 jurisdictions in order to assist directors and in-house counsel of national and international companies in making well-informed judgements about the risks they are taking, and to provide a valuable starting point for the private practice lawyers advising them.

Each chapter has been written by a lawyer who is expert in the field and provides guidance on the duties of directors and the claims that may be brought against them in the relevant jurisdiction. In addition, commentary is included on the prevailing claims culture and the availability of indemnification and directors' and officers' liability (D&O) insurance. Chapters have been structured identically for ease of reference and to assist the reader when comparing different jurisdictions.

I would like to thank the individuals and law firms that devoted considerable time and care in contributing their chapters to make this book the valuable resource that it is. I am particularly grateful for their efforts to produce consistently structured chapters, despite the diverse natures of the legal systems concerned. This, I believe, is one of the main distinctions of this book. I would also like to thank my firm, Reynolds Porter Chamberlain LLP, and its marketing department (Sarah Yetman in particular), for supporting this project. Thanks are also due to Kenneth Underhill for his assistance on the insurance regulatory aspects of the UK chapter. Most of all, I would like to thank Alison Clarke, a senior lawyer at Reynolds Porter Chamberlain, who spent countless hours reviewing each chapter and providing valuable guidance to our contributors. I am quite sure the book would not have been possible without her considerable skill and dedication.

Finally, several chapters in this book note recent legislative change. The position regarding directors' liabilities and protection continues to evolve rapidly. Further change is inevitable.

Edward Smerdon is a partner in the international risks and reinsurance department at City of London law firm Reynolds Porter Chamberlain LLP. He specialises, and has 12 years' experience, in the field of directors' and officers' liability, and is currently involved in claims against directors in the United Kingdom, the European Union and the United States. As an expert on liability, he has been well placed to advise upon and develop insurance products to protect directors, and indemnification arrangements between directors and their companies. In doing so, Mr Smerdon has become a leading authority on the interrelationship between D&O insurance and indemnification, and lectures widely on the subject.

Argentina

Sheila Böhm
Martín G Argañaraz Luque
Allende & Brea Abogados

1. Directors' duties

1.1 Nature of the duties

The Argentine Companies Law (19550)[1] contains provisions that set out:

- specific standards that must be met by the directors of a *sociedad anónima*[2] (SA) when discharging their duties; and
- certain tasks that they must carry out.

Each director has a duty of loyalty and care. Section 59 of the Companies Law provides that directors must, in handling the SA's business and affairs, "act with the loyalty and care of a good businessman". Non-compliance with such a standard makes them jointly and severally liable for the damage resulting from their acts or omissions. Section 274 of the Companies Law states that the directors are jointly and severally liable with regard to the SA, the shareholders and third parties if they do not carry out their duties according to the standards provided for under Section 59. They are also liable for the violation of laws, company bylaws or their implementing resolutions, and for any other damages resulting from wilful misconduct, abuse of authority or gross negligence.

The Companies Law contains specific provisions on the duty of care and loyalty required from directors. These include the following:

- Directors cannot compete with the SA in which they serve unless this has been expressly authorised by the shareholders' meeting;[3]
- Directors must disclose any conflict of interest to the board and the statutory auditor, and cannot participate in decisions of the board concerning such a matter;[4] and
- Directors cannot enter into contracts with the SA unless certain conditions are met ('interested director' transactions).[5]

1 Law 19550, April 3, 1972, BO April 25 1972, as amended (Arg).
2 A *sociedad anónima* is a legal entity organised and existing under the laws of Argentina. It is similar to a corporation.
3 Section 273 of the Companies Law. The possible conflict of interest that arises if a director is also a director of a competing SA is judged on a case-by-case basis.
4 *Ibid*, Section 272.
5 *Ibid*, Section 271.

Section 271 of the Companies Law states that contracts entered into between the SA and one or more of its directors are permissible if they relate to the activity of the SA and are executed at arm's length (ie, under market conditions). If this is the case, no prior approval or validation by any corporate body is required. However, if those requirements are not complied with, the transaction can be executed only with the prior approval of the board of directors (the interested director(s) are not involved in any decisions concerning the matter)[6] or, if the board meeting cannot be held due to a lack of quorum, with the prior approval of the statutory auditor. If the SA has no statutory auditor, an ordinary shareholders' meeting should be convened for the purpose of approving the execution of the contract.[7] Any contract executed without prior approval is null and void. Even if the board of directors or the statutory auditor approves the contract, the board must disclose this transaction at the annual shareholders' meeting. If the shareholders' meeting does not approve the contract or if a judicial decision invalidates that approval, the directors and the statutory auditor are jointly and severally liable for the damage caused to the SA, without prejudice to the liability of the shareholders that approved the contract.[8]

Under the Companies Law, a conflict of interest is presumed where a director is also a shareholder of the SA. As a result, he cannot vote at a shareholders' meeting to approve his own tenure as director.[9] For the same reason, directors may not hold a shareholder's proxy to vote at a shareholders' meeting.[10]

For listed companies, the standard set out in the Companies Law is reaffirmed and broadened by Section 8 of Decree 677/01.[11] This provides that directors, officers and statutory auditors must be loyal and diligent in discharging their duties. They must:

- ensure that, without exception, the SA's interest or the shareholders' common interests prevail over any other interest, including those of the controlling shareholders;
- abstain from obtaining any personal benefit from the SA other than remuneration for their position; and
- organise and implement preventive systems and mechanisms to protect the SA's interest to reduce the risk of conflicts of interest in their relationship with the SA, or in the relationships of others linked to the SA with respect to the SA. This duty refers to:
  - activities in competition with the SA;
  - the use or appropriation of corporate assets;
  - the fixing of remuneration or proposals in that regard;
  - the use of non-public information;
  - the usurpation of business opportunities for their own benefit or for the benefit of third parties; and
  - in general, all situations that create, or might create, a conflict of interest affecting the SA.

---

6 4 Ricardo Augusto Nissen, *Ley de Sociedades Comerciales* 360 (Editorial Ábaco de Rodolfo Depalma ed, second ed 1995).
7 *Ibid.*
8 *Ibid*, at 361.
9 Section 241 of the Companies Law.
10 *Ibid*, Section 239.
11 Decree 677/01, May 22 2001, BO May 28 2001, as amended and complemented (Arg).

Section 15 of Decree 677/01 has also created the audit committee to reduce the potential for a conflict of interest. This must be comprised of at least three members of the board of directors, the majority of whom must be independent in accordance with the criteria set out in Argentine securities laws and regulations.

Section 77 of Decree 677/01 sets out specific duties for directors, as follows:

- They are forbidden to use the SA's assets and any confidential information for private purposes;
- They are forbidden to usurp or allow others to usurp, whether by act or omission, business opportunities of the SA;
- They are obliged to perform the duties only for the purposes for which those duties have been entrusted by the law, the bylaws, the shareholders' meeting or the board of directors; and
- They are obliged not to create direct or indirect conflicts of interest with the SA when discharging their duties.

The director has the burden of proof where there is any doubt about compliance with the duty of loyalty.

Finally, in the case of listed companies, interested transactions (which include only those transactions involving a relevant amount[12] executed between, among others, the SA and its directors and officers) must comply with a specific procedure set out in Section 73 of Decree 677/01.[13]

1.2 Standard of care

The term 'standard of care' when applied to a 'good businessman' indicates technical capacity, experience and knowledge.[14] To evaluate compliance with this standard, the following will be taken into account:

- the dimension of the SA;
- the corporate purpose;
- the generic duties of a director and the specific duties entrusted to a particular director;
- the circumstances in which the director acted (urgency, information, etc); and
- how the duty of care was fulfilled.[15]

The duty of loyalty also requires that directors and officers not put their personal interests ahead of those of the SA. To comply with their duty, they must act in pursuit of the SA's interest and its corporate purpose.

---

12 One per cent of the net worth of the SA as shown in the latest approved financial statements, as long as the transaction exceeds the equivalent of Ps100,000 ($30,000 approximately).

13 This procedure requires, among other things, that certain information related to the interested transactions (background and records) be available prior to the approval of the interested transactions by the board of directors and the audit committee.

14 Isaac Halperín, *Sociedades Anónimas* (Corporations) 453 (Ediciones Depalma Buenos Aires, 1974).

15 *Ibid.*

1.3 To whom the duties are owed

As a general rule, directors of an SA are not personally liable to the SA or any third parties. Decisions taken in a regular manner are considered to be decisions of the SA.

However, as mentioned above, directors and officers owe duties to, and are jointly and severally liable to, the SA, the shareholders and any third parties for damages arising from:

- breach of their fiduciary duty;[16]
- violation of the law, the bylaws and their implementing resolutions;[17] and
- wilful misconduct, abuse of authority or gross negligence.[18]

Where an alternate director is substituted, he is liable for his decisions.

The bylaws can provide for the creation of an executive committee to manage the ordinary business of the SA, whose actions will be monitored by the board.[19] This does not exclude or limit the liability of the members of the board of directors.[20] In addition, the board of directors is empowered to appoint managers (whether directors or not) to execute such acts within the SA's ordinary course of business as duly delegated by the board.[21] Again, this does not relieve the directors from liability.[22] Managers must comply with the same fiduciary duties imposed on directors and, thus, are also accountable towards the SA and third parties to the same extent as directors (but they are not jointly liable with the rest of the managers)[23] for the performance of their duties.[24]

1.4 Common defences to and exemptions from liability

The defences to liability asserted by directors and officers are diverse and include:

- the statute of limitations;
- the delegation of particular duties to specific directors;
- the prior valid approval of the performance of the director;
- the claim that a business decision was adopted diligently that cannot be judicially reviewed as far as its merits, opportunity or convenience is concerned;
- the claim that a transaction was executed under market conditions; and
- failure to establish the elements of the cause of action.[25]

16 Sections 59 and 274 of the Companies Law.
17 *Ibid*, Section 274.
18 *Ibid*.
19 *Ibid*, Section 269.
20 *Ibid*.
21 *Ibid*, Section 270.
22 *Ibid*.
23 4 Nissen, n 6 above at 356.
24 Section 270 of the Companies Law.
25 For instance, for the responsibility of directors to arise, there must be damage and causality between breach and damage (see, for example, 4 Nissen, n 6 above at 375, 379).

(a) ***Exemption from liability***

There are two important exemptions from liability and they are both included in Section 274 of the Companies Law:

- If the liability results from a decision of the board of directors,[26] a director who attended the board meeting, who participated in the adoption of a resolution or who had personal knowledge of a resolution that violates the law or the company bylaws will not be held liable for damages caused by such violation if he leaves written, precise and concrete notice of his disagreement with such resolution in the minutes of the board meeting if present, or as soon as he learns of the resolution if absent,[27] and gives notice of it to the statutory auditor[28] of the SA before his liability is reported to the board of directors, the statutory auditor, the shareholders' meeting or any competent governmental authority, or before a judicial action is filed against the board members; and
- If the duties of the board of directors were personally assigned to certain directors by the bylaws or by the shareholders' meeting, the attribution of liability will be made taking into account the individual performance of each director. For this attribution of liability to apply, both the decision adopted by the shareholders' meeting and the appointment of such persons must be registered with the appropriate Office of Corporations.[29]

In the case of listed companies, Section 76 of Decree 677 indicates that the registration has been complied with when the information is provided to the *Comisión Nacional de Valores* (Argentina's Securities and Exchange Commission) and the self-regulated entity where the SA's shares are listed, without prejudice to the registration in the Office of Corporations.

(b) ***Expiration of liability***

Section 275 of the Companies Law provides that the liability of directors and officers towards the SA expires upon:

- the approval of their performance by the annual shareholders' meeting;
- the shareholders' resignation of the right to sue the directors; or

---

26 Halperín, n 14 above at 455.

27 *Ibid.*

28 In the event the SA does not have a statutory auditor (in the situations permitted by the Companies Law), the doctrine understands that the dissenting director has no liability when he has left written precise and concrete notice of his disagreement with a resolution in the minutes of the board meeting and requested at the same time that a shareholders' meeting be called to note the resolution that would potentially generate directors' liability. If the statutory auditor is present at the board meeting, it is sufficient for the dissenting director to leave his disagreement in writing in the minutes of the meeting (see, for example, Ernesto Eduardo Martorell, *Los Directores de Sociedades Anónimas* 409 (Ediciones Depalma Buenos Aires, second edn, 1994) (1990)).

29 See 4 Horacio Roitman, *Ley de Sociedades Comerciales Comentada y Anotada* 557 (La Ley ed, 2006) (arguing that in the cases where the assignment of duties is duly proven and registered, the director will be judged individually for his acts or omissions in accordance with the obligations imposed upon him); see also 4 Nissen, n 6 above at 383 (arguing that the registration of the assignment of duties to directors is relevant only when the liability of directors is sought by third parties pursuant to the 'individual suit' set forth in Section 279 of the Companies Law, since the decisions adopted by the shareholders' meetings assigning specific duties to directors should be presumed known by the members of the SA).

- a settlement approved by the shareholders' meeting. In such case, settlement with one director benefits all the others.[30] If the settlement is of a litigious claim, it will not be binding unless it has been filed with the appropriate judge and signed by the interested parties.[31]

In any event, liability will not be extinguished if it arose from a violation of the law, company bylaws or their implementing resolutions and if shareholders representing at least 5% of the capital stock oppose it.

The termination of liability is effective only with regard to the SA, and not third parties.[32] It is not effective in the case of bankruptcy, even if the shareholders have agreed to it.[33]

2. Who can bring claims

Two types of action can be brought against directors to redress the injury caused by a breach of fiduciary duty: a corporate suit and an individual suit. The former intends to restore the SA's net worth - that is, to benefit the SA directly, not the shareholders. The suit can be brought by:

- the SA itself;
- the shareholders of the SA in certain situations for the benefit of the SA (this suit is known as a corporate suit *uti singuli*);[34] and
- third parties, but only in the event of the bankruptcy of the SA.[35] In such case, the claim must be filed by the court-appointed receiver of the reorganisation proceeding or, in case of omission by the receiver, by third parties individually.[36]

The individual suit seeks to compensate shareholders and third parties for the damage suffered by them personally or to their net worth due to the wilful or negligent acts or omissions of the directors.[37] This is a direct suit, not a derivative suit, filed by the shareholder or third party on his own account.

2.1 The company (and its liquidators)

The SA can bring a claim against the directors following a resolution of the shareholders' meeting. This decision can be adopted even if it was not included on the meeting's agenda when it is a direct consequence of an item included on such agenda. The adopted resolution will enable the removal of the affected director(s), who will then have to be replaced.

---

30 See Martorell, n 28 above at 417.
31 See 4 Nissen, n 6 above at 392.
32 See Martorell, n 28 above at 415.
33 In this case, the liability suit will be filed pursuant to Section 278 of Law 19550.
34 See 4 Nissan, n 6 above at 394.
35 *Ibid.*
36 *Ibid.*
37 *Ibid.*

In the case of bankruptcy, a corporate suit may be filed by the receiver of the reorganisation proceeding or, in case of omission, by the receiver or by individual creditors.[38] For example, a corporate suit was filed by an SA and continued by the receiver where the court found that the influence of a former director had created a crisis that resulted in the bankruptcy of the company, given that it had worsened its economic difficulties.[39]

2.2 The shareholders for the benefit of the company

The shareholders may bring an action to benefit the SA in the situations described below.

If the shareholders' meeting decides to bring an action against directors, but the SA fails to do so within three months of the date of the decision, the suit can be brought by any shareholder, irrespective of his shareholding.[40] This is not to say, however, that the expiry of the three-month period precludes the SA from filing suit against the directors. The SA can bring such suit until the applicable three-year statute of limitations has expired.[41] In both cases, the suit should be brought only against the director responsible for the damage caused to the SA.

However, if the shareholders' meeting relieves the directors from liability, a claim can still be brought if the directors' liability arises from a breach of the law, the company bylaws or their implementing resolutions, and if shareholders holding at least 5% of the capital stock dissent to the waiver, as this resolution is not binding on the dissenting shareholders.[42] In addition, the dissenting shareholders are entitled to bring a claim against those shareholders who approved the release from liability.[43] However, if the dissenting shareholders do not hold 5% of the capital stock, they must bring an action to contest the resolution of the shareholders' meeting (as without such a minimum percentage, the shareholders' resolution is valid and binding) and cumulatively bring an action against the directors.[44] Therefore, the prior or simultaneous judicial declaration of the resolution as null and void is required.

Similarly, if the dissenting shareholders hold at least 5% of the capital stock but the liability of the directors does not arise from a breach of the law, the company bylaws or their implementing resolutions, those shareholders must contest the shareholders' resolution as a requirement to file, simultaneously or subsequently, a suit seeking the liability of the directors.[45] In all such cases the suit will be brought against both the SA and the directors, since the latter will remain in office until a judicial declaration of liability is issued, triggering their removal and replacement. However, if the directors do not remain in office, the suit should be filed against them only.

---

38 Section 278 of the Companies Law.

39 Court of Appeals in Commercial Matters, Section D, October 5 2004, *Establecimientos Metalúrgicos Crespo SA* v *Carlisi, Angel*, La Ley (2004–E-849) (Arg).

40 Section 277 of the Companies Law.

41 The statute of limitations starts to run as of the date that liability was imputed to the directors by the SA.

42 See 4 Nissen, n 6 above at 396.

43 *Ibid* at 397.

44 *Ibid* at 397 to 398.

45 *Ibid* at 398.

In the case of listed companies, Section 75 of Decree 677/01 provides that the corporate suit *uti singuli* described above can be brought by the shareholders to seek:

- compensation on behalf of the SA for the damage it suffered; or
- compensation for the partial damage suffered indirectly by the shareholders in proportion to their respective interests, in which case the monetary compensation will be for their own benefit instead of the SA's.

In addition, when the defendant director (or officer) is sued for the total amount of damages claimed to have been suffered by the SA, he can opt to settle with the plaintiff shareholders for compensation of the indirect damages they suffered, in proportion to their respective interests.

2.3 The shareholders on their own account

An individual suit can be filed by the shareholders and may be brought as a sole remedy or in addition to the corporate suit.[46] As mentioned above, this action seeks to compensate for damages directly suffered by shareholders due to the conduct of the directors. No prior resolution of the shareholders' meeting is needed and the pursuit of this action against directors does not affect the functioning of the SA because the directors remain in office.

Where the plaintiff ceases to be a shareholder of the SA during the prosecution of the action, he can nevertheless continue with the proceedings, as the compensation arises from damage caused to his own net worth.[47]

For this action to proceed, the conduct of the directors must have caused direct personal damage to the net worth of the shareholder filing the suit.[48]

The most common causes of direct personal damage include:

- denying a shareholder access to the shareholders' meeting;
- preventing the casting of a vote;
- preventing the exercise of pre-emptive rights;
- not liquidating dividends already approved and made available;
- distributing fictitious dividends; and
- not providing documentation that proves the status of a shareholder.[49]

2.4 Third parties

Third parties may also bring an individual suit. The definition of 'third parties' is broad and covers all those who are not shareholders of the SA and who have suffered damage as a result of the actions of the directors.[50] Some examples include:

- employees of the SA for claims against directors based on fraud with respect to labour or social security laws;[51]
- holders of convertible bonds; and

---

46 See 4 Nissen, n 6 above at 409.

47 Mariano Gagliardo, *Responsabilidad de los Directores de Sociedades Anónimas*, 644 to 645 (Abeledo-Perrot ed, second edn 1994); see also 4 Roitman, n 29 above at 601 to 602.

48 See 4 Roitman, n 29 above at 599.

49 *Ibid* at 602.

50 *Ibid* at 603.

51 *Ibid.*

- holders of debentures and bonds individually considered, or the trustee in his capacity as legal representative of the holders of debentures and bonds of the SA[52].

3. Claims culture

3.1 Litigation

The Companies Law is a federal law and its provisions do not differ substantially between listed and non-listed companies.

The liability of directors and officers is laid down mainly in Sections 59 and 270 to 279 of the Companies Law, although these are complemented by other specific regulations (eg, tax, labour, customs, securities, environmental and administrative regulations).

Although no statistics exist that allow us to quantify the situations that give rise to most disputes, we can assert that the vast majority of corporate litigation filed in Argentina concerns non-listed or family companies. The main source of conflict relates to managerial vacancies on the governing body, with the shareholder-heirs fighting to participate.

There are also other cases seeking the annulment of increases of capital stock; accusations relating to the abuse of majorities, non-payment of dividends or the transfer of assets or activities to other companies controlled by controlling shareholders or directors; and general liability suits filed against directors and officers.

Usually, these claims also involve the judicial intervention of the sued company,[53] although the courts grant this preventive measure restrictively.

The accusations levelled against directors and officers are varied. Even though the Companies Law contemplates specific situations that give rise to liability, the generic standards described therein that must also be followed by directors and officers in handling the business and affairs of the SA (ie, the duty of loyalty and the "care of a good businessman") have broadened the scope of the acts and omissions of directors and officers that may be attacked judicially. To date, the doctrine and jurisprudence have not created rules that shield directors and officers from liability, as has happened in certain countries such as the United States, with its business judgement rule. This lack of protection afforded to the business decisions adopted by directors and officers opens the door to questions about the management of the SA in its entirety, which results in an increase in litigation.

The lawsuits filed against directors personally are not always successful because they generally refer to situations imputable to the SA. However, claims against directors usually succeed where it is proved that they acted fraudulently, negligently or with gross negligence.

---

52 See Gagliardo, n 48 above at 644.

53 'Judicial intervention' as the term is used here is a provisional remedy that may be granted by a court where appropriate when the acts or omissions of directors put the SA in serious danger (Section 113 of the Companies Law). If granted, the intervention may entail the appointment of a receiver or court administrator whose duties will be determined by the judge (Section 115 of the Companies Law).

3.2 Ability to bring class actions

Class actions filed against the directors and officers of a company by its own shareholders do not proceed.

Few lawsuits are filed against officers and directors by third parties on their own account. Those that have been filed have involved, among other things, claims asserting that corporate structures were used to defraud third parties which, when proven, led the courts to pierce the corporate veil.

There have been cases in which consumer associations sue companies (although not their directors and officers) based on claims relating to the commercial activities of the company. In such cases, the companies have frequently questioned the legitimate interest of the consumer associations to pursue these lawsuits.

3.3 Funding of claims and whether loser pays

The court determines the allocation of legal expenses when it issues its decision. The determination of judicial fees is made in accordance with parameters established by law. The general principle is that the losing party must pay all legal expenses, unless there are reasonable reasons, according to the court's discretion, for the losing party to have defended his position, in which case the court may determine that each party should pay his own expenses.

The amounts of indemnification are determined by the court and the losing party is obliged to pay that amount only. In many cases, the costs of the wining party may be higher than the amount awarded.

The risk of an adverse costs award is a significant deterrent against frivolous claims. At the same time, most jurisdictions require the payment of certain fees and expenses simultaneously with the filing of the lawsuit, which can also play a role in this regard.

The court also determines the attorneys' fees. In corporate lawsuits, the extent of the work performed by the attorneys and the results obtained are taken into account, although the value of the company's assets cannot be used as the basis for such determination. The law that regulates attorneys' fees also allows clients to enter into agreements with attorneys whereby the client agrees to pay a percentage (usually up to a maximum of 30%) of the amount awarded as attorneys' fees.

3.4 Plaintiffs' bar

The plaintiffs' bar does not exist in Argentina as it does in the United States and other countries.

3.5 Procedural barriers

(a) Statute of limitations

As the Companies Law does not specify the applicable statute of limitations for liability lawsuits, defendants have raised the statute of limitations as a defence.

In corporate suits, corporate suits *uti singuli* and individual suits filed by the shareholders, the majority opinion prevailing in the doctrine and jurisprudence is that a lawsuit should be commenced within a three-year timeframe.[54] In the case of corporate suits or corporate suits *uti singuli* filed by dissenting shareholders holding at least 5% of the capital stock of the SA, the statute of limitations starts to run from the date on which the shareholders' meeting either declares or rejects the directors' liability.[55] In the case of corporate suits filed by any shareholder in case of inaction by the SA, the statute of limitations starts to run three months after the date of the shareholders' meeting at which the decision to bring the lawsuit was made.[56] For lawsuits filed by dissenting shareholders that do not hold at least 5% of the capital stock of the SA, the statute of limitations starts to run from the date of the shareholders' meeting that must be challenged.[57]

With regard to claims filed by third parties, the applicable statute of limitations depends on the particular action filed;[58] in the event that there is no specified statute of limitations, the applicable statute of limitations is two years.

(b) *Approvals required*

A corporate suit filed by the SA requires a prior resolution of the shareholders' meeting. However, once the decision to file the action against a director has been adopted, the remaining directors are obliged to bring the action. Non-compliance with such shareholders' resolution results in liability for those other directors.[59] Conversely, approval is not required for shareholders to file either:

- a corporate suit on behalf of the SA once the requirements described in section 2.2 are met; or
- an individual suit whereby an individual shareholder seeks to redress any personal and direct damage suffered as mentioned in section 2.3.

4. Indemnification rights

4.1 When the company can indemnify

Argentine law does not allow the bylaws of an SA to limit or exclude the legal provisions dealing with the liability of directors and officers.[60] This notwithstanding, once the event giving rise to liability has taken place, the shareholders may waive their right to sue the directors by approving their performance, expressly waiving the right to bring a claim or settling with them as long as:

- the liability does not arise as a consequence of a violation of the law, the company bylaws or their implementing resolutions; and

---

54 The statute of limitations applied in all these cases is set forth in Section 848 of the Commercial Code (Arg). But see 4 Nissen, note 6 above at 410 (arguing that the applicable statute of limitations for the individual suit set forth in Section 279 of the Companies Law is two years, regardless of whether the lawsuit is filed by a shareholder or a third party).

55 See 4 Roitman, n 29 above at 583.

56 *Ibid*, 584.

57 *Ibid*.

58 But see 4 Nissen, n 6 above at 410 (arguing that the applicable statute of limitations is the two-year term set out in Section 4037 of the Civil Code (Arg)); see 4 Roitman, n 29 above at 602 (arguing that the individual suit of liability prescribes two years after the damaging event took place).

59 See 4 Roitman, n 29 above at 591.

60 See Gagliardo, n 48 above at 519 to 520 (arguing that the doctrine rejects the inclusion of agreements limiting the liability of directors); see also Martorell, n 27 above at 415 (arguing that the liability of directors cannot be extinguished in advance concerning an event that has not yet taken place).

- there is no opposition from shareholders holding at least 5% of the capital stock.[61]

The issue of reimbursement and indemnification of directors by the SA is not explicitly contemplated in the Companies Law or Decree 677/01. However, it is widely understood that a director is entitled to reimbursement by the SA of any legal fees and expenses incurred in defending any lawsuits brought by shareholders or third parties. If the lawsuit is dismissed, the director has right to reimbursement against the SA because those expenses arose due to his capacity as a director.[62] However, directors are not entitled to reimbursement if the SA files the action because the shareholders' resolution deciding to bring an action against directors is seeking their removal. The court will determine the allocation of legal fees and expenses.[63] Finally, if a director is ordered by the court to pay any compensation personally to the shareholders and third parties, the director must pay this compensation, without prejudicing any reimbursement action that he may have against the SA.

4.2 Formalities for indemnification

A company may use its bylaws to outline the situations in which reimbursement is possible. It may also define those situations by way of a shareholders' resolution, as long as those situations are inherent to the performance of the directors' duties. Alternatively or additionally, directors and officers can seek protection by entering into indemnity agreements or hold-harmless letters with the shareholders of the SA or any other third party, or by availing of the coverage provided by D&O insurance policies. These are issued by insurance companies that are registered with the local insurance authorities.

In the case of listed companies, Section 74 of Decree 677/01 allows the SA to purchase insurance to cover the civil liability of its directors with respect to risks inherent to the performance of their duties, unless the company bylaws provide otherwise.

4.3 How indemnification works

There is no specific procedure that must be followed for indemnification. In the event of judicial proceedings, the defendant director may join the SA as a third-party defendant.

4.4 What cannot be indemnified

As mentioned in section 4.2, reimbursement will proceed if the situations giving rise to liability are inherent to the performance of the directors' duties. Personal obligations of directors unrelated to the tasks or duties inherent to their position cannot be indemnified or reimbursed by the SA.

Directors are not generally entitled to reimbursement or indemnification from the SA for penalties and fines imposed in cases involving gross negligence, wilful misconduct or criminal behaviour.

---

61 See Gagliardo, n 48 above at 520.
62 Halperín, n 14 above at 461.
63 *Ibid.*

5. D&O insurance

5.1 Ability of D&O insurance

Argentine law allows directors and officers to seek protection by, among other things, availing of D&O insurance policies issued by insurance companies that are registered as such with the local insurance authorities.

The Superintendence of Insurance approved the issue of D&O insurance policies for the first time in 1996. Currently, the Argentine subsidiaries of major insurance companies offer such coverage. These policies were designed on a 'claims-made' basis. They are enforceable because the Superintendence of Insurance approved this type of coverage as it has both a period of retroactivity and an extended reporting period.

However, in *Barral de Keller* a civil court stated at the end of 2006 that insurance policies designed on a claims-made basis were unconstitutional. It is worth noting that:

- in this case the policy had neither a period of retroactivity nor an extended reporting period; and
- while the ruling applies only to this case, it is now a precedent for future disputes.

The Supreme Court of Justice has not yet ruled on the issue.

The local D&O insurance policies offered on the Argentine market are basically structured as follows:

- Insured persons - provides coverage to directors and officers for losses, including defence costs, arising from claims filed against them for any wrongful acts;
- Corporate reimbursement - reimburses a corporation for its losses when the corporation must indemnify its directors and officers for claims filed against them;
- Employment practices liability coverage - provides coverage to directors and officers (and other employees in a similar position) for losses resulting from claims brought by employees for sexual harassment, failure to promote, etc; and
- Entity security coverage - provides coverage to the corporation itself for losses resulting from security claims.

Most cases in the Argentine insurance market relating to D&O coverage are based on the payment of defence costs relating to employment practices liability. However, it is expected that the number of claims (and their complexity) covered by a D&O policy will drastically increase in the near future, as there is a tendency to sue not only SAs, but also their directors and officers.

5.2 Local rules on cover provided under a non-domestic D&O policy

Argentine law provides that only foreign insurance companies approved by the Superintendence of Insurance may insure people, companies or assets domiciled or located in Argentina.

Foreign insurers may apply for registration with the superintendence through either a subsidiary incorporated in Argentina or an Argentine branch of a foreign company. However, a branch will be authorised to carry on insurance business in Argentina only if the laws of the country where the head office is incorporated provide reciprocal rights to an Argentine insurance company.

Additionally, if a parent company of an Argentine subsidiary obtains a global policy from a non-domestic insurer, the policy must be nationalised in Argentina (ie, issued through an Argentine insurance company with the same terms and conditions as the global policy). Otherwise, it could be interpreted that the Argentine subsidiary is not complying with local regulations.

It is therefore forbidden to insure risks of Argentines outside of Argentina. However, if a risk is insured abroad, Argentine law allows for the imposition of a fine of up to 25 times the value of the premium on the insured and the intermediary (or broker).[64] The insurance policy will be considered null and void and the insurance company will face a fine of up to Argentine Ps100,000 (approximately $30,000). The directors, officers and/or any other employees in a similar position will be jointly liable for the payment of the fine.[65]

64 Law 12988, Section 2.
65 Law 20091, Section 61.

Australia

Richard Midgley
Jodie Potts
Anthony Scott
Moray & Agnew Solicitors

1. Directors' duties

1.1 Nature of the duties

In Australia, directors' duties arise pursuant to equity, the common law and statute.[1] The primary statute governing directors' obligations and responsibilities is the Corporations Act 2001.[2] The statutory duties imposed by the Corporations Act exist in parallel with common law and equitable duties. Directors should also be cognisant of multifarious obligations, the general law and a number of other key statutes imposed: Commonwealth trade practices and state fair trading legislation, employment laws, environment protection laws, occupational health and safety laws, equal opportunity laws, taxation laws and the privacy laws will be of widespread relevance.[3]

(a) *Duty of care, skill and diligence*

Both the common law and statute impose duties of care and skill on directors. Section 180(1) of the Corporations Act reflects, and to some extent refines, the common law duty of care. It provides that directors owe a duty to exercise their powers and discharge their duties with a degree of care and diligence that a reasonable person would exercise in their position.

(b) *Duty to act* bona fide *in the interests of the company*

As a result of the director's fiduciary relationship with the company, equity imposes on directors the obligation to use their powers *bona fide* in the best interests of the company.[4] Similar duties also arise under common law and pursuant to statute. Section 181(1) of the Corporations Act provides that directors must exercise their powers and discharge their duties in good faith in the best interests of the company.

(c) *Duty to exercise powers for proper purposes*

A separate duty is imposed on directors to exercise their powers for proper purposes. This duty arises pursuant to equity, the common law and statute.

---

1 The duties discussed may be owed by persons other than those who have been appointed to the position of director. See the definition of 'director' in Section 9 of the Corporations Act. Many of the Corporations Act duties apply to officers that include directors.
2 Unless noted otherwise, all acts cited are statutes of the Commonwealth of Australia.
3 Detailed consideration of all of these obligations is beyond the scope of this chapter.
4 *Chew v R* (1991) 5 ACSR 473.

(d) ***Duty to avoid conflicts of interest***

Given the fiduciary relationship between directors and the company, directors owe a duty not to enter into arrangements in which they have a conflicting personal interest or which possibly may conflict with the company's interests. Section 182(1) of the Corporations Act also provides that directors must not improperly use their position to gain an advantage for themselves or someone else, or cause detriment to the company.

(e) ***Duty not to make improper use of information***

Section 183 of the Corporations Act provides that directors must not improperly use information obtained as a director of a company to gain an advantage for themselves or someone else or to cause detriment to the company.

(f) ***Duty to prevent insolvent trading***

Section 588G of the Corporations Act imposes a duty on directors to prevent insolvent trading by the company and to prevent a company from trading if to do so would result in insolvency.

1.2 Standards of care

(a) ***Duty of care, skill and diligence***

The nature and extent of the duty imposed upon directors by Section 180(1) of the Corporations Act and the common law are similar.[5] In determining whether directors have exercised reasonable care and diligence, one must ask what an ordinary person, with the knowledge and experience of the directors, might be expected to have done in the circumstances.[6] What is required of a particular director in the circumstances varies according to a range of factors, including:

- the size and business of the company;
- the position held by the director; and
- the experience or skills that the director held himself out as having.[7]

To some degree, directors are entitled to rely upon others in discharging their duty of care unless they know, or ought to know, facts that would deny such reliance on others.[8] As a minimum, directors are required to:

- become familiar with the fundamentals of the business in which the company is engaged;
- remain informed about the activities of the company; and
- ensure a general monitoring of corporate affairs and policies by way of regular attendance at board meetings.[9]

The 'sleeping director' will be accorded little sympathy by Australian courts.

---

5 *Sheahan v Verco* [2001] SASC 91 at 97; *Vines v Australian Securities & Investments Commission* [2007] NSWCA 75.

6 Per Santow J in *Australian Securities and Investments Commission v Adler* (2002) 42 ACSR 80.

7 *Daniels v Anderson* (1995) 16 ACSR 607.

8 *Daniels v Anderson*, above.

9 Per Santow J in *Australian Securities and Investments Commission v Adler*, above.

(b) ***Duty to act* bona fide *in the interests of the company***

The test to determine whether directors have acted *bona fide* is subjective.[10] A breach of the obligation to act *bona fide* in the interests of the company involves a consciousness that what is being done is not in the interests of the company and deliberate conduct in disregard of that knowledge.[11] Although there is some debate as to whether contravention of Section 181 requires deliberate conduct on behalf of the directors, recent case law suggests that a similar test is likely to be adopted in respect of Section 181.[12]

(c) ***Duty to exercise powers for proper purposes***

The courts have adopted a two-step approach in determining whether directors have breached their duty to act for proper purposes. The first step is to identify the objective purpose for conferring the power upon the directors. The second is to identify the subjective purpose for which the power was exercised and whether that purpose falls within the objective purpose.[13]

(d) ***Duty to avoid conflicts of interest***

Directors will be in breach of their duty to avoid conflicts of interest if there is a real and sensible possibility of conflict.[14] Equity will apply the duty to avoid conflicts strictly. A director's intentions or motives in breaching the duty are irrelevant.[15] A director of a company who is also a director of another company must not exercise his powers for the benefit or gain of the second company without clearly disclosing the second company's interests to the first company and obtaining the first company's consent.[16]

(e) ***Duty not to make improper use of information***

Directors are not permitted to use information acquired because of their position to gain a benefit for themselves, or someone else, or to cause a detriment to the company. Whether directors have breached this duty will depend on the particular factual circumstances of each case. However, simple disregard of a company's internal procedures and guidelines does not equate to improper use of information.[17]

(f) ***Duty to prevent insolvent trading***

Directors contravene Section 588G if they are aware, at the time the company incurs the debt, that that the company was insolvent or would become insolvent as a result of incurring that debt.[18]

---

10 *Howard Smith Ltd v Ampol Petroleum Ltd* [1974] 1 NSWLR 68.
11 *Marchesi v Barnes* [1970] VR 434.
12 *Australian Securities & Investments Commission v Maxwell* [2006] NSWCA 1052.
13 *Howard Smith Ltd v Ampol Petroleum Ltd*, above.
14 *Howard Smith Ltd v Ampol Petroleum Ltd*, above.
15 *Bray v Ford* [1895–99] All ER Rep 1009.
16 *Bray v Ford*, above.
17 *Adler v ASIC* [2003] NSWCA 131.
18 Section 588G(2) of the Corporations Act.

1.3 To whom the duties are owed

Directors owe duties to the company as a whole - that is, to the shareholders.[19] However, in certain circumstances, directors may owe additional duties to other persons, such as individual shareholders[20] and beneficiaries of trusts of which the company is a trustee.[21] Although directors do not owe a duty of care directly to creditors, they must take into account the interests of creditors, especially in respect of their obligations to prevent insolvent trading.[22]

Traditionally, directors of wholly owned subsidiary companies were not permitted to act in the best interests of the holding company. Section 187 of the Corporations Act now permits directors of wholly owned subsidiaries to act in the best interests of the holding company if the constitution of the subsidiary expressly authorises the director so to act.

Directors do not owe a general duty to act in the interests of employees.[23] However, the company and its directors will be subject to specific legal obligations in respect of employees arising, for example, under various laws concerning employee entitlements and prohibited conduct such as unlawful discrimination.

Directors may be personally liable at law in varied circumstances. For example, they may be personally liable to third parties in negligence in certain circumstances for misleading conduct proscribed by fair trading legislation or under provisions of the Corporations Act relating to misleading information concerning securities.

1.4 Common defences to and exemptions from liability

Various statutory defences are potentially available to directors under the Corporations Act. Some of these are discussed below.

Generally, provided there is no fraud or oppression of minority shareholders, the general meeting may condone a breach of duty by directors other than a breach of statutory duty.[24]

Directors will not escape liability for damages for breach of duty merely because the default of another person caused or contributed to the loss suffered by the claimant. However, it is necessary to establish that the alleged breach of duty caused the relevant loss to the claimant in an action for damages.[25] Accordingly, if causation cannot be established, directors may escape liability.

Damages in respect of some causes of action may be able to be reduced by reason of the fault of another concurrent wrongdoer or the claimant pursuant to legislation providing for apportionment of liability.

---

19 *Greenhalgh v Arderne Cinemas Ltd* [1950] 2 All ER 1120.
20 *Coleman v Myers* [1997] 2 NZLR 225 and *Brunninghausen v Glavanics* (1999) 46 NSWLR 538.
21 *Hurley v BGH Nominees Pty Ltd (No 2)* (1984) 37 SASR 499.
22 *Walker v Wimborne* (1976) 137 CLR 1.
23 *Parke v Daily News Ltd* [1962] 2 All ER 929.
24 *Angas Law Services Pty Ltd (In liq) v Carabelas* (2005) 215 ALR 110.
25 *Gold Ribbon (Accountants) Pty Ltd (in liq) v Sheers* [2006] QCA 335.

(a) *Business judgement rule*

Section 180(2) of the Corporations Act provides that directors who make a business judgement[26] will have discharged their duty of care in respect of the judgement if they:

- made the judgement in good faith for a proper purpose;
- do not have a material personal interest in the subject matter of the judgement;
- inform themselves about the subject matter of the judgement to the extent they reasonably believe to be appropriate; and
- rationally believe that the judgement is in the best interests of the company.[27]

Directors will be unable to rely on the business judgement rule if they failed to make a business judgement or, to the extent that they did, failed to establish that they made it in good faith for a proper purpose.[28]

(b) *Delegation of powers*

Directors may defeat claims for breach of duty if they have responsibly delegated their powers.[29] Section 190 of the Corporations Act provides that directors who delegate their powers are responsible for the exercise of those powers as if they exercised the power themselves, unless they believed on reasonable grounds:

- that the delegate would exercise the power in conformity with the directors' duties; and
- in good faith and after making proper inquiries (if required), that the delegate was reliable and competent in relation to the power delegated.

(c) *Reliance on information or advice provided by others*

Directors commonly rely on information or advice provided to them by others in exercising their powers. The issue of whether such reliance is reasonable may arise in proceedings issued against directors for breach of duty. Section 189 of the Corporations Act provides that reliance on information or advice provided to directors by employees, advisers and other directors will be presumed to be reasonable if the reliance was made in good faith and after the directors made an independent assessment of the information or advice, having regard to the directors' knowledge of the company and the complexity of the structure and operations of the company.

(d) *Disclosure of interest*

Directors who have material personal interests[30] in matters relating to the affairs of the company must give notice of those interests to the other directors.[31] The notice must include the nature and extent of the interest.[32]

---

26 'Business judgement' means any decision to take or not take action in respect of a matter relevant to the business operations of the company (see Section 180(3) of the Corporations Act).

27 The director's belief that the judgement is in the best interests of the company is a rational one unless it is one that no reasonable person in his position would hold (see Section 180(2) of the Corporations Act).

28 Per Santow J in *Australian Securities and Investments Commission v Adler*, above.

29 Section 198D of the Corporations Act.

30 'Material personal interest' is not defined in the Corporations Act.

31 A number of exceptions to this rule are set out in Section 191(2) of the Corporations Act.

32 Sections 191 to 195 of the Corporations Act.

(e) ***Defences to insolvent trading***

Section 588H of the Corporations Act provides for several defences to proceedings brought for contravention of the directors' duty to prevent insolvent trading, including the following:

- The directors had reasonable grounds to expect, and did expect, that the company was solvent and would remain solvent even if it incurred the debt;
- The directors had reasonable grounds to believe, and did believe, based on information provided to them by a competent and reliable person responsible for providing directors with adequate information about whether the company was solvent, that the company was solvent and would remain solvent even if it incurred the debt;
- The directors did not take part in the management of the company at the time the debt was incurred because of illness or for some other good reason; or
- The directors took all reasonable steps to prevent the company from incurring the debt.

(f) ***Court's power to grant relief***

Section 1318 of the Corporations Act gives the court a discretionary power to excuse directors for breaches of duties if the directors have acted honestly and, having regard to all the circumstances, the court considers that the directors ought fairly to be excused from liability. The court will probably be reluctant to grant relief under this provision in cases where the director has acted negligently, but honestly, where the breach is significant.[33]

2. Who can bring claims

2.1 The company (and its liquidators)

(a) ***Claims by the company***

A company is permitted to issue proceedings in its own name against its own directors, officers or other third parties.

Generally, the power to commence proceedings falls within the wide powers of management vested in the board of directors subject to the constitution of the company and the Corporations Act. [34]

A purported ratification of authority by shareholders was held invalid after legal proceedings had been commenced without authority of the board, which was deadlocked. It was held that while a limited power for shareholders to act in cases of necessity may be implied, there was no general reserve power to act.[35]

As discussed in section 2.2, a court may permit derivative proceedings in the name of the company if the board is unable to act, for example, by reason of a conflict of interest in commencing proceedings against directors for breach of duty.

33 *Vines v Australian Securities & Investments Commission,* above.

34 For example, Sections 198A and 198E of the Corporations Act. An attempt to issue shares by a general meeting was held invalid in *Saad v Doumeny Holdings Pty Ltd* [2005] NSWSC 893.

35 *Massey v Wales* (2003) 57 NSWLR 718, at paras 45 to 49.

Typically, the company may claim that directors have:

- failed to act in the best interests of the company and for a proper purpose;
- made an improper use of their position; or
- failed to exercise the level of care and diligence expected, subject to the business judgement rule.[36]

(b) *Claims when the company is insolvent*

A court-appointed liquidator has a statutory power to commence proceedings in the name of the company under Section 477(2)(a) of the Corporations Act. [37]

Once appointed, a liquidator is obliged to prepare a report for the Australian Securities and Investments Commission (ASIC) commenting on the causes of the company's failure and whether any further enquiry is desirable.[38] If it appears to the liquidator that, among other things, an officer or employee has committed an offence in relation to the company, or that a person who has taken part in the administration or management of the company has been guilty of any negligence, default, breach of duty or breach of trust, or has misapplied or retained any property of the company, then this must be reported to ASIC.[39]

The liquidator will also need to realise the assets of the company, which would include an assessment of possible claims against directors. The former directors are required to provide the liquidator with a report as to the affairs of the company. The liquidator also has the power to access the books of the company, and the right to examine certain officers of the company on oath and require production of documents from them.[40] The liquidator can also apply to the court to examine any other person about the examinable affairs of the company and require production of documents.[41]

If the company has no or few assets, the liquidator's investigations may be limited in the absence of third-party funding, as the liquidator is not generally obliged to incur any expense unless there is sufficient available property.[42] Third-party litigation funding is available in Australia.

A liquidator does not need court approval or approval of the creditors to commence a proceeding, but will often consult creditors, or a creditors' committee, about proposed proceedings. Section 479 of the Corporations Act requires a liquidator to have regard to any directions given by a resolution of the creditors or contributories at a general meeting, or by any committee of inspection. The liquidator may approach the creditors to seek funding for a proposed action.

A wider range of remedies are available to a liquidator against directors, officers and others beyond claims otherwise available to the company. Section 598 of the

---

36 Section 180(2) of the Corporations Act.

37 A liquidator in a voluntary winding-up can exercise the same powers as a court-appointed liquidator (Section 506(1)(b) the Corporations Act); an administrator may exercise any power the company would have if not under administration (Section 437A of the Corporations Act); and an administrator under a deed of company arrangement has powers as set out in the deed of arrangement.

38 Section 476 of the Corporations Act.

39 Section 533 of the Corporations Act.

40 Sections 596A and 597 of the Corporations Act.

41 Sections 596B and 597 of the Corporations Act.

42 Section 545 of the Corporations Act and *Clasquin SA v AAR International Pty Ltd* (1989) 15 ACLR 9. Some funding, however, may be available from ASIC through the Assetless Administration Fund.

Corporations Act enables a liquidator to seek a relief for any fraud, negligence, default, breach of trust or breach of duty in relation to a company. Part 5.7B of the Corporations Act provides further relief for voidable transactions that the company may have entered into such as unfair preferences, uncommercial transactions, insolvent transactions, unfair loans to the company and unreasonable director-related transactions.[43] A liquidator may also bring a claim against a director for insolvent trading.[44]

2.2 Minority shareholders on behalf of the company (derivative actions)

A statutory mechanism is available for derivative actions. Members and former members of the company, members and former members of related companies, and officers and former officers of the company may apply to the court to bring such a proceeding. [45] Derivative actions under general law have been abolished.[46]

Leave of court is required to bring a statutory derivative action. It must be demonstrated that it is probable that:

- the company will not itself bring the proposed proceeding;
- the applicant is acting in good faith;
- the bringing of a derivative proceeding is in the best interests of the company; and
- the proceeding involves a serious issue to be tried.[47]

While there is a rebuttable presumption against granting leave for claims against third parties if the company has decided not to pursue them,[48] the court must grant leave if the statutory criteria are satisfied. The burden of proof is on the applicant.[49]

To prove good faith, an applicant must show that he honestly and reasonably believes there is a good cause of action with reasonable prospects of success. If the proposed proceeding is for a collateral purpose, this may be an abuse of process and indicate an absence of good faith.[50] It is more difficult for a former shareholder or officer with nothing to gain directly from the action to establish good faith.[51]

The 'best interests of the company' criterion requires consideration of the benefit to and welfare of the company as a whole, as well as the interests of creditors if the company is insolvent.[52] The court may consider the degree to which the company may be affected by the proposed proceeding including the prospects of a successful recovery and the consequences of adverse costs orders. An applicant may be required to indemnify the company for costs and provide security as a condition of leave being granted.[53]

---

43 See generally Sections 588E to 588FJ of the Corporations Act.
44 Section 588G of the Corporations Act.
45 Section 236 of the Corporations Act.
46 Section 236(2) of the Corporations Act.
47 Section 237(2) of the Corporations Act.
48 Section 237(3) of the Corporations Act.
49 *Re Varsity Queensland Pty Ltd* [2006] QSC 356; *Swansson v Pratt* (2002) 20 ACLC 1.
50 *Chahwan v Euphonic Pty Ltd* [2006] NSWSC 1002; *Swansson,* above.
51 *Magafas v Carantinos* [2006] NSWSC 1459.
52 *Carpenter v Pioneer Park Pty Ltd* 211 ALR 457; *Charlton v Barber* [2003] NSWSC 745.
53 *Magafas,* above; *John Herbert McLachlan v Christoher Stephen De Vere* [2006] NSWSC 959; *Fiduciary* v *Morning Star Research Pty Ltd* [2005] NSWSC 442.

Authority suggests that a proceeding against a director or officer of the company for compensation is at least *prima facie* in the interests of the company.[54]

The requirement for there to exist a serious question to be tried[55] does not require a detailed review of the merits of the proposed proceeding or the resolution of evidence in dispute, which ordinarily will be a matter for trial. The test should filter out proposed claims that are frivolous or vexatious.

Ordinarily, written notice of the application seeking leave, together with the reasons for applying, should be given to the company at least 14 days before the application. However, the court has discretion to grant leave in the absence of such notice.[56]

Current authority supports the availability of the statutory derivative action notwithstanding that the company is in liquidation, although some opposing views have been expressed.[57]

The statutory derivative procedure does not limit the type of claim that can be brought, provided the criteria in Section 237 of the Corporations Act are satisfied. Derivative claims can be brought against company directors, officers, professional advisers or other third parties. The procedure can be used to ensure a company defends a claim[58] or even to pursue an appeal against an unsuccessful claim made by the company.

2.3 Shareholders on their own account

Where a company seeks to amend the rights of holders of a class of shares and not all members of the class agree, members holding at least 10% of the votes in the class may have the court set aside the amendment to their rights if the court is satisfied that the alteration would be unfairly prejudicial.[59] The application must be brought within one month of the variation, cancellation or modification to the shareholders' rights.[60]

In addition, the court has wide powers to intervene where conduct or proposed conduct of company affairs, or an actual or proposed resolution of members or a class of members, is contrary to the interests of the company as a whole. It also has power to intervene where conduct or proposed conduct is oppressive to, unfairly prejudicial to or unfairly discriminatory against a member or members.[61] Former members can apply for an order if removed from the register because of a selective reduction or where the application relates to the circumstances in which they ceased to be a member.[62]

There remains debate about whether and to what extent a member might be entitled to seek relief under Section 1324 of the Corporations Act for a wrong done to the company.[63]

---

54 *Magafas*, above; *Maher v Honeysett and Maher Electrical Contractors Pty Ltd* [2005] NSWSC 859.

55 *American Cyanamid v Ethicon Ltd* [1975] 1 All ER 504 at 510.

56 Section 237(2)(ii) of the Corporations Act.

57 *Charlton*, above; *Roach v WinnotePty Ltd (in liq)* [2001] NSWSC 822; *Brightwell v RFB Holdings Pty Ltd (in liq)* (2003) 171 FLR 464; *Carpenter v Pioneer Park Pty Ltd (in liq)* (2004) 211 ALR 457; *cf: BL & GY International Co Ltd v Hypertec Electronics Pty Ltd* (2001) 164 FLR 268 and the comments of Siopis J in *Promaco Conventions Pty Ltd v Dedline Printing Pty Ltd* [2007] FCA 586, at paras 34 to 38.

58 *Maher*, above.

59 Section 246D of the Corporations Act.

60 Section 246D(2) of the Corporations Act.

61 Sections 232 and 233 of the Corporations Act.

62 Section 234 of the Corporations Act.

63 *Mesenberg v Cord Industrial Recruiters* (1996) 39 NSWLR 128; *cf Airspeak Pty Ltd v Jetstream Aircraft Ltd* (1997) 15 ACLC 715; *Emlen Pty Ltd v St Barbara Mines Ltd* (1997) 15 ACLC 1107; *Port Kennedy Golf Country Club Pty Ltd v Port Kennedy Resorts Pty Ltd* [1999] WASC 253.

Examples of wrongful conduct include:

- an increase in share capital to dilute a minority's interests;
- amendment of the company constitution to enable an improper acquisition of minority interests[64] or to qualify a right to vote;[65]
- a decision by the majority not to bring proposed proceedings against their own actions;[66] and
- dealings between the company and entities related to the majority.[67]

Generally, directors' fiduciary duties are owed only to the company and not to the shareholders, unless the particular relationship creates fiduciary duties, but in that event such duties are likely to be limited.[68]

Where a member seeks damages for a breach of duty that was also owed to the company such that the company itself could sue, the member cannot bring a claim for loss that "would be made good if the company's assets were replenished through action against the party responsible for the loss".[69] A shareholder may nonetheless have personal claims against directors - for example, for misrepresentations inducing them to invest or by reason of the particular relationship or arrangements with directors. In such circumstances, the courts will be conscious of avoiding double recovery.[70]

Where a subscribing shareholder is induced by misrepresentation to acquire shares, he may still be able to make a statutory claim against the company without first being required to rescind the subscription contract.[71] Such a claim may be postponed to creditors under Section 563A of the Corporations Act in the event of liquidation. However, if the shareholder was not allotted shares but acquired them from a third party, then his claims will rank equally with creditors in the liquidation.[72] Claims against directors are not subject to these potential restrictions.

2.4 Third parties

Generally, a contractual claim by a third party would be against the company alone; although, depending on the circumstances, directors may have owed a personal duty of care to the third party. They may be liable to the third parties as accessories to misleading and deceptive conduct by the company.[73] Alternatively, if the directors themselves were engaged in misleading conduct, a direct claim may be brought against them under, for example, state fair trading legislation.[74]

---

64 *Gambotto v WCP Ltd* (1995) 182 CLR 432.

65 *Shears v Phosphate Co-op Co of Australia Ltd* (1988) 14 ACLC 747.

66 *Biala Pty Ltd v Mallina Holdings Ltd (No 2)* (1993) 11 ACLC 1082.

67 *Re Bright Pine Mills Pty Ltd* (1969) VR 1002.

68 *Charlton v Barber* [2003] NSWSC 745.

69 *Johnson v Gore Wood & Co* [2002] 2 AC 1, per Lord Bingham at paras 35 to 36. See also *Gould v Vaggelas* (1984) 157 CLR 215; *Chen v Karandonis* [2002] NSWSC 412; *Willoughby v Clayton* Utz [2005] WASC 47; *Thomas v D'Arcy* (2005) 23 ACLC 393; *Rodgers v ANZ Banking Group Ltd* [2006] QSC 190.

70 *Johnson*, above.

71 *Cadence Asset Management Pty Ltd v Concept Sports Ltd* (2005) 147 FCR 434 in relation to a claim under Section 729 of the Corporations Act; cf *Webb Distributors (Aust) Pty Ltd v Victoria* (1993) 179 CLR 15.

72 *Sons of Gwalia Ltd v Margaretic* (2007) 232 ALR 232.

73 Section 75B of the Trade Practices Act 1974. To be a party to the contravention requires proof of knowledge of the essential facts giving rise to the contravention – *Yorke v Lucas* (1985) 158 CLR 661.

74 *Houghton v Arms* (2006) 231 ALR 534.

There are also other circumstances in which directors may be responsible for conduct involving the company. For example, a director may be responsible for conduct in connection with misleading statements in a disclosure document,[75] a financial product or the provision of a financial service,[76] or for insolvent trading.[77] While directors may be obliged to have regard to the interests of creditors if the company is insolvent or about to become insolvent, no general independent duty is owed by directors to creditors.[78]

Where the company appears unable to meet its liabilities, including alleged liabilities, to third parties, claims against directors are more likely by creditors, such as ordinary trade creditors and financiers, customers or other persons with which the company has had dealings.

Additionally, the introduction of the proportionate liability regime in Australia[79] may result in the conduct of directors being more closely considered by defendants for the purposes of alleging contributory negligence against a company. A defendant director might also seek to deflect responsibility to other directors or officers in an attempt to reduce his own liability.

Generally, there are no specific formalities required for third-party claims, save for compliance with the relevant rules of court, but there are exceptions - for example, to bring a claim for insolvent trading, a creditor must obtain the written consent of the liquidator or seek leave of the court after giving appropriate notice to the liquidator.[80]

3. Claims culture

3.1 Litigation

The incidence of more active marketing by plaintiff lawyers and perhaps a greater awareness of rights, as well as the expansion of tort law and statutory remedies for misleading conduct and procedures for class actions, may have contributed to an increased perception of a compensation culture.[81] The swift rise of insurance premiums following the collapse of the HIH Insurance Group and the reduction of insurance capacity in Australia made tort reform a political issue, resulting in wide-ranging reform affecting substantive rights to pursue claims and new proportionate liability regimes in both federal and state jurisdictions.

It has been suggested that claims activity is generally lower following this tort reform.[82] This could be due to a number of factors in addition to the reforms, such as buoyant economic conditions, increased regulatory control and better risk management. There may also have been a spike in claims before the proposed reforms took effect. The use of alternative dispute resolution is widespread and, in practice, a large proportion of claims are compromised before trial. Litigation is more actively managed by the courts, which encourage parties to mediate before trial.

---

5 Section 729 of the Corporations Act.
76 Section 1041H of the Corporations Act.
77 Sections 588R and 588T of the Corporations Act.
78 *Spies v R* (2000) 173 CLR 529.
79 Provisions have been introduced in each jurisdiction (eg, Part VIA of the Trade Practices Act 1974 (Cth)).
80 Sections 588R, 588S and 588T of the Corporations Act.
81 S Clark and R McInnes, "Unprecedented reform: The new tort law" (2004) 15 ILJ 99.
82 JP Morgan/Deloitte 2006 General Insurance Industry Survey, December 7 2006.

The nature of a case against directors will influence the outcome. Where the claim relates to the wrongful acquisition or diversion of assets or exploitation of corporate opportunities by directors, the impropriety of the conduct, if proven, may be obvious. In cases of misrepresentation, where there has been some disclosure of information which has turned out to be incorrect, liability may be strict or, to the extent the representation related to future matters, the directors may have to prove they had reasonable grounds for the representation at the time it was made. Liability of directors as accessories is more difficult to establish. In a claim for breach of the directors' duty to exercise care and diligence, the business judgement rule reduces the prospect of a claim succeeding, as even a disastrous decision will not necessarily be a breach. Most cases will be factually dependent.

3.2 Ability to bring class actions

Class actions are permitted at federal level and in all state jurisdictions in Australia. Section 33C of the Federal Court Act 1976 typically establishes the procedural requirements.

The key criteria which must be satisfied to bring a class action under Section 33C are that the claims:

- are brought by seven or more persons against the same person;[83]
- are in respect of, or arise out of, the same, similar or related circumstances; and
- give rise to a substantial common issue of law or fact.

The 'claims' by each group member against the respondent need not be the same causes of action. [84]

The need for the claims to be against the 'same person' can be problematic where there are a number of respondents. In *Philip Morris (Australia) Ltd v Nixon*,[85] the applicants conceded that each member of the class was required to have a claim against each respondent. The court supported that concession. However, in *Bray v F Hoffman-La Roche Ltd*, [86] the majority expressed the view that statements in *Philip Morris* on this issue were incorrect, and that while the representative party had to have a claim against each respondent, the group members need not, provided the other necessary conditions in Section 33C of the Federal Court Act were satisfied. The position remains unsettled.[87]

The next requirement is the need for the claims to be in respect of, or arise out of, the same, similar or related circumstances. The meaning of 'related' depends on

---

83 In the event it becomes apparent there are fewer than seven persons, the court retains discretion to permit the class action to continue.

84 *Rod Investments (Vic) Pty Ltd v Clark* [2006] VSC 342, at para 36; *Hunter Valley Community Investments Pty Ltd v Bell* [2001] FCA 201.

85 (2000) 170 ALR 487.

86 (2003) 130 FCR 317.

87 Subsequent Federal Court decisions have followed the *Philip Morris* decision and suggested the comments of the majority in *Bray* were *obiter* (see *Johnstone v HIH Insurance Ltd* [2004] Federal Court Act 190; *Guglielmin v Trescowthick (No 2)* [2005] FCA 138. In *Rod Investments*, above, Justice Hansen assumed, without deciding, *Philip Morris* was correctly decided). However, the *Bray* position was supported in *Milful v Terranora Lakes Country Club Ltd* (2004) 214 ALR 228.

its context and requires practical judgements in each particular case as to whether there exists a sufficient degree of connection between the claims.[88]

The substantial common issue of fact or law requirement is potentially more problematic in multi-respondent cases. The 'substantial' element means 'real' or 'of substance', rather than 'large', 'of special significance' or 'would have a major impact on the litigation'.[89]

(a) *Outline of procedure*

No leave of court is required to commence a representative proceeding. The material facts in the pleading usually satisfy the elements required by Section 33C of the Federal Court Act.

Selection of the representative party or parties as the named applicant(s) in the proceeding is significant because generally only an applicant is exposed to liability for the respondent's costs, as other group members are immune.[90]

Once commenced, notice must be given to group members of the representative proceeding and their right to opt out before a specified date.[91] The court must approve the form and content of the notice and how it is to be given. A failure of a group member to receive or respond to a notice does not affect a step taken or order made in the proceeding.[92] A judgment in a representative proceeding will bind all members of the group unless they have opted out. [93]

Notice, with court approval, must also be given to group members prior to any settlement of the representative proceeding.[94] Court approval of the settlement itself is necessary.[95] Factors which the court will consider in approving settlement include:

- the amount offered to each group member, the prospects of success and the likelihood of group members obtaining judgment for an amount significantly in excess of the settlement offer;
- the advice received from counsel and any independent expert on issues in the proceeding;
- the likely duration and costs of the matter proceeded to judgment; and
- the attitude of group members to the proposed settlement.[96]

The court has discretion as to how any trial is to be conducted, but may determine issues between the representative and the respondent and the common issues first, and then reliance and damages issues for group members later. A separate trial may also be ordered in relation to any claims by a respondent against a cross- respondent, but those

---

88 See, for example, *Connell v Nevada Financial Group Pty Ltd* (1996) 139 ALR 723, where separate written and oral misrepresentations to various group members at different times were found to be sufficient. Where representations to thousands of shareholders in financial documents released to the public over a five-year period inducing shareholders to purchase or retain shares were also held to be sufficient.

89 *Wong v Silkfield Pty Ltd* (1999) 199 CLR 255 at para 28.

90 Section 43(1A) of the Federal Court Act.

91 Section 33X of the Federal Court Act.

92 Section 33Yof the Federal Court Act.

93 Section 33ZB of the Federal Court Act.

94 Section 33X(4) of the Federal Court Act.

95 Section 33V of the Federal Court Act.

96 *Williams v FAI Home Security Pty Ltd (No 4)* (2000) 180 ALR 459 at paragraph [19]; *Darwalla Milling Co Pty Ltd v F Hoffman-La Roche Ltd (No 2)* [2006] FCA 1388.

parties may be bound by earlier findings of fact or law. If the court can make a reasonably accurate assessment of the total liability to group members, then an aggregate assessment may be made.[97]

(b) *Popularity of class actions*

Class actions relating to personal injury claims as a result of defective or contaminated products or activities of large corporations were prevalent during the period of development of class actions. Attention has now turned towards economic loss cases and, in particular, so-called 'securities fraud' cases. Shareholders' claims have received a boost in recent times through rulings of the High Court on litigation funding[98] and shareholder rights.[99]

(c) *Other forms of group action*

Multi-claimant actions can generally also be brought by way of representative procedures. However, difficulties with such procedures may emerge, as they do not deal extensively with important issues such as identification of the class, the extent of persons bound by the outcome and distribution of any damages out of a global settlement sum.

Joinder of claimants as parties to one action is another possibility where some common issues of law or fact would arise if separate proceedings were instituted and if the rights to relief are in respect of, or arise out of, the same transaction or series of transactions.[100] However, the claimants, as parties to the action, would each participate in the conduct of the proceeding and be liable in respect of costs.

Court rules generally enable the courts to order separate proceedings to be consolidated, heard together or one after the other, or to stay a proceeding pending the hearing of another. The courts generally have discretion to order consolidation if desirable to do so, particularly where some common issues of fact or law exist and the rights to relief are in respect of, or arise out of, the same transaction or series of transactions.[101]

A 'test case' procedure might also be adopted, but this would often depend on agreement between claimants and the defendant about the extent to which relevant findings made in the test case will be binding as between the defendant and other claimants.

3.3 Funding of claims and whether the loser pays

The burden of funding a claim can be significant, although conditional fee agreements such as 'no win, no fee' arrangements with plaintiff law firms are now relatively common in Australia and are discussed further below.

97 Section 33Z(1)(f) of the Federal Court Act.
98 *Campbells Cash & Cash Pty Ltd v Fostif Pty Ltd* (2006) 229 ALR 58.
99 *Sons of Gwalia* and *Cadence Asset Management*, above.
100 Federal Court Rules Order 6, rule 2
101 For example Federal Court Rules Order 29, rule 5.

The High Court of Australia has also confirmed the right of third parties to enter into funding arrangements with claimants under which the funder is entitled to receive a share of the proceeds if the claim is successful.[102]

Liquidators, in particular, have for some time been entering into third-party funding arrangements in order to fund recovery actions either with litigation funders or with creditors.[103]

Subject to the court's discretion, costs ordinarily follow the event and a losing party will be ordered to pay the successful party's costs. Importantly, in a class action, only the named representative is exposed to the defendant's costs, whereas group members are not. The 'loser pays costs' principle can be a significant potential deterrent to claims without substance.

The court usually assesses costs payable by a losing party. These may, depending on the jurisdiction, accord with a court scale of rates applicable for the various tasks or having regard to charge-out rates and work performed. Costs are usually ordered on a party/party basis rather than a solicitor/client basis, unless some special reason exists, such as a failure to accept an offer of compromise or unreasonable conduct on the part of a particular party. In general, party/party costs cover costs which were reasonable and necessary for the conduct of the litigation and solicitor/client costs cover all costs unless unreasonable. Typically, there will be a shortfall between costs recovered from an unsuccessful party and actual costs.

The courts have discretion to order that security for costs are provided which is particularly relevant to cases funded by third parties for an impecunious claimant. The introduction of proportionate liability may also increase costs, as more defendants may need to be joined to ensure the prospect of a full recovery, or to limit liability, for any loss suffered.

3.4 Plaintiffs' bar

Several prominent Australian firms are generally regarded as plaintiff law firms and one such firm has recently become a listed company on the Australian Stock Exchange. They act in claims including major class actions ranging from securities actions to product liability cases and actively promote their services in these areas. They are alert to events that may give rise to claims and are able to deploy significant legal and managerial resources for the litigation. They have established relationships with some litigation funders.

Solicitor fee arrangements are subject to obligations imposed in each particular jurisdiction in Australia. Generally, solicitors can enter into conditional fee arrangements where they do not charge unless the claimant is successful. These are often 'no win, no fee' retainers, but the claimant may still have to meet disbursements and could also be subject to adverse costs orders. Some jurisdictions permit a modest percentage 'uplift' in fees if a conditional fee arrangement is entered into and the claim is successful.[104]

---

102 *Campbells*, above

103 *UTSA Pty Ltd (In liq) v Ultra Tune Australia Pty Ltd* (1996) 21 ACSR 457 and under Section 564 of the Corporations Act, funding creditors can seek a greater percentage of any recovery proceeds.

104 For example, in New South Wales and Victoria an uplift limited to 25% of fees is currently permitted.

3.5 Procedural barriers

Provided that the claimant can establish a cause of action against a director, no particular formality is required to bring a claim against a director.[105]

The limitation period for a claim against directors will depend on the cause of action relied upon. Generally, claims in tort, contract and misleading and deceptive conduct are barred after six years from the accrual of the cause of action. Where loss forms part of the cause of action, establishing when loss is first suffered - and accordingly when time starts to run – can be difficult.[106] Rights to extend the limitation period vary between jurisdictions.

In a class action, limitation periods are suspended until either the group member opts out of the proceeding or the proceeding is finally determined without finally disposing of the group member's claim.[107] However, constitutional issues arise concerning the validity of such provisions.

4. Indemnification rights

4.1 When the company can indemnify

Depending on the allegations made against the directors, a company may provide an indemnity against liability and defence costs in respect of civil proceedings, criminal proceedings and regulatory proceedings. The extent of the indemnity available will be governed by the limitations provided in Division 1 of Part 2.D2 of the Corporations Act and Section 77A of the Trade Practices Act, and general principles relating to illegality.

Division 1 of Part 2.D2 of the Corporations Act sets out certain restrictions on the extent to which a company can indemnify its directors for liabilities and defence costs.[108] Section 199A(2) of the Corporations Act provides that a company, including a related company, must not indemnify[109] a director against any of the following liabilities incurred as a director of the company:

- a liability owed to the company or a related company;
- a liability for a pecuniary penalty order or a compensation order for breaching, among other things, Sections 180 to 183 and Section 588G of the Corporations Act; and
- a liability that is owed to someone other than the company or a related body corporate and did not arise out of conduct in good faith.

The restrictions imposed by Section 199A(2) do not apply expressly to a liability for legal costs. The ability of a company to indemnify its directors in respect of legal costs is dealt with separately in Section 199A(3) of the Corporations Act.

---

105 Some procedural issues are, however, discussed in section 2.

106 In *Commonwealth of Australia v Cornwell* [2007] HCA 16, a claim was allowed more than 30 years after the relevant misrepresentations.

107 Section 33Z of the Federal Court Act.

108 Section 199A(1) of the Corporations Act also prohibits a company from exempting a director from a liability to the company incurred as a director of the company.

109 "To indemnify" in Section 199A of the Corporations Act and Section 77A of the Trade Practices Act 1974 includes an indemnity by agreement or by making a payment, and whether directly or through an interposed entity.

Section 199A(3) provides that a company, or a related company, must not indemnify a director against legal costs incurred in defending an action for a liability incurred as a director if the costs are incurred:

- in defending or resisting proceedings in which the director is found to have a liability for which he could not be indemnified under Section 199A(2);[110]
- in defending or resisting criminal proceedings in which the director is found guilty;
- in defending or resisting proceedings brought by ASIC or a liquidator for a court order, if the grounds for making the order are found by the court to have been established;[111] or
- in connection with proceedings for relief to the director under the Corporations Act in which the court denies the relief.[112]

Note 4 to Section 199A(3) refers to a company's right to give directors a loan or advance in respect of the legal costs pursuant to Section 212 of the Corporations Act. Section 212 provides that member approval is not necessary where a company enters into an agreement to make a payment (whether by way of advance loan or otherwise) in respect of legal costs incurred by a director in defending an action for liability incurred as a director of the company. However, if Section 199A applies to the costs, the director must repay the amount paid if the costs become costs for which the company must not give the director an indemnity under that section. It is also a requirement of Section 212 that it is reasonable in the circumstances for the company to enter into such an agreement with the directors.[113]

Section 77A of the Trade Practices Act prohibits a company from indemnifying its directors against a pecuniary penalty for a contravention of the restrictive trade practices provisions in Part IV of the act, and any legal costs incurred in defending or resisting proceedings in which the person is found to have such a liability.[114]

Similarly, a company may legally lend moneys to directors to defend proceedings for contraventions of the restrictive trade practices provisions in the Trade Practices Act on the basis that such moneys are repayable if the proceedings are successful.[115]

Directors should also be aware of the effect of Section 199B of the Corporations Act, which prohibits a company, or related company, from paying a premium for a contract insuring a director against a liability (other than one for legal costs) arising out of:

- conduct involving a wilful breach of duty in relation to the company; or
- a contravention of Section 182 or 183 of the Corporations Act.[116]

---

110 For the purposes of Section 199A(3), the outcome of proceedings is the outcome of the proceedings and any appeal in relation to the proceedings (Section 199A(3)(4)).

111 Section 199A(3)(c) does not apply to costs incurred in responding to actions taken by ASIC or a liquidator as part of an investigation before commencing proceedings for the court order.

112 For example, an application pursuant to Section 1318.

113 Section 212(3) of the Corporations Act sets out the factors which must be taken into consideration when determining reasonableness.

114 Section 77A of the Trade Practices Act 1974.

115 This possibility is suggested in the explanatory memorandum for these provisions when introduced into the Trade Practices Act 1974.

116 As discussed above, these provisions deal with the directors' duties not to misuse their position or make improper use of information.

4.2 Formalities for indemnification

Indemnification of directors is permissive in nature. The limitations on a company's right to indemnify its directors are set out in Sections 199A and 199B of the Corporations Act and Section 77A of the Trade Practices Act. Other limitations may exist under general law principles relating to illegality.

A company's constitution may include indemnities in favour of directors. It is common for Australian companies to provide indemnities to directors, which are usually recorded in a deed. The nature and extent of the indemnity will vary depending on the agreement reached between the directors and the company. However, any provision that purports to indemnify a person against a liability prohibited by Section 199A or 199B the Corporations Act is void to the extent that it contravenes those provisions.[117]

Companies are not obliged to enter into indemnity agreements with their directors. Directors should request that the company indemnify them against liability and defence costs to the full extent permitted by the law. Any such agreement should be recorded in writing and should set out the mechanisms by which directors may enforce the indemnities so as to avoid any future disputes. Directors should seek specific legal advice before signing any such agreement to ensure that the indemnity is drafted in the widest permissible terms.

4.3 How indemnification works

Directors should ensure that the company's constitution permits indemnification of directors. If indemnification is available, it is common for the ambit of the indemnity to be defined in a deed. The deed may contain provisions dealing not only with the scope of the indemnity, but also with procedural requirements for its enforcement.

4.4 What cannot be indemnified

A company may indemnify directors in relation to proceedings where allegations of gross negligence, wilful misconduct, criminal behaviour or a liability to the company is alleged, including advancing defence costs. The mere making of an allegation, without more, does not preclude an indemnity.[118] However, if such liability is established by a determination of a court, then the restrictions in Sections 199A and 77A and the general law are enlivened and such an indemnity may be rendered void. Any advance defence costs must then be repaid.

Companies are not permitted to indemnify directors for penalty or compensation orders for breaches of a number of provisions of the Corporations Act, including Sections 180 to 183 and Section 588G or for penalties for contravention of Part IV of TPA 1974. General principles of illegality may also intervene to preclude indemnification by the company in respect of other penalties.

---

117 Section 199C(2) of the Corporations Act.

118 *ASIC; In the Matter of Lanepoint Enterprises Pty Ltd ACN 110 693 251 v Lanepoint Enterprises Pty Ltd ACN 110 693 251; ASIC; In the Matter of Bowesco Pty Ltd ACN 008 915 357 (Receiver and Manager Appointed) v Bowesco Pty Ltd ACN 008 915 357 (Receiver and Manager Appointed) (No 2)* [2006] FCA1493.

5. D&O insurance

5.1 Availability of D&O insurance

Directors' and officers' liability insurance is widely available in Australia. There are significant differences between policies available in the Australian market.

The scheme of a common form of cover provides indemnity to the insured persons for loss arising from claims first made during the period of insurance. This insurance covers claims arising from wrongful acts committed by the insured persons in connection with the performance of their duties as a director or officer of the named company. The definition of 'loss' will usually extend to costs incurred by the insured persons in the defence or settlement of claims with the insurer's consent, as well as to liabilities to third parties pursuant to a judgment or settlement.

In addition, the policy will usually indemnify the named company for loss for which it is permitted to indemnify the insured persons arising from such claims. The company will not be covered for its own liability to third parties, although policies are sometimes extended to provide limited 'entity cover' in respect of particular risks. Directors' and officers' liability cover is also sometimes combined with other covers in a broad-form liability policy arranged by the company. Further, directors may be entitled to the benefit of a range of third-party liability policies arranged by the company or standalone legal expense policies.

Personal directors' and officers' cover is available in Australia. Such cover may be particularly worthy of consideration by directors who are members of multiple boards who are retiring from a board, or where directors consider that the terms of any insurance arranged on behalf of all of the directors of the company may be insufficient.

5.2 Local rules on cover provided under a non-domestic D&O policy

Directors, whether resident or non-resident, may have the benefit of D&O insurance arranged outside Australia, but covering Australian risks. For example, a parent company of a resident subsidiary might obtain a global policy from a non-domestic insurer, which covers directors of the subsidiary.

Issues may arise as to whether Australian law applies to such policies. In Australia, the primary statute regulating contracts of general insurance[119] is the Insurance Contracts Act 1984.[120] The act contains a wide range of provisions affecting the rights and remedies of both the insured and insurers. Significant modifications to the common law position are effected. Broadly speaking, the reach of the act extends to contracts of insurance, or proposed contracts, the proper law of which is an Australian state or territory.[121]

119 Section 9 of the act sets out details of exempt contracts (eg, contracts of reinsurance).

120 The Commonwealth government has proposed a range of amendments to the act that are currently in the form of an exposure draft of a bill to amend the act. The proposed reforms include new provisions that would widen the application of the act to contracts entered into, or proposed to be entered into, by persons domiciled in Australia and that provide, or would provide, cover against risk of loss or damage occurring in Australia. Some state legislation is also relevant.

121 What is the proper law will be determined by the rules of private international law. In determining this issue, the existence of an express provision in the contract specifying that the proper law is a foreign law of the issue is not determinative: see Section 8 of the Insurance Contracts Act; *Akai v Peoples Insurance Co Ltd* (1995) ANZIC 61–254. Contracts of insurance relating to Australian risks sometimes provide expressly that Australian law applies. Choice of law provisions should be the subject of specific advice.

A range of statutes regulates general insurance business in Australia. The Insurance Act 1973 is of particular importance. It is an offence for a person other than a body corporate or, subject to certain conditions, a Lloyds' underwriter, to carry on general insurance business in Australia.[122] Authorisation or specific exemption under the act is then a precondition to the lawful carrying on of general insurance business in Australia.[123]

The Australian Prudential Regulation Authority regulates authorisation and revocation of authority.[124] Compliance with certain prudential standards is mandated. There are specific provisions in the act relating to the carrying on of insurance business in Australia by Lloyds' underwriters.[125] Complex issues can arise in relation to contracts of general insurance made with an unauthorised insurance company.

122 Sections 9 to 10 of the Insurance Act 1973.

123 'Insurance business' is defined as "the business of undertaking liability, by way of insurance (including reinsurance) in respect of any loss or damage, including liability to pay damages or compensation, contingent on the happening of a specified event".

124 Information concerning the regulation of general insurance business is available on the website of the Australian Prudential Regulatory Authority at www.apra.gov.au.

125 See Part VII of the Insurance Act 1973. The Commonwealth government has foreshadowed amendments to the act to provide for a new regime in relation to the authorisation of direct offshore foreign insurers.

Bermuda, the British Virgin Islands and the Cayman Islands

Robert Briant
Kevin Butler
Graham Collis
Christian Luthi
Conyers Dill & Pearman

The powers of directors of a Bermuda, British Virgin Islands (BVI) or Cayman company are prescribed by the company's memorandum of association and bylaws/articles of association, and the relevant companies statutes:

- the Companies Act 1981 (the Bermuda Act);
- the BVI Business Companies Act 2004 (the BVI Act); and
- the Companies Law (2004 Revision) Act (the Cayman Act).

Directors' powers may extend to include the exclusive management of the company's business and the exercise of all its powers, except for those powers that the law requires requires be exercised by the company's shareholders in general meeting.

1. Directors' duties

1.1 Nature of the duties

The common law of Bermuda, BVI and Cayman provides that directors have a duty to exercise their powers carefully (the duty of skill and care), and with good faith and honesty (fiduciary duties).

(a) *Duty of skill and care*

A director must discharge his duties with skill, care and diligence. He is not required to give continuous attention to the affairs of the company. A director's duties are to be performed only at periodic board meetings. He is not bound to attend all board meetings, but he should attend them when he is reasonably able to do so.

Directors may, and in appropriate circumstances should, rely on the advice of independent outside advisers, provided that the directors have reason to believe that the advisers are appropriately qualified and the directors exercise their independent discretion in respect of the advice.

A director will not be liable for the acts of co-directors or other company officers solely by virtue of his position. A director is entitled to rely on co-directors or company officers, as well as subordinates who are expressly charged with day-to-day management, provided such reliance is honest and reasonable and the director is satisfied that the delegates have the requisite skills to discharge the functions delegated to them. However, the board cannot absolve itself from all responsibility to the company by delegating its powers to others. The board should require a regular flow of information from its delegates to ensure that they are fulfilling their obligations satisfactorily.

Directors who fail in their duty of skill and care will be regarded as negligent in the performance of their duties and will be liable to the company for any damage caused by their negligence.

(b) *Fiduciary duties*

A director's fiduciary duties require that he act honestly and in good faith, use his powers for proper purposes, not put himself in a position where his interests conflict with those of the company and not make secret profits. ·

(c) *Duty to act honestly and in good faith*

Directors must act in what they consider to be the best interests of the company and its present and future shareholders. If the company is insolvent, or nearly so, the directors must also have regard to the interests of creditors. It is for the directors, in the exercise of their business judgement, to determine how the business of the company should be conducted. In general, the courts of Bermuda, BVI and Cayman will interfere with a decision of a director only if there is evidence of bad faith or if the court believes that no reasonable director could come to the conclusion that the decision in question was in the interests of the company.

The Bermuda Act deems a director not to be acting honestly and in good faith if he fails to provide the company's auditors, when requested, with information concerning his remuneration or benefits, or if he fails to disclose his interest in a material contract with the company or its subsidiaries.

(d) *Duty to exercise powers for a proper purpose*

Directors may exercise only those powers given to them by the company's memorandum of association and bylaws/articles of association, and must exercise those powers only for the purposes for which they were intended.

(e) *Duty to avoid conflicts of interest*

Directors must not put themselves in a position where there is an actual or potential conflict between their personal interests and their duties to the company, or between their duty to a third party and their duty to the company. If they do so, any contract with the director may be voided by the company and the director will be liable to account to the company for any profits. A director, may, however, be interested in a contract with the company if permitted by the bylaws/articles of association or if authorised by a meeting of shareholders.

The nature of a director's interest in any arrangement with the company should be declared by the director at the board meeting that considers the arrangement. If a director becomes interested in a contract with the company after it is made, the director should disclose this interest to the board at the first opportunity.

A 'nominee' who, with the consent of the company, represents the interests of his appointor on the board is not in breach of his duty to the company, provided that he preserves a substantial degree of independent discretion in the exercise of his powers and, if a conflict arises between the interests of the company and those of the appointor, he does not subordinate the interests of the company to the interests of his appointor. A nominee director may not pass confidential information to his appointor.

A director is not prohibited from acting as a director of a competing company unless there is a real possibility of conflict. However, in such circumstances, a director must not exploit an opportunity belonging to his company, fetter his discretion on the exercise of his powers or subordinate the interests of his company to the interests of the competitor.

(f) ***Duty not to make secret profits***

A director is prohibited from making secret profits from his use of corporate assets, opportunities or information, and is liable to account to the company for such profits or for any losses the company may suffer. Such profits will include secret commissions, bribes and the use of trade secrets. If the director exploits an opportunity that came to him by virtue of his directorship, he is liable to the company whether or not the profits would otherwise have gone to the company. It is no defence for a director to claim that he acted honestly and in good faith, but approval of the act by the company's shareholders in a general meeting will absolve the director from liability.

(g) ***Statutory duties and obligations***

The Bermuda Act, the BVI Act and the Cayman Act impose additional specific duties and obligations on directors and companies. Where the obligation is placed on the company, the directors are responsible for ensuring proper compliance with the law.

(i) *The Bermuda Act*

The Bermuda Act imposes a range of duties on directors with regard to the operation of the company. These include:

- maintaining accounts and statutory registers and records;
- making certain information available to shareholders and the public; and
- such other general duties as are contained within Part VI of the Bermuda Act.

The Bermuda Act also sets out the circumstances under which directors will have civil or criminal liability or be liable for default fines.

Directors are responsible for the payment of dividends which, pursuant to the Bermuda Act, may be made only where they have reasonable grounds to believe that the company is and, after payment of the dividend, will be able to pay its liabilities as they become due, and that the realisable value of the company's assets will not be less than the aggregate of its liabilities and its issued share capital and share premium accounts.

If a director knows that a prospectus contains a material misrepresentation, he commits a criminal offence. There are also civil and criminal penalties for directors who permit the allotment of shares or the provision of financial assistance in connection with the acquisition of company shares in contravention of the Bermuda Act.

It is the duty of the directors to keep proper books of account and, unless waived by all directors and all members of the company, the directors are obliged to lay before the company in general meeting audited financial statements for the relevant period prepared in accordance with generally accepted accounting principles.

It is not lawful for a Bermuda company to make a loan or enter into a guarantee, or to provide security in connection with a loan to a director (which includes his spouse and children and companies where any of them control more than 20% of their capital or loan debt), except with the consent of shareholders holding in the aggregate not less than nine-tenths of the total voting rights of all shareholders of the company having the right to vote.

Any conveyance, mortgage, delivery of goods, payment or other act relating to property made or done by or against a company in the six months before the commencement of winding-up, with a view to giving one creditor a preference over another, will, in the event of the company being wound up, be deemed a fraudulent preference and be invalid.

The Bermuda Criminal Code Act 1967 prescribes offences for misleading statements and practices, market manipulation and insider dealing in respect of shares listed on the Bermuda Stock Exchange.

(ii) *The BVI Act*

This provides that a director shall exercise his powers as a director for a proper purpose and shall not act, or agree to the company acting, in a manner that contravenes the BVI Act or the memorandum or articles of association of the company.

Subject to the BVI Act and a company's memorandum and articles of association, a company has, irrespective of corporate benefit, full capacity to carry on or undertake any business or activity, do any act or enter into any transaction with full rights, powers and privileges. No act of a BVI company and no transfer of an asset by or to a company is invalid only by reason of the fact that the company did not have the capacity, right or power to perform the act or to transfer or receive the asset.

The BVI Act requires that a director of a company, after becoming aware that he is interested in a transaction entered into or to be entered into by the company, disclose the interest to the board of the company. However, the director is not required to comply with this requirement if the transaction or proposed transaction is or is to be entered into in the ordinary course of the company's business and on the usual terms and conditions. Disclosure is not made to the board unless it is made or brought to the attention of every director on the board, but the failure by a director to disclose his interest does not affect the validity of the transaction entered into by the director or the company. A director who fails to disclose his interest commits an offence and is liable, on summary conviction, to a fine of $10,000.

A transaction entered into by a BVI company in respect of which a director is interested is voidable by the company unless the director's interest was disclosed prior to the company entering into the transaction or did not need to be disclosed. However, a transaction is not voidable if the material facts of the interest of the director are known by the members of the company and the transaction is approved or ratified by resolution of the members, or the company received fair value for the transaction. A director who is interested in a transaction may:

- vote on a matter relating to the transaction;
- attend directors' meetings at which matters relating to the transaction arise;
- be included for the purposes of a quorum; and
- sign documents on behalf of the company or do other things in his capacity as a director that relate to the transaction.

Further, the avoidance of a transaction does not affect the title or interest of a third party in or to property which that party has acquired if the property was acquired by the third party for valuable consideration and without knowledge of the improper circumstances under which the transferor acquired the property from the company.

Directors of a BVI company may, by resolution, authorise a distribution - including a dividend – to the shareholders, provided that they are satisfied on reasonable grounds that immediately after the distribution, the value of the company's assets will exceed its liabilities and the company will be able to pay its debts as they fall due. An action may be brought against the directors for failing to ensure the company satisfies this solvency test.

Before issuing shares for consideration other than money, the directors of a BVI company must pass a resolution stating:

- the amount to be credited to the company for the issue of the shares;
- their determination of the reasonable present cash value of the non-money consideration; and
- that, in their opinion, the present cash value of the non-money consideration for the issue is not less than the amount to be credited to the company for the issue of the shares.

The directors are also responsible for ensuring that the company keep a register of all relevant charges created by the BVI company showing:

- the date of creation of the charge or, if the charge is a charge existing on property acquired by the company, the date on which the property was acquired;
- a short description of the liability secured by the charge;
- a short description of the property charged;
- the name and address of the trustee for the security or, if there is no such trustee, the name and address of the chargee;
- the name and address of the holder of the charge; and
- details of any prohibition or restrictions, if any, contained in the instrument creating the charge on the power of the company to create any future charge

ranking in priority to, or equally with, the charge.

The BVI Act requires BVI companies to observe the following requirements, and a director who knowingly permits the company to breach them will be liable to a penalty for every day or part thereof that the breach continues:

- not to carry on business that is expressly prohibited;
- to maintain accounts and records in accordance with the BVI Act;
- to maintain a registered office and registered agent in accordance with the BVI Act; and
- to file compliant articles of dissolution on the company's dissolution.

(iii) *The Cayman Act*

This provides that a director may be liable on summary conviction to a fine or to imprisonment for a variety of offences, including where:

- in relation to a reduction of share capital, the director wilfully conceals the name of any creditor entitled to object to the reduction or wilfully misrepresents the nature of the debt or claim of any creditor, or aids, abets or is privy to any such concealment or misrepresentation;
- the director wilfully authorises or permits any distribution or dividend to be paid in contravention of the Cayman Act under which a company is prohibited from making a distribution or paying a dividend to its shareholders out of the share premium account unless, on the date the distribution is made or the dividend is paid, the Cayman company is able to pay its debts as they fall due in the ordinary course of business;
- the director knowingly or wilfully authorises or permits any payment out of capital to effect a redemption or purchase of its own shares which is not lawful unless, following the date on which the payment is proposed to be made, the company is able to pay its debts as they fall due in the ordinary course of business; or
- the director makes or permits the making of an annual declaration required by the Cayman Act knowing it to be false.

In addition, the Cayman Act provides that a director will be liable to a penalty if he knowingly and wilfully authorises or permits a contravention of the following requirements:

- to keep a register of members;
- to file with the registrar of companies a notice of increase of share capital or, in the case of a company limited by guarantee, a notice of increase of shareholders;
- to display its name on notices, correspondence, bills of exchange, cheques or the like in the manner directed by the Cayman Act;
- to keep a register of mortgages;
- to keep a register of directors and notify the registrar of companies of any change therein within 30 days of the change;

- to annex or embody in its articles of association a copy of every special resolution passed by the shareholders; and
- in the case of an exempted company, to ensure it does not carry on any business in Cayman in contravention of Part VII of the Cayman Act.

Directors of a Cayman company must exercise their general duty to exercise skill and care in financial matters. It is the responsibility of the directors to ensure that the company fulfils its obligations to keep proper books of accounts as required by the Cayman Act.

A Cayman company is capable of exercising all functions of a natural person of capacity irrespective of corporate benefit and no transaction will be invalid as exceeding the company's powers merely because the company has no capacity to enter into it. However, a director may be held liable for loss or damage to the company as a result of an unauthorised transaction.

The Cayman Act also provides, with respect to a segregated portfolio company, that a director may incur personal liability if the segregated portfolio company breaches the Cayman Act by not contracting properly in the name of a segregated portfolio. However, such director may be relieved of such personal liability if he can satisfy the Cayman court that he ought fairly to be so relieved because:

- he was not aware of the circumstances giving rise to his liability and, in being so not aware, he was not fraudulent, reckless or negligent, and did not act in bad faith; or
- he expressly objected and exercised such rights as he had as a director, whether by way of voting power or otherwise, so as to try to prevent the circumstances giving rise to his liability.

1.2 Standards of care

Common law requires that a director exercise such care and diligence in the performance of his duties as an ordinary person would be expected to take on his own behalf. In addition, a director must perform his duties with such skill as would reasonably be expected of a person with his knowledge, experience and qualifications. A director is not expected to possess any particular skills merely by virtue of his office, but where he has any special knowledge or expertise, he should give the company the benefit of that when performing his duties. A director should, however, acquaint himself with sufficient knowledge and understanding of his company's business to enable him properly to discharge his duties as director.

The legislation in each of Bermuda, BVI and Cayman, however, increases the degree of care and skill that must be exercised by directors, in each case holding them to an objective standard.

(a) Bermuda

Directors of a Bermuda company must exercise the care, diligence and skill that a reasonably prudent person would exercise in comparable circumstances.

(b) ***BVI***

The BVI Act provides that a director of a BVI company must exercise the care, diligence and skill that a reasonable director would exercise in the same circumstances, taking into account, but without limitation:

- the nature of the company;
- the nature of the decision; and
- the position of the director and the nature of the responsibilities undertaken by him.

(c) ***Cayman***

In Cayman, a director of a company must exercise the care, diligence and skill that a reasonably prudent person would exercise in comparable circumstances.

1.3 To whom the duties are owed

Directors' fiduciary duties are owed to the company only, and not to the shareholders or any other person. In certain circumstances, however, directors may, by their conduct, put themselves in a position of owing fiduciary duties to the shareholders as well as to the company, as would be the case where they make a recommendation to shareholders concerning a takeover offer.

If directors make dividends in excess of the amount permitted by the Bermuda Act, they may be personally liable to creditors for such excess. In addition, directors may be personally liable to creditors where they exceed their borrowing powers as set out in the bylaws. Also, directors may be personally liable for pension or tax remittances that the company fails to pay.

A director of a Bermuda company will be liable to pay compensation to all persons who subscribed for shares in reliance on a prospectus and for any loss or damage the subscribers sustain by reason of any untrue statement in the prospectus, unless the director had reasonable grounds to believe that the statement was true.

1.4 Common defences to and exemptions from liability

A director will be absolved from liability for a breach of his common law fiduciary duties if the company's shareholders, in general meeting, ratify the relevant breach, either before or after it takes place. In such circumstances, the company will cease to have a cause of action and will have no standing to bring a claim against the director. There are also statutory exemptions from liability.

In any proceedings against directors for breach of their duty of skill and care, the company must prove that such breach resulted in a loss to it. Where the claim alleges that the directors failed to take appropriate action, the company must establish that the loss would not have occurred had the relevant action been taken.

The Bermuda Act provides that in any proceedings for negligence, default, breach of duty or breach of trust by a Bermuda company against a director, the court may relieve him, either wholly or partly, from any liability on such terms as the court thinks fit if it appears to the court that such director is or may be liable in respect of the negligence, default, breach of duty or breach of trust, but that:

- he has acted honestly and reasonably; and
- having regard to all the circumstances of the case, including those connected

> with his appointment, he ought fairly to be excused for the negligence, default, breach of duty or breach of trust.

The Bermuda Act also provides that, in the event that a director is found to be liable for damages, unless it is proved that he knowingly engaged in fraud or dishonesty, he will be liable only for a percentage of the plaintiff's total loss based upon his proportionate share of responsibility for that loss and will have no liability in respect of any judgment entered against any other parties to the action.

2. Who can bring claims

2.1 The company (and its liquidators)

Where a director breaches his fiduciary duties or commits some other wrong against the company, the company may, like any other person, sue the director. It is the directors who have the authority under the company's constitution to commence litigation in the company's name. Where a company is in liquidation, action may be brought by the liquidator in the company's name. As a general rule, shareholders do not have standing to enforce a company's legal rights through court proceedings.

The rule in *Foss v Harbottle* states that where a wrong is done to a company, *prima facie* the only proper plaintiff is the company itself. In practice, however, since the offending directors usually control the company on the board and in shareholder meetings, no action is brought. As such, it is only when a company goes into liquidation and a liquidator takes control of the company from the directors that a complaint is brought.

The Bermuda Act, the BVI insolvency legislation and the Cayman Act all expressly stipulate that a company may be wound up by the court if the court is of the opinion that it is "just and equitable" that this should happen.

In general, the bases for a winding-up order under the relevant statutory provisions have been held to include the following:

- The substratum of the company has disappeared;
- There is deadlock or disagreement in the management of the company;
- There has been some fraud on the minority (see above) or illegality; or
- There has been mismanagement or misapplication of the company's funds.

(a) Bermuda

If, in the course of a winding-up of a Bermuda company, it appears that any business of the company has been carried on with the intent to defraud creditors of the company or creditors of any other person, or for any fraudulent purpose, which includes continuing to trade while knowing that there is no realistic prospect that the company will be able to pay creditors in full, the Bermuda court, on application of the liquidator or any creditor of the company, may, if it thinks proper, declare that any persons who were knowingly party to the carrying on of the business in that manner will be personally responsible, without any limitation of liability, for all or any of the debts or other liabilities of the company as the court may direct. In addition, a director may be liable on conviction to imprisonment in respect of falsification of books or records, and in connection with actions intended to defraud shareholders or creditors of the company.

In the event that the liquidator or the official receiver, or any creditor or contributory of a Bermuda company in liquidation, complains to the Bermuda court that a director has misapplied or is liable to account for company property, or is guilty of misfeasance or breach of trust in relation to the company, the court may compel the director to account for such property with interest and to contribute such sum to the assets of the company by way of compensation as the court thinks just.

(b) *BVI*

Where a liquidator of a BVI company proves to the BVI court that a director has carried on the company's business with intent to defraud its creditors or other persons, or for any fraudulent purpose, or knowing that there was no reasonable prospect that the company would avoid insolvent liquidation, the court may order the director to make such contribution to the BVI company's assets as it considers proper.

In addition, if, on the application of a liquidator of an insolvent BVI company, the BVI court is satisfied that a director has misapplied or become accountable for assets of the company or has committed any misfeasance or breach of duty in relation to the company, the court may order the director to account for the assets with interest and pay compensation for any misfeasance or breach of duty that it considers proper.

(c) *Cayman*

If, during the course of the winding-up of a Cayman company, it appears that any past or present director, manager, official or other liquidator or any officer of a company has misapplied moneys of the company or been guilty of any misfeasance or breach of trust in relation to the company, the Cayman court may order any such person to repay any moneys so misapplied, together with interest, or to contribute such sums of money to the assets of the company by way of compensation as the court thinks just.

The liquidator may also, with the direction or approval of the Cayman court, institute and conduct a prosecution against a director or past director who is guilty of any offence in relation to the company for which he is criminally responsible.

2.2 Minority shareholders on behalf of the company (derivative actions)

It is possible, in certain circumstances (the so-called 'exceptions to the rule' in *Foss v Harbottle*), for a shareholder to enforce the company's rights by suing the wrongdoers on behalf of the company. In such circumstances, the shareholder is enforcing a right of action derived from the company.

The exceptions to the rule of *Foss v Harbottle*, which sets out the circumstances where a shareholder has standing to bring a derivative action on behalf of the company, are as follows:

- The act complained of is illegal or is outside the corporate capacity of the

company as set out in its memorandum of association;
- The act complained of constitutes a 'fraud on a minority' of the company's shareholders in circumstances where the wrongdoers themselves are in control of the company. For this purpose, a 'fraud on a minority' includes common law fraud, as well as where certain shareholders receive advantages in which the other shareholders are entitled to participate;
- The company has taken an action without obtaining the required shareholder authorising resolution; or
- The act complained of infringes the personal rights of shareholders, such as the right to vote or a pre-emptive right.

In a derivative action, the wrongdoers are made defendants in the action and the company is also joined as a nominal defendant so that it will be bound by the judgment. If the action is successful, any award will go to the company, not the shareholder. A plaintiff shareholder may, at the commencement of a derivative action, apply to the court for an order that the company will indemnify him against the costs of the action, whether the action succeeds or not. The court will order the company to indemnify the plaintiff if, in its view, the legal action constitutes a reasonable and prudent course to take in the interests of the company.

A derivative action may be brought only with the leave of the court (see section 3.2), where it is in the interests of the company to do so and it is brought in relation to acts or conduct which (subject to the company's bylaws) are not capable of authorisation or subsequent ratification by the company. There are no requirements that a company must have refused to bring a claim, nor are there any requirements that a percentage of shareholders have approved the action.

2.3 Minority shareholders on their own account

In a personal action, the shareholder sues in his own name and on his own behalf in respect of a breach of his rights as a shareholder. A complainant may bring a personal action if he is:

- prevented from exercising his voting rights;
- deprived of the benefit of a pre-emption right;
- refused the right to requisition a shareholders' meeting; or
- otherwise denied a right conferred on him in the bylaws or articles of association of the relevant company.

Generally, the remedies available against the company in such circumstances will be limited to a declaration or injunction to enforce the shareholder's rights rather than damages.

(a) Bermuda

The Bermuda Act provides that where the Bermuda court, on the application of a shareholder, is satisfied that the directors have managed the company in a way that is oppressive or prejudicial to the interests of some part of the shareholders, including the applicant, and is of the opinion that the facts would justify an order to wind up the company on the grounds that it was "just and equitable", but is also of the opinion that to do so would unfairly prejudice that part of the shareholders, then the court may make such order as it thinks fit. In such circumstances, the court may make an order that regulates the management of the Bermuda company's business or practices in the future, or requires certain shareholders to buy the shares of other shareholders.

(b) *BVI*

The BVI court may, on the application of a member or a director, make an order directing a BVI company to comply with, or restrain a company or director from engaging in conduct that contravenes, the BVI Act or the company's memorandum or articles of association. A member of a company who considers that the company's affairs have been, are being or are likely to be conducted in a manner that is, or that any act or acts of the company have been or are likely to be, oppressive, unfairly discriminatory or unfairly prejudicial to him may apply to the court for an order; the BVI court may, if it considers it to be just and equitable, grant such order as it thinks fit.

(c) *Cayman*

Shareholders representing not less than one-fifth of the issued shares of a Cayman company for the time being issued or, where the company's share capital is not divided into shares, one-fifth of the total number of shareholders on the register of members of the company may apply to the Cayman court to appoint one or more inspectors to examine the company's affairs and report to the court in such manner as the court may direct. All directors, officers and agents of the company are under a duty to produce for examination by a court-appointed inspector all books and documents in their custody or power, and any inspector may examine the officers and agents under oath in relation to the company's business. Any officer or agent who refuses or neglects to produce any book or document that has been requested by the inspector, or to answer any questions relating to the affairs of the company, may incur a penalty in respect of each such offence. The report of the inspector is admissible in any legal proceedings as evidence of the opinion of the inspector in relation to any matter contained in the report.

2.4 Third parties

(a) *Bermuda*

The Bermuda Act permits the minister of finance to appoint an inspector to investigate the business of a Bermuda exempted company. If the investigation reveals that the company or its directors have deliberately contravened the Bermuda Act, the minister may cause a petition to be made to the court for the company to be wound up. If, on the other hand, the inspector's report evidences that the exempted company's business is being managed in a manner detrimental to the interests of shareholders or creditors, the minister may require the company to take such measures as he considers necessary in relation to its affairs.

(b) *BVI*

The BVI Act permits a shareholder or the registrar of corporate affairs to apply to the court for an order directing that an investigation be conducted of the company and any of its affiliates. The BVI court may make any order it thinks fit with respect to an investigation of the company, including the production of documents and the examination under oath of any individual, and may order the publication of a report.

Generally in Bermuda, BVI and Cayman, creditors, employees and other parties with whom the company has contracted may bring claims. A subscriber for shares in the company may have a contractual claim against a company in respect of the issue of shares.

3. Claims culture

3.1 Litigation

The court systems of Bermuda, BVI and Cayman are all based on the English court system. The English Rules of the Supreme Court, which were in effect in 1999 with some amendments, are incorporated into Bermuda legislation under the Rules of the Supreme Court 1985 (as amended in 2005) (the Bermuda Rules). BVI has adopted rules modelled on the English Civil Procedure Rules 2000, namely the Eastern Caribbean Supreme Court Civil Procedure Rules 2000 (the BVI Rules). Procedure in the Grand Court of the Cayman Islands is regulated by the Grand Court Rules 1995 (the Cayman Rules) which, like the Bermuda Rules, are modelled on the English Rules of the Supreme Court.

Decisions in each jurisdiction frequently cite and apply English case law, and decisions of the Court of Appeal for England and Wales and the House of Lords are regarded as highly persuasive and are generally followed in the Bermuda courts. Decisions of first instance English courts (ie, the trial courts) and Commonwealth courts are also cited in each jurisdiction. Their persuasiveness depends upon their relevance and the strength of the judicial reasoning and the standing of the judge. Decisions of the Judicial Committee of the Privy Council are formally binding on the courts of each jurisdiction. The claims culture in each jurisdiction is heavily influenced by the claims culture in England and Wales.

Over the last 15 years, with the growth of international business, the courts of each jurisdiction have had to deal with increasingly sophisticated litigation to meet the demands placed upon them by international business. Each jurisdiction has sought to equip itself to deal with commercial litigation. For example, in 2005, with the introduction of the amendments to the Bermuda Rules, a Commercial Court was introduced in Bermuda. The BVI government has now committed to providing a separate Commercial Court by the end of 2007. This will operate within the Eastern Caribbean Supreme Court, based in the BVI.

The number of claims and the level of sophistication of claims in each jurisdiction have increased over the past 20 years as international business has matured. While it is difficult to generalise, in the company law context, disputes take the form of:

- disputes between shareholders *inter se*;
- minority oppression and/or just and equitable winding-up proceedings; and
- claims arising in the context of insolvency.

Claims against directors and officers of companies are usually brought in the context of liquidation. To the extent that a claims culture in relation to claims against directors and officers can be identified, it is perhaps best characterised as being influenced by five significant factors.

First, broad indemnification provisions for directors in relation to any acts, with the exception of fraud and dishonesty, combined with indemnities for legal costs, will deter claims against directors, as claims must be alleged that fall outside the scope of the indemnity. In Bermuda, for example, claims brought against directors that would otherwise be covered by indemnification provisions in the company bylaws will be struck out.

Second, the company itself must bring any claim against directors. Typically, these will be brought by liquidators or minority shareholders through derivative actions (discussed below). Under company law principles in each jurisdiction, a shareholder will not have a direct right of action against a director. The shareholder's only remedy will be to claim against the company. The company, in turn, may then claim against the director.

Third, as a general rule, a shareholder will not be entitled to claim a loss which is reflective of the loss suffered by the company against a director or third party. This will normally include damage arising from loss of profits the company would otherwise have made which is suffered by the company at the hands of some other party, including a director. Such losses will include claims for diminution of the value of a company. The shareholder in this situation can recover only consequential losses to him personally, which are not losses suffered by, or which could otherwise have been recovered by, the company.

Fourth, relief granted against companies and directors will, in any event, be compensatory only. Typically, punitive damages will not be awarded.

Fifth, for reasons discussed below, the costs associated with proceedings in all jurisdictions will be high.

For the above reasons, claims by shareholders, in particular group claims, are rare.

BVI has introduced director disqualification procedures following the UK model. It is anticipated that the availability of these new remedies will increase potential actions against directors in the BVI.

3.2 Ability to bring class actions

In line with their English roots, the procedure rules in each jurisdiction do not provide for class actions or group litigation orders, but provide for 'representative actions'. The procedural rules of each jurisdiction permit representative actions to be brought by representatives of a large class of persons who have the same interest in the proceedings. The Cayman Rules and the Bermuda Rules provide that proceedings may be commenced by one or more representatives without leave, but defendants can challenge the formation of the class after the proceedings have commenced. Under the BVI Rules, the court must appoint a representative. As a general rule, all the parties represented will be liable on any judgment against the representative but such a judgment may not be enforced without leave. The validity and binding character of the judgment cannot be challenged by the party represented, except on facts particular to his case (eg, where he is not a member of the class).

A defendant may challenge the appropriateness of a representative action in each jurisdiction if the representative and the class he represents do not have a common interest or a common grievance. If other parties have a separate interest, then they should not be part of the representative class.

Company shareholders may also instigate derivative actions in each jurisdiction. The purpose of such actions is to permit a shareholder to sue on behalf of the company for a wrong done to the company where there has been a fraud on a minority. It extends beyond fraud at common law in the sense that it includes an abuse or misuse of power by the majority that could not otherwise be approved by the company at a general meeting. As such actions are brought by a minority shareholder standing in the company's shoes, leave of the court to continue a derivative action after it has been commenced must be obtained. In BVI, derivative actions are regulated by the BVI Act which provides (as from January 1 2007) that derivative actions be conducted under procedure set out in Section 184C of that act. Derivative actions can be brought only with the leave of the court. In such cases the test is whether:

- the action is in the interests of the company;
- the member is acting in good faith; and
- the proceedings are likely to succeed, balanced against the likely cost of the proceedings; and
- an alternative remedy is available.

The legal basis for an action is still governed by the general principles referred to above.

3.3 Funding of claims and whether the losing party pays

The cost framework in each jurisdiction renders it potentially expensive for plaintiff shareholders if they lose their claim. The relevant bar rules in Bermuda and the Cayman Islands prohibit attorneys from charging contingency or conditional fee arrangements. In BVI, such arrangements are not the norm, although they are not regulated by legislation. Attorneys charge on a 'time spent' basis. In each jurisdiction, the normal order as to costs is that the loser pay the winner's costs. In Bermuda, the party in whose favour the costs order is made will recover what are deemed to be reasonable fees paid. Such fees approach those actually paid to attorneys and will include disbursements such as experts' fees, travel expenses and, if reasonable, foreign attorneys' fees. Cayman and BVI currently have a system of prescribed costs whereby the successful party is awarded costs according to a scale calculated by reference to the value of the case, unless there are special reasons that take it outside that scale. In Cayman, parties tend to recover approximately two-thirds to three-quarters of their costs, while in BVI the scales are much lower. In each jurisdiction, the courts have the power, in exceptional circumstances, to award costs on an indemnity basis. This cost regime deters parties from bringing unmeritorious or adventurous claims.

3.4 Plaintiffs' bar

The bars in each jurisdiction are not organised specifically into plaintiffs' bars (or, for that matter, defendants' bars), and there is no plaintiffs' bar as that term is understood in the United States.

3.5 Procedural barriers

Formalities for bringing claims against directors are discussed above. The company must bring claims against directors if they relate to loss occasioned to the company. Usually such a claim, if a derivative action, requires leave of the court at an early stage. Claims by shareholders where the company is in liquidation will require the approval of the liquidator (and possibly a creditors' committee) and the approval of the court. The law of each jurisdiction generally imposes limitation periods on the prosecution of certain claims. The length of the period is based on the nature of the underlying cause of action.

4. Indemnification rights

4.1 When the company can indemnity

(a) Bermuda

The Bermuda Act provides that a Bermuda company may, in its bylaws or in a contract, indemnify its directors and other persons against any liability which, by virtue of any rule of law, would otherwise be imposed on them in respect of any negligence, default, breach of duty or breach of trust, and which is incurred by them in defending any civil or criminal proceedings, except in cases where it is determined by the court that the liability arises from the fraud or dishonesty of the director. In addition, a company may advance moneys to a director to cover the expenses of defending any proceedings against him. In the event that the court finds that the director has acted fraudulently or dishonestly, the director will be obliged to repay to the company any money provided for his defence.

(b) BVI

The BVI Act provides that a BVI company may indemnify against all expenses, including legal fees, and against all judgments, fines and amounts paid in settlement and reasonably incurred in connection with legal, administrative or investigative proceedings, any person who is or was a party, or who may be made a party, to any threatened, pending or completed proceedings, whether civil, criminal, administrative or investigative, by reason of the fact that the person is or was a director of the company, or is or was, at the request of the company, serving as director of, or in any other capacity is or was acting for, another body corporate or a partnership, joint venture, trust or other enterprise, provided that such person acted honestly and in good faith in what he believed to be in the best interests of the company and, in the case of criminal proceedings, the person had no reasonable cause to believe that his conduct was unlawful.

(c) ***Cayman***

The Cayman Act is silent with respect to the indemnification of directors. As such, Cayman law would look to the common law, which allows for such a contract of indemnity provided it is not against public policy. A Cayman company may, in its articles of association or by contract, indemnify its directors and other persons against any liability which, by virtue of any rule of law, would otherwise be imposed on them for any negligence, default, breach of duty or breach of trust, and which is incurred by them in defending any civil or criminal proceedings, except in cases where it is determined by the court that such indemnity would be against public policy. As is the case with Bermuda and BVI, indemnities that cover fraud, dishonesty or criminal activity of the director would be against public policy and not enforceable.

4.2 Formalities for indemnification

There are no formalities in Bermuda, BVI and Cayman for the grant or enforcement of indemnification rights.

4.3 How indemnification works

The right to indemnification must be contained in the company's bylaws or articles of association, or in a contract between the director and the company.

4.4 What cannot be indemnified

(a) ***Bermuda***

A Bermuda company cannot indemnify a director in respect of any act where a court finds that the director has been fraudulent or dishonest.

(b) ***BVI***

A BVI company cannot indemnify a director where he has not acted honestly and in good faith in what he believes to be the best interests of the company or where he had reasonable cause to believe that his conduct was unlawful.

(c) ***Cayman***

A Cayman company cannot indemnity a director where such indemnity would be against public policy (eg, indemnifying against fraud, dishonesty or criminal activity).

5. D&O insurance

5.1 Availability of D&O insurance

(a) Bermuda

Whether or not a Bermuda company may otherwise indemnify its directors, the Bermuda Act permits a company to purchase and maintain insurance for the benefit of its directors in respect of any loss or liability attaching to them for any negligence, default, breach of duty or breach of trust.

(b) BVI

The BVI Act permits a company to purchase and maintain insurance in relation to any person who is or was a director against any liability asserted against the person and incurred by the person in his capacity as a director, whether or not the BVI company has the power to indemnify the person against the liability.

(c) Cayman

Although the Cayman Act is silent with respect to the purchase and maintenance of insurance to cover any loss or liability attaching to directors in respect of any negligence, default, breach of duty or breach of trust, such policies would not be against public policy and are allowed in Cayman.

5.2 Local rules on cover provided under a non-domestic D&O policy

There are no regulations in Bermuda, BVI or Cayman which restrict companies from purchasing D&O policies issued by non-domestic insurers, and there is nothing to prevent the directors of a company from being included as beneficiaries on a global D&O policy issued by a non-domestic insurer to the company's parent company.

Non-resident insurers are not entitled to carry on business in Bermuda, BVI or Cayman, but that does not prevent them from selling policies to Bermuda, BVI or Cayman companies from their overseas offices. It is very unlikely that an overseas insurer will be able to obtain permission to establish a branch in, or send representatives to, Bermuda, BVI and Cayman to sell its policies. There are, however, some resident exempted companies that are authorised to sell D&O policies in the domestic markets.

Brazil

Marcelo Mansur Haddad
Julia Santoro de Camargo
Mattos Filho, Veiga Filho, Marrey Jr e Quiroga Advogados

1. Directors' duties

1.1 Nature of the duties

Brazil is structured under a codified law system. The primary statutes governing directors' obligations and responsibilities are:

- the Corporations Law (6404/76), which is periodically amended;
- the Civil Code; and
- several specific federal laws that create liability for directors and officers, including in relation to finance, bankruptcy, tax, the environment, labour, consumers and competition.

Under Brazilian law, the two main types of commercial entity are corporations (*sociedade anônima*) and limited liability companies (*sociedade de responsabilidade limitada*).

A corporation is governed by the Corporations Law and is managed by a board of officers comprising at least two members. This may be subject to supervision by a board of directors (comprising at least three members) pursuant to the limits and conditions set out in the company bylaws. The existence of a board of directors is mandatory for certain companies (eg, publicly traded companies).

Limited liability companies are governed by the Civil Code and subsidiarily by the Corporations Law. A limited liability company is managed by one or more officers pursuant to the terms and conditions set out in the articles of association.

Hence, the duties of directors and officers have codified and statutory sources. These may be found not only in the Corporations Law, but also in the Civil Code, in addition to the provisions of specific bylaws and articles of association.

Regarding the types of duty commonly imposed on directors and officers, Chapter XII, Section IV of the Corporations Law sets out several duties and liabilities of directors and officers, as follows:

- the duty of diligence and care;
- the duty to act in the company's interest;
- the duty of loyalty;
- the duty of confidentiality;
- the duty to avoid situations giving rise to a conflict of interest; and
- the duty to inform any shareholder, investor or the market about information relevant to the company.

In addition, the Civil Code also establishes a duty of diligence and loyalty, among other duties, and limited liability company officers also have a duty to provide specific standards of care. These are outlined below.

1.2 Standards of care

According to Brazilian law, directors and officers are not personally liable for obligations undertaken on behalf of the company when acting in compliance with the applicable laws, its bylaws or articles of association. However, they will be personally liable before the company, the shareholders or quota holders (ie, the limited liability company partners), and any third party for losses caused by their acts and/or omissions where these:

- are performed or incurred by wilful misconduct or fault;
- breach the law or any corporate document; or
- breach their legal duties.

'Fault' would include any negligent act or omission of the relevant director or officer. However, there are no defined parameters to establish whether an act or omission of a director or officer is negligent. Nevertheless, it is possible to say that a director or officer would not be at fault where he performed all acts that would be expected of a skilled and experienced professional.

The main standards of care required from directors and officers to avoid any civil liability are:

- to comply with any corporate law or act;
- to act diligently on behalf of the company and, in the case of directors, expressly to disapprove or vote against any decision of the board that is negligent, breaks any law or corporate act, or may be considered as wilful misconduct;
- not to perform any act on behalf of the company that would result in individual benefit, including the execution of loans, the receipt of any moneys or the assumption of any obligations, without statutory or management authorisation;
- not to interfere in any transaction in which his interests conflict with those of the company;
- to act with loyalty and keep confidential information regarding the company's business;
- to keep confidential any information not disclosed to the public, obtained as a result of his position, which may influence the price of the company's securities;
- to enter into agreements on behalf of the company only under reasonable and equitable conditions, equivalent to those prevailing in the market;
- to inform the shareholders/quota holders of any rights or benefits to which they may be entitled; and
- if publicly traded, to inform the market about relevant acts or facts of the company.

Moreover, an officer will be liable for the acts of other officers if he:

- agrees with such act;
- is negligent in detecting such act; or
- does not prevent such act from happening, where possible.

In principle, directors are jointly liable for the decisions taken by the board of directors, except where one of them disagrees with a decision or resolution in writing, or informs the competent management body or audit committee (if installed) of their disagreement.

Finally, under Brazilian law, civil liability is classified as objective (strict liability) or subjective. The civil liability of directors and officers is subjective, so in order to be entitled to an indemnification right, one must prove their fault connected to a particular loss or damage. However, civil liability may be objective (strict liability) where the law expressly establishes this or where the activity usually carried out by the company may cause risk or damage to the rights of third parties.

1.3 To whom duties are owed

The directors' duties are basically owed to the company. However, since the acts or omissions of directors and officers may cause loss or damage to any person or entity, including investors, shareholders, quota holders, partners, creditors, employees or any third party, their duties are owed to everyone that may be directly or indirectly affected by such acts or omissions.

1.4 Common defences to and exemptions from liability.

A common defence for directors and officers is based on the fact that their civil liability is essentially subjective or, as mentioned above, based on fault. The Civil Code provides four basic requirements that must be evidenced by a claimant to entitle him to be indemnified:

- the existence of an act or omission;
- the occurrence of damage;
- fault of the person who performed the act or incurred the omission (eg, negligence); and
- a link between the act or omission and the damage suffered.

If any of these requirements is not duly evidenced, the claimant will, in principle, have no right to indemnification.

It is often the case that a claimant is unable to provide enough evidence of fault on the part of the directors and officers to be entitled to indemnification. In such cases the liability of directors or officers in relation to the claimed damage shall not be recognised or triggered.

However, this argument does not apply where the liability of a director or officer is of an objective nature, since under Brazilian law, such liability does not require evidence of fault (eg, liability for acts or omissions that violate competition laws or relate to product liability issues).

In addition to the defences mentioned above, certain others are available to directors or officers, as follows:

- where the directors or officers are acting in compliance with the bylaws or articles of association (ie, regular acts of management) - in such case, if the damage results from an act or omission duly supported by law or the corporate documents, the company will be solely liable for such damage; and
- where a director expressly disagrees in writing with an act or omission of the board of directors or any decision passed by it, or informs the competent management body or audit committee (if installed) of his disagreement (see section 1.2).

2. Who can bring claims

2.1 The company (and its liquidators)

According to Brazilian law, the company is a competent claimant and is entitled to bring a lawsuit against directors or officers for losses caused to its assets. For corporations, however, such a claim requires the prior approval of an ordinary or extraordinary general shareholders' meeting, under a majority quorum (a so-called 'corporate action').

If the shareholders' approval is obtained, the relevant director or officer can no longer act on behalf of the company and must be replaced at the same shareholders' meeting which approves the filing of the corporate action.

The lawsuit against the director or officer must be filed before the Brazilian courts within three months of the date of the respective shareholders' meeting.

If the corporate lawsuit is not filed within this three-month period, any shareholder is entitled to initiate proceedings against the relevant director or officer on behalf of the company. In this case, notwithstanding that the claim is brought by a shareholder, the company (rather than the shareholder) is the beneficiary of the respective indemnification, provided that the shareholder recovers from the company all costs and expenses arising from the lawsuit, up to the amount of the indemnity due.

Under Brazilian bankruptcy and insolvency laws, a liquidator or administrator is not entitled to file a civil liability claim against a director or officer on behalf of an insolvent or bankrupt company, as the civil liability of such director or officer is verified under the bankruptcy or insolvency procedure by the competent court or authority.

2.2 Minority shareholders on behalf of the company (derivative actions)

In addition to the situation described in section 2.1, if the ordinary or extraordinary general shareholders' meeting decides not to file a corporate lawsuit against a director or officer, any shareholder representing at least 5% of the company's capital stock is legally entitled to file a claim on behalf of the company (a so-called 'derivative lawsuit').

Again, in this case the company is the beneficiary of the respective indemnity, provided that the minority shareholder who filed the derivative action recovers from the company all costs and expenses arising from such claim, up to the amount of the indemnity due.

2.3 Minority shareholders on their own account

Pursuant to corporate law, the corporate or derivative lawsuits described above do not preclude an individual shareholder or quota holder from bringing a claim on his own account where his individual right or interest has been damaged by the directors' or officers' acts or omissions. There is no need for any corporate approval to file such a lawsuit and any award will directly benefit the claimant, not the company.

Any civil liability claim to be filed by minority shareholders against the directors or officers must satisfy the following requirements for subjective civil liability:

- the occurrence of an act or omission;
- the evidence of the respective loss or damage;
- the link between such act or omission and the loss or damage; and
- the agent's fault.

2.4 Third parties

The corporate or derivative lawsuits described above do not preclude a third party who has been directly damaged by an act or omission of a certain director or officer from bringing a claim on the same basis as mentioned above. The third party must provide evidence of:

- the occurrence of an act or omission;
- the respective loss or damage;
- the link between such act or omission and the loss or damage; and
- the agent's fault.

These claims are usually initiated by former employees, creditors and other individuals or entities that have suffered damage as a result of a decision of the directors or officers. However, such claims often fail as the personal liability of the officer or director, as well as the liability of the company itself, cannot be established. These types of lawsuit are often used to put pressure on the company.

3. Claims culture

3.1 Litigation

In Brazil, there is no litigation culture as far indemnities are concerned. Similarly, there is no litigation culture regarding the liability of directors or officers. This is mainly because a judge will grant an indemnity only up to the amount of the actual damage the claimant has suffered. The claimant is not entitled to receive any other amount, such as punitive damages. Even moral damages, if granted, do not represent substantial amounts of money. Although some commentators suggest that indemnification for moral damages should be sufficiently high to persuade agents not to repeat their acts or omissions, this is the minority view.

Recently, some claimants have litigated against both companies and their officers and directors at the same time, with the clear intention of putting pressure on the latter. However, in most such cases the claimants do not have a very good case against the directors or officers, as they cannot show that their loss resulted from individual fault. For this reason, insurance coverage for defence costs is often more relevant than for indemnities due to third parties.

Generally speaking, most lawsuits filed against directors or officers that may have a chance of success relate to labour and, to a lesser extent, tax issues.

3.2 Ability to bring class actions

The Corporations Law establishes the possibility for shareholders to bring derivative actions against a director or officer, under the terms and conditions mentioned therein. However, under Brazilian law, this is not regarded as a 'class action'.

According to Brazilian law, class actions are used to defend the common interests of a collective group, whether organised (normally through associations) or not, and may be filed by the federal, state or local public prosecutor's office, regulatory agencies, foundations, state-controlled companies and associations in general. They are normally used to protect public, non-individualised (eg, environmental, consumer, economic) interests. Thus, class actions are not usually brought against directors or officers. However, if a director or officer is personally liable for an environmental or consumer accident, the above entities could start a class action against him.

3.3 Funding of claims and whether loser pays

The plaintiff pays the initial court costs of a lawsuit (normally 1% of the amount under dispute). However, as mentioned above, when shareholders file a corporate or even a derivative lawsuit, the company must reimburse them for the respective costs (up to the amount of the indemnity) if they are successful. However, if a lawsuit is unsuccessful, the shareholders, as the losing party, will bear all costs.

Under Brazilian procedural law, the losing party is generally required to pay the winning party's costs. These include legal fees and court costs, such as court charges (including the above-mentioned 1%) and the fees of any experts appointed by the judge, among others.

However, Brazilian law states that the judge will determine the amount corresponding to the winning party's legal fees to be paid by the losing party. These can vary from 10% to 20% of the condemnation amount and may not necessarily reflect the amount the winning party is actually paying to its counsel.

In addition, the parties may enter into a fee agreement, whereby they establish that each party will pay its own costs.

Brazilian lawyers may enter into agreements, on a case-by-case basis, to establish success fees that may represent part of the indemnity awarded. However, according to the bylaws of the Brazilian Bar, Brazilian lawyers are not allowed to work on a *pro bono* basis, except in certain specific circumstances. This is regulated by the Brazilian

Bar. Brazilian counsel commonly receive a retention fee in addition to any contingency fee agreed by the parties.

Unmeritorious or unfounded claims are penalised under Brazilian procedural law. The plaintiff (ie, the losing party) in such a case will be ordered to pay:

- a penalty of up to 1% of the amount awarded;
- an indemnity for losses caused by the filing of the claim in a sum of up to 20% of the amount awarded; and
- the legal fees (as explained above) and court costs incurred by the other party.

These potential costs usually deter plaintiffs from filing unmeritorious or unfounded claims.

3.4 Plaintiffs' bar

This concept is not known in Brazil. Normally, in cases where a large number of individuals or entities are affected, they organise themselves through associations or similar institutions and hire a lawyer to defend their rights.

Any class action filed in Brazil must satisfy the conditions and requirements, and must be filed under the circumstances, described in section 3.2. Thus, a class action cannot be brought against a director or officer for any purpose other than the protection of public, non-individualised interests or by claimants other than the entities mentioned in section 3.2.

3.5 Procedural barriers

Under Brazilian law, the statute of limitations for civil liability claims is three years from the date of knowledge of the damage or loss. In the specific case of claims against directors and officers, this three-year period begins on the date on which the balance sheet for the year when the violation took place was presented or approved by the partners of the company.

To commence a lawsuit against a director or officer, the plaintiff must be resident in Brazil and must have real estate assets in the jurisdiction. If a non-resident wishes to start a lawsuit, it must guarantee court costs and the legal fees of the winning party. This rule does not apply to execution or foreclosure proceedings; lawsuits against directors and officers are normally not foreclosure proceedings.

4. Indemnification rights

4.1 When the company can indemnify

A company can indemnify its directors and/or officers for any damage that has arisen from regular acts of management (including, without limitation, legal costs, attorneys' fees and indemnities due to third parties). As directors and officers are generally not personally liable for regular acts of management, indemnification is exceptional and is usually limited to court and defence costs. In such cases the director should be indemnified in full for court and defence costs. The company can pay these fees in advance, but if the director or officer is shown to be at fault, he must refund them.

The conditions under which a company will indemnify its directors and officers in connection with any claims against them will already have been established by way of a private agreement. In our understanding, such an agreement - commonly known as an indemnification agreement or hold-harmless letter - should be restricted to indemnification arising from regular acts of management. If it is broadly adopted to cover wilful misconduct of directors and officers or faulty acts or omissions, it may be challenged by the shareholders and quota holders and may have to be annulled.

If the agreement between the parties does not allow defence costs and attorneys' fees to be advanced by the company, the relevant director or officer will still be indemnified once a final decision has been issued by the judge or arbitrator, as long as it is established that he did not commit wilful misconduct or act at fault.

4.2 Formalities for indemnification

The formalities under which indemnities will be paid to directors and officers are generally set out in the relevant law, and may be further specified in an indemnification agreement or hold-harmless letter which observes the restrictions set out in section 4.1.

In any event, it is recommended that such an agreement or hold-harmless letter receive the prior approval of the majority of shareholders or quota holders, to mitigate the risk of subsequent challenge by them.

4.3 How indemnification works

The payment of indemnification must comply with the company's corporate documents, as well as any indemnification agreement or hold-harmless letter.

4.4 What cannot be indemnified

Pursuant to the Corporations Law, directors and officers will be personally liable (and therefore will not be indemnified) towards the company for loss and damage caused by their acts or omissions when they:

- demonstrated wilful misconduct or fault; or
- violated applicable laws or the bylaws or articles of association of the relevant company.

If there is subjective (not strict) liability on top of that, the following requirements must be satisfied:

- An act or omission must exist;
- Damage or loss must have occurred;
- The fault of the individual responsible for the act or omission must be shown; and
- There must be a link between the act or omission and the damage or loss.

Therefore, if the company is willing to indemnify an individual director or officer for acts or omissions - even where the company has expressly agreed to do so by means of an indemnification agreement or hold-harmless letter - the shareholders, quota holders or investors may challenge any indemnification paid by the company.

5. D&O insurance

5.1 Availability of D&O insurance

Insurance transactions are basically regulated by the Civil Code, Decree-Law 73/66, Complementary Law 126/07 and several specific regulations issued by the Brazilian insurance authority.

D&O insurance coverage is classified and regulated by the Brazilian insurance authority as a 'damage insurance contract' (*contrato de seguro de danos*). It is defined as civil liability insurance covering losses and damage resulting from claims made by third parties against the insured, based on his acts or omissions as manager (director or officer) of a company. It also covers legal costs and attorneys' fees, which are paid in advance by the insurer. The insurer must approve in advance the fees to be paid to legal counsel and may sometimes veto the service provider.

According to local rules, D&O policies can be structured as:

- occurrence policies (ie, the insurer will pay the indemnity provided that the loss occurred during the policy period and the insured claims coverage from the insurer during the policy period or within the statute of limitations); or
- claims-made policies (ie, the insurer will pay the indemnity provided that the loss occurred during the policy period or a certain retroactive period offered by the insurer and any third party presented its claim during the policy period, the complementary period or supplementary period, if applicable).

Nevertheless, most policies are structured as claims-made policies.

Any company incorporated under Brazilian law as a corporation or a limited liability company can purchase D&O insurance. The insured will be any director or officer duly elected or nominated according to the applicable law and the corporate documents. Moreover, many policies include anyone vested with representative powers before third parties. Nearly all policies extend D&O coverage to former directors and officers or attorneys-in-fact.

The coverage sold under D&O insurance is usually extended to officers and directors who are also appointed by the principal as an officer or director of a non-profitable foundation or association linked to the principal, provided that this foundation or association is not a pension fund.

Finally, in certain circumstances, it is not only the directors and officers who are insured by a D&O policy, but also the principal itself. This may occur, for example, where coverage for the issuance of securities is purchased.

5.2 Local rules on cover provided under a non-domestic D&O policy

Complementary Law 126/07, which governs the opening up of the Brazilian reinsurance market, and National Council of Private Insurance Regulation 165/07, which regulates this complementary law, provide that Brazilian residents (individuals and legal entities) may purchase insurance from abroad relating to risks located in Brazil only in the following circumstances:

- The cover is unavailable in Brazil;
- The cover relates to risks abroad for the benefit of Brazilian individuals who

are travelling offshore and for the duration of such travel;

- The cover is envisaged in international treaties duly ratified and confirmed by the Brazilian Congress; or
- The cover has been contracted abroad pursuant to the legislation in force prior to the enactment of Complementary Law 126/07 (ie, Decree-Law 73/66).

Generally, the Brazilian insurance authority will consider unavailable in Brazil any cover that is denied by three different local insurers.

In view of the above, and considering that local insurers commonly offer D&O insurance, the purchase of non-domestic D&O cover may be interpreted as against Brazilian law. However, it is still debatable whether Brazilian law can validly restrict the acts of non-resident entities or individuals when their assets are located offshore, especially when the coverage is for the benefit of a Brazilian resident.

All D&O policies purchased in Brazil are submitted to local law and the rules issued by the Brazilian insurance authority in respect to their form and certain mandatory provisions. Foreign companies are not authorised to sell insurance products in the Brazilian territory.

Canada

Bruno Floriani
Natasa Karambatsos
Marvin Liebman
Lapointe Rosenstein, LLP

1. Directors' duties

The Constitution Act, 1867 (Canada) governs the manner in which powers are divided among the governing authorities of each of Canada's 10 provinces and three territories. Section 92 of the Constitution Act, 1867 confers on provincial governments jurisdiction over the incorporation of companies with provincial objects. Canadian courts have held that the federal government's residuary power to legislate with respect to peace, order and good government includes the power to enact laws governing the incorporation of companies with objects other than those that are provincial in nature. As a consequence of this dichotomy, both federal and provincial legislation governing corporate law, and the duties of corporate directors thereunder, exist. The issue of directors' liability and indemnification is examined primarily from the perspective of federal corporate law (ie, the Canada Business Corporations Act) and other applicable federal legislation, with noteworthy provincial differentiations mentioned throughout the text.

1.1 Nature of the duties

(a) Duty of care and fiduciary duty of directors

The statutory duty of directors is to manage and supervise the business and affairs of the corporation. Specifically, directors must:

- act honestly, in good faith and in the best interests of the corporation (the fiduciary duty); and
- exercise the care, diligence and skill that a reasonably prudent person would exercise in comparable circumstances (the duty of care).

The fiduciary duty requires that a director subordinate his personal interests to those of the corporation. For example, a director may not use confidential information received in his capacity as a director to his own advantage. A director is also forbidden from misappropriating a business opportunity that could be of interest to the corporation that he serves.

The fiduciary duty includes an obligation to inform the corporation of a conflict of interest arising from an actual or potential divergence of a director's personal interests from those of the corporation. Consequently, directors must disclose in writing or cause to be entered into the minutes of a board of directors' meeting the nature and extent of any interest they may have in a current or projected material contract or transaction with the corporation. This requirement applies if a director:

- is a party to the contract or transaction in question;
- is a director or officer, or an individual acting in a similar capacity, of a party to such contract or transaction; or
- has a material interest in a party to such contract or transaction.

A director required to make this disclosure is entitled to vote on a resolution to approve the contract or transaction only if the contract or transaction:

- is entered into with an affiliate of the corporation;
- relates primarily to the remuneration of the director; or
- is entered into for the purpose of providing the indemnity or insurance under Section 124 of the Canada Business Corporations Act (D&O liability).

A director who fails to disclose any such interest in an accurate, complete and timely manner, or who fails to abstain from voting, may be compelled to reimburse the corporation or its shareholders for any gain derived from the contract or transaction. In addition, such contract or transaction may also be declared null and void by a court of law. In such case a defence based solely on the fact that a true conflict never materialised is insufficient; entering into a *potential* conflict of interest suffices to trigger a director's personal liability. This principle is consistent with the common law principle that a fiduciary who acts with the object of deriving a personal benefit cannot subsequently seek to validate an otherwise invalid act by showing that the act was advantageous to the corporate beneficiary.

The duty of care requires that a director exercise reasonable care, prudence and skill in managing the affairs of a corporation. Attendance at meetings, compliance with reasonable policies and reliance upon professional counsel are generally perceived as characterising a sound and reasonable stewardship of a corporation's affairs. Directors may fulfil their responsibilities, where reasonable in the circumstances, by conferring certain responsibilities on third parties and by relying on management and financial statements. However, directors must inquire as to whether reasonable grounds exist to question the content of financial statements or other information provided to them.

(b) Duties in the event of insolvency or bankruptcy

A corporation's insolvency or bankruptcy broadens a director's exposure to personal liability in the form of claims which may include:

- claims by employees for debts arising from their employment;
- claims under the Excise Tax Act (Canada) for the payment of unremitted goods and services tax (essentially, a value added tax on the supply of products and services);
- claims by governmental authorities for the deduction, remittance and payment of income tax, employment insurance premiums, the Canada Pension Plan (or its provincial equivalent) contributions and certain other payroll and source deductions;

- claims by the corporation against directors who vote in favour of or consent to certain corporate finance actions; and
- claims under the Bankruptcy and Insolvency Act (Canada). If a corporation commits an offence under the Bankruptcy and Insolvency Act, any officer, director or agent of the corporation who directed or authorised the commission of the offence is a party to, and guilty of, the offence and is liable on conviction to the punishment associated with the offence, whether or not the corporation has been prosecuted or convicted.

Insolvency and restructuring legislation also provides that where a court finds that a bankrupt corporation has paid a dividend other than a stock dividend, or redeemed or purchased for cancellation any shares of the share capital of the corporation, at a time when the corporation was insolvent or in circumstances where such act rendered the corporation insolvent, and where the directors had reasonable grounds to believe that this would be the case, the directors may be jointly and severally liable for the amount of the dividend, the proceeds of the redemption or the purchase price, respectively, which has not been otherwise recovered by the corporation.

In the event of a corporation's insolvency, directors will continue to owe their fiduciary duty solely to the corporation and not to any particular shareholder, creditor or other stakeholder. However, directors may take into consideration the interests of the corporation's various stakeholders provided that they do not disregard entirely the interests of a particular group.

(c) ***Offences under corporate statutes***

The federal, provincial and territorial corporate statutes generally create director and officer-related offences that are punishable by fine and/or a period of imprisonment. While the offence provisions of each corporate statute differ, this section provides a general overview of certain commonly invoked offence provisions of the Canada Business Corporations Act.

Circumstances in which directors and officers of a corporation governed by the Canada Business Corporations Act will be guilty of an offence for failing to comply with their statutory duties include the following.

(i) *Capital impairment*

Directors have a duty to maintain the capital of the corporation, failing which they are personally liable to the corporation for impairing its capital in violation of applicable provisions of the Canada Business Corporations Act. For example, a director who consents to resolutions authorising the following commits an offence:

- the issuance of shares before consideration therefor is paid in full; or
- the payment of dividends or the purchase or redemption of shares in situations where the corporation is insolvent or otherwise fails to satisfy the solvency tests enumerated in the Canada Business Corporations Act.

(ii) *Insider trading*

Directors and officers of a corporation who are guilty of insider trading (the purchase or sale of a security of a corporation by an insider of that corporation who has certain confidential information) will be liable to the person from or to whom the securities were sold or purchased, as the case may be, and will be required to compensate that person for any damages sustained as a result of the purchase or sale. Directors and officers who are guilty of insider trading will also be accountable to the corporation for any advantage received or receivable by them as a result of the purchase or sale.

(iii) *Insider tipping*

Directors and officers of a corporation who are guilty of insider tipping (the communication of certain confidential information by an insider to another person who then purchases or sells a security of the corporation) must compensate any person who subsequently sells securities of the corporation to, or purchases securities of the corporation from, the person to whom the insider disclosed the confidential information.

(iv) *Record maintenance*

Directors have a duty to maintain certain records for the corporation in accordance with the provisions set forth in the applicable corporate statute. Directors who, without reasonable cause, contravene the provisions dealing with the preparation, maintenance and safekeeping of corporate records are guilty of an offence.

1.2 Standards of care

The Supreme Court of Canada has affirmed that the standard of care to which directors are subject is an objective standard, albeit an objective standard that takes into consideration the factual circumstances surrounding a particular occurrence. Recall that the duty of care requires the care, diligence and skill that a reasonably prudent person would exercise *in comparable circumstances*. The decisions of directors and officers must be reasonable business decisions in light of all circumstances, including prevailing socio-economic conditions, of which they were or ought to have been aware. Directors who, in the absence of any reasonable suspicion as to their veracity, adopt a course of action in reliance on reports issued by professionals such as lawyers, accountants, engineers, appraisers or any other person whose profession lends credibility to a statement made by that person may, if necessary, avail themselves of a defence of reasonable care.

Courts generally respect the business decisions of Canadian directors and officers as long as the decisions do not involve fraud or self-dealing, and are made on an informed basis in what the director or officer honestly believes to be the best interests of the corporation. It is generally accepted that directors and officers who have acted honestly and with care for the benefit of the corporation should not be personally liable for mere errors in judgement. The Supreme Court of Canada recently held that courts are ill-suited and should be reluctant to second-guess the application of business expertise to the considerations that are often involved in corporate decision-making.

Consequently, if directors and officers have acted with due care in what they honestly consider to be the best interests of the corporation, Canadian courts will defer to their business judgement.

1.3 To whom the duties are owed

(a) *The corporation*

A director owes a fiduciary duty to the corporation. Consequently, decisions made by a director must always be in the best interests of the corporation and not those of the director himself or of a particular constituency of the corporation (eg, a controlling shareholder, a class of shareholders, creditors or others), irrespective of whether such constituency has nominated or appointed such director.

(b) *Holders of securities*

Though uncommon, directors may also owe a separate and distinct fiduciary duty directly to the holders of securities of a corporation (ie, shareholders and holders of debt obligations of the corporation). The Supreme Court of Canada has held that a fiduciary relationship may exist where a person, alone, has the ability to exercise some discretion or power to affect another's legal interests in circumstances where the other person is particularly vulnerable. Whether this principle of law can be relied upon by a holder of securities of a corporation will be a question of fact.

While a direct duty of directors to holders of securities of the corporation will rarely be found to exist, the consideration and furtherance of their interests may be necessary for a director to fulfil his duty to act in the best interests of the corporation properly. For example, the directors of a corporation that is the target of a takeover generally have the obligation to take steps to maximise shareholder value.

(c) *Creditors*

Directors and officers do not owe a duty directly to creditors (including contracting parties in favour of whom the corporation has undertaken obligations) of the corporation. However, directors of some corporations - particularly deposit-taking institutions or other companies that routinely receive sums of money in trust - may owe a duty directly to the beneficiaries of any trust monies.

(d) *Duty to employees*

Personal liability for amounts owing to employees and for payroll source deductions owing to government authorities are among the most significant areas of personal liability facing directors in Canada. Many provinces impose personal liability on directors for employee wages and related amounts under both their corporate statutes and their employment legislation. Employees seeking recourse often choose to avail themselves of the employment legislation, as governmental authorities charged with the application of such legislation may pursue a claim on their behalf by way of administrative proceedings. In those provinces where employment legislation imposes personal liability on directors for termination and severance pay, opting to initiate proceedings against the directors of a corporation under employment legislation may also be preferable.

The majority of the corporate statutes in Canada also impose liability on directors for salary arrears and other amounts owing to employees of a corporation; these statutes do not impose such liability on officers of the corporation. The corporate statutory provisions that make directors liable to 'employees' of the corporation generally apply to all employees of the corporation without regard to rank. Consequently, members of middle and senior management may initiate proceedings under corporate statutory regimes whereas they may be excluded from the ambit of employment legislation. The Canada Business Corporations Act provides that directors are personally liable for all service-related debts owing to employees up to a maximum amount equivalent to six months' wages provided the director was, in fact, a director at the time the employee services were performed. However, an employee will succeed in his claim for such amounts only if he meets one of the following conditions:

- The corporation has been successfully sued for the debt within six months of it becoming due but complete execution of the judgment has been unsuccessful;
- The corporation has commenced liquidation and dissolution proceedings or has been dissolved and a claim for the debt has been proved within six months of the earlier of the date of commencement of the liquidation and dissolution proceedings and the date of dissolution; or
- The corporation has made an assignment, or a bankruptcy order has been made against it, under the Bankruptcy Act and a claim for the debt has been proved in the six months following the date of the assignment or bankruptcy order.

The personal liability of directors for unpaid service-related debts is joint and several. Consequently, if both plaintiff and defendant are directors, the plaintiff is not barred from relief under the Canada Business Corporations Act. However, he will have to share the responsibility of paying any such relief.

(e) *Duty to the public*

Directors and officers of a corporation owe no special duty to the public at large, but may become personally liable in contract or tort if their actions are judged to be personal and outside the scope of their authority as agents for the corporation. In addition, directors' obligations to ensure a corporation's compliance with applicable environmental statutes and the triggering of their personal liability in cases where they fail to do so can be seen as a statutory reflection of the duty of directors to the public.

1.4 Common defences to and exemptions from liability

The defences available to a director or officer will be determined by the elements of the offence which he is purported to have committed. In addition to the failure of a plaintiff to establish the elements of its cause of action, the corporate statutes of Canada provide for a number of defences which may be set up by directors or officers in connection with allegations directed towards them under such statutes. This section provides a brief overview of the most commonly available defences for directors and officers of corporations governed by the Canada Business Corporations Act.

No provision in a contract, the articles, the bylaws or a resolution relieves a director or officer from his duty to act in accordance with the Canada Business Corporations Act or its regulations; nor can such a provision relieve a director or officer from liability for a breach thereof. In addition, it is not a defence to personal liability under the Canada Business Corporations Act for a director to allege that he did not attend a board meeting. Nor is it sufficient that a director have abstained or voted against a resolution. To avoid responsibility for any resolution or action taken at a board meeting, one's dissent must be recorded. A director absent from a meeting is deemed to have consented to resolutions passed thereat unless, within seven days of becoming aware of the resolution, he causes his dissent to be recorded in the minutes of the meeting or sends a dissent to the registered office of the corporation. A director can set up his registered dissent to avoid liability for a number of offences and breaches which the board of directors may be accused of having committed and which are expressly listed in the Canada Business Corporations Act (ie, issuing shares for inadequate non-cash consideration, declaring dividends or otherwise paying out moneys to shareholders when the corporation is insolvent or which render the corporation insolvent, or failing to pay employee wages) where he exercises the care, diligence and skill that a reasonably prudent person would have exercised in comparable circumstances, including reliance, in good faith, on the corporation's financial statements or a professional report.

There now exists a due diligence defence in the Canada Business Corporations Act in respect of liability for an undervalued issuance of shares, improper declaration of dividends, improper purchase or redemption of shares, unpaid employee wages and non-compliance with the Canada Business Corporations Act, the constitutive documents or any unanimous shareholder agreement. The due diligence defence is broader than a reliance in good faith defence, as a director may invoke that he acted upon the report of a person whose profession lends credibility to his statement to demonstrate the director's due diligence, but need not prove such reliance to succeed in the above defence. Conversely, a reliance in good faith defence does exist with respect to any liability arising under an alleged breach of the fiduciary duty or duty of care by a director of a corporation governed by the Canada Business Corporations Act. For such a defence to succeed, a director must prove actual reliance on either:

- financial statements presented to the director by an officer of the corporation or in a written report of the auditor of the corporation; or
- a report of a person whose profession lends credibility to a statement made by such professional.

The absence of intent may be set up as a defence by a director or officer in relation to certain offences. This defence is commonly invoked by directors and officers who are accused of having authorised or acquiesced to fraudulent preferences (a constituent element of which is a dominant intent to prefer) given by a corporation to one of its creditors in a bankruptcy situation. The determination of intent is an objective determination.

The scope of liability and the defences available to directors under provincial legislation vary considerably across Canada, and defences available to directors and officers in one province may not be available in another. For example, there is absolute personal liability on directors for the costs of remediation of a contaminated site if they are found to be 'responsible persons' within the meaning of the Waste Management Act (British Columbia). Consequently, a due diligence defence is unavailable to directors in such cases. Conversely, the Environment Quality Act (Quebec) specifies that every director or officer who authorises or, through advice or encouragement, leads the corporation to refuse or neglect to comply with an order under such act, or to discharge a contaminant into the environment, commits an offence. A defence of due diligence and absence of intent may be set up by a director or officer accused of breaching the latter provision, although the onus is on such director or officer to establish that the offence was committed without his knowledge or consent and despite measures taken to prevent its commission.

2. Who can bring claims

2.1 The company

A corporation may bring a claim against a director or officer where such person has acted in breach of his fiduciary duty, his duty to act diligently or his statutory or regulatory duties. The decision to bring such claim is subject to the same formalities required to bring suit in general.

Where a corporation is insolvent, the decision to bring suit against a director or officer is that of the trustee in bankruptcy. Pursuant to the Bankruptcy Act, the trustee may, with the permission of the inspectors named by the various creditors, bring, institute or defend any action or other legal proceeding relating to the property of the bankrupt. The Bankruptcy Act further provides that a creditor of the bankrupt is entitled to request that the trustee take any proceeding that, in the creditor's opinion, would be for the benefit of the corporation. In the event that the trustee fails to acquiesce to such request, the creditor may seek an order from the court authorising him to bring suit in his own name and at his own expense.

2.2 Holders of securities on behalf of the company

A derivative action is a lawsuit in which one or more complainants sue in the corporation's name to remedy or prevent an injury to the corporation. The corporate statutes of Canada typically permit a holder of securities of a corporation to apply to a court to bring an action in the name of the corporation or any of its subsidiaries, or to intervene in an action to which the corporation is a party in order to prosecute, defend or discontinue an action on behalf of the corporation. The foregoing are all variations of derivative actions.

The court must approve each proposed derivative action and complainants must typically satisfy a number of conditions before a court will grant derivative relief. For example, the Canada Business Corporations Act provides that a complainant cannot bring a derivative action if it has not first shown that:

- it has given reasonable notice to the directors that an application is intended to be made if the directors do not bring, defend, prosecute or discontinue an action;
- it is acting in good faith; and
- it appears to be in the interests of the corporation that the action be brought, prosecuted, defended or discontinued.

A complainant need not be a minority shareholder to exercise a derivative action under the Canada Business Corporations Act. By way of example, each of the following persons can be a 'complainant':

- a current or former registered holder or beneficial owner of a security of a corporation or its subsidiary;
- a current or former director or officer of a corporation or its subsidiary; or
- any other person who, in the discretion of a court, is a proper person to make such an application.

A derivative action under the Canada Business Corporations Act relates only to the enforcement of the rights of a corporation and not those of individual shareholders. The following are examples of cases where a derivative action may be invoked:

- actions against directors or officers for a breach of the fiduciary duty or duty of care owed to the corporation; and
- actions for an injunction to prevent a threatened injury to the corporation.

2.3 Shareholders on their own account

The corporate statutes of Canada allow a shareholder and certain other persons with legitimate standing (eg, creditors) to apply to the court for a broad range of remedies when directors unfairly disregard the complainant's interests. Shareholders of a corporation, whether they be minority or majority shareholders, may seek a remedy against the corporation and its directors by bringing proceedings for:

- oppression, where the shareholder complains that the board of directors has acted in an oppressive or prejudicial manner and asks the court to address his complaint. In the latter case, it may be possible to obtain judgment against a corporation's directors personally. A recent decision by the Ontario Court of Appeal upheld an order requiring a director to pay C$97,000 to the corporation so as to enable the creditor of such corporation to recover its judgment. The creditor in this case successfully sued for relief under the oppression provisions of the Business Corporations Act (Ontario), which reflect those set out in the Canada Business Corporations Act; or
- compliance, where the shareholder seeks a court order compelling the directors to comply with the articles, bylaws, shareholder agreement or governing corporate statute.

2.4 Third parties

Pursuant to the Canada Business Corporations Act and a number of other provincial corporate statutes, creditors and other stakeholders, including contracting parties, of a corporation who are not current or former holders or beneficial owners of a security of said corporation are not entitled, as of right, to remedies for oppression. They may do so only if they are qualified, at the discretion of the court, to be a proper person to make an application. Although the determination of who is a 'proper person to make an application' is fact specific, secured and unsecured creditors (including the Crown) of pecuniary and non-pecuniary obligations (ie, contracting parties) and shareholders of parent corporations have both been held to be such persons. The Supreme Court of Canada has recently recognised that creditors' interests become increasingly relevant as a corporation's finances deteriorate. This factor will be significant when courts consider whether a creditor is a 'proper person' with the requisite standing to bring an oppression remedy claim.

3. Claims culture

3.1 Litigation

Canadian litigation culture is not as favourable to plaintiffs as that of the United States. Judicially imposed caps on punitive damages, limited damage awards for non-pecuniary losses and the absence, in most Canadian jurisdictions, of jury trials for civil matters are several factors that serve to discourage large awards. Conservative views with respect to the judicial award of moral and punitive damages have been adopted to avoid clogged court dockets and the swelling of insurance premiums, and are consistent with the Canadian legal principle that damage awards should be commensurate with the actual and proven value of damages sustained.

3.2 Ability to bring class actions

Class actions, as a procedural vehicle by which legal proceedings are instituted against corporate directors and officers, have recently gained in popularity, particularly in the context of corporate insolvency. This is especially true in Quebec, where the increase in class actions against directors has arisen primarily as a result of recent legislative changes permitting class actions in securities matters. Moreover, this surge in class action litigation is also attributable to the relatively low threshold for certification in Quebec and the recent enactment of procedural amendments which substantially curtail a defendant's ability to challenge certification.

Ontario has also enacted legislation which facilitates the institution of class action proceedings, albeit by investors who purchase securities in Ontario. Secondary market investors may now institute proceedings against issuers and their directors where a document or a public declaration made by the issuer contains false representations or the issuer fails to disclose material information in a timely manner. Unlike similar legislation in the United States, a plaintiff need not prove that the defendant intended to deceive, manipulate or defraud the plaintiff, or that the defendant was reckless or wilfully blind. By eliminating the need for an investor to prove specific reliance, this legislation may have the effect of expanding the number of securities-related class actions in Ontario brought against directors. However, the projected increase in such litigation may be tempered by the recent enactment of amendments which provide that the prevailing party is entitled to costs, notwithstanding anything in the Courts of Justice Act (Ontario) and the Class Proceedings Act (Ontario).

In sum, the wider scope of liability resulting from the above-described amendments increases the number of potential civil claimants in Canada, making it reasonably foreseeable that securities-related class actions against issuers and their directors will become more popular. However, at present, the fact remains that the overwhelming majority of director liability cases proceed as individual actions.

3.3 Funding of claims and whether loser pays

(a) Cost awards

The question of whether a losing party may be required to pay a successful party's costs is provincially regulated and therefore contingent on the Canadian province in which the action is being instituted. Typically, costs are awarded by civil courts to a successful party and cover judicial costs (eg, filing costs) and fees (ie, nominal tariff in respect of legal fees). Only exceptionally would amounts in excess of the tariff be awarded to compensate for legal fees incurred by the successful party.

The percentage of a successful party's expenses that will be recoverable is discretionary; Canadian provinces and territories have each developed a set of factors to be considered when awarding costs in litigious proceedings. For instance, the Courts of Justice Act (Ontario) provides that, subject to the provisions of another act or rules of court, the award of costs of and incidental to a proceeding or a step in a proceeding are at the entire discretion of the court, and the court may determine by whom and to what extent the costs shall be paid. However, where the proceedings instituted in Ontario against a defendant are class action proceedings, the Class Proceedings Act (Ontario) provides for a different cost award mechanism; a successful defendant has a *prima facie* entitlement to costs except where the court, in its discretion, chooses not to award such costs because the action is a test case, raises a novel point of law or is in the public interest. As previously mentioned, this may serve as a disincentive to plaintiffs wishing to sue the directors or officers of a corporation by way of a class action lawsuit.

(b) Funding and fee agreements

Rules governing fee agreements between the parties to a judicial proceeding and their respective legal counsel are provincially regulated. For example, contingency fee arrangements, including conditional fee arrangements, were not permitted in Ontario prior to 2002. However, as a means of promoting access to justice, Ontario contingency fee arrangements were legalised in 2002 subject to the provisions of the Solicitors Act (Ontario).

The Supreme Court of Canada recently stipulated that the risk premium to which a solicitor may be entitled by virtue of a contingency agreement entered into with a successful plaintiff will not be considered when an award of indemnity costs is ordered. A defendant has no knowledge of the private arrangements between the plaintiff and his counsel, and thus has no means of measuring the risk of engaging in litigation if such arrangements are considered in the award.

3.4 Plaintiffs' bar

As damage awards in Canada have traditionally been compensatory in nature and thus limited to indemnifying plaintiffs for proven losses, class action tort litigation has not yet reached a level of popularity or profitability to warrant the development of a network of trial lawyers with the sophistication and influence of the plaintiffs' bar in the United States. However, given the recent trend in Canadian legislation and courtrooms towards awarding punitive damages of increasing importance, directors and officers may soon face a Canadian version of the plaintiffs' bar.

3.5 Procedural barriers

Except for the formalities which must first be satisfied in certain types of proceeding (eg, class actions and derivative actions), procedural barriers precluding the advancement of a claim against a director or officer are few. The expiration of the applicable limitation period is the procedural barrier common to all forms of action instituted against directors and officers of a corporation. The limitation periods vary depending on the provincial or territorial legislation applicable to the judicial proceedings and on the provision allegedly breached by a director or officer.

4. Indemnification rights

4.1 When the company can indemnify

A corporation may, in certain circumstances, indemnify its directors and officers in respect of liabilities incurred in such capacity, including defence costs.

As the costs, charges and expenses incurred in defending an action can be substantial, it is not uncommon for a director or officer to request that a corporation advance such amounts. Certain provincial corporate statutes do not permit such advances and expressly state that the amounts to be indemnified must have actually been incurred to be reimbursed. However, the Canada Business Corporations Act expressly permits the advance of costs to directors, although it requires a director to repay the amounts so advanced if he does not meet the statutory standard necessary for indemnification (see section 4.2). However, such an advance is permitted only where the director has acted honestly, in good faith and in the best interests of the corporation. In the case of a criminal or administrative action or proceeding that is enforced by a monetary penalty, the director must also have had reasonable grounds to believe that his conduct was lawful.

An indemnity agreement may also be drafted so as to require expressly the corporation to advance funds to a director for the purpose of covering ongoing costs and expenses prior to the final resolution of a claim, action or proceeding (subject to the director undertaking to repay the advances received if defence or appeal of such director is found to be without merit).

4.2 Formalities for indemnification

Canadian corporate statutes allow a corporation to indemnify its directors and officers provided that they acted honestly, in good faith and in the best interests of the corporation. With respect to liability for criminal or administrative actions, the individual must also have had reasonable grounds to believe that the conduct was lawful in order to be indemnified. To this end, both permissive and mandatory indemnification provisions have been set forth in the Canada Business Corporations Act.

First, the Canada Business Corporations Act permits a corporation to indemnify a current or former director or officer of the corporation against all costs, charges and expenses, including an amount paid to settle an action or satisfy a judgment, reasonably incurred in respect of any individual in respect of any civil, criminal, administrative, investigative or other proceeding in which the individual is involved because of that association with the corporation or other entity, provided that the director or officer in question:

- acted honestly, in good faith and in the best interests of the corporation or, as the case may be, in the best interests of another entity for which the individual acted as director or officer or in a similar capacity at the corporation's request; and
- in the case of a criminal or administrative action or proceeding punished by a monetary penalty, had reasonable grounds to believe that his conduct was lawful.

Second, the Canada Business Corporations Act renders mandatory the payment by the corporation of all amounts reasonably incurred by a director to defend an action to which he is a party by reason of his previous or current role as a director if such director is found not to be at fault and has complied with the conditions above. Under the corporate statutes of certain provinces (eg, Alberta and New Brunswick), the entitlement of a director or officer to the mandatory indemnity is contingent on the satisfaction by such director or officer of a third requirement that he be "fairly and reasonably entitled to indemnity". However, under the corporate statutes of other provinces (eg, Prince Edward Island and Quebec), there exist no mandatory indemnification provisions.

There is little case law relating to the mandatory indemnity provisions set out in Canada's various corporate statutes and the scope of such provisions remains largely ambiguous where, for example, an action against a director is terminated or charges are withdrawn. It is also unclear whether a director or officer who succeeds on a procedural technicality is entitled to receive the mandatory indemnity.

Directors and officers may further reduce their exposure to personal liability through the inclusion of indemnity provisions in the bylaws of the corporation or an indemnity agreement with the corporation.

Corporate bylaws in Canada often include indemnification provisions to ensure that the corporation is bound to indemnify its directors in situations where the legislation merely provides for permissive indemnification by the corporation. However, since the indemnification provisions stipulated in a corporation's bylaws do not constitute a binding agreement between the corporation and its directors, a director cannot prevent the provisions of the bylaws from being amended.

An indemnity agreement is an agreement whereby the corporation, a third party (eg, a majority shareholder) or both agree to indemnify the directors or officers of the corporation against claims that may be made against them as a result of the performance of their duties. Indemnity agreements offer stability of coverage insofar as the scope of indemnification provided for in such agreements may not be modified without the consent of the director benefiting therefrom. Often, directors and officers who are party to such agreements will strive to ensure that a number of criteria are met or items provided for. For example, a director or officer will often seek to extend indemnification to circumstances where he is simply a witness or participant in, rather than a party to, any proceedings.

The value of indemnity agreements is questionable in the event of a corporation's insolvency. A director or officer will often require that a corporation undertake to purchase and maintain an insurance policy which offers meaningful and sufficient liability coverage to such director or officer.

Finally, other protection mechanisms can be structured by the corporation to ensure the indemnification of its directors, although such mechanisms are rarely used. For instance, it is possible to create a trust specifically designed to segregate funds that will indemnify the directors and, in certain cases, third parties to whom the directors would normally be personally liable.

4.3 How indemnification works

Generally, the procedure to be followed in respect of statutory indemnification in Canada is largely determined by the corporation with no need for either the corporation or the indemnified party to resort to the court system of the relevant jurisdiction. However, provincial statutes may provide for certain exceptions. For instance, the Companies Act (Prince Edward Island) requires that "the consent of the company [be] given at any general meeting" before an indemnity may be paid to a director or officer by the corporation.

Further, the Canada Business Corporations Act and the majority of the provincial corporate statutes provide that if a director or officer seeks an indemnity with respect to a derivative action or an action brought by the corporation, he must obtain the approval of the court. However, this requirement will not apply to corporations created under certain provincial statutes (eg, Quebec, Nova Scotia and Prince Edward Island).

4.4 What cannot be indemnified

There are two important limitations to the statutory ability or obligation of a corporation to indemnify a director or officer for the liabilities incurred in the discharge of his duties.

First, the mandatory indemnity provision set out in the corporate statutes of Canada does not compel a corporation to indemnify its directors or officers for amounts paid to settle an action or satisfy a judgment. This limitation results from the condition that a mandatory indemnity is payable only where the director or officer susceptible to such indemnification is substantially successful on the merits of his defence.

Second, in the case of a derivative action commenced by the corporation, the indemnity does not extend to the amounts paid to settle an action or satisfy a judgment. This exception is premised on the improbability that a director called upon to defend a derivative action which is subsequently lost or settled has been acting in the corporation's best interest.

Directors who vote for, or consent to, a resolution authorising an indemnity payment which is contrary to an applicable corporate statute are generally liable on a joint and several basis to restore to the corporation any unrecovered sums, unless they succeed in showing that their decision was based on their reliance, in good faith, on certain financial statements or professional reports.

5. D&O insurance

5.1 Availability of D&O insurance

A corporation may purchase and maintain insurance for the benefit of a director or officer against any liability incurred by the latter in the discharge of his duties. A corporation, on the same basis, may also purchase and maintain insurance policies for its directors and officers who acted as directors or officers of another corporation at the request of the corporation. The majority of the corporate statutes currently in force in Canada, with few exceptions (eg, Quebec, Prince Edward Island and Nova Scotia), have provisions which govern or apply to D&O insurance.

D&O policies traditionally include liability and indemnification coverage. Liability coverage insures directors and officers for loss for wrongful acts for which they are not indemnified by the corporation and generally includes damages, judgments, settlements, costs and defence costs. In contrast, indemnification coverage does not provide direct contractual protection to the individual directors and officers of a corporation, but insures the corporation for amounts it is legally required to pay to indemnify its directors and officers. D&O insurance contracts are typically written on a 'claims-made and reported' basis. Claims-made policies differ from regular occurrence-based contracts in that coverage is triggered by claims made against the directors and officers during the policy period for wrongful acts committed before or during the policy period. A claims-made policy will cover only claims made against the directors or officers during the policy period, irrespective of when the act giving rise to the claim may have occurred.

The corporate statutes of Canada which contain provisions applicable to D&O insurance generally prohibit a corporation from purchasing and maintaining insurance for the benefit of its directors and officers against any liability arising from their failure to act honestly, in good faith and in the best interests of the corporation. If the policy provides for such coverage, the corporation is prohibited from paying the related insurance premium. However, the Canada Business Corporations Act and the Business Corporations Act (British Columbia) contain no restrictions on the actions of directors and officers that may be insured.

5.2 Local rules on cover provided under a non-domestic D&O policy

Generally speaking, but subject to prescribed exceptions, insurance companies that act as insurers within a given province must be authorised and licensed to do so by applicable provincial regulatory bodies. The definition of 'acting as an insurer' and the criteria that need be met to obtain a licence vary from province to province. The absence of a licence generally precludes a non-domestic insurer from providing a policy to a resident policyholder. Subject to the applicable provincial definition of 'acting as an insurer' or an equivalent expression, a foreign parent corporation is usually not precluded from subscribing to an umbrella D&O policy covering directors and officers of its domestic subsidiaries from an insurance company in the foreign parent corporation's home jurisdiction. However, doing so may raise questions of private international law with regard to the validity of any choice of law provisions, and such a policy may be subject to any provincial civil laws of public order governing relationships between insurers and insureds.

Colombia

José Francisco Mafla
Carlos Umaña
Brigard & Urrutia

In 1995 Law 222 introduced significant innovations to the directors' liability regime, among other improvements in corporate law. In line with contemporary corporate law, Law 222 adopted a regime based on fiduciary duties which was, to a certain extent, inspired by the US experience.

Section 24 of Law 222 (included as Section 200 of the Commercial Code), the cornerstone of directors' liability, provides that directors are jointly and severally liable without limitation for damages wilfully or negligently caused to the company, its shareholders or third parties.

Law 222 does not explain the concept or characteristics of a 'director', but rather provides the following exhaustive list of individuals who are deemed to be directors:

- the legal representative (officer);
- the liquidator (officer in liquidation proceedings);
- the manager of an ongoing concern;
- the members of the board of directors; and
- whoever performs or has such functions according to the company bylaws.

1.1 Nature of the duties

Law 222 establishes three different general duties and certain specific obligations.

(a) *Duty of good faith*

This implements a general legal principle imposing certain standards of behaviour on all those engaging in legal transactions. The Colombian Constitution imposes a general obligation to act in good faith on both authorities and individuals.[1] Likewise, there is a general presumption of good faith; so the burden of proof generally falls on the party claiming otherwise.[2]

In practice, the duty of good faith requires parties to execute and perform transactions with a true and correct intention, and to undertake all actions needed to ensure that this is achieved.

The duty of good faith means that directors must reach informed and fair decisions through a fair decision-making process. Directors must give the board sufficient information to allow them to discharge their responsibilities to the company. Individual directors cannot request specific information from the

1 Section 83 of the Constitution.
2 Section 177 of the Code of Civil Procedure.

management if this information is confidential. Further, directors are allowed to rely on the opinions of advisers and experts, as long as they have been carefully selected based on objective criteria.

Moreover, a fair decision-making process is generally associated with an unbiased approach which aims to advance the interests of the company. To achieve this, major companies in Colombia establish internal policies and procedures that apply to material decisions, such as investments and the selection of contractors.

(b) Duty of care

In order to prevent mismanagement of the company, directors must comply with a duty of care.

(c) Duty of loyalty

As in other jurisdictions, this is not specifically defined and its scope can change depending on specific circumstances. It can operate as a catchall provision to cover specific prohibitions and any actions by the directors that may cause harm to the company.

In theory, the nature of the duty of loyalty does not differ from that in common law jurisdictions, requiring the fiduciary to act in the best interests of the company.

(d) Specific obligations

These are minimum obligations set out in Law 222, as follows.

(i) *Take steps adequately to carry out the corporate purpose*

Pursuant to this obligation, and based on the corporate purpose doctrine under Colombian law,[3] the directors must always seek to carry out the corporate purpose and cannot make any decision that goes against it.

This is very important, given that Colombian law generally requires that the corporate purpose of companies is limited to certain industrial or commercial activity or activities and their related transactions. Accordingly, as further explained below, any act beyond the scope of this purpose could compromise the directors' liability in respect of the company and affected third parties.

Although this obligation does not require the director to assure the financial success of the corporate venture, it nevertheless requires him to commit to achieving specific corporate goals by means of an agreement.

(ii) *Ensure compliance with bylaws and other applicable laws and regulations*

Directors must be aware of all legal provisions and bylaws, and make every effort to ensure compliance (eg, delegating functions adequately and hiring appropriate legal counsel where advisable).

Although ensuring compliance may seem complicated, if directors try to establish adequate control systems to oversee management breaches or non-compliance by the company, their liability should not be compromised.

---

3 Superintendence of Companies, Resolution 360-1498, July 31 1997.

(iii) *Ensure that the statutory auditor is allowed to perform its duties*
The duties and activities of the statutory auditors depend on the directors' support, as the latter could easily block or affect them. This duty mainly requires directors to deliver all necessary information so that the statutory auditors can carry out their duties.

(iv) *Guard and protect the company's confidential information*
Pursuant to this obligation, directors must refrain from disclosing or taking advantage of any confidential information held by the company and undertake all measures to ensure that such confidentiality is preserved. Any breach of this duty would compromise the liability of the defaulting director.

(v) *Refrain from misusing privileged information*
This obligation has a different but associated scope from that concerning confidential information, as here disclosure of proprietary information could also involve improper use of privileged information whenever the information is both confidential and privileged; there are times when maintaining confidential privileged information that should have been disclosed implies the improper use of the same (eg, when securities or other regulations impose an obligation to reveal a corporate transaction). In certain cases it can result in penalties and criminal liability.

(vi) *Afford equitable treatment to all shareholders and respect their inspection rights*
Even though directors are usually appointed and supported by the majority of the shareholders, they must not discriminate between majority and minority shareholders. The Commercial Code states that directors must advance the interests of the company as a whole in line with the interests of the shareholders. They do not just represent groups of shareholders – they represent all of them.

Commentators have generally identified the following common examples of discrimination:

- only allowing certain shareholders to enter the corporate offices;
- holding private meetings with some shareholders and not with others; and
- bias when entering into agreements with shareholders and their companies.

(vii) *Refrain from acting, directly or indirectly, in case of a conflict of interest except when duly authorised*
This prevents directors from taking advantage of corporate opportunities and engaging in transactions that would cause a conflict of interest (interested directors' transactions) to arise with the company. [4]

Competition or taking undue advantage of corporate opportunities happens when, without adequate corporate approval, directors undertake activities in connection with assets, services, transactions, individuals or markets pursued by the company.

4 Superintendence of Companies, External Notice 20/1997 and Law 155/1959.

A conflict of interest occurs where directors have a personal interest in a decision that prevents them from exercising unbiased judgment.

In both cases the following rules apply:

- A directors is directly involved in these situations or via a third party as an agent or 'straw man'; and
- The interest or activity concerned may belong to directors or related persons.

If there is sufficient approval from the shareholders, this overturns the prohibition.

Approval by the shareholders should comply with the following requirements:

- It must be granted *ex ante*, not after the director has engaged in the conflicting transactions;
- Full prior disclosure is required – the director must provide all necessary information to allow shareholders to make an informed decision;
- If the interested director is also a shareholder, he should not take part in the discussion or approval; and
- Approval cannot be delegated to the board of directors or any corporate body other than the shareholders' assembly.

1.2 Standards of care

Pursuant to Law 222,[5] the 'good businessman' standard applies to directors. In theory, this standard differs from the 'reasonable person in similar circumstances' standard in the United States, in that it is abstract and does not consider the particular circumstances of directors and their decisions. However, courts tend to take a case-specific approach when deciding on matters of liability, so the practical implications are probably similar.

Scholars[6] believe that the 'good businessman' standard is more demanding than the classic *paterfamilias* standard which civil law jurisdictions have inherited from Roman law. It requires certain knowledge, skills and attitudes typical in the business community, thus allowing a wider scope of action and risk assumptions in corporate ventures.

However, given that these duties have recently been introduced, there is no significant case law or administrative decisions as to the specific elements involved and scope of the standard of care.

1.3 To whom duties are owed

Duties are owed first to the company, second to the shareholders and, to a limited extent, to third parties in specific cases.

1.4 Common defences to and exemptions from liability

According to general rules of civil liability and based on Section 200 of the Commercial Code (as amended by Article 24 of Law 222), to bring an action against

---

5 Section 23 of Law 222.

6 Francisco Reyes, *Derecho Societario*, Volume I.

directors, plaintiffs must argue and demonstrate:

- the director's breach of an obligation;
- the level of scienter in the conduct (negligence or wilful misconduct);
- the existence of losses or damages; and
- causation between the defendant's act and the plaintiff's losses or damages.

Defendants have the opportunity to rebut the existence of any of these elements and avoid liability.

Section 24 of Law 222 introduced an additional significant liability exemption in special circumstances: directors who were unaware of the act or omission, or who voted against it, will not be subject to liability.

There is a legal presumption of negligence whenever there is a breach of a legal provision or of the company bylaws. Further, any limitation on directors' liability included in the bylaws is ineffective.

If a legal entity acts as a director, both the legal entity and its corresponding legal representative may be held liable.

2. Who can bring claims

2.1 The company

Law 222 introduced the direct company claim.[7] The company itself has a right to bring a claim against its directors in case of wrongdoing, to recover any incurred losses or damages. Accordingly, any recovery goes to the company treasury and not to the shareholders or creditors.

Given that these claims come from the company itself, they require a decision of the shareholders' assembly. Some special rules apply to this decision:

- The decision may be adopted at any shareholders' meeting (ordinary or extraordinary), even if it is not included on the agenda.[8]
- The meeting may be convened by directors, the statutory auditor or the Superintendence of Companies. As a special rule, the meeting can also be convened by shareholders holding at least 20% of the outstanding shares.[9]
- If a majority of the shareholders are represented at the meeting, the decision may be made by a majority of the attending shares.[10]
- Directors who are also shareholders can take part in the meeting and the vote.[11]
- In the case of incumbent directors, the decision causes automatic removal.[12]
- Once a decision is made, the legal representative (officer) (or the liquidator during a liquidation procedure) must file the corresponding suit.[13]

---

7 Section 25 of Law 222.
8 Francisco Reyes, *Derecho Societario*, Volume I.
9 Section 25 of Law 222.
10 Section 25 of Law 222.
11 Francisco Reyes, *Derecho Societario*, Volume I.
12 Section 25 of Law 222.
13 Section 25 of Law 222.

- Other directors, shareholders, the statutory auditor or certain creditors may bring a derivative action if the lawsuit is not filed within three months of the decision.[14]

2.2 Minority shareholders on behalf of the company

Although shareholders may bring derivative actions, these are a subsidiary alternative claim. This right becomes available only three months after the shareholders decided to bring the claim, if the company's legal representative has not filed the claim.

Any derivative action requires the prior approval of the shareholders, so if the directors have the support of the majority of shareholders, there will be no derivative action against them.

Any recovery from a successful action goes to the company treasury, as it is brought on behalf of the company.

2.3 Minority shareholders on their own account

Shareholders are also entitled to claim against directors to obtain redress of personal damages, which must be direct and certain. So-called 'reflected damages'[15] (ie, company damages allegedly affecting shareholders) are usually not treated as direct.

Direct damages may comprise the following:

- lack of payment of decreed dividends;
- denial or delay of annotations regarding ownership rights in the stock ledger;
- disruption of inspection rights; or
- violations of pre-emptive rights.

Such claims do not require prior approval by the shareholders' meeting and any recovery goes directly to the shareholder, not to the company treasury. Liability must be proved by satisfying the elements mentioned in section 1.4.

Finally, class action proceedings are also available as discussed in section 3.2.[16]

2.4 Third parties

Without prejudice to their rights against the company, third parties (ie, creditors and contractual parties) may also claim against the directors based on the general tort regime whenever the damage reaches a certain level and is caused by a director rather than the company.[17]

Events triggering direct liability to third parties are as follows:

- wilful or negligent activities by directors beyond the scope of their powers;
- events where the company is liable but insolvent and cannot repair the corresponding damage; and
- cases where directors' liability is established by statute.

---

14 Section 25 of Law 222.
15 Francisco Reyes, *Derecho Societario*, Volume I.
16 Law 472/1998.
17 Gabino Pinzón, *Sociedades Comerciales*, Volume I.

Any recovery goes directly to the third party and not to the company treasury. Liability must be proved by satisfying the elements mentioned in section 1.4.

3. Claims culture

3.1 Litigation

Although reforms have been introduced, the Colombian judicial system lacks efficiency and there is always a backlog of cases. A final ruling can take years, so in most cases the parties prefer to settle claims privately.

There is not a strong compensation culture in Colombia, and although directors' duties and liability have become common topics in corporate governance documents and legal literature, there has not been a major increase in claims following the introduction of Law 222. Any claims are brought directly by the company, but these are not always successful.

3.2 Ability to bring class actions

Class actions were introduced by the Constitution in 1991 and were further developed by Law 472/1998. They are available to groups of potential plaintiffs that have sustained damages from the same situation. The state attorney general and the local attorney general may file class actions on behalf of any individual or group of individuals.[18]

Class actions may be used by shareholders against directors if, in addition to the general requirements for bringing a judicial claim, the following special requirements are met:

- The class consists of at least 20 members, of whom at least 20 must be specifically identified, although not all of them need be actually named; and
- The claim must be common to all members.

Class actions must be filed through an attorney. If there is more than one attorney, a class committee will be created. The court will recognise the attorney representing the greatest number of victims as the coordinator. However, the class committee can also appoint an attorney.[19]

After a class action has been filed and before the beginning of discovery, individuals may join the class action procedure by filing a brief stating:

- their name;
- the damage suffered;
- the source of the damages; and
- their interest in becoming part of the action and their commitment to abide by any future decision.

If an individual does not join the action, he can still benefit from any decision after it is issued by filing this brief within 20 days of publication of the decision, provided that this is not barred by the statute of limitations. However, these

18 Section 48 of Law 472/1998.
19 Section 49 of Law 472/1998.

claimants cannot request extraordinary or exceptional damages and cannot recover legal fees and expenses.[20]

3.3 Funding of claims and whether loser pays

Courts do not charge for proceedings.[21] Nevertheless, as a general rule, the losing party will be required to pay the winning party's costs, such as:

- all proven court expenses (eg, experts' fees, service fees, guardian *ad litem* fees); and
- attorneys' fees established pursuant to the fixed amounts set out in Resolution 1887/2003 of the Higher Council of the Judiciary.

At least in connection with attorneys' fees, the assessed amount normally does not reflect the true costs incurred by the winning party.

The loser faces the risk of a claim for damages caused by the initial claim, especially where provisional remedies are involved. However, this does not usually deter claimants from bringing unmeritorious or frivolous claims.

Attorneys' fees generate additional costs, as the plaintiff must hire a lawyer to represent him before the court. These fees are agreed independently between attorney and plaintiff according to market standards, and can incorporate options such as conditional or contingency agreements, in an amount of up to 50% of the judgment.

There are a number of judicial alternatives to enforce judgments and force the losing party to pay; however, any recovery depends on the solvency of the losing party at the moment of effective payment.

3.4 Plaintiffs' bar

Colombia lacks a consolidated and unified plaintiffs' bar, and lawyers and law firms generally act independently. However, contingency fees are becoming increasingly common and attorneys' networks are growing; in turn, these are both strengthening the position of trial lawyers.

3.5 Procedural barriers

As noted above, actions to be brought on behalf of the company (by the company itself, by the shareholders or by the statutory auditor) require the prior approval of the shareholders pursuant to the requirements of the bylaws.

On the other hand, a general statute of limitations of five years applies to all claims to be brought in connection with directors' liability resulting from conduct attributable to the director.[22]

---

20 Section 55 of Law 472/1998.
21 Section 6 of Law 270/1995.
22 Section 235 of Law 222.

4. Indemnification rights

4.1 When the company can indemnify

There are no specific rules on directors' indemnification and the topic is therefore governed by general liability and indemnification rules. There is no significant case law on this point.

While it is uncertain whether a company can indemnify directors in relation to negligence, pursuant to a basic civil liability rule, it is clear that parties cannot exonerate one another for future wilful misconduct or gross negligence.[23] The basic directors' liability rule, as quoted above, states that directors will be jointly and severally liable, without limitation, for damage wilfully or negligently caused to the company, its shareholders or third parties.[24]

Accordingly, it is not clear whether the company can indemnify at all, and whether the labour or services agreements by which directors and officers are hired can specify events, limits and other details concerning indemnification rights. Based on these rules, we would argue that directors cannot be indemnified by the company in any circumstances.

4.2 Formalities for indemnification

In the event that indemnification is accepted as a hypothetical event, given the lack of rules on this point, there are no legal formalities for indemnification rights. Such formalities could possibly be agreed between the company and the directors.

4.3 How indemnification works

There is no set legal procedure for indemnification, so the company and the concerned directors or officers can agree the procedure between them.

4.4 What cannot be indemnified

As there is debate even as to whether directors' indemnification by the company is absolutely prohibited, it is not certainly possible to indemnify damages caused by the director's wilful misconduct or gross negligence. Directors are not entitled to file claims against the company for damages or to recover amounts paid as a result of penalties imposed upon them for violation of their duties.

5. D&O insurance

5.1 Availability of D&O insurance

D&O insurance policies are available to cover the risk of any director or any individual who performs direction or management of the company. This includes the members of the board, the officers, the liquidators and the representatives of ongoing concerns. Such policies are becoming increasingly popular with companies, which usually take out one policy to cover all directors.

---

23 Section 1522 of the Civil Code.
24 Section 24 of Law 222 (included as Section 200 of the Commercial Code).

5.2 Local rules on cover provided under a non-domestic D&O policy

Colombian residents cannot purchase non-domestic insurance policies, unless these are used for travelling abroad.

However, if they have the prior authorisation of the Finance Authority, foreign insurers can still sell insurance in Colombia on a case-by-case basis. The Finance Authority has stated that when granting authorisation, it will take into account:

- the situation on the Colombian market;
- the offer of insurance products by Colombian insurers;
- the cost of insurance premiums;
- coverage at a national, regional and worldwide level; and
- the reinsurance market.[25]

If the parent company of a Colombian-resident subsidiary obtains a global policy from a foreign insurer to cover the subsidiary, it would violate the prohibition against purchasing non-domestic insurance policies. This notwithstanding, no penalties would be imposed on the parent company, the subsidiary or the foreign insurer; but if the parent company pays the premium for the global policy and this is then reimbursed by the subsidiary, it will not be allowed to deduct the payments for tax purposes.

The following customary D&O insurance exclusions have been identified:

- wilful misconduct;
- third-party personal injury;
- physical damage to assets;
- environmental liability;
- fines and penalties;
- securities issuances; and
- claims against insured persons notified or informed prior to the policy.

5.3 Other D&O liability issues

(a) *Criminal liability*

In general, directors are subject to criminal liability in the following instances:

- The directors are guilty of forgery in the event that they:
  - order, tolerate, make or hide alterations to the financial statements of the company;
  - issue false certificates or furnish false information to the authorities; or
  - falsely represent the names of shareholders or directors of the company with a view to inducing third parties to subscribe for shares.[26]
- The directors are guilty of the undue use of privileged information if they use such information for their own benefit or for that of a third party.

---

25 Section 188 of the Financial System Statute (Decree 663/1993).

26 Chapter III of the Criminal Code and Section 10 of Law 43/1990.

The directors are not entitled to file claims against the company for damages or for the recovery of amounts paid as a result of penalties imposed upon them due to their criminal liability. (Criminal liability may entail civil liability for damages to third parties.)

The criminal liability of directors is the subject of growing interest in Colombia as a result of recent cases involving alleged violations of rights relating to the environment, the patrimony of shareholders and third parties, the so-called 'public trust' and the public administration in general. However, a detailed discussion of these matters is beyond the scope of this chapter.

Tax rules establish three main events of criminal liability by the legal representatives of a company:

- not paying income tax that has been withheld from a third party within two months of such withholding or issuing incorrect withholding tax certificates to third parties, except where another individual in the company has been expressly appointed as liable before the tax administration;[27]
- not paying value added tax charged to third parties within one month of the corresponding two-month period;[28] and
- introducing to the country merchandise valued at more than 100 minimum monthly salaries (approximately $19,000) through inappropriate ports of entry or hiding such merchandise from the customs authorities.[29]

(b) Tax obligations

Directors may also be liable for minor breaches that do not amount to criminal offences. Accordingly, directors who are responsible for compliance with procedural tax obligations (ie, filing of tax returns and supporting information) are liable in case of breach; they may be forced to pay fines or the amount that is owed and subject to additional penalties.

(c) Accounting obligations

Directors are responsible for ensuring adequate company accounting and compliance with the relevant accounting rules. Accordingly, fines and other penalties may be imposed where the directors are responsible for breaches in this regard or should have avoided them.[30]

(d) Foreign exchange obligations

Directors are liable if the company breaches its foreign exchange obligations and considerable fines may be imposed directly on them. Foreign exchange obligations include reporting and updating on:

- foreign investment in the company;
- the company's foreign debts;

---

27 Sections 665 and 666 of the Tax Statute.
28 Sections 665 and 666 of the Tax Statute.
29 Sections 319 to 322 of the Criminal Code.
30 General Accounting Statute (Decree 2649/1993).

- import and export levels; and
- investments abroad.[31]

Further, directors who sign and present a foreign exchange declaration in their own name or on behalf of the company may be liable for the veracity of the information presented and must keep a physical archive of all signed originals and the supporting documents.

(e) *Customs obligations*

The same liabilities and responsibilities as apply for tax matters apply for customs matters.

31 See Colombian Foreign Exchange Regime (Central Bank Resolution 8 of 2000, External Central Bank Notice DCIN 83 of December 16 2004).

France

Virginie Bozonnet
Philippe Delecluse
Sarah Xerri-Hanote
Vovan & Associés

1 Directors' duties

1.1 Nature of the duties

(a) General duties

Under French law, there is an implicit presumption of competence on the part of any director to the extent that no legal rule - with the exception of those applicable to certain regulated professions or activities for which directors must possess specific qualifications, training or management experience – lays down any general conditions or levels of knowledge necessary to be a company director.

Anyone can potentially become a director, provided he is of age and is free to carry out commercial activity in France. Individuals with criminal convictions cannot become directors.

As the director is elected by the general assembly, the shareholders must ensure that the person to whom they intend to entrust the management of their company is professionally competent.

If an individual accepts the position of director, he deems himself fully capable of doing the job and will be responsible to the general assembly.

Under the French regime, the following must be established for a director to incur liability:

- wrongdoing;
- loss or damage; and
- a causal link between the wrongful act and the loss or damage.

Therefore, even if the company's affairs are in a poor state, this does not in itself constitute evidence of wrongdoing by an individual director.

There are two main categories of wrongful act or 'fault' (*faute*) in France:

- faults of commission, resulting from acts of management (eg, unfair competition, breach of level of authority, reckless acts); and
- faults of omission (eg, lack of interest in the management of the company, inadequate accounting, failure to supervise staff).

The legal texts governing the liability of directors come from various different sources and the rules are similar regardless of whether liability is sought by the company itself or by third parties. Article 1850 of the Civil Code governs the liability of directors of the different kinds of private company (*société civile, société en nom collectif* and *société en commandite*). Article L223–22 of the Commercial Code governs the liability of directors of limited companies (*sociétés à responsabilité limitée*). Finally, Articles L225–251, L225–252 and L227–8 of the Commercial Code govern the liability of directors of public companies (*sociétés anonymes* and *sociétés par actions simplifiée*).

In addition to the obligations directly linked to his management function, a director is bound to the shareholders by a number of duties both during and after his period of office.

(i) *During the period of office*

In office, the director is bound by an obligation of loyalty towards the company and his partners. As a result, he must abstain from indulging in any activity that competes with the company he represents. This non-compete obligation is imposed upon the director by law, without any need for a non-compete clause.

It is possible to detect here the influence of a key concept in US company law: that of 'fiduciary duties', which comprise a duty of care and a duty of loyalty *stricto sensu*.

Under this duty of loyalty, directors have been accused of not having revealed to a shareholder who had expressed the desire to sell his shares that the director knew of someone interested in acquiring them, and of having then bought them himself before selling them on at a higher price to the interested buyer.[1] Similarly, other directors have been accused by shareholders wishing to sell shares of having concealed from them that negotiations were ongoing with a third party with a view to purchasing them or making a capital contribution.[2]

(ii) *After termination of office*

The director remains bound to the shareholders of the company by his duty of loyalty, even after his office has been terminated.

This obligation is founded on case law.[3] It means that under Article 1382 of the Civil Code, a former director can still be liable, on the grounds that any wrongful act which causes damage to another person obliges its author to compensate for such loss.

One of the obvious consequences of this obligation is that it does not permit acts of unfair competition. In practice, an ex-director is not forbidden from setting up a similar enterprise,[4] but he must avoid systematically enticing the staff of the former company, denigrating the former company or causing confusion in the minds of the clientele.[5]

Moreover, the director should take care not to create a new enterprise before he formally ceases his duties as director.[6]

---

1 Cass com, February 27 1996, 94–11.241.

2 Cass com, May 12 2004, 00–15.618, JCP éd E 2004, No 1393, note F-G. Trébulle, D 2004, p 1600, Obs A Lienhard, JCP E 2004, 1510, Obs Caussain, Deboissy and Wicker, Dr sociétés 2004, No 139, Obs F-G Trébulle, Rev sociétés 2005, p 140, note L Godon.

3 Cass com, February 10 1998, 95–21.893, Rev sociétés 1998, p 546, note Coquelet; cf also articles by M Buy, Dr & patr 1999, 69, p 48, and L Godon.

4 Cass req, February 8 1911, DP 1912, I, p 173 ; Cass com, June 30 1992, 90–18.662; TGI Guéret, October 13 1992, Bull Joly (Cass req, February 8 1911, DP 1912, I, p 173 ; Cass com, June 30 1992, No 90–18.662; TGI Guéret, October 13 1992, Bull Joly.

5 Cass com, February 16 1976, No 74–14.546, Bull civ IV, 49, p 44.

6 Cass com, June 7 1994, No 92–13.935, Rev sociétés 1995, p 275, note Vatinet.

This is an important point in practice. It is possible to consider – by analogous application of the rules governing all employees - that nothing prevents a director from preparing for future activities in competition with the company of which he is still a director during the notice period following his resignation (eg, by going through the formalities of setting up a company). However, the director would incur liability if this new company began trading before the notice period had expired. The Supreme Court has been very clear on this point, approving a court of appeal decision that a director in this position "fell short of his obligations of loyalty and fidelity towards the companies of which he was the manager".[7]

In its ruling of February 12 2002, the Supreme Court also held that the surname of the ex-director had featured on brochures advertising his new company while he was still a director at his previous company. This caused confusion. However, the manager in question did not have a management role in the new company, "a fact which underlined the unnecessary nature of the use of his name".

(b) *Specific duties*

Independently of the duties mentioned above, which are common to all directors, company directors are liable for any wrongful acts which they commit while carrying out their duties. This may result from:

- civil fault through the violation of regulatory or legal provisions, a violation of the statutes or a management error; or
- criminal fault resulting from a violation of specific regulations.

(i) *Liability resulting from civil fault*

The company or the partners alleging the wrongful act of a director must supply proof of such wrongdoing. Wrongdoing may arise at various points in the life of a company.

Incorporation: The founders and directors are liable for any loss or damage to third parties caused by any irregularity which affects the incorporation of the company or its cancellation, and arising from a failure to observe the basic preconditions or the conditions of form or publicity.

As regards the fundamental preconditions, where it is not possible to incorporate the company, those who have acted in its name are jointly, severally and indefinitely liable for their actions, unless the company, once ultimately incorporated, frees them from liability by taking over these actions on its own account. If the company is incorporated and subsequently cancelled, or if resolutions made following its incorporation are cancelled, an action for liability may be launched against those persons responsible for the nullity. This action is time-barred for three years after the final decision to cancel the company (after exhaustion of any recovery).

As regards the conditions of form or publicity, an action will be based on loss or damage resulting from either:

- failure to make an obligatory inclusion in the statutes; or

7 Cass Com, February 12 2002, 00–11.602, JCP E 2002, 1603, p 1776, note Monnet, Dr & patr 2002, 104, p 94, Obs Poracchia, Dr sociétés 2002, 146, Obs Bonneau, Bull Joly 2002, p 617, note Saintourens.

- failure to carry out registration formalities with the Companies Register.

Those potentially liable are the founders of the company and its initial directors. They are deemed jointly and severally liable for loss or damage caused by their negligence, even if the nullity is not formally confirmed. Such action is time barred for 10 years either from the date of registration or from the modified registration in the Companies Register.

Wrongful acts committed by directors at the time of incorporation of the company may be held against them - in particular, when penalties are imposed as a result of administration or liquidation proceedings - if the court considers that the company's resources upon incorporation were insufficient to allow it to prosper. In this way, a lack of sufficient equity capital to enable the company to function normally[8] will constitute a fault of 'inadequate or excessive investment'.[9]

Breaches of legal or regulatory provisions: Once the company has been incorporated, the directors must scrupulously follow the general and particular rules of company law, as failure to do so will constitute a wrongful act. This applies to:

- breach of the rules on the convening of meetings (eg, failure to convene an annual meeting; breach of the duty of communication to shareholders; ignorance of the rules on competence, quorum and majority; failure to observe publication formalities); and
- publication of incorrect accounts, and irregularities in drafting formal accounts and in the payment of dividends.

As a result of various financial scandals in the United States and Europe, and following the introduction of the Sarbanes-Oxley Act in the United States, France passed the Financial Security Law of August 2 2003 to restore investor confidence in the market, clarify the rules on the punishment of stock market offences and improve corporate governance, as well as ending the use of company boards as mere 'rubber-stamping' devices.

Violation of statutes: The liability of directors may be sought where they have failed to observe statutory provisions in addition to legal or regulatory stipulations (eg, where a director entered into an agreement without obtaining the prior authorisation of shareholders).

Management wrongdoing: Directors are liable for any action that is contrary to the interests of the company and for which they are responsible. The definition of liability for 'management wrongdoing' is very broad, and extends from simple negligence to fraudulent operations. To avoid liability it is necessary to demonstrate that the director showed sufficient diligence – this is essentially an obligation of best efforts on the part of the director. Case law will seek to identify any behaviour that strays from that of a 'prudent, diligent and active' director.

---

8 Cass Com, March 19 1996, 94–12.004, Bull civ IV, 91, p 77.

9 Cass Com, November 23 1999, 97–12.834, BRDA 2000, 5, p 4.

Management fault consists of:

- imprudence or lack of foresight in the management of corporate funds;
- misuse of the position of director in furtherance of personal aims, which translates into a misappropriation of funds; and
- negligent inaction, without there necessarily being any breach of law.

Case law defines management fault by the following examples:[10]

- signature of a lease that is prejudicial to the company;[11]
- complicity in the breach of a contract by having a machine manufactured by a third party in disregard of contracts signed between the company and the plaintiff;[12]
- fiscal fraud;[13] and
- negligence in causing a company to be liable to compensate for loss or damage in respect of unfair competition.[14]

Termination of office: Although every director is free to resign, liability may still be sought where resignation occurs under circumstances that could be described as improper (eg, publishing the reasons for resigning or causing the company difficulties because of the abruptness of the decision).

Ex-directors may still be liable for wrongful acts committed during their office which came to light only after their departure, within the applicable statute of limitations. In principle, this lasts for three years, barring exceptional cases.

(ii) *Liability resulting from criminal fault*

In exercising his functions, a director must act across a number of different spheres. In so doing, he is exposed to a number of potential criminal offences, in particular those under:

- labour law (health and safety rules, industrial accidents, restraint of trade union rights);
- environmental law (pollution, classified premises);
- transport law;
- general criminal law (fraud, theft, breach of trust, receipt of stolen goods, abuse of powers of signature, forgery and use of forgery, defamation);
- insolvency law (bankruptcy, fraudulent insolvency);
- economic law (conspiracy to defraud or abuse of dominant position, false publicity); and
- fiscal law (obstruction of the collection of tax due).

Criminal offences specific to company law and the stock market also exist, such as:

- abuse of power and of voting rights;
- distribution of fictitious dividends;

10 *Mémento Francis Lefebvre Sociétés Commerciales*, 5435.
11 Cass Com, June 8 1963, Bull III No 254.
12 Cass Com, January 19 1965, Bull III No 57.
13 Cass Com, October 14 1974, Bull Joly 1975.477 som.
14 CA Paris, March 21 1984, BRDA 1984/11 p 9.

- presentation of false accounts;
- failure to produce accounts;
- misappropriation of funds;
- market manipulation;
- insider trading; and
- publication of false information.

Where a director commits a criminal offence, in addition to criminal penalties he may incur civil third-party liability in case of loss or damage to a third party.

To obtain compensation for its loss, the company, represented by its associates or its legal representative, as well as any third-party victims of the criminal offence committed by the director, can either file a civil action against the director or take action independently before a court of civil jurisdiction.

If the victim chooses to file a civil action before a criminal judge, it is for the criminal judge to evaluate the loss sustained and to establish the amount of damages to which the victim is entitled in compensation.

If the victim takes action before a civil judge even though a criminal action has been launched, the civil judge is obliged to defer judgment until the criminal jurisdiction has been decided.

1.2 Standards of care

Generally speaking, as in Anglo-Saxon countries, directors have a duty of attention - they must:

- act prudently and reasonably, in good faith and in the best interests of the company;
- refrain from acting in their own interest; and
- obviously respect the laws and regulations currently in force.

In particular, a director must manage the company responsibly, ensuring that the decisions which he takes are for the sole benefit of the company as a whole and that his overall standard of management corresponds to that which shareholders are normally entitled to expect of any director. Consequently, the director must exercise particular vigilance in all acts of management of the company. However, if the company's affairs are in a poor state, this does not in itself constitute evidence of wrongdoing by the director.

A director must seek prior approval from the management body or *ex post* approval from the general assembly, depending on the legal status of the company, for the conclusion of any contract with another group company or with another company of which he is also a director, unless the contract in question may be considered to be a customary agreement reached under normal operating conditions. A list of such agreements must be given to the shareholders in the form of a special report.

The director of a company which is quoted on a regulated market must also report periodically to the shareholders by means of annual, half-yearly or quarterly reports. The auditors of the company must submit these reports for revision. They will inform the shareholders of the results of the audit and any eventual qualifications on the information contained therein.

In order to prevent and penalise abuses on the part of company directors, and to moderate the powers given to them by statute, the law allows partners and other directors to seek the liability of a culpable director in the name of the common interest (*'ut singuli'* and *'ut universi'* actions). These are discussed further below.

However, the size of the company or the composition of its board of directors may make such an action difficult to pursue. In practice, the size of a company may be an obstacle to the dissemination of information and may make it difficult to bring the shareholders together (a necessary prerequisite for an action against a director).

In the same way, the composition of decision-making bodies within the firm may hamper the progress of such actions, especially in companies with majority family ownership.

In 1998 the Viénot Report introduced principles of corporate governance, largely borrowed from the Anglo-Saxon world, into French law. They aim to moderate the powers of directors, and ensure that their responsibilities and loyalties lie towards the company and its shareholders, by establishing effective control in the hands of the board of directors.

In order for shareholders to exercise control over the management body, principles of corporate governance have been established to improve transparency and the dissemination of information within the company, and to give more weight to stakeholders in corporate decisions by creating study committees. The purpose of these committees is consultative and they are essentially designed to gather opinions.

The development of this kind of structure, especially in larger groups, allows for the various situations that arise in the business life of a firm – and even specific situations - to be analysed and appropriate solutions found or necessary changes implemented. The devolved role of these committees may relate to a variety of areas (eg, auditing, remuneration, organisation or technology). Their conclusions should serve to support proposals submitted to the decision-making bodies, whose roles they may not usurp.

Certain listed companies have also adopted the recommendation of the Viénot Report by requiring the presence of independent directors on the board of directors. Their voting powers afford a degree of balance in decision-making with the majority directors.

An independent director cannot be an employee or the chairman or chief executive of the company or a group company, and must not have occupied such a position for at least three years. He also cannot be an important shareholder of the company or a group company, or be linked in any way to a significant and habitual commercial or financial partner of the company or a group company.

1.3 To whom the duties are owed

The directors may incur liability if they do not respect the obligations implicit in their duty towards the company, its shareholders and third parties.

(a) ***The company***

The company may seek the liability of the directors and take action based on loss or damage caused by one or more directors and suffered by the company as a whole. The company's legal representatives will undertake such an action. If all directors are guilty, the action may be launched on an individual basis by a shareholder or group of shareholders.

(b) ***Shareholders***

The shareholders may seek to establish the liability of the directors and pursue an individual action, based on their personal loss or damage caused directly by one or more directors and suffered by one or more shareholders.

(c) ***Third parties***

Third parties would mainly include corporate creditors that seek to claim compensation on grounds of wrongdoing by a director leading to insolvency. They might also be competitors and clients, or even employees. Third parties may act against a director to obtain compensation for their loss only if the director has committed a personal fault separate from the exercise of his duty. If this is not the case, the company is solely liable to third parties.

1.4 Common defences to and exemptions from liability

The first and essential defence is to demonstrate that the necessary conditions for invoking the liability of the directors are not met. These are as follows:

- a wrongful act (fault);
- loss or damage that is direct, certain and personal, and has infringed an acquired right. This may be difficult to determine (eg, a short-term loss may later be translated into a profit); and
- a causal link between the fault and the loss or damage. Proof of this may also be hard to provide, as a number of factors may come into play (eg, some acts that occurred before the launch of the action, when viewed in a different context, might actually count in mitigation).

The onus is on the plaintiff to prove his loss, the damage and the causal link.

Means of exemption are quite limited. The first principle is that "clauses in the statutes limiting the powers of directors are not opposable against third parties".

Further, under Article L225–253(1) of the Commercial Code, "any clause in the statutes having the effect of submitting the exercise of a corporate action to the prior opinion or authorisation of the general meeting of shareholders is deemed invalid". Finally, according to Article L225–253(2) of the Commercial Code, "no decision of the annual general meeting may have the effect of extinguishing a liability action against the directors for a fault committed in the fulfilment of their office". As a result, the discharge granted to the directors by the annual general meeting upon the expiry of their term of office does not, in principle, exonerate them from future liability for their acts.

A director can also attempt to exonerate himself from liability by delegating certain of his powers to others within the company. In effect, certain offences may be blamed on the director, but may be due not to his actions but rather to those of other employees.

It is a principle of criminal law that no one can be liable for actions other than of his own doing. However, there is an exception to this, in that directors are often held liable for offences committed by their employees. In criminal law, liability will arise either due to a specific stipulation of the law or because the director will personally have committed a fault due to a failure on his part in the supervision or management of his staff or in the general organisation of his company. In civil law, on the other hand, liability will arise from the confirmation of a criminal offence or a failure on behalf of the chief executive in his general duty of supervision. However, third parties may also invoke the principle that an employer is liable for the acts of its employees.

In criminal cases, a director may divert the liability incumbent on him for the acts of company employees by proving the delegation of powers to the person responsible for the offence. Such delegation is common in larger undertakings, which are harder to control directly due to the size of their workforce.

With regard to third-party civil liability, by proving the defence of delegation of powers a director can avoid liability. However, the need to identify an individual whom the victims can hold liable, and the fact that there are certain responsibilities which a director cannot delegate, often lead to the undertaking itself being held liable or the director being found guilty of a breach of his personal obligations, which by their nature are impossible to delegate.

2. Who can bring claims

A person who has suffered loss or damage resulting from the wrongful act of a director can launch a civil third-party action or a criminal action where an offence has been committed.

2.1 The company (and its liquidators)

A distinction must be drawn here between companies involved in insolvency proceedings (which is the situation in most such cases) and solvent companies.

(a) Insolvent companies

Reforms were introduced by the enactment of the Law on the Court Protection of Companies on July 26 2005, which allows directors and officers to avoid incurring liability.

Under the act, directors no longer risk personal liability during judicial protection proceedings or administration proceedings. This means that they cannot be sued if, despite their wrongful acts, the company may still be rescued. Financial penalties thus may no longer be sought during administration or protection proceedings. There is a new obligation to meet corporate debts, which comes into effect only during official receivership proceedings (ie, liquidation subject to judicial supervision). This is also the case for an 'action for insufficiency of assets', the successor to the old 'action for making up a balance sheet deficiency', which may be launched only once a rescue or recovery plan has been completed or in case of official receivership.

In the same way, personal bankruptcy, a ban from management and fraudulent bankruptcy can no longer be pronounced during protection proceedings, but only in the period of official receivership.

Insolvency regulations apply to all directors, whether in law or in fact. Actions filed against directors are brought before the commercial court which is presiding over the insolvency proceedings.

This law has introduced changes to the personal liability of directors. It has completely reshaped the types of action by which directors' liability is incurred in insolvency proceedings. The old 'action to make up a balance sheet deficiency' has been transformed into an 'action for insufficiency of assets'; and the old system of penalties during insolvency proceedings for the most serious wrongful acts has been replaced with an obligation to meet corporate debts.

Moreover, in the event of liability for either insufficiency of assets or breach of the obligation to meet corporate debts, joint liability is no longer automatic where there are several directors. It is simply stated that the court "may" declare the directors jointly and severally liable by reasoned decision.

Similarly, Article L652–1 of the Commercial Code provides in its last paragraph that if one of the wrongful acts contributing to the obligation to meet corporate debts is confirmed, there are no longer grounds for an action for insufficiency of assets. This means that if the fault in question also represents a fault of management, the director will be penalised only on the basis of the obligation to meet corporate debts. This is expected to absorb the liability for insufficiency of assets and thus to minimise the directors' exposure to personal risk.

(i) *Liability for insufficiency of assets*

In insolvency proceedings, this applies to directors of a private entity as well as to those who are permanent representatives of entities as directors.

An action for insufficiency of assets may be brought by the official administrator, the liquidator or the public prosecutor.[15] Moreover, in the collective interest of the creditors, the court may be solicited by the majority of creditors nominated as controllers if the official receiver has not launched an action after having been formally requested to do so.

In effect, third parties lose all possibility of action themselves, unless this is based upon a wrongful act allegedly committed by the director after the commencement of insolvency proceedings.[16]

When the resolution of judicial protection proceedings, administration proceedings or official receivership gives rise to an insufficiency of assets, the court may decide that the debts of the entity should be borne, in whole or in part, by the directors or by those who contributed to the fault of management. If there are several

15 Article 651 of the Commercial Code.
16 Cass Com, March 14 2000, Bull Joly, 2000, p 602, § 133, note J-J Daigre.

directors, the court may, in a reasoned decision, find them jointly and severally liable. The statute of limitations for such an action is three years from the date of the judicial decision pronouncing the official receivership or the resolution of the protection/reorganisation plan (Article L651–2 of the Commercial Code).

Three conditions must be met for such an action to be launched,[17] which are identical to those previously required to bring an action for making up a balance sheet deficiency:

- an insufficiency of assets of the company, assessed as of the date on which the action for is brought and not as of the date of the commencement of insolvency proceedings;
- a wrongful act by the director:[18] The Supreme Court has classified the following behaviour as wrongful acts:
  - delay in issuing a declaration of insolvency,[19] which must occur within 45 days of insolvency;
  - abusive and deliberate continuation of trading while insolvent with the intention of profiting from the assets of the company to the personal benefit of the directors;[20]
  - failure in the duty of supervision of a venture capital company; and
  - dereliction of duty which aggravated the liabilities of the company;[21] and
- a causal link between the above elements.

If the court considers the action to be justified, it will sentence the director(s) responsible for the management errors to compensate for the insufficiency of assets in full or in part. The damages will be allocated to the company's funds and will be used to pay its creditors.

In the event of non-payment by the director of the full debt he incurs as a result of the action for insufficiency of assets, he will be exposed to personal bankruptcy proceedings.

(ii) *Obligation to meet corporate debts*

The same parties that are entitled to bring an action for insufficiency of assets can initiate this action.

Under Article L652–1 of the Commercial Code, in the course of official receivership proceedings, the court may order that a director in law or fact pay the whole or a part of the debts of the company, where the director committed one of the following faults and this contributed to insolvency:

- disposed of the goods of the company as though they were his own;
- used the entity as a front to conceal his actions, having carried out business for his own personal gain;

---

17 Article L651–2 of the Commercial Code.
18 *Lamy Sociétés Commerciales.*
19 Cass Com, January 8 2002, 98–22.833.
20 Cass Com, October 20 1992, 90–17.916.
21 Cass Com, October 30 2000.

- used company goods or credit in a manner contrary to the company's interest and to his own ends, or in favour of another entity or company in which he held a direct or indirect interest;
- abusively continued to trade in deficit, for his own interests, in such a way as would inevitably lead to the insolvency of the entity; or
- embezzled all or part of the assets or fraudulently increased the liabilities of the entity.

In the event that more than one director is liable, the court will take account of the degree of fault of each to determine the share of the corporate debt to be attributed to him. In a reasoned judgment, it may declare them to be jointly and severally liable.

The amounts recovered are used to pay off the creditors.

The statute of limitations is three years from the date of the commencement of official receivership.

(iii) *Personal penalties*

Apart from the penalties described above, the director may also be subject to the following personal penalties:

- a ban against directing, managing, administering or controlling any commercial enterprise or trade. The new law limits the duration of this penalty to 15 years. The duration of the ban should be proportionate to the director's behaviour; and
- personal bankruptcy,[22] particularly in case of wrongful acts such as those listed in Article L652–1 of the Commercial Code (obligation to meet corporate debts).

Such actions may be brought by the court either on its own initiative or at the request of the administrator, the creditors' representative, the liquidator or the public prosecutor.

(iv) *Criminal penalties*

Fraudulent bankruptcy is punishable by five years' imprisonment and a fine of €75,000, and other criminal penalties specific to insolvency law. Fraudulent bankruptcy is found where the director has:

- bought shares below their value or employed ruinous means to obtain funds with the intention of delaying the commencement of administration proceedings;
- embezzled or concealed all or part of the company's assets;
- fraudulently increased the company's liabilities;
- drawn up fictitious accounts or removed the accounting documents of company, or failed to draw up accounts where required to do so by law; or
- kept accounts in a manifestly incomplete or irregular manner with regard to legal provisions.

---

22 Articles L653–1 and following of the Commercial Code.

Criminal proceedings may be launched either directly by the public prosecutor or through a complaint filed by the administrator, the creditors' representative or the liquidator.

(b) *Solvent companies*

Where there is a situation which is prejudicial to the company, the company's legal representative may initiate a recovery action against the director responsible (an action '*ut universi*'). This procedure aims to obtain compensation for a collective loss or damage to the company. If the director is convicted, the company will be the sole recipient of eventual damages.

The liquidator may bring this kind of action in the event of amicable dissolution of the company, up until the dissolution procedure has closed.

It is normally the duty of a director, acting as the company's legal representative, to launch a recovery action against another director in the name of and on the account of the company as soon as he judges that the latter has caused loss or damage to the company.

Such an action, which may be brought only in the sole interest of the company, may not be made subject to the prior agreement of any corporate body - whether the board of directors, the management board or even the general assembly of shareholders.

However, in the event of obvious inaction or obstruction by a director in pursuing a liability action against an individual, the board of directors or the general assembly may solicit the company's legal representative to launch such proceedings. The director will incur liability if he fails to execute the decisions of these bodies.

Where the legal representative is also the director responsible for the fault, the legislature has provided an alternative – an action *ut singuli*, discussed below.

2.2 Minority shareholders on behalf of the company

The law permits one or more partners or shareholders to launch an action in the name of and on the account of the company against its directors (an action *ut singuli*). This procedure aims to obtain compensation for a collective loss or damage to the company. If the director is convicted, the company will be the sole recipient of eventual damages.

This kind of action may be launched by:

- any partner or shareholder acting as an individual, whatever his shareholding; this right of action is lost as soon as the individual ceases to be a member of the company, even though the wrongdoing might have occurred prior to his departure from the company;
- a group of partners or shareholders nominated from among the partners or shareholders. In a limited liability company, this right of action is available to a group of partners representing at least 10% of the capital,[23] while in a

23 Article 45 of the Decree of March 23 1967.

public limited company, the shareholders may form a group if they represent at least 5% of the capital (this percentage is progressively reduced for companies whose share capital is greater than €750,000);[24] and

- an association of shareholders in listed companies, provided that:
  - the shareholders have been listed on the shareholders' register in their own name for at least two years;
  - the shareholders between them hold at least 5% of the voting rights of the company (this percentage is progressively reduced for companies whose capital is greater than €750,000); and
  - the statutes of the association have been sent to the Financial Markets Authority.

2.3 Minority shareholders on their own account

Although a partner or shareholder has the right to bring an action on behalf of the company, he may act in his own name and on his own account only if he has suffered a personal loss distinct from that suffered by the company. In bringing a personal action, the partner or shareholder is a third party towards the company. Consequently, the directors are liable in regard to the partner or shareholder only for wrongful acts that can be separated from their position as directors.

Case law has been slow to recognise the existence of a direct and personal loss or damage to a partner or shareholder which is not a consequence of a loss already suffered by the company.

Thus, an action brought by a shareholder seeking compensation for the loss of value of his stock as a result of a wrongful act committed by a director is not admissible, since the loss in question is only a corollary of the damage suffered by the company.[25]

Similarly, the Supreme Court[26] specifies that "the offence of misappropriation of funds only occasions a direct and personal loss to the company itself and not to each of the shareholders".

That said, in another ruling[27] the court found that if the subject of a criminal complaint filed by a shareholder in the name of the company for the illegal appropriation of an interest by civil servants recruited by the company and ex-ministers who had responsibilities in the company's sector of activity also constituted an abuse of the credit of the company, then there was direct damage to the shareholder. Such direct personal loss or damage was also found by the Criminal Division of the Supreme Court in a case involving another offence possibly committed by a director: the presentation and publication of inaccurate accounts.[28]

---

24 Article 200 of the Decree of March 23 1967.
25 Cass com January 15 2002 66; CA Versailles September 13 2005.
26 Cass crim, December 5 2001, 01–80.065, Bull Joly 2002, p 492, note Le Nabasque.
27 Cass crim, November 21 2001, 01–81.178, Bull Joly 2002, p 398, note S Messaï.
28 Cass crim, January 30 2002, 01–84.256, JCP E 2002, 14, p 592.

2.4 Third parties

Third parties may not act against a director if the fault attributable to him was committed in the performance of his duties. Any fault which is separable from those functions may have the effect of piercing the corporate veil and allowing third parties to act directly against the directors.

In principle, a director acts in the name and on account of the company. The third party then has the company itself as a contractual partner and only the company's liability may be sought.

The personal liability of the director may, in principle, be admitted on an exceptional basis. Although this condition is not set out in any legal text, it is for this purpose that case law has required that the director have committed "a fault separable from his functions which may be imputed to him personally"[29] before holding him liable.

Examples of faults separable from a director's functions have included:[30]

- the corruption of a civil servant to obtain for a client of the company a permit to transform residential premises into commercial premises;[31]
- counterfeiting and forgery of labels;[32] and
- abuse of office.[33]

While jurisprudence has never defined the notion of a fault that is separable from a director's functions, a recent Supreme Court ruling has nonetheless specified that where a director has committed "intentionally a fault of particular gravity not compatible with the normal exercise of his corporate functions",[34] this constitutes a fault separable from his functions.

Notwithstanding this attempt at a definition, in practice, the liability of company directors with regard to third parties is only rarely recognised in case law. It always requires the existence of a fault that may be separated from the exercise of the corporate function of the director.[35]

3. Claims culture

3.1 Litigation

For many years most cases against directors arose during insolvency procedures.

However, the approach traditionally taken towards directors' and officers' liability has evolved in the wake of financial scandals such as Enron and Parmalat, which have hit a large number of small investors. Many associations and societies representing minority shareholders have been created to take a united stand against the directors of large quoted groups (eg, the Association for the Defence of Minority Shareholders).

---

29 Cass Com, January 22 1991, RF compt, May 1991, p 62, note Ph Reigné.

30 *Lamy Sociétés Commerciales*, No 659 and Maxence Laugier, *L'introuvable responsabilité du dirigeant social envers les tiers pour fautes de gestion*? Bull Joly Sociétés, December 2003.

31 Cass civ 1re, October 6 1998, 95–12.519.

32 CA Bordeaux, January 24 2000, Juris-Data, 121080.

33 CA Paris, March 22 2002, BRDA 2002, 11, p 3.

34 Cass Com, May 10 2003, Rev Sociétés, July-September 2003, p 479, note J-F Barbièri.

35 Cass Com, July 1 2003, 1078 F D.

These organisations seek compensation for losses affecting minority shareholders. They bring them together in large numbers - sometimes many hundreds at a time.

Suits against directors, even of healthy companies, have become a much more regular feature of French business life. The large majority of cases still arise as a result of insolvency procedures, and these are the cases most likely to succeed. Actions against solvent companies are rarer.

3.2 Ability to bring class actions

This chapter has already explored the possibilities available to a group of shareholders or an association to take action against directors.

The subject of class actions has been a hot topic in political, consumer and legal circles in France for a number of years.

As a result of former President Chirac's appeal in his 2005 New Year address to introduce a form of French class action, a working party representing all interested stakeholders – consumers, business, the law and academics – spent 18 months producing a report. Luc Chatel, a politician who has championed class actions for many years, lodged a private members' bill.

The key concern of the French legislature has been to avoid the abuses which are seen to exist in the US system: especially where entrepreneurial lawyers appear to benefit far more than the victims from class actions launched on their own initiative. The US system is deemed to have laid huge costs at the door of business, far more than the simple reparation of damage caused.

A draft law finally gained the approval of the Council of Ministers - the final stage before presentation to parliament - in November 2006. Unfortunately, it was not possible to push the draft law through Parliament before the presidential elections in May 2007 and in January 2007 the project was suspended.

Some key features of the draft law are as follows:

- A class action could be brought only by approved consumer associations.
- It could relate only to individual material damages (and loss of use) of under €2,000;
- The system would be 'opt in' (ie, victims would have to make a positive choice to join the action); and
- The action would involve two stages – a decision on the principle of liability followed by negotiation on the quantum of damages.

The kind of group action that the draft law envisages would allow compensation for a material loss undergone collectively by consumers if a professional had not met his contractual obligations. Typically, cases would include overcharging, incorrect deliveries and other claims relating to small sums that an individual consumer would not generally pursue.

This draft law, something of a compromise, has pleased none of the different stakeholders that would be most affected by it: consumer associations claim that it does not go far enough, while in business and insurance circles it represents a threatening and costly new development.

Consumer associations have criticised not only the limited scope of the draft, but also the cumbersome legal machinery it lays down.

Business interests, through MEDEF (the French employers' association), estimate the cost of the US class action system at 1% of gross domestic product. To the French economy, this would be the equivalent of €16.5 billion.

Nevertheless, the draft law appeared to meet with broad approval in legal and political circles. However, given the delays that have resulted from the elections, it is impossible to say when or even whether it will be re-presented in its current form.

As things stand, there is thus not yet a well-honed system of class actions in place in France.

3.3 Funding of claims and whether loser pays

The principle in France is that the losing party should pay the costs of proceedings and the irrecoverable expenses of the winning party. In practice, these include the legal costs of the winning party.[36]

A request for costs is presented to the court, which has sole discretion to accept or reject it in whole or in part. In theory, the parties must produce invoices approved by their lawyers to justify any expenses. In practice, it is often the case that no receipts are produced and the judge awards what he considers to be an appropriate sum.

Awards of costs in France are usually far lower than in other countries, rarely exceeding €15,000. The relatively small size of costs awards does not, in practice, dissuade plaintiffs from acting, even if they have doubts about the strength of their case.

Lawyers may be allowed to take a success fee by agreement with their clients but this may not represent the total amount of their fees. They cannot solicit instructions, advertise or compete with the police force by carrying out their own inquiries. This body of rules diverges quite sharply from the US system.

3.4 Plaintiffs' bar

As French law does not yet allow for class actions, the concept of a plaintiffs' bar is not recognised.

3.5 Procedural barriers

The main procedural barrier in France is the statute of limitations which applies to the liability of directors and officers.

A liability action against the directors of a commercial company becomes time barred three years after the date on which the loss occurred or, if it has been hidden, from the date of its discovery.

As stated above, the legal representative has full powers to launch a legal action on behalf of the company against any person, including another director.

Whether an action is taken by the directors or by the shareholders, no obstacle may be placed in its path: any clauses in the statutes disclaiming liability or making the right to act subject to approval by the general assembly are deemed to be null and void.

---

36 Article 700 of the New Code of Civil Procedure.

4. Indemnification rights

4.1 When the company can indemnify

The company will be entitled to indemnify a third-party victim when the wrongful act of the director is committed in the performance of his functions (ie, where he has acted in the name and on behalf of the company and has thus engaged the company exclusively with regard to the third party, which the company must indemnify if the act carried out by the director ultimately triggers third-party liability).

On the other hand, the company will never be called upon to indemnify the director where he is personally responsible for the misappropriation of funds, particularly where certain corporate structures are involved (eg, a public limited company or a limited company), since the debt which is incumbent on the director himself cannot be paid by the company.[37] Examples of this would include:

- the company covering the director's legal expenses for defending himself in a personal case; or
- the company reimbursing the cost of fines imposed on the director.

The approach is similar when paying for defence costs. As soon as a court has ruled that the director has not exceeded his capacity, the company may advance his defence costs. The company (through its management body) should pay careful attention to the manner in which the case is launched. If, from the start, the opposing party alleges a wrongful act that can be separated from the director's functions, it would be prudent to leave the director to cover his legal costs himself. If it is ultimately decided that the director did act within his capacity, then indemnification of those costs by the company is legal and valid, and *post facto* reimbursement of any costs advanced by the director is admissible.

However, if it is found that the director did commit a wrongful act outside his capacity, then he must pay his own defence costs. If the company paid an advance, the director must pay it back.

4.2 Formalities for indemnification

The framework for indemnification is strict: either the director will have acted within his capacity and the company, being responsible for his actions, may indemnify him as part of its normal management procedures; or he will have acted outside it and the company cannot indemnify.

The decision to indemnify is taken by the management body (eg, the board of directors for a public limited company or the managing partner in the case of a limited liability company) and under its responsibility, which implies that the funds must be recovered against the director if he has acted outside his capacity as director. Failing this, the management body exposes itself to action for misappropriation of funds.

A prior agreement between the director and the company is admissible, provided it respects the rules outlined above.

---

37 Cass Crim, February 20 2002.

4.3 How indemnification works

As stated in section 4.1, a company cannot indemnify a director for wrongful acts for which he is personally responsible. Consequently, there is no procedure for the indemnification of the director by the company in such an eventuality.

If the director is found liable for a fault which is separable from his functions, the director must pay compensation for the entire loss or damage to the shareholders, the company or the third party. This compensation takes the form of damages.

The director must personally pay any penalty.

4.4 What cannot be indemnified

Criminal penalties imposed upon a director cannot be indemnified; nor can his defence costs in criminal proceedings.

4.5 Cases of cumulative liability

In principle, where there is more than one director, each is liable for his own individual faults and is not responsible for the faults of the others.

However, there is a possibility of joint and several liability or liability *in solidum* of the directors if several have committed the wrongful acts alleged by the victim.

In cases of joint and several liability, or an obligation *in solidum*, the victim has the right to claim against each of the responsible parties. Subrogatory recoveries between the directors after payment will then establish the final contribution owed by each director.

The company cannot indemnify a director for acts for which he was personally responsible. However, in certain companies or groups, the company will issue a letter of comfort for the benefit of the director – although the legality of this practice is disputed.

5. D&O insurance

5.1 Availability of D&O insurance

A proliferation of lawsuits against directors has led to the development and growth of D&O insurance in France. The first insurers to offer this coverage were from the London market, followed by some US companies after the stock market crash on Wall Street. These were followed by French insurers. D&O insurance has become much more common on the French insurance market.

(a) The insured

Under the D&O policy, the insured is by definition distinct from the persons whose activity is insured and which may prove detrimental to others.

The company takes out the insurance for the account and the benefit of all its directors in office. French market practice is that directors never take out their own insurance.

Each year the company must pay a premium, which is determined once the underwriters have analysed the risk. As D&O insurance premiums are paid by the company itself, the French tax authorities accept that these may be deducted from taxable profits.

The insurer's analysis of the risk consists of an examination of:

- the financial documents of the company;
- its statutes;
- its management methods;
- its sector of activity; and
- its relationships with suppliers and customers.

A detailed questionnaire is sent to the company taking out the insurance, which must fill in this document and supply all information required to evaluate the risk.

The limits of coverage will vary according to the wishes or needs of the insured.

(b) *Beneficiaries*

Only those categories of director specified in the policy may benefit from the coverage.

Coverage is not automatically accorded to *de facto* directors, whose coverage must be expressly included. This is the case for the majority of French policies.

Directors of companies whose office expires during the insured period (due to resignation, dismissal or the fact that they have not been re-elected) are covered by the policy for acts carried out during their term of office.

If a director dies, his heirs will benefit from the coverage, as they may still be sued in their capacity as heirs to his liabilities.

Depending on the wording of the policies, coverage may also be extended to directors of subsidiaries.

Other extensions commonly offered on the French market include those to:

- directorships held in minority shareholdings;
- financial consequences and defence costs indemnifiable by the insured company or its subsidiaries, where the legislation of a country so allows;
- employees in the context of employment legislation;
- claims linked to financial securities; and
- the company as policyholder and its subsidiaries, excluding financial securities.

(c) *Scope of coverage*

Directors are usually covered for the financial consequences of the liability which they may incur through "faults, errors, omissions, inaccuracies and false interpretations, violations of legal and regulatory texts" committed towards third parties in the exercise of their duty.

The definitions of 'third party' and 'the insured' in the policy wording are of key importance. In fact, any person or entity not listed as an insured is considered to be a third party.

The term 'third party' generally includes not only shareholders taking action for their own account with the intention of obtaining compensation for a personal loss or damage distinct from that of the company, but also shareholders taking action *ut singuli*, (ie, in the name of the company against the directors with the intention of obtaining compensation for loss or damage suffered by the company). The question of coverage for an action *ut universi* is not positively addressed in the different policies available on the market. In practice, there is some difficulty in considering the company as policyholder to be a third party in relation to its directors, who are its representatives. Fear of collusion between the directors in law and the office holder who endorses their liability is often present, as the insurer then risks providing an indirect source of financing to the company.

It further includes third parties *per se*: various creditors, suppliers and clients, the state and public services.

The award made by the court to the victim will be paid either directly by the insurer, which is usually the case, or by the director, who will then recover from insurers.

The amount of indemnity paid does not constitute taxable income for the director.

(d) Exclusions

In addition to the exclusion of deliberate wrongdoing by the insured (which the Supreme Court has defined as a premeditated desire to cause the loss or damage as it occurred and not simply to create the risk that such loss or damage might happen), the following exclusions usually feature in D&O policies on the French market:

- penalties, fines, taxes and delay penalties owed by directors and officers under criminal, fiscal, customs and excise or social law;
- actions launched by family members of the accused director;
- actions between the insureds themselves, except where the director is a shareholder and acts as such;
- consequences arising from the utilisation of the position of company director for personal gain or in favour of another company in which an insured has a direct or indirect interest;
- actions deriving from personal benefits or remuneration which the insureds have awarded to themselves;
- actions deriving from social conflicts;
- all bodily injury and material damage losses, as well as pure financial loss resulting from activities of the company;
- consequences of any pollution or environmental damage;
- consequences of any natural catastrophe;
- consequences of the commitment of the insureds to any commercial or financial performance (the policy is not intended to cover any performance bond or guarantee in respect of the company's operations); and
- specific exclusions, such as exclusions relating to the United States, Canada and the United Kingdom, where the geographic scope of the contract is worldwide.

5.2 Local rules on cover provided under a non-domestic D&O policy

The Treaty of Rome applies to the benefit of insurers in France as well as those in other EU member states. Consequently, insurance companies in the European Union benefit from the following principles:

- Freedom of establishment (Article L362–1 of the Insurance Code) - the passport system means that a licence issued to an insurer by the supervisory authorities of the EU member state in which its head office is located is valid across the whole of the European Union. Any insurer from an EU member state has the right to establish a branch office in France and to undertake insurance operations, as stated in Article L310–1 of the Insurance Code, for which it has been authorised by the authorities in its home country, on the condition that the French minister for the economy and finance receives prior notification from the home country authorities.
- Freedom of services - again, this is due to the passport system, which allows an insurer established in one EU member state to practise in another member state without having to be established there. Once again, the home country authorities are competent to supervise and verify the conditions under which the necessary licences are issued to the insurer in question.

Insurance companies from outside the European Union must obtain a licence from the Ministry of the Economy and Finance for authorisation to underwrite in France. French insureds cannot take out insurance in France with insurers which are not authorised in this way.

D&O cover is not compulsory and is not specifically regulated in France. It is therefore possible for French directors to benefit from D&O insurance in the context of a master policy taken out by the parent company of their group with a company which is not authorised to underwrite in France, provided that the insurance is taken out outside France by the parent company, whose head office is situated outside French territory.

However, it is necessary to ensure that the scope of the coverage includes the specific risks that may be incurred by the French director, particularly with regard to risks attached to suits against the directors during insolvency proceedings. The insureds may prefer to take out a local policy.

Germany

Oliver Sieg
Nörr Stiefenhofer Lutz

Germany has a mature and professional directors' and officers' liability (D&O) insurance market. Both the market and the legal regime are becoming increasingly sophisticated due to continuing advancements regarding directors' liability risks and insurance law and coverage issues, driven by case law and legislative developments. Further changes to directors' duties may be expected as a result of decisions pending in the Federal Court of Justice.

The ongoing reform of corporate law aims to guarantee transparency in company operations and supervision at management level. The German government initially presented a draft Act on Increasing Liability for False Information Relating to Capital Markets, but the draft has since been withdrawn amid widespread criticism of the proposed strict liability of directors. Plans for an amended version of the act have not yet been announced.

A new version of the Insurance Contract Act will come into force in January 2008, which will have a significant impact on liability insurance.

1. Directors' duties

German law on directors' liability distinguishes between liability towards the company (internal liability) and liability towards third parties, such as contractual partners or shareholders (external liability).

Internal liability is based on a breach of duties arising from the position of director, the contract of employment or tort. Internal liability is subject to statutory rules that tie in with the position of director. It applies to directors, shadow directors and *de facto* directors.

There are no general statutory rules on directors' external liability; just a few specific provisions on contingent liability for taxes are set out in Sections 69 and 34 of the General Tax Act. Otherwise, liability towards third parties is governed by civil law, in particular tort law.

1.1 Nature of the duties

With regard to directors' duties, the law distinguishes between managing directors and supervisory directors. For corporate governance purposes, it is usual to have a two-board system comprising a management board and a supervisory board. The duties owed to the company by managing and supervisory directors are set out below.

The rules of general civil law apply to both executive and supervisory directors. Accordingly, under certain circumstances, directors might have duties towards a contracting third party (eg, a duty to clarify the subject matter of the contract). Directors may not affect the legal interests of third parties by tort.

(a) *Internal duties*

The statutory basis of internal liability depends on the type of company for which the director is acting:

- The Stock Corporation Act sets out rules on the liability of directors in stock corporations;
- The Limited Liability Company Act regulates the liability of directors of limited liability companies; and
- The Cooperative Society Act governs the liability of directors in cooperative societies.

The liability of managing directors in stock corporations is set out in Section 93(2) of the Stock Corporation Act. The liability of supervisory directors is based on Section 116, which refers mainly to Section 93.

The managing directors of limited liability companies are liable according to Section 43(2) of the Limited Liability Company Act. Limited liability companies are not obliged to have a supervisory board. If a supervisory board has nonetheless been established, the liability of supervisory directors is governed by Section 52 of the Limited Liability Company Act, which refers to the relevant provisions of the Stock Corporation Act.

Section 34(2) of the Cooperative Society Act regulates the liability of managing directors and Section 41, in connection with Section 34, regulates the liability of supervisory directors.

Different provisions basically follow the principles of Section 93 of the Stock Corporation Act, and relevant case law, regarding the liability of managing directors in stock corporations.

(i) *Managing directors*

Some specific duties of managing directors are expressly defined in special provisions. Directors are also obliged to conduct business in a proper manner.

Managing directors are under a specific duty to provide information. Pursuant to Section 90(1) of the Stock Corporation Act, managing directors in stock corporations are obliged to inform the supervisory board about relevant corporate planning, the company's financial standing and any important business dealings. According to Section 42a(1) of the Limited Liability Company Act and Section 33(1) of the Cooperative Society Act, directors must provide the shareholders with annual accounts. The duty to inform, or to obtain consent from, the supervisory board can also arise from the company bylaws. Directors of listed stock corporations must release *ad hoc* announcements in compliance with Section 15 of the Securities Trading Act.

Some other duties are specifically provided for in law, such as duties regarding:

- accounting (Section 91 of the Stock Corporation Act; Section 41 of the Limited Liability Company Act; Section 33 of the Cooperative Society Act);

- maintenance of capital (Section 93(3) of the Stock Corporation Act; Section 43(3) of the Limited Liability Company Act; Section 34(3) of the Cooperative Society Act);
- filing for bankruptcy (Section 92(2) of the Stock Corporation Act; Section 64(1) of the Limited Liability Company Act); and
- confidentiality obligations (Section 93(1)(3) of the Stock Corporation Act; Section 34(1)(2) of the Cooperative Society Act).

The blanket clauses in Section 93(1) of the Stock Corporation Act, Section 43(1) of the Limited Liability Company Act and Section 34(1) of the Cooperative Society Act are the catch-all provisions on the duty of directors to conduct business according to the standards of a prudent businessperson. Conduct of business includes both legally required decisions and entrepreneurial decisions. Entrepreneurial decisions concern future developments and are based on predictions and assessments.

Legally required decisions must comply with the statutory rules, bylaws and guidelines of the company, the directives of shareholders and instructions agreed in the employment contract. Managing directors are obliged to assess the company's financial standing on a regular basis. Where tasks are delegated, directors must take proper measures (ie, select the appropriate employees carefully and supervise them periodically). These duties are clarified in Section 91(2) of the Stock Corporation Act, implemented in the scope of the Control and Transparency in Business Act, which came into force in 1998. According to Section 91(2), directors must take appropriate measures to monitor and detect at an early stage any developments that could endanger the existence of the company.

Since November 2005, Section 93(1) of the Stock Corporation Act – implemented in the scope of the Act on the Integrity of Companies and Modernisation of the Stock Corporation Law – has set forth the German equivalent of the business judgement rule with regard to entrepreneurial decisions. Section 93(1) states that directors are not liable for mistakes within the scope of their discretion to make entrepreneurial decisions.

The business judgement rule complied with the prevailing case law at the time of implementation. However, by using general legal terms, the legislature deliberately left it to case law to develop directors' liability in this regard. The business judgement rule encourages directors to take on entrepreneurial risks, but at the same time prevents them from acting rashly or improvidently at the expense of investors and employees.

(ii) *Supervisory directors*

The duties of supervisory directors are broadly similar to those of managing directors. However, the specifics corresponding to the function of the supervisory board must be taken into consideration. Pursuant to Section 111 of the Stock Corporation Act, the central duty of the supervisory board is to control and supervise the management of the company. The supervisory directors must obtain all necessary information in order to do this.

The supervisory board decides on the remuneration of the managing directors. Supervisory directors may become liable if this amount is considered to be too high. The recent *Mannesmann* judgment of the Federal Court of Justice, referring to payments to directors in the Vodafone takeover, has attracted particular interest in this regard.

Additionally, the supervisory board has a duty to assert and enforce claims of the company against the management. In its judgment of April 21 1997, the Federal High Court of Justice found that members of the supervisory board are obliged to bring claims against the management, otherwise they are exposed to liability. The Federal Court of Justice has also clarified duties which supervisory members must observe if they are to control entrepreneurial decisions by the management. The business judgement rule must also be applied accordingly.

(b) External duties

There are no general statutory rules on external liability that tie in with the position of director; just a few specific provisions on contingent liability for taxes are set out in Sections 69 and 34 of the General Tax Act. Otherwise, third parties are confined to general civil law, such as contractual or tort law. Third parties may include creditors, contracting parties, purchasers of securities and shareholders.

Contractual claims against directors are considered in Section 311(3) of the Civil Code, which states that contractual duties can arise in relation to persons who are not party to the contract themselves. This is particularly the case if the third party had undue influence in negotiations or on the outcome of the contract. Such liability is subject to strict requirements and is rarely assumed.

Tort law provides for liability for financial loss only in case of breach of protective legal provisions (Section 823(2) of the Civil Code). Penal law is generally considered to protect a third party (eg, in the case of fraud or embezzlement), but requires intent. In principle, liability due to negligence requires infringement of specific legal interests, such as ownership or corporate integrity. However, the Federal Court of Justice recently found, in its January 24 2006 judgment in *Kirch v Breuer*, that directors can be liable for financial loss where there is negligent interference with a third party's right to its established business enterprise.

The principles of external liability also apply to each shareholder. However, directors' liability in relation to shareholders based on breach of their duties is also considered in Section 117(2) of the Stock Corporation Act. According to that provision, members of the management or supervisory board who have breached their duties are jointly and severally liable together with any third party that influenced them to act against the interests of the company.

Managing directors of limited liability companies owe certain duties to the shareholders directly. These include the duty to prevent payments that affect the nominal capital. If there is negligent breach of this duty, the managing directors are jointly and severally liable to shareholders pursuant to Section 31(6) of the Limited Liability Company Act.

Shareholders, as third parties, also have recourse to civil law. If a company bylaw affects the shareholders' rights, this will justify a claim in tort.

1.2 Standards of care

Unless stated otherwise, German law requires negligence as a standard of care with regard to claims for compensation of damages. This applies to both internal and external liability. Pursuant to Section 276(2) of the Civil Code, a director is negligent if he fails to exercise due diligence according to the circumstances. Directors are obliged to act as prudent businesspersons (Section 93(1) of the Stock Corporation Act; Section 43(1) of the Limited Liability Company Act). They are required to anticipate and avoid an unlawful result. This is referred to an abstract standard of care (ie, the standard of care of a reasonably diligent person with the knowledge, skill and expertise that may be expected of a director). Special knowledge or competence of the specific director, or contractual agreements, may increase the standard of care.

Tort law in connection with criminal offences requires intent. The criminal courts have a tendency to expand the scope of contingent intent with respect to white-collar crime.

According to Section 93(1) of the Stock Corporation Act, the business judgement rule applies with regard to liability for entrepreneurial decisions. This section provides that: "A breach of duty has not occurred if the director may reasonably assume to act on the basis of appropriate information to the benefit of the company."

The starting point of the business judgement rule is the director's perspective. The director must regard his decision as of benefit to the company. The standard for assessing whether the director 'may' have regarded his decision as of benefit to the company is provided by the word 'reasonably'. According to case law, a director's assumption would be unreasonable if he incorrectly assessed the risk connected with the entrepreneurial decision and thereby acted irresponsibly. A decision would be considered to benefit the company if it served to increase its profits and competitiveness on a long-term basis. The decisive point in assessing the interests of the company is the time at which the decision was taken.

Further, the director must have reasonably assumed that he was making a decision based on appropriate information. The preamble to Section 93(1) expressly states that entrepreneurial decisions are often based on instinct, experience and intuition with regard to future developments, as well as a sense for the market and the reactions of customers and competitors. It must also be remembered that entrepreneurial decisions are often subject to extreme time pressure.

The appropriateness of the information must be assessed on the basis of:

- the time available in which to make the decision;
- the importance and nature of the decision; and
- a consideration of general economic standards.

It will be considered whether external analyses should have been obtained. The business judgement rule does not state that the director must obtain expert reports or analyses as a matter of course.

In fact, the courts do not always respect the directors' discretion to make entrepreneurial decisions, but often try to retrace the decision based on the outcome. Whether the preparations were appropriate preparation is broadly subject to court assessment. There are few guidelines on which a director may rely, to be on the safe side. Even external professional advice in support of the decision will not necessarily prevent directors' liability.

1.3 To whom duties are owed

The directors' primary duty is to the company, not to third parties (this includes shareholders). Any relationship between the third party and the company must be established by contract. Any actions of a director constituting a claim in tort are attributed to the company, so a third party will usually assert a claim against the company. The company then may have recourse against the director. Against this background, directors are usually exposed to internal liability.

However, a third party may also directly hold directors liable for compensation of damages according to the principles of external liability. Such external liability is principally observed in case of the company's insolvency.

1.4 Common defences to and exemptions from liability

Directors' liability generally requires that a director have negligently breached his duties and thereby caused damage to the company. The company, as claimant, must substantiate the alleged breach of duty and bears the burden of proof with regard to damage and causation. Negligence on the part of the director is assumed. The director can exculpate himself in this regard.

These principles also apply to former directors. However, as German procedural law does not, in principle, provide for the right to disclosure/discovery of documents in the possession of the opposing party, the Federal Court of Justice has found that former directors are entitled to have access to the files and documents necessary for their defence against any asserted claims.

Directors are, in principle, jointly and severally liable. This does not apply if the responsibilities are attributed to a single director; in such case, only the director in charge of the respective department can be held liable. Liability of the other directors may also arise if it can be shown that they neglected their organisational duties and ignored apparent indications that their co-director had breached his duties.

The company is generally restricted in waiving claims against directors, corresponding to the limits of indemnification as set out in section 4.1.

2. Who can bring claims

2.1 The company (and its liquidators)

The supervisory board asserts claims against managing directors in a stock corporation. The management board in turn asserts claims against the supervisory directors. The respective board must decide to bring an action against a director. Pursuant to Section 77(1) of the Stock Corporation Act, the executive board of a stock corporation conducts the company's business jointly and unanimously, unless provided otherwise by the company bylaws (ie, the joint conduct of business combined with majority decisions). In principle, a decision of the supervisory board requires majority approval. However, deviations are possible, according to the bylaws.

In a limited liability company, the shareholders' meeting is the competent body to assert claims against managing or supervisory directors. Decisions are made by the majority. Under Section 47 of the Limited Liability Company Act, this provision may also be altered in the company bylaws.

In case of insolvency, the liquidator is entitled (and obliged) to pursue the claims of the company.

2.2 Minority shareholders on behalf of the company (derivative actions)

The Act on the Integrity of Companies and Modernisation of the Stock Corporation Law, which came into force in November 2005, strengthened the position of shareholders in stock corporations by introducing measures for shareholders to enforce the assertion of claims of the company against directors. German law does not have derivative action rights in favour of a single shareholder, but only in favour of a minority of shareholders.

According to Section 147 of the Stock Corporation Act, claims against directors must be asserted if a majority of the shareholders' meeting so decides. Shareholders that together hold 10% of the share capital or a total amount of €1 million can appoint certain representatives for the assertion of claims.

Additionally, shareholders that together hold 1% of the share capital or a total amount of €100,000 are entitled to assert claims of the company against directors themselves (Section 148 of the Stock Corporation Act). To counterbalance the low thresholds and avoid improper actions, the legislature constituted proceedings in two stages. First, shareholders can move for admission of the assertion of claims. The parties in this pre-trial hearing are those responsible for asserting claims (ie, the members of the supervisory board, regarding claims against managing directors). The court will grant admission under the following conditions:

- Shareholders must prove that they acquired their shares prior to publication of the alleged breaches of duty and alleged damages, and that they requested the company to assert the claims itself and set an appropriate time limit for the company; and
- The facts justify the assumption that damage was caused to the company based on improbity or gross breach of the law or bylaws.

The admission of claims is excluded if the claims were contrary to the predominant interests of the company. After admission of the assertion of claims by court order, shareholders can file an action against the directors within three months, but only after requesting that the company again bring claims itself within an appropriate timeframe. The subsequent judgment is effective towards the company and all shareholders.

2.3 Minority of shareholders on their own account

Like any third party, shareholders can bring claims against directors based on general civil law, but without any cause of action derived from their capacity as a shareholder. Shareholders can make claims on their own account in the case of prospectus liability or where there has been a breach of information requirements, such as for the immediate release of *ad hoc* notices. Shareholders can also hold directors liable on the basis of Section 117 of the Stock Corporation Act.

2.4 Third parties

Third parties can sue directors for claims based on external liability. Third-party claims mainly arise when the company becomes insolvent. The social security authorities and the tax administration may be third-party claimants with regard to contributions for employees or unpaid taxes. If there has been a delay in filing a petition for insolvency, liability can be based on tort in relation to creditors. For customers, claims might arise based on the director's negligence with regard to the duty to inform in connection with the contract of special personal reliance. Tort law also includes the liability of directors for negligence with regard to products that have been placed on the market or for environmental pollution. Employees can also hold directors liable for breach of the prohibition against discrimination (see Section 611 of the Civil Code).

3. Claims culture

3.1 Litigation

Litigation on directors' liability has consistently increased over the last 10 years. There are many reasons for this.

Numerous financial scandals and insolvencies around the turn of the century brought the issue of directors' liability to the attention of both the public and the legislature. In the last few years, new rules on directors' duties and standards of care have been implemented.

Moreover, companies have become increasingly willing to make claims against their directors. Since the Federal Court of Justice expressly stated that supervisory directors would expose themselves to liability if they refrained from asserting claims against managing directors without good cause, supervisory directors must consider the company's interests with regard to management. The legislature has also allowed claims to be brought against directors. In addition, the Act on Capital Investor Sample Proceedings, which came into force in 2005, has made it easier for investors to assert claims as a collective. Overall, the position of shareholders has strengthened significantly. This exerts additional pressure on (supervisory) directors to bring a claim in the company's interests.

The fact that D&O insurance has become more prominent in the German market may also be a factor. Companies sue their directors with the primary aim of obtaining the D&O insurance. Where the company and the director being sued cooperate, it is very difficult for insurers to obtain the necessary information to mount a successful defence against the asserted claims. Another aspect to be considered is that the German court system is relatively cost efficient.

According to the principles of internal liability, the company usually holds the directors liable. Creditors usually make third-party claims against directors where the company has filed for bankruptcy. Foreign claims (ie, those brought before foreign courts pursuant to foreign law) are another source of third-party claims.

In Germany, there has been a recent tendency to increase the scope of criminal liability for directors. The standard for contingent intent has been expanded. In its *Kinowelt* decision of November 22 2005 the Federal Court of Justice stated that by exceeding the scope for discretion in entrepreneurial decisions, directors would be guilty of an intentional breach of fiduciary duties. This is not covered by D&O insurance.

3.2 Ability to bring class actions

German procedural law does not have the equivalent of a class action in US law. However, the Act on Capital Investor Sample Proceedings introduced the procedural instrument of a 'sample proceeding'.

A sample proceeding is an option if numerous plaintiffs have each filed a statement of claim based on common factual or legal issues. The court will establish a motion of either the plaintiff or the defendant as a sample proceeding. The court's decision is binding on all plaintiffs that joined the motion. While the sample proceeding is ongoing, all other proceedings of the joining plaintiffs are stayed. Once the sample proceeding has been decided, the joining plaintiffs can file the sample decision in their proceedings. The judge is then bound to follow the sample decision irrespective of whether the plaintiff concerned had made the decisive arguments.

At present, the Act on Capital Investor Sample Proceedings is a separate law that amends the Code of Civil Procedure. It refers only to capital investor claims. In November 2010 the law will be reviewed to evaluate whether the sample proceeding should be implemented in the Code of Civil Procedure and should apply to all civil procedures.

3.3 Funding of claims and whether loser pays

Under Sections 91 and following of the Code of Civil Procedure, the losing party in a lawsuit is, in principle, liable for all necessary judicial and extrajudicial costs. However, this is true only for the statutory lawyers' fees and assumes that the losing party is capable of reimbursing advanced fees. If the court grants only part of the claim and dismisses the rest, there are two possible solutions:

- Each party bears the *pro rata* costs corresponding to the lost part of the claim; or
- The parties share the court fees and each bears its own costs.

To give a rough idea of procedural costs in Germany, court and lawyers' fees of one plaintiff and one defendant based on an amount of €1 million would add up to about €50,000.

(a) Judicial costs

The plaintiff must pay judicial costs in advance. Judicial costs include the court fees as well as certain expenses of the parties (eg, costs incurred in obtaining evidence). Normally, a first-instance civil lawsuit ending with a judgment takes three court fees (No 1210 schedule of costs). The three court fees are reduced to one if the proceedings are determined by:

- withdrawal of the action, a judgment based on a defendant's acknowledgement or a claimant's renunciation;

- an arrangement after receiving a court order; or
- a declaration of settlement (No 1211 schedule of costs).

The amount of one court fee is calculated on the basis of the value of the matter in dispute. In connection with the Court Fees Act, a schedule is provided which shows the basic fees and any *pro rata* increase relating to the disputed amounts.

(b) Extrajudicial costs

Extrajudicial costs include lawyers' fees and certain expenses of the parties (eg, the cost of travelling to the hearings).

In principle, the prevailing party can claim for compensation of lawyers' costs only in the amount of statutory fees for one lawyer. These are set out in the Lawyers' Remuneration Act. Lawyers' fees are calculated on a *pro rata* basis, corresponding to the value of the matter in dispute. Under vocational and professional law, solicitors are by bound to charge statutory fees as a minimum. Higher fees charged on an hourly basis, as usually agreed on in commercial actions, are not recoverable and must be borne by the respective party.

Contingency fees are currently prohibited. However, in a decision of March 7 2007 the Federal Constitutional Court ruled that in future, the legislature must allow exceptions in special circumstances.

3.4 Plaintiffs' bar

German law has no equivalent of the plaintiffs' bar. Advertising by law firms is strictly curtailed. German law provides for neither class actions nor contingency fees.

3.5 Procedural barriers

Shareholders that bring claims against directors on behalf of the company must first seek admission for the claim (see section 2.2). Other than that, there are no specific procedural features of claims against directors.

Under German law, a time bar is regarded not as procedural barrier, but rather as a concept of material law. Claims based on directors' internal liability are time barred after five years, irrespective of the claimant's knowledge. The same applies to claims of shareholders based on Section 117 of the Stock Corporation Act. Claims on the basis of general civil law are subject to regular limitation rules. Pursuant to Sections 195 and 199 of the Civil Code, the regular limitation period is three years, starting from the end of the year in which the claim arose and in which the claimant first knew or did not know about the facts of the claim.

4. Indemnification rights

4.1 When the company can indemnify

(a) Defence costs

Permission for indemnification depends on whether the company itself has claims against the director and can waive these claims. In third-party proceedings the question of whether the director also breached duties in relation to the company and thereby established internal liability can usually be determined only after a final decision of the proceeding. The director is entitled to indemnification of defence costs in advance, as long as the company can recoup this if the director loses in the civil or criminal proceeding. This director's claim is based on rights arising from his employment contract (Section 670 of the Civil Code).

If the director successfully defends the third-party claims, the procedural costs are borne by the other party. This includes the director's legal costs, but only in the amount of statutory fees. However, white-collar crime lawyers are usually paid on an hourly basis and these costs will exceed the statutory fees. The director must pay these fees even if the claim is dismissed or he is acquitted. According to legal commentators, there are good reasons for the company to pay the excess to the director, based on the company's fiduciary duties.

In principle, if the director loses in a civil or criminal proceeding, defence costs cannot be indemnified. Claims based on Section 670 of the Civil Code are limited in case of contributory negligence on the part of the claimant.

(b) *Directors' right to indemnification for compensation to third parties*

The internal liability of directors of stock corporations is mandatory. Therefore, any indemnification commitment of a stock corporation to its directors by agreement will be ineffective, if third-party claims are based on breach of a director's duty in relation to the company. For the same reason, a director is not entitled to indemnification pursuant to Section 670 of the Civil Code. The stock corporation would be obliged to indemnify a director with regard to third-party claims only if the director were liable to third parties without having breached his duties to the stock corporation.

In contrast, the liability of directors in limited liability companies may be waived, in principle. Prior commitment to indemnification is possible. However, in the event of intentional breaches of duty, prior commitment to indemnification by limited liability companies is excluded by general civil law. The question of whether prior indemnification is possible in the event of gross negligence is subject to legal dispute. There are no precedents expressly dealing with this issue. Some decisions of the Federal Court of Justice suggest that prior indemnification for gross negligence is possible, but these have been criticised by legal commentators.

(c) *Voluntary indemnification by the company for directors' compensation to third parties*

According to prevailing legal literature, voluntary indemnification by a stock corporation subsequent to a ruling against a director is possible within the scope of Section 93(4) of the Stock Corporation Act. This provides that the stock corporation can waive or settle claims against directors only after three years and only if the shareholders' meeting consents (and there is no opposition by a minority of shareholders that together hold 10% of the share capital).

A limited liability company cannot waive claims against directors based on breach of certain duties if compensation is needed to satisfy creditors of the company (eg, indemnification is impossible for breaches of duties concerning maintenance of capital). Also, a limited liability company cannot waive claims based on a director's delay in filing an insolvency petition. The same applies to claims based on breach of duties in connection with an increase in the nominal capital.

(d) ***In case of settlement***

In case of a settlement (ie, no court finding with regard to the director's breach of duty, the competent body for asserting claims against the director must determine whether the director breached his duty to the company. If the board confirmed that there had been a breach of duty, the company would not be obliged to make the settlement payment. With regard to voluntary indemnification, the principles outlined in section 4.1 apply. If the board decided that the director did not breach his duties, he would be entitled to indemnification pursuant to Section 670 of the Civil Code.

4.2 Formalities for indemnification

A director is basically entitled to indemnification based on rights set out in his employment contract (Section 670 of the Civil Code). The directors' rights are limited by principles of internal liability. Voluntary indemnification by the company is restricted by rules on waivers of claims against directors (see section 4.1).

4.3 How indemnification works

There is no special procedure to be followed with respect to indemnification, other than that outlined in section 4.1.

4.4 What cannot be indemnified

For the limits of voluntary indemnification, see section 4.1.

5. D&O insurance

5.1 Availability of D&O insurance

D&O insurance has been established since the mid-1980s. Most listed stock corporations and increasing numbers of small and medium-sized companies carry D&O insurance for their directors. The fact that D&O insurance is mentioned in the Corporate Governance Codex released by the government indicates that it is a generally accepted product on the German market.

In 2005, the estimated annual premium volume was in the range of €400 million to €600 million. The D&O market for small and medium-sized companies is highly competitive and therefore softening, whereas the D&O market for those larger companies listed on the stock exchange is still considered a 'hard' market.

5.2 Local rules on cover provided under a non-domestic D&O policy

Non-domestic insurers may provide cover to resident policyholders subject to German insurance regulatory law. EU-based insurers can exercise privileged rights pursuant to EU law compared with non-EU-based risk carriers. German regulatory law does not refer to so-called *'Korrespondenzverträge'* (ie, contracts concluded at the initiative of a resident policyholder with a non-domestic insurer that does not do business in the German market).

(a) *Non-EU insurers*

Insurers based in non-EU states are subject to Sections 105 to 110 of the Insurance Regulatory Act. According to Section 105(1), non-EU insurers require permission to underwrite risks on the German market through an intermediary. Where this is the case, correspondence contracts are prohibited to preserve transparency.

The insurer must establish a branch on German territory and keep any business records there. The insurer must appoint a main representative for that branch. The representative need not necessarily be German, but must have his or her permanent residence in Germany, be able to speak German and know the basics of German insurance law. The branch must be entered in the Commercial Register at the residence of the main representative. Case law treats the branch as a legal person. The location of the branch defines the insurer's place of jurisdiction.

The insurer is obliged to provide a solvency margin in the amount of the business written through the branch. A certain amount (guarantee fund) of this capital resource must be kept in Germany and the rest within the European Union. Additionally, the insurer must provide a certain amount as caution money. Exceptions can be made for those insurers that have received permission in another EU member state.

(b) *EU-based insurers*

Insurers based in EU member states or in the European Economic Area as defined by law are subject to Sections 110a and following of the Insurance Regulatory Act. Specific rules apply for Lloyd's of London pursuant to Section 110b of the act.

Insurers from EU member states that are subject to EU directives are allowed to write business on the German market through branches or intermediaries without any specific permission from the German regulatory authority. This does not apply to insurers based in a European country that is not subject to EU directives. In such cases the regulatory authority of the insurer's country of origin regulates the finances. In all other cases, the German authority is responsible for the regulation of insurers acting on the German market. Insurers must comply with German statutory rules that protect the public interest.

(c) *Coverage of resident subsidiary under non-domestic global policy*

The question of whether the parent company of a German subsidiary can obtain insurance coverage for the subsidiary under a global insurance policy from a non-domestic insurer is disputed with regard to admissibility under German regulatory law. Thus far, this issue has not been resolved, but some insurers have issued local policies.

(d) *German law on D&O insurance*

There are no special statutory rules on D&O insurance. Any legal questions arising from, or in connection with, D&O insurance must be appraised according to general statutory rules, as well as according to the parties' agreements in the specific insurance contract (limited by compulsory legal provisions). The relevant statutory rules are contained in the Insurance Contract Act and the Civil Code.

Hong Kong

Declan McDaid
Deacons

1. Directors' duties

1.1 Nature of the duties

Until July 1 1997, Hong Kong was under the direct rule of the United Kingdom, so decisions of the High Court in London (and the appellate courts) were binding in Hong Kong. Accordingly, both the codified law (ordinances) and the common law have been heavily influenced by the United Kingdom over the past 150 years. While High Court decisions are no longer binding, they remain highly influential. Hong Kong has stamped its mark on the legal framework since the handover, but much of the legislation that underpins the legal system can be traced back to the United Kingdom, so in many respects the systems are inextricably linked and to many the similarities will be obvious.

The Companies Ordinance (Cap 32) does not define the term 'director', except to state that it includes any person occupying the position of a director, irrespective of title (Section 2(1)).

A director, whether executive or non-executive (the duties are the same), stands in a fiduciary relationship to the company and the fiduciary duty that flows from the relationship is owed to the company alone (not to a shareholder - even a majority shareholder or parent company - but to all members of the company, both present and future). Directors operate collectively as a board and act as agents of the company. As such, they must:

- act in good faith in the best interests of the company as a whole;
- exercise the powers given to them under the articles of association; and
- not allow any conflict of interest to arise between their duties as directors and any personal interests.

There is no one source of directors' duties in Hong Kong, so there is scope for latitude when interpreting the precise nature and scope of their duties. The duties, rights and powers of a director are derived from:

- the interpretation of the common law;
- the rules of equity;
- the Companies Ordinance; and
- the various rules and codes of practice that exist in Hong Kong (eg, the Main Board Rules Governing the Listing of Securities on the Stock Exchange of Hong Kong Limited (the Main Board Listing Rules), the Rules Governing the

Listing of Rules on the Growth Enterprise Market of the Stock Exchange of Hong Kong Limited (the GEM Listing Rules), and the Guide for Directors of Listed Companies (in particular, Appendices 10 and 14 (the Model Code for Securities Transactions and Code of Best Practice)).

(a) ***Main Board and GEM Listing Rules***

Rule 3.08 of the Main Board Listing Rules and Rule 5.01 of the GEM Listing Rules reflect the features of collective responsibility that are important to the regulatory authorities in Hong Kong. Both the Main Board Listing Rules and the GEM Listing Rules require that a director:

- act honestly and in good faith in the interests of the company as a whole;
- act for proper purpose;
- be answerable to the issuer for the application or misapplication of its assets;
- avoid actual and potential conflicts of interest and duty;
- disclose fully and fairly any interest in contracts with the issuer; and
- apply such degree of skill, care and diligence as may reasonably be expected of a person of his knowledge and experience.

(b) ***Companies Ordinance***

The Companies Ordinance defines some directors' duties; however, these deal more with procedural matters than meeting fiduciary duties and/or duties of care, diligence and skill to a standard at least corresponding to those required by the common law in Hong Kong. While this list is not exhaustive, some of the more significant duties that arise by virtue of the Companies Ordinance are as follows:

- duty to obtain prior company approval for the allotment of shares by directors (Section 57B);
- duty to convene an extraordinary general meeting upon request (Section 113);
- duty to attach a directors' report to the balance sheet (Section 129D);
- duty to convene a company meeting at the request of an auditor who has resigned (Section 140B);
- duty to obtain prior company approval for the disposal by the directors of fixed assets of the company (Section 155A);
- duty to include in notices of resolutions an explanation of their effect and the particulars of any relevant interests of directors (Section 155B);
- duty to shareholders regarding the prospectus or statements in lieu (Section 155C);
- duties regarding retention of the register of directors and secretaries (Section 158A);
- duty to make disclosures for the purposes of Section 158 (Section 158B);
- particulars on directors' emoluments and pensions (Section 161);
- particulars on loans to officers (Section 161B);
- general duty to make disclosures for the purposes of Sections 161 and 161B (Section 161C);
- disclosure by directors of material interests in contracts (Section 162);

- duties relating to contracts with a sole member who is also a director (Section 162B); and
- duty of a director or past director to disclose payment for loss of office and so on, made in connection with the transfer of shares in the company (Section 163B).

There are also a large number of duties created by enactments that are well outside the traditional ambit of company law.

(c) ***Companies Register guidelines***

Many of the most important features dealing with the general responsibilities and liabilities of directors derive from various sources, including the constitution of the company and case law based on the decisions of numerous judges over the years. These general duties are conveniently set out in the Non Statutory Guidelines on Director's Duties issued by the Companies Register in April 2006. It is intended that all directors should read the guidelines and it is recommended that all companies give a copy of the guidelines to new directors irrespective of whether they organise induction training. While the Companies Register is at pains to stress that the statements in the guidelines are principles only and are not intended as exhaustive statements of the law, they are fairly comprehensive. The general principles of directors' duties are as follows.

(i) *Duty to act in good faith for the benefit of the company as a whole*

A director must exercise his discretion and judgment in good faith in the best interests of the company and not for any hidden agenda that is contrary to the wellbeing of the company. This means that a director owes a duty to act in the interests of both the company and all present and future members. In carrying out this duty, a director must (as far as practicable) have regard to the need to achieve fair and reasonable outcomes for its members.

(ii) *Duty to use powers for a proper purpose for the benefit of members as a whole*

A director must exercise his powers purely for the purposes for which they were conferred and the exercise of a director's powers must always be for the benefit of the company. In considering whether a director has used any power properly, a court will apply a four-stage test which will involve identifying:

- the power;
- the proper purpose for which the power was granted;
- the substantial purpose for which the power was actually used; and
- whether that purpose was proper.

Further, to establish a breach it is not necessary to establish dishonesty; a breach can occur even if a director has acted in good faith.

(iii) *Duty not to delegate powers except with proper authorisation and duty to exercise independent judgement*

Unless expressly authorised to do so by the company's constitution or any resolution, a director of a company must not delegate any powers and must at all times exercise independent judgement in relation to any exercise of his powers for the benefit of the company.

(iv) *Duty to exercise care, skill and diligence*

A director of a company must exercise the care, skill and diligence (at least to the standards required under Hong Kong law) that would be exercised by a reasonable person with the knowledge, skill and experience reasonably expected of a person in such position. In determining whether a director has fulfilled this duty, the court will also consider whether he has exercised the care, skill and diligence that would be exercised by a reasonable person with any additional knowledge, skill and experience that the director may have.

(v) *Duty to avoid conflicts between personal interests and interests of the company*

A director of a company is in a fiduciary relationship with the company and must not allow personal interests to conflict with the interests of the company. Any contract in which the director has a personal interest which conflicts with the interests of the company is voidable by the company. Further, a court will expect a very high standard of honesty from all fiduciaries.

(vi) *Duty not to enter into transactions in which the directors have an interest except in compliance with the requirements of the law*

There are complex statutory provisions dealing with the areas in which conflicts of interest are most likely to arise (ie, service contracts, loans to directors and dealings in shares). A director must not authorise or procure or permit the company to enter into any such transaction, or enter into any such transaction himself, unless he has fully complied with these statutory provisions.

(vii) *Duty not to gain advantage by exploiting the position of director*

A director must not use his position as a director to gain (directly or indirectly) an advantage for himself or someone else, or which is to the detriment of the company.

(vii) *Duty not to make unauthorised use of company property or information*

A director must not use company property or information, or any opportunity that presents itself to the company, for personal gain, except where the use or benefit has been disclosed to the company in general meeting and the company has consented to it. If there is no disclosure a conflict of interest and duty will arise. It makes no difference that personal gain secured is one which the company could not itself have made if the director had not used his or her own resources, or that the director acted in good faith.

(ix) *Duty not to accept personal benefit from third parties conferred due to position of director*
A director or former director must not accept any benefit from a third party that is conferred because of the position held and the powers conferred on him by virtue of that position, or by way of reward for any exercise of his powers as a director. The company can confer a benefit, provided that it has consented to it by ordinary resolution or the benefit is necessarily incidental to the proper performance of any of the directors' duties. If the benefit is not disclosed, any profit belongs to the company and the director is under a duty to account for it.

(x) *Duty to observe the company's memorandum and articles of association and resolutions*
A director must abide by the company's constitution and act in accordance with resolutions that are made in accordance with the company's constitution.

(xi) *Duty to keep proper books of account*
A director must take all reasonable steps to ensure that proper books of account are kept, and that these give a true and fair view of the state of affairs of the company and fully explain its transactions. To avoid breaching the fraudulent trading provisions in Section 275 of the Companies Ordinance, a director must not allow the company to incur further debt knowing that there is no reasonable prospect of avoiding insolvency.

1.2 Standards of care

For the past six or seven years there has been an ongoing review of the Companies Ordinance, and part of that debate has been whether to codify and bring certainty to the standards of care demanded from directors. To date, codification has not taken place because the perception in Hong Kong as to whether there has been a breach of duty turns on the facts arising in each particular case. Accordingly, not every eventuality could be provided for and any codification would therefore have to be supplemented with guidelines. These would not necessarily provide directors with a clear picture as to how they should best serve the interests of the company. Further, there is a belief that any codification could operate to stifle judicial intervention to change case law in order to reflect developments in other jurisdictions.

The law on negligence is therefore at the heart of the assessment of the standards of care, skill and diligence required under Hong Kong law, which directors must apply when carrying their duties to the company. The actual standards of skill and care demanded of directors in Hong Kong can be traced back to Justice Romer's comments in *Re City Equitable Fire Insurance Ltd* [1925] Ch 407 at 428: "A director need not exhibit in the performance of his duties a greater degree of care and skill than may reasonably be expected from a person with his skill and experience."

The basis of a director's liability in Hong Kong arises independently of any contract or fiduciary relationship and will require some measure of active participation in the wrong before it will amount to a breach. The mere fact of being a director would not be sufficient for liability to attach.

1.3 To whom the duties are owed

As set out above, directors' duties are primarily owed to the company. The directors represent the interests of the company as a whole and as such will generally owe duties to the shareholders collectively as a group, but not individually.

While the directors' duties primarily focus on the interests of the company, three categories of person can be identified as those most likely to be directly affected by the directors' duties: individual shareholders, creditors and employees. Directors' duties in respect of these three categories are discussed in more detail in the next section.

However, while these categories are obvious, the laws of Hong Kong in the form of ordinances and the common law offer many opportunities for directors to incur liability.

1.4 Common defences to and exemptions from liability

In the absence of bad faith or fraud, there is limited scope for a director to escape liability by asking the company to ratify his breach of duty.

In a consultation paper dated July 2001, which was part of the first phase of the Corporate Governance Review, the government identified what would constitute a corporate wrong as follows:

- breach of a director's duty of loyalty;
- negligence; or
- exercise of a director's powers for an improper purpose.

While shareholders of the company may ratify such wrongs, they cannot ratify certain types of conduct, including:

- illegal transactions such as theft;
- financial assistance or the distribution of capital in breach of the Companies Ordinance;
- misappropriation of assets so as to constitute a fraud on the company; and
- misappropriation of assets by shareholders or directors.

There is some difficulty in determining what can and cannot be ratified, but certain general principles help to identify certain types of conduct which cannot be ratified after the event. For example, where the substance of a transaction is damaging to the company and is to the personal gain of the wrongdoers, it will not be capable of ratification.

Accordingly, directors who find themselves accused of a breach of their duties to the company will escape liability if their acts are ratified in a general meeting following full and frank disclosure of all relevant information. Any attempt to ratify acts must involve full and frank disclosure; if the disclosure falls short in any way, the purported ratification will be ineffective. Further, any ratification by a company before it enters into liquidation will not be effective if the transaction amounts to a fraud on the creditors.

Section 358 of the Companies Ordinance empowers the court to relieve the directors and/or the officers of the court of any liability in respect of negligence, default and breach of duty of trust where, after considering all available evidence, the court concludes it would be fair for those persons to be excused because they acted fairly, reasonably and honestly. The ability to grant such relief under Section 358 applies to proceedings brought by or on behalf of a company against its directors and officers, and proceedings instigated to enforce the terms of the Companies Ordinance. Under this section, the burden falls upon the applicant to show that the action taken was honest and reasonable. However, if established, the court may relieve the director of blame either totally or partially as it sees fit (there is considerable judicial discretion here).

Under Section 165(1) of the Companies Ordinance, a director may be entitled to an indemnity from the company for losses and liabilities incurred in exercising the powers granted by the company's constitution (see section 4).

The law on negligence sits alongside these statutory provisions, and while it is often difficult to establish a breach of duty of care because the breach may consist of a straightforward commercial misjudgement, it is usually easier to establish a breach of a fiduciary duty because this will often involve an element of dishonesty which will be much easier to highlight. Moreover, in Hong Kong, private companies are often structured and run by families on a patriarchal system, with the board composed of family members, so any 'breaches' may be looked at more sympathetically.

2. Who can bring claims

2.1 The company and its liquidators

(a) The company

As an abstract body, a company cannot be responsible for its actions – this responsibility falls on its directors and officers, whose primary duties are to the company. The company is the most significant potential claimant for claims of breach of duty, because the wrong is done to the company and therefore the ability to sue rests with the company.

In Hong Kong, the rule in *Foss v Harbottle* [1843] 2 Hare 461 applies and the basis for the rule is that directors are not in a fiduciary relationship with individual shareholders. However, there are some notable exceptions:

- where the act complained of is *ultra vires*;
- where the action complained of was an invasion of the member's personal rights; and
- where the wrongdoer is effectively in complete control of the company, so it would be impossible for the company to take any action on its own behalf.

Numerous provisions throughout the Companies Ordinance also allow the company to police the actions of directors and/or officers, and some allow the company to take action against a director.

(b) *The liquidator*

A director who is knowingly party to fraudulent trading may, when the company is being wound up, be made personally liable for the company's debts or other liabilities and be subject to criminal penalties. The imposition of criminal penalties requires a very high standard of proof, in that it must be shown conclusively that the business was carried on with the intention of defrauding the creditors.

Under Section 275 of the Companies Ordinance, upon application to the High Court by the official receiver, the liquidator or any creditor or contributory of the company (ie, a shareholder), the court may, if it thinks it proper so to do, declare that any persons who were knowingly party to fraudulent trading shall be personally liable, without limitation, for all debts or other liabilities of the company as the court may direct, and will order those persons to contribute to the assets of the company as it sees fit.

Fraudulent trading is a little-used remedy in Hong Kong. To satisfy the standard of proof required, it must be established that the accused:

- made decisions which were not in the interests of the company; and
- did so in the knowledge that, at a time of incurring greater liabilities, the company was insolvent and in no position to clear its debts.

If the above points are determined on the facts, then fraud or dishonesty may be established, subject to:

- a subjective test as to the state of mind/motives of the accused (as what seems like fraud may only be negligence); and
- an objective test as to whether the accused fulfilled his duty to preserve the assets of the company (eg, if a director takes a risk in using company assets which no director could honestly believe to be in the interests of the company and which is prejudicial to the rights of others, then that director has acted fraudulently).

The civil remedy in Section 275 of the Companies Ordinance in relation to insolvent trading requires a burden of proof on a par with that required in criminal proceedings. The perception in Hong Kong is that this 'criminal aspect' to fraudulent trading is important; those who participate in such activities should be aware that the penalty for their behaviour might extend beyond mere fines and could result in imprisonment.

Under Section 276 of the Companies Ordinance, current and past directors of a company that is in the process of being wound up may become liable or accountable for any money or property that has been misapplied or retained. They are thereby guilty of misfeasance or breach of duty in relation to the company. Section 276 is commonly known as the 'misfeasance provision' and is actionable on the suit of the official receiver, the liquidator or any creditor or contributory. Under Section 276, assistance may be sought from the court to investigate the conduct of:

- anyone who participated in the formation or promotion of the company;
- any past or present officer; or

- any liquidator or receiver of the company (including a particular director or officer or a group of directors).

Following the investigation, if the court finds that an individual is guilty of a misfeasance or breach of duty, it may order him to repay or restore any money or property, plus interest, or to contribute such sum to the assets of the company by way of compensation as the court thinks fit. This provision is also rarely used.

2.2 Minority shareholders on behalf of the company

In Hong Kong (and several other Asian jurisdictions), many listed companies are controlled by families, on the basis of a patriarchal system. This often creates an imbalance between the controlling family shareholders and the minority shareholders.

The principle of 'majority rule' among shareholders is fundamental under Hong Kong law, as it is under English company law. Therefore, if a majority of shareholders do not support the company in bringing a claim against the directors, it cannot usually proceed. Accordingly, until Section 168A of the Companies Ordinance was enacted, minority shareholders' rights to bring claims on behalf of the company were restricted, in that *locus standi* could be established only if there was a fraud on the minority and the wrongdoers were in control of the company. Such cases are unusual because the structure of the company often makes it very difficult to obtain the evidence needed to meet the very high burden of proof. Further, Hong Kong is an expensive arena within which to litigate and there is no contingency/conditional fee system.

Section 168A of the Companies Ordinance provides minority shareholders with a statutory basis on which to bring a claim against the directors on behalf of the company for 'misfeasance' - defined by Section 168BB as "fraud, negligence, default in compliance with any enactment or rule of law, or breach of duty". It is therefore no longer necessary to establish fraud on the minority to bring a shareholder action under the statutory regime, as is required under common law.

One of the problems with Section 168A from the perspective of the minority shareholders is that the term 'unfair prejudice', as used in the Companies Ordinance, is not defined therein; nor, as far as we can ascertain, has it been defined judicially. It is possible that the words have not been defined because a strict definition would fetter judicial discretion. A judge would have to ensure that all elements of the definition were present before deciding that there had been unfair prejudice, rather than being able to look at any potential wrongdoing in the round. Section 168A has not been widely used, possibly because of the uncertainty surrounding the degree of evidence which would be required to establish unfair prejudice. Another reason for this, as set out above, is that the claim is brought for the benefit of the company, so any damages belong to the company and the shareholder will not benefit directly. The costs involved are very likely to outweigh any benefit. Further, under Section 168A, a shareholder must apply to the court for leave to commence the statutory action.

At the hearing for leave, the court will consider whether:

- there is a serious issue to be tried;
- proceedings are in the interest of the company; and
- having regard to the above, there has been any approval or ratification.

Directors facing an unwanted shareholder derivative action can seek ratification to stop the action from proceeding beyond the application for leave (Section 168BF(2) of the Companies Ordinance).

If leave to continue the action is given, the court is likely to order, among other things, that the company indemnify the shareholder who has brought the action on its behalf for all past and future costs incurred.

2.3 Minority shareholders on their own account

Directors' duties are owed to the company. Only in very limited circumstances, which are not precisely defined, will a shareholder be entitled to bring an action against the directors in his own name.

In Hong Kong, the law relating to directors' duties to shareholders is complex. However, operating as an agent and making statements which induce shareholders to invest in the company may give rise to causes of action. This is considered more fully in section 2.4.

A more common situation is where a minority shareholder complains that his personal rights have been violated by the directors, causing unfair prejudice. There is also a personal element to Section 168A(2)(b) of the Companies Ordinance, as the shareholder must establish unfair prejudice.

2.4 Third parties

In general, directors do not owe any fiduciary duties to third parties. This state of affairs arises because the decision to incorporate with limited liability and register under the Companies Ordinance protects the company from trading debts in the absence of fraud.

(a) General

In Hong Kong, as a general rule, when directors deal with third parties during normal commercial transactions, they bind the company in their capacity as its officers. The principle governing this relationship has grown out of the same strain of common law, equity and statue as the law in England and Wales (ie, a company is a separate legal entity), and third parties that deal with the company should realise that the corporate veil protecting all limited liability companies will be lifted only in certain limited circumstances

The first is where a director who is also the principal shareholder uses the corporate entity to commit fraud against a third party. In such circumstances the court will allow the corporate veil to be lifted to expose the true nature of the fraud. In effect, in these cases the company will have been formed as a device, stratagem or mask for the effective carrying on of a business and will therefore be a sham.

The second exception focuses on the liability of a company director for negligent misstatement. The authoritative statement by the House of Lords in *Williams Natural Life Health Foods Ltd* [1998] 1 WLR 831 has been applied in Hong Kong several times since the decision was handed down. The principle is that in making a misstatement to a third party, a director may assume personal responsibility if there is a very clear indication that a personal assumption of risk by the director was anticipated. The crux of the matter is whether a third party could reasonably be said to rely on the director's personal responsibility as opposed to relying on the company's corporate responsibility.

The third exception concerns directors' dealings in shares as an agent for an individual shareholder and the accuracy of statements and documents when shares are being issued.

(b) *Creditors*

As a general rule, directors are not personally liable to creditors of the company, unless they are contracting on their own account or have provided a personal guarantee at the insistence of a party with which the company is dealing.

To avoid doubt, it should be made abundantly clear on whose behalf a director is entering into a contract. If there is any doubt and a director signs a contract, issues a cheque or orders goods, the director may become personally liable to honour the terms of the contract. Section 26 of the Bills of Exchange Ordinance provides that to avoid personal liability on a cheque, a director must endorse it to the effect that he is signing it only in a representative capacity. Under Section 93 of the Companies Ordinance, if a company cheque does not bear the name of the company, the director who signs it is guilty of an offence.

This general rule is supplanted when a company is insolvent, as the company's assets must then be applied for the benefit of the creditors ahead of the shareholders. (This is discussed in more detail in the following section.) However, if the director's or officer's intention is to defraud creditors or prefer one creditor over others he may be liable to a fine and/or imprisonment. Under Section 266 of the Companies Ordinance, certain transactions can be deemed fraudulent and therefore invalid, the test being whether any such transaction would have been a fraudulent transaction if committed by an individual in bankruptcy. Section 267 of the Companies Ordinance focuses on floating charges and is designed to prevent insolvent companies from creating preferences.

In certain circumstances, directors may also owe a duty to creditors as a result of their actions if, at common law, the creditors are entitled to pierce the corporate veil and look to the remaining assets to satisfy their claims. As set out above, besides fraud, the established grounds for piercing the corporate veil are arguments of personal responsibility, agency, trust and enemy alien. Each case must be judged on its own facts

The corporate veil can also be pierced by statute with the result that personal liability may be imposed on certain individuals. For example:

- Section 31 of the Companies Ordinance dictates that if a company has been carrying on business for more than six months without having at least two members, the sole member shall be liable for the debts of the company;

- Section 93(5) deals with the use (and misuse) of a company's seal, and again can impose personal liability on a shareholder who has used the seal unless the company accepts liability; and
- Section 344(6) allows a company that is not commercially active to become dormant to avoid the administration required under the Companies Ordinance for active companies and imposes personal liability on any shareholder who ought to have known that the company was dormant.

(d) *Regulatory authorities*

One of the most significant pieces of legislation to be enacted in Hong Kong in recent years is the Securities and Futures Ordinance, which came into force on April 1 2003. The Securities and Futures Ordinance introduced the concept of dual filing, and requires listing documents and various categories of corporate communications to be filed with both the Securities and Futures Commission (SFC) and the Stock Exchange of Hong Kong. This dual filing enables the SFC to enforce deliberate or reckless misstatements by investigation and prosecution where appropriate. In short, the SFC is primarily responsible for enforcing laws relating to the securities and futures industries. As mentioned earlier, it may commence criminal proceedings and impose compensatory penalties on directors and officers.

(e) *Investors who are mis-sold shares*

Under Section 40 of the Companies Ordinance, directors may be liable to pay compensation to subscribers in the context of an initial public offering where subscribers suffer a loss because of any untrue or misleading statements made in the prospectus issued for the initial public offering. Each director of the company at the time of the issue of the prospectus is also liable to imprisonment and a fine unless he can prove that the statement was immaterial or that he had reasonable grounds to believe, and did so at the time, that the statement was true. Accordingly, under Section 40 of the Companies Ordinance, both civil and criminal liability can arise. The Protection of Investors Ordinance makes it a criminal offence to induce someone into investing by a fraudulent or reckless misrepresentation.

Section 107 of the Securities and Futures Ordinance provides that where a fraudulent or reckless misrepresentation is made to induce a subscriber to enter into an agreement to acquire, dispose, subscribe for or underwrite securities, the director at the time the misrepresentation was made has committed an offence and is liable on indictment to a fine of HK$1 million and imprisonment for seven years. Further, under Section 108, regardless of whether the director has already incurred any other liability, he will also be liable to pay compensation by way of damages to a subscriber for any pecuniary loss that the subscriber has suffered because he relied on the director's misrepresentation, unless it can be proved that the director did not authorise the misrepresentation.

The extent of the liability does not cease there. Under Sections 383 and 384 of the Securities and Futures Ordinance, a director who makes a statement to the SFC in support of an application in purported compliance with the requirements of the ordinance, but which he knows is reckless, false or misleading, will have committed an offence on indictment and is liable to a fine of HK$1 million and imprisonment for two years. Section 391 governs directors' civil liability for false or misleading public communications concerning securities and futures contracts. The director will be liable to pay compensation by way of damages to the public (or a group of persons comprising members of the public) for any pecuniary loss sustained as a result of any actions they took or failed to take because they relied on documents given to them by the director.

(f) ***Employees***

When debating issues relating to either long-term or short-term strategies, directors should always consider any impact a decision may have on the interests of their employees. Under Sections 31 and 63A of the Employment Ordinance, they will commit an offence and be personally liable for a fine if they employ someone or fail to terminate someone's employment when it is obvious that person's wages cannot be paid when they fall due.

3. Claims culture

3.1 Litigation

Hong Kong is now a highly regulated market and while it cannot yet be compared to the United Kingdom and the United States in terms of a 'blame culture', there has been an increase in shareholder activism and the exercise of shareholders' rights. Without the limitations built into the litigation rules, there would be a lot more claims. Cultural factors, too, tend to direct those with grievances away from direct confrontation.

The litigation culture in Hong Kong (as in many other Asian countries) has changed significantly since the 1997 financial crisis. Over the last six or seven years there has been a significant increase in regulatory activity. Initially, this could be explained as a reaction to the collapse of the markets, but more recently it may be linked to the extremely buoyant initial public offering market. The link is obvious, as regulatory activity usually manifests itself in the form of investigations and inquiries by bodies such as the SFC and the Hong Kong Stock Exchange focusing on non-compliance with the Listing Rules.

The increase in shareholder actions has also resulted in an upturn in claims against companies and their directors. Throughout Asia, many listed companies are controlled by families and run on a patriarchal basis. Also, traditionally, the government played a significant role in the corporate landscape. However, this landscape is now changing, and while a decade or so ago mere lip service was paid to corporate governance, the penalties that can now be imposed on directors and officers mean that this has been replaced with solid corporate governance policies. Not the least of these, in terms of Hong Kong and Asian companies, has been the introduction of the non-executive director to the board, which has forced a lot of companies to become more transparent.

3.2 **Ability to bring class actions**

Order 15, Rules 12 and 13 of the Rules of the Supreme Court allow for certain types of representative action. Order 15, Rule 12 permits an unincorporated club which does not have legal capacity to sue in its own name to enforce the interests of its members by an action in the name of its president or representative. This provision can also be invoked by certain associations unique to Hong Kong such as a '*heung*' or a '*t'ong*'. Order 15, Rule 13 allows for the representation of interested parties who cannot be identified. However, apart from these rules there is no specific provision in Hong Kong for US-style class or group actions. Accordingly, the only way shareholders can seek redress on behalf of the company is by way of derivative actions.

3.3 **Funding of claims and whether loser pays**

Hong Kong is an expensive jurisdiction in which to litigate. The courts operate civil proceedings on a 'loser pays' or 'costs follow the event' basis, inasmuch as, subject to the discretion of the presiding judge, an unsuccessful claimant pays the successful defendant's costs or *vice versa*. A successful plaintiff or defendant can usually expect to recover only a proportion of his costs, by way of either negotiation or a formal determination of costs. Traditionally the successful plaintiff can expect to recover only in the region of 65% to 75% of his costs; this is often a significant deterrent to the commencement of actions.

Claims are generally funded by the claimant, who pays for the litigation privately. A Legal Aid Department does provide means-tested assistance to litigants, but it is unlikely that public funding would be available for claims against directors. Access to the courts is one of the fundamental rights constitutionally protected by the Basic Law. However, if the cost of litigation is prohibitive for some sections of society, they are effectively denied access to justice. A growing number of litigants in Hong Kong have no legal representation. This would suggest that a large proportion of the community do not qualify for legal aid and so cannot afford to engage solicitors to litigate on their behalf.

As matters stand, it is unlawful for a solicitor or barrister to enter into a conditional or contingency fee arrangement for a claim involving the institution of legal proceedings. On July 9 2007, the Conditional Fees Subcommittee of the Law Reform Commission released a report on conditional fees which recommended that the status quo be maintained. The primary reason for the decision not to introduce conditional fees was the absence of an insurance market which could provide affordable insurance (called 'after-the-event' insurance) to cover the opponent's legal costs if the legal action failed. So although the introduction of conditional fees has been debated in Hong Kong, they are still unlawful.

3.4 **Plaintiffs' bar**

In Hong Kong, there is no organised plaintiffs' bar that focuses on the bringing of claims against directors. This is attributable in part to the fact that shareholder awareness is still developing and the regulatory authorities are particularly active. This creates a perception that an effective system of checks and balances is in place.

3.5 **Procedural barriers**

As set out above, Section 168 of the Companies Ordinance provides that shareholder derivative actions may be commenced only with leave from the court.

Section 4(1)(a) of the Limitation Ordinance (Cap 347) prescribes that a civil action for breach of contract or tort will generally be time barred if it is not instituted within six years of the date of the breach.

Section 26(1) of the Limitation Ordinance provides that where an action is based on the fraud of a defendant and there has been deliberate concealment of a fact which may have had an impact on the plaintiff's ability to realise there were grounds to commence proceedings, the limitation period will not begin to run until discovery of the fraud or when, with reasonable diligence, it could have been discovered.

4. Indemnification rights

Until the new Section 165 of the Companies Ordinance became effective on February 13 2004,[1] Section 165 was (although never challenged) largely interpreted as allowing a company to provide a director with an indemnity provided that:

- in the context of a civil case, the case was dismissed; or
- when facing criminal charges, the director was acquitted.

The company could then seek reimbursement from an insurer. Many thought that, subject to the exemption set out above, the old Section 165 prevented a company from insuring the liabilities of its directors. The new Section 165 reforms the law by clarifying and improving this situation in several ways:

- The product can now be purchased legitimately;
- An acquittal or dismissal is no longer a prerequisite of indemnity or cover; and
- While it is still not permissible to buy fidelity cover against fraud, cover can be provided in relation to the defence of actions involving fraud.

4.1 When the company can indemnify

The new Section 165(1) of the Companies Ordinance states as follows:

> *Any provision, whether contained in the articles of a company or in any contract with a company or otherwise, for exempting any officer of the company or any person employed by the company as auditor from, or indemnifying him against, any liability to the company or a related company that by virtue of any rule of law would otherwise attach to him in respect of any negligence, default, breach of duty or breach of trust of which he may be guilty in relation to the company or related company shall, subject to subsections (2) to (4), be void.*

Section 165 (2) permits a company to:

indemnify any officer of the company, or any person employed by the company as auditor, against any liability incurred by him:

1 See Commencement Notice LN 267 of 2003, published on December 12 2003.

(a) in defending any proceedings, whether civil or criminal, in which judgment is given in his favour or in which he is acquitted; or
(b) in connection with any application under section 358 in which relief is granted to him by the court.

By virtue of Section 165(1), any attempt to exempt any officer of the company or any person employed by the company from liability to the company or a related company which, by virtue of the operation of the common law, would otherwise attach in respect of negligence, default or breach of duty will be void subject to Sections 165(2) and (3).

Otherwise, this section enables the company to indemnify any director or officer of the company for any obligation incurred by him in defending any criminal or civil proceedings in which:

- the director or officer is acquitted;
- the judgment is given in his favour; or
- in respect of an application under Section 358 of the Companies Ordinance, the appropriate relief is granted by the court.

(a) Claims by the company

On paper, a company can provide a director with what appears to be a true indemnity in respect of personal losses incurred while carrying out company business (this indemnity is meaningful only while the company is solvent).

However, Section 165(1) of the Companies Ordinance takes precedence over any such indemnity and, with the force of statute, operates to control the indemnity or indemnities that companies can give to directors via the articles of association. This renders void any agreement between a director and the company that provides any indemnity above and beyond the cost of defending proceedings in which the director is acquitted or the case dismissed.

(b) Criminal, regulatory and civil proceedings

The indemnity by the company can be availed of only where the director is innocent or the case against him is been discontinued; a conviction or judgment will result in the company seeking repayment of any sums advanced. Section 165(2) cannot indemnify criminal fines and regulatory penalties.

The requirement of innocence significantly waters down the indemnity that can be provided and restricts the ability of the company to negotiate an out-of-court settlement because no decision has been made in respect of the underlying proceedings.

(c) Third parties

Claims by third parties are relatively rare and focus on circumstances in which a court will be prepared to pierce the corporate veil. These situations are subject to Section 165(2), so notwithstanding the reform to the Companies Ordinance that improves the situation for directors, a company will be able to provide only limited comfort to directors.

In all cases, however, the new Section 165(3) of the Companies Ordinance changes the position somewhat with regard to a company's ability to purchase insurance to provide more extensive protection (see below).

4.2 Formalities for indemnification

There are no formalities for indemnification, save those set out in Section 165(1) of the Companies Ordinance.

4.3 How indemnification works

There is no specific procedure for indemnification.

4.4 What cannot be indemnified

As set out in section 4.1, indemnification is not permitted in respect of criminal fines and penalties, or other than in the circumstances set out in Section 165.

5. D&O insurance

5.1 Availability of D&O insurance

D&O insurance is widely available in Hong Kong. Demand for this product is increasing, prompted by the clarity of the new Section 165 of the Companies Ordinance and the heightened focus on corporate governance and transparency demanded by the regulators.

Section 165(3) of the Companies Ordinance now makes it clear that the insurer from which the product is purchased can provide cover for wrongful acts (anything which would constitute a breach of the duties set out in detail earlier is likely to constitute a wrongful act). Although cover is wide, fraud and fraudulent misrepresentation will be either expressly excluded or deemed excluded on grounds of public policy. When considering the indemnity to be provided, it must be borne in mind that in the absence of any insurance, the indemnity a company can provide is limited by the operation of Section 165(2). Accordingly, the issues addressed below, while dealt with in broad and general terms, apply both when there is insurance and when there is not.

5.3 Local rules on writing insurance business in Hong Kong

Under Section 6 of the Insurance Companies Ordinance (Cap 41), the Insurance Authority may prohibit any person from carrying on insurance business in or from Hong Kong. The exceptions to this are authorised insurers, Lloyd's and associations of underwriters.

A company wishing to carry on insurance business in or from Hong Kong may apply to the Insurance Authority for authorisation to do so under the Insurance Companies Ordinance. For the purposes of the Insurance Companies Ordinance, a 'company' is an entity formed and registered under the Companies Ordinance and includes companies incorporated outside Hong Kong to which Part XI of the Companies Ordinance applies. (Part XI deals with the establishment of a place of business in Hong Kong by a company incorporated outside Hong Kong.)

Authorisation to carry on insurance business in or from Hong Kong will be granted only to those insurers that meet the authorisation requirements stipulated under Sections 8(2) and (3) of the Insurance Companies Ordinance. These focus on capital, solvency, fitness of management and adequacy of reinsurance arrangements. An insurer applying for authorisation must meet certain other conditions as set out in the Authorisation Guidelines issued by the Insurance Authority. These seek to ensure that the applicant insurer is financially sound and competent to provide the insurance cover it seeks authorisation to write. These conditions must be met at the outset and will continue to apply while the insurer is authorised.

As set out above, insurers wishing to offer D&O products in Hong Kong to Hong Kong companies may have to seek authorisation. Where matters become complicated is where the parent company of a resident subsidiary obtains a global policy from a foreign insurer purporting to 'offer' the resident subsidiary D&O cover. In this context the question that must be addressed is whether the foreign insurer is conducting insurance business in Hong Kong (a detailed examination of this issue is beyond the scope of this chapter).

6. China

6.1 Legislative framework

In 2006 China updated its companies and securities legislation. The revised Company Law imposes duties of loyalty and due diligence on the directors and officers of a company; if breached, the directors can be held jointly and severally liable for their actions.

Chapter VI of the Company Law sets out in detail the qualifications required of company directors, supervisors and senior managers. Article 147 specifies who may and may not take on the role of director, supervisor and/or senior manager. For example, a person may not assume such a position if he:

- has been convicted of corruption, bribery or "disruption of the order of the socialist market";
- has been declared bankrupt;
- has acted as a legal representative of a company which has had its business licence revoked or been ordered to close down; or
- is unable to pay a relatively large amount of personal debt.

If an appointment is made in violation of Article 147, the appointment will be void; if any of the circumstances giving rise to a violation arise while the individual concerned is serving as a director, supervisor or senior manager, then the appointment will be terminated automatically.

Article 148 demands compliance with laws of the land and the company's articles of association and, most significantly, imposes a fiduciary duty on directors, supervisors and senior managers towards the company. However, the most significant provisions of the law are Articles 149 and 150. Article 149 provides as follows:

A director or senior management personnel shall not:

- *misappropriate company funds;*

- *deposit company funds in a bank account opened in his/her name or in the name of others;*
- *use company funds to make loans to others or provide guarantee for others without the consent of the board of shareholders, a shareholders' general meeting or the board of directors and in violation of the provisions of the articles of association of the company;*
- *enter into contracts with the company or carry out transactions with the company in violation of the provisions of the articles of association of the company or without the consent of the board of shareholders or a shareholders' general meeting;*
- *abuse his/her duties and powers to seize commercial opportunities of the company for himself/herself or others or engage in similar business as the company's on his/her own or with others without the consent of the board of shareholders or a shareholders' general meeting;*
- *pocket the commissions for transactions between the company and other parties;*
- *disclose company secrets arbitrarily; and*
- *do any other act which violates his/her fiduciary duties towards the company.*

Income received by directors and senior management personnel in violation of the aforesaid provisions shall belong to the company.

Article 150 provides that "[a] director, supervisor or senior management personnel who violates the provisions of laws and administrative regulations or the articles of association of the company in his/her performance of duties and powers and causing the company to suffer damages shall bear compensation liability".

While the duties imposed on directors and officers under Articles 149 and 150 bear striking similarities to those in other jurisdictions such as Hong Kong and the United Kingdom, it must be borne in mind that China is a country in transition. In those other jurisdictions, corporate governance issues have developed over many decades, while China is making the shift from a planned, state-run economy to a market-orientated economy in less than 20 years.

6.2 D&O insurance

The Chinese stock market came into existence in 1990 and in less than 20 years has grown to become the fourth largest in the world (behind stock markets in the United States, Japan and Germany). The corporate governance culture in China is still in its infancy and the level of sophistication required to appreciate the subtleties of risk transfer via D&O insurance is thus still developing. However, given the exposure that companies such as China Life and Pacific Internet now face in other jurisdictions, it will not be long before Chinese companies begin to appreciate the benefits that such risk transfer programmes offer.

Against this background, Article 92 of the Insurance Law provides a statutory basis for listed companies to buy liability insurance for directors, supervisors and/or senior management of limited companies. The statutory basis for the purchase of such insurance was devised from the Guiding Principles of Establishing an Independent Director System in Limited Companies and the Code of Corporate

Governance for Limited Companies, which supplements the Company Law. Article 39 of the code dovetails neatly with Article 148 of the Company Code. This would suggest that any negligence or breach of duty must be honest and without fraud or personal gain.

Companies that opt to purchase D&O insurance must do so through a company licensed to write such business by the China Insurance Regulatory Commission and the policy providing cover must be issued locally. The market for D&O insurance is quite small, but new companies are in the process of securing authorisation to write this class of business. Companies that are not incorporated in China trading through local subsidiaries may look to non-licensed insurers for cover or rely on the parent company's global programme. However, there are no rules and regulations governing the ability of non-licensed insurers to write business in the China, so in the long run, it may be safer to purchase cover from a local licensed provider.

Hungary

Dezsõ Perlaki
Burai-Kovács & Partners

According to the Act on Business Associations (IV/2006), the executive officers (also often called directors) or a board comprised of executive officers will manage the company. 'Management' means passing decisions which allow the company to operate, other than those reserved to the supreme body or other company organ (shareholders' meeting, members' meeting, supervisory board) under the memorandum of association.

The management of general and limited partnerships is handled by the member or members entitled to act in the capacity of executive officers. One or more managing directors carry out the management of limited liability companies.

The management of (public or private) companies limited by shares is carried out by the management board, except where its powers have been delegated to a single executive officer under the statute of private limited companies.

The statute of public companies limited by shares may also contain provisions to delegate management and supervisory functions to the board of directors (one-tier system). In this case the (public or private) limited company has no supervisory board and the members of the board of directors are treated as executive officers.

According to the provisions laid down in the memorandum of association, the management of a group is carried out by the director as an executive officer or by the management board functioning as a body.

The most common form of company in Hungary is the limited liability company.

Pursuant to the new Act on Business Associations, which came into effect on July 1 2006, the executive officers may not serve under contract of employment; they rather act under a service contract and their legal position is governed by the provisions of the Civil Code relating to service contracts. However, if the executive officer is also employed by the company in a different position, the rules of the Labour Code (Act XXII/1992) will still apply.[1]

The definition of an 'executive officer' or 'director' is to be found in Sections 21 to 32 of the Act on Business Associations. The Labour Code also provides a definition of 'leading positions' – that is, key positions in a company. Those holding such positions are deemed to be employees and the Labour Code governs their liabilities, rights and obligations.

1 As of September 1 2007, executive officers may act based on the employment relationship again. However, this will not affect their liability.

1. Directors' duties

1.1 Nature of the duties

The Act on Business Associations and the company's articles of association govern the duties of the executive officers. However, other legal regulations are also provided for in the Civil Code (Act IV/1959), such as the Act on Bankruptcy Proceedings and Liquidation Proceedings and the Act on Accounting.

(a) *Duties of the directors and officers*

Executive officers are responsible for the day-to-day management, representation and operation of the company. However, the company's supreme body may limit the powers of such officers in relation to the management of the company where authorised by law or the articles of association.

The executive officers of the company act as legal representatives towards third parties before the court and other authorities. The statutory right of representation of the executive officers may be limited in the articles of association or may be distributed among several executive officers. Any limitation or division of the right of representation shall be null and void towards third parties.

The executive officers are responsible for notifying the court of registration about:

- the foundation of the company;
- any amendment of the articles of association or the statutes;
- the rights, facts and data to be entered in the Companies Register and changes thereto; and
- any other data required by law.

Unless otherwise provided by law, at the request of the members (shareholders), the executive officers must provide information about the affairs of the company and allow the inspection of its books and documents. In the event of an executive officer's failure to comply with such request, then at the request of the member concerned the court of registration may instruct the company to provide the information in question and/or to allow for inspection.

Unless otherwise provided by the articles of association, executive officers shall exercise employer's rights over company employees. If the company has a management body, the various functions for exercising employer's rights will be distributed among the members of this body as instructed in the articles of association or in the management body's internal rules of procedure, if the articles of association do not provide for this.

Executive officers must treat all business secrets of the company as strictly confidential. In Hungary, it is quite common for the service contract of an executive officer to contain a so-called confidentiality clause, which regulates this obligation in detail.

Executive officers bear joint and several liability towards the company for any damage resulting from incorrect data, rights or facts notified to authorities, or from any delay in filing or failure to file the notification.

An executive officer may not acquire any shares – other than shares in public limited companies – in any business organisation whose main business activity is similar to that of the company, and may not accept an executive office in a company or cooperative whose main business activity is similar to that of the business association, unless permitted by the articles of association of the company affected or unless the supreme body of the company has given its consent. A competition clause is frequently included in the service contracts of executive officers. This means that after they leave the company, the executive officer cannot act as an executive officer of a competitor for a certain period of time against payment of an agreed fee.

An executive officer and his close relatives or common law spouse may not conclude any transactions falling within the scope of the main activities of the company in his own name or on his own account, unless this is specifically permitted by the articles of association.

The articles of association may specify that the above restriction applies to any company whose main business activity is similar to that of the company or to transactions falling within the scope of activities of the business association.

An executive officer and his partner or close relatives cannot be elected as members of the supervisory board at the same company. The executive officers are liable for any infringement of the above prohibition; the claims for damages caused to the company by this infringement may be enforced for a period of one year after it occurs.

The statutes of private companies limited by shares or the articles of association of limited liability companies can contain provisions that assign the right to appoint and remove management board members and managing directors, establish their remuneration and allow certain peremptory resolutions to be passed subject to the prior consent of the supervisory board. In this case, members of the supervisory board will also be treated as executive officers and, according to the provisions of the Civil Code, will have unlimited, joint and several liability for damages caused to the company by adopting such resolutions.

(b) ***Special duties of the directors of a company under liquidation***

These are to:

- prepare a closing inventory, annual report, simplified report or simplified balance sheet as of the date preceding the start of liquidation proceedings, as well as tax returns and a closing balance sheet following the distribution of profit. These must be delivered to the liquidator and the tax authorities within 45 days of the start of the liquidation proceedings;
- prepare a list of the documents that may not be discarded or are classified as confidential, and deliver such documents to the liquidator, as well as archive material and information regarding pending affairs;
- file a declaration with the liquidator and the competent environmental protection agency within 30 days of the start of liquidation proceedings to determine whether there are any remaining environmental damages or

hazards that may result in penalties or other payment obligations, or expenses connected to the clean-up of such damage;
- disclose information to the liquidator regarding all transactions in the Bankruptcy Act;
- inform without delay the employees, cooperative members, trade unions and workers' councils about the start of the liquidation proceedings; and
- inform the beneficiaries of the claims regarding the start of liquidation proceedings within 30 days.

If the company goes into liquidation, the executive officer of a company may be subject to a fine of up to 50% of his income from the company in the year preceding the liquidation proceedings (or up to Ft1 million if his income cannot be determined) for any breach of the obligations prescribed for the executive officers above, or for providing any false information. The fine may be imposed even if the individual is no longer employed by, or in any work-related contractual relationship with, the debtor, or is no longer a member or an executive officer of the debtor. However, the court shall notify the executive officer of the possibility of imposing a fine in the above cases.

According to the Act on Business Associations, if there is any threat to the solvency of the company, the executive officers must give priority to the company's creditors. In the event that non-compliance with this obligation is verified and the company is deemed to be insolvent, then under the Bankruptcy Act, the executive officers may be financially liable to the company's creditors (ie, the creditors are entitled to bring an action during the liquidation proceedings for the court to establish that the former executives of the business failed properly to represent their preferential rights).

1.2 Standards of care

These are governed by the Act on Business Associations and the Bankruptcy Act. Other general principles are set out in Sections 474 to 482 of the Civil Code.

Executive officers must discharge their duties relating to the company's internal affairs and its bodies and other officers in person; no representation is allowed.

Executive officers must conduct the management of the company with due care and diligence, and give priority to the interests of the company.

Executive officers must discharge their duties independently and are superseded only by legal regulations, the articles of association and resolutions of the company's supreme body. They cannot be instructed by the members (shareholders) of the company, with one exception: the member of the single member company (those with a sole shareholder) may instruct the executive officer in writing.

1.3 To whom duties are owed

As a general rule, the executive officers shall be liable to the company in accordance with the general provisions of civil law for damage caused by any infringement of the law or any breach of the articles of association, resolutions of the company's supreme body or their management obligations. Their liability is joint and several if they are authorised to sign jointly for the company.

In the latter case, according to the general rules of civil law, the liability of the executive officers towards one another shall be divided in proportion to their respective degrees of responsibility. Liability for damages shall be divided in equal proportions if the degree of responsibility cannot be established. In certain cases duties are owed towards the shareholders. This is merely an obligation to provide information regarding the affairs of the company so as to enable the shareholders to check the books, to convene the shareholders' meeting and so on. However, these rights should be exercised in good faith, always taking into account business interests and any confidential information held by the company.

Special duties are owed towards the court of registration, the liquidator and the creditors, as described in section 1.1.

1.4 Common defences to and exemptions from liability

The company shall be liable for damages caused to third parties by an executive officer when acting in an official capacity.

The executive officers are liable to the company only in accordance with the general rules of the civil law for damages. The executive officers may be exempt from liability if they can prove that they have acted in a manner that could generally be expected from a person in their position in any given situation (ie, the Act on Business Associations requires an increased level of care and diligence from executive officers).

The rules of civil law state that the liability of an executive officer can be limited or excluded in advance in relation to the exclusion of liability for breach of contract. Any liability for a breach of contract that has damaged life, physical integrity or health, and that has been caused wilfully, by gross negligence or by a felony offence, cannot be validly excluded. Liability for breach of contract cannot be excluded or restricted, unless the disadvantage incurred can be offset by the adequate reduction of the consideration or by some other advantage. In the service contract concluded by the company and the executive officer, the parties are entitled to limit or exclude liability for damages caused by simple negligence. Reducing the salary of the executive officer can offset any disadvantage incurred.

As mentioned above, the sole member (shareholder) may instruct the executive officer in writing. The executive officer is required to carry out these instructions, but in such case he is exempt from the general liability of executive officers.

Where executive officers are vested with a joint right of representation or where the company is managed by a body, the liability of executive officers for damages to the company shall be joint and several according to the provisions of the Civil Code pertaining to joint negligence. If the damage results from a decision of the management body, any member who did not take part in the decision-making process or who voted against it shall be exempt from liability.

The articles of association may contain provisions for the company's supreme body to evaluate on an annual basis the work of the executive officers in the previous financial year. They can then grant a discharge of liability to certain executive officers.

Granting a discharge of liability constitutes the supreme body's verification that, during the period under review, the executive officers in question gave priority to the interests of the business. The discharge of liability will be abolished if a subsequent court ruling declares that the information on which the discharge of liability was based was false or incomplete. However, this is allowed only within the general limitation period.

Any executive who can verify that he has taken all reasonable measures to reduce the losses of creditors in a situation where there is a danger of insolvency shall not be held responsible in any court proceedings where the creditor or the liquidator enforces his claim against the former executive officer on the grounds that the executive officer failed properly to represent the preferential rights of creditors in the three years prior to the start of liquidation proceedings.

2. Who can bring claims

2.1 The company (and its liquidators)

The company can lodge a claim against an executive officer for damages caused when acting in an official capacity under the regulations provided by civil law.

Following termination of the company without a legal successor, claims for damages may be brought against the executive officers by the members (shareholders) at the time the company was deleted from the Companies Register by the court of registration, within one year of the final ruling.

If, during the existence of the company, the member (shareholder) had limited liability, the member (shareholder) may enforce a claim up to the share due to him from the assets of the company distributed upon termination. If the company has been deleted from the Companies Register at the end of a liquidation procedure and creditors still have outstanding claims, the members are not entitled to enforce their claims against the executive officers, as this would affect the unsatisfied creditors.

During the liquidation proceedings, any liquidator may bring an action before the court to show that the former executives of the business failed properly to represent the preferential rights of creditors in the three years prior to the start of liquidation proceedings in the wake of any situation bearing a potential danger of insolvency (including the clean-up of any environmental damage), in consequence of which the company's assets diminished to the extent specified. A situation is considered to carry a potential danger of insolvency as of the date on which the business executives were or should have been able to predict that the business could not satisfy the company's liabilities as they fell due. If several persons caused damage, their liability shall be joint and several.

If an executive did not deposit and publish the debtor's annual report (consolidated annual report) before the start of liquidation proceedings in accordance with specific legislation, injury to the creditors' interests shall be presumed.

2.2 Minority shareholders on behalf of the company (derivative actions)

If the supreme body of a company has refused a request to enforce a claim against the executive officers, or if the company's supreme body failed to adopt a decision regarding a proposal that has been properly presented to establish the liability of an executive officer, a group of members (shareholders) controlling at least 5% of the votes may, under penalty of forfeiture of rights, enforce the claim themselves on behalf of the company. The court proceedings must take place within 30 days of the meeting of the company's supreme body at which the resolution was taken.

The claim is lodged by the minority shareholders, but in the name of the company. The company must advance the court duty and costs. In practice, this means that the minority shareholders will have to advance these costs and then be reimbursed by the company if they win. If they lose and the company had advanced the costs, the minority shareholders must reimburse the company.

2.3 Minority shareholders on their own account

The shareholders, minority shareholders included, may not bring direct actions against executive officers acting in this capacity. (The only exception to this is described in section 2.1).

However, as a special procedure for the enforcement of claims, those members (shareholders) controlling at least 5% of the voting rights may, at any time, request that the company's supreme body be convened, indicating the reason and the purpose thereof. (The articles of association may also grant this right to members (shareholders) controlling a lesser percentage of the votes.)

If management fails to comply with this request within 30 days, the court of registration will convene a meeting of the company's supreme body within 30 days of the submission of the request or shall empower the members to convene such a meeting.

2.4 Third parties

(a) General

The general rule is that the company will be liable for damages caused to third parties by its executive officer when acting in his official capacity. These third parties can bring claims against the company only according to the provisions of civil law.

(b) Creditors (following final conclusion of the liquidation)

An exception to the general rule is that within a 90-day forfeit deadline following the final conclusion of liquidation proceedings, any creditor may bring an action for the court to establish the liability of the debtor's former executive and to order this executive to satisfy any debtor's claims that have not yet been satisfied. If more than one creditor files for action within this timeframe, the court will consolidate these actions and obtain an award equivalent to dividends on the claims.

If a final decision in the lawsuit is not adopted by the final conclusion of liquidation proceedings, the forfeit deadline will commence on the day following the that on which the final court ruling in the lawsuit is adopted.

3. Claims culture

3.1 Litigation

There are no statistical reports detailing how often directors are sued, how frequently shareholders, companies and third parties enforce claims against the executive officers and how 'claimant friendly' the Hungarian courts are. The official statistics include only the number of pending and finished civil, commercial, criminal and labour cases. (It seems that companies do not like to go public about problems with their executive officers.)

More information is available on cases where executive officers sue companies because their employment contract has been illegally terminated. Here the courts are more claimant friendly.

We are not yet aware of general court practice on lawsuits between directors and companies based on the new regulations, as the status of directors is regulated by the Civil Code, not the Labour Code.

3.2 Ability to bring class actions

In Hungary, there are no legal means by which a legal action can be brought on behalf of a group of people; the Code of Civil Procedure regulates only the joinder of parties, whereby the parties or claims are united in a single lawsuit.

However, consumer organisations are entitled to bring claims on behalf of hundreds or even thousands of consumers to obtain judicial orders against corporations that cause injury or damage to consumers (ie, they can represent the collective interest of consumers).

3.3 Funding of claims and whether loser pays

The costs of litigation comprise:

- court costs;
- cost of an expert opinion;
- translation costs;
- cost of acquiring of official documents (eg, excerpts of registration, notarised certificates); and
- attorneys' fees.

According to the Code of Civil Procedure, the court costs (including all fees and duties) will be assessed by the court based on the certification of such costs and on any other legal provisions that regulate the maximum amount of these fees.

The 'duty' (*illeték*) is the cost of litigation that must be paid to the Treasury. The general rule is that the claimant must advance these costs. In certain cases (eg, labour law, some administrative procedures) the costs need not be paid because of the nature of the procedure (ie, objective exemption of duty). In certain cases the claimant need not pay the costs because of his financial situation.

Generally, the loser pays. However, in labour law cases, if the claimant was an employee, the costs will be borne by the Treasury even if he loses the lawsuit.

The basis of costs in civil proceedings will be the value of the subject matter of the proceedings at the time of the initiation of the proceedings, or the value of the claim or part of claim disputed in proceedings for legal remedy.

In court proceedings the rate is 6% or a minimum of Ft7,000 and a maximum of Ft900,000.

The reduced duty is 10% of the duty on litigious proceedings if:

- the plaintiff withdraws his claim during the first hearing;
- the legal action is suspended during first hearing and is dismissed as a result of suspension;
- the defendant acknowledges the claim during the first hearing or satisfies the claim prior to the first hearing;
- the parties reach a settlement during the first hearing; or
- the parties jointly file for dismissal during the first hearing.

The reduced duty is 30% of the duty on litigious proceedings for a case dismissed by suspension following the first hearing, due to the plaintiff's withdrawal or if jointly requested by the parties. It is 50% of the duty on litigious proceedings if a settlement is concluded following the first hearing.

Attorneys' fees are usually specified in a letter of assignment and are subject to agreement by the parties. The parties can also agree:

- a success fee, which might be based on the financial outcome of the case; or
- a lump sum.

The general practice is to agree a fee based on the time spent on the case.

A Ministry of Justice order on attorneys' fees states that these should basically reflect the amount in dispute and the complexity of the case. However, the parties do not have to observe this regulation if they agree otherwise.

In such case the court is entitled to reduce the fee if it considers that it is too high compared to the sum in dispute, but the agreement between the parties is not affected (instead, the losing party need only reimburse the costs fixed by the court).

As a general rule, the court costs are paid in advance by the claimant and all costs, including the legal fees of both parties, are paid by the losing party at the end of the procedure. (See section 2.2 on special cases involving the enforcement of claims by minority shareholders on their own account but on behalf of the company.)

Previously, as litigation before the labour courts involved no financial consequences as to costs, and there was need for the claimant to engage a lawyer before the first and second-level courts (the district county courts), there was nothing to stop claimants from bringing claims without foundation. The fact that in civil law costs must now be paid in advance might deter unmeritorious litigation.

3.4 Plaintiffs' bar

In Hungary, there is no organised claimant lawyer network where information is shared and lawyers can target directors with lawsuits quickly. There are only the regional bar associations established in each county, which unite all practice lawyers within that area. The Hungarian Bar Association includes all regional bar associations. Information and experiences are shared informally.

3.5 Procedural barriers

Generally, claims can be brought only against the company, which can then lodge a claim against the executive officer. The five-year statute of limitations applies. This is excluded where the damage results from criminal conduct and the statute of limitations for such conduct is more than five years, in which case the longer period applies.

Following termination of the company without a legal successor, claims for damages may be brought against the executive officers by the members (shareholders) for a period of one year following deletion of the company from the Companies Register by the court of registration.

There are no special formalities in relation to claims to be brought against executive officers.

Unless provided for by the internal rules of the company (or the board), no prior approval is required from the shareholders to commence litigation against a director.

4. Indemnification rights

4.1 When the company can indemnify

Generally, the company can indemnify its executive officers where this has been contractually agreed (ie, indemnification generally cannot be considered as mandatory unless the parties have so agreed).

This rule applies to the whole question of indemnification.

Mandatory indemnification is required where the director was instructed by the sole member of the company (see sections 1.3 and 1.4).

Indemnification might cover any claims arising out of, or in connection with, defence and other costs incurred by the officer.

There are no restrictions on the advancement of costs.

In a claim against a director, if a settlement is reached before trial, the costs connected with the settlement and their reimbursement must be agreed with the company in advance.

4.2 Formalities for indemnification rights

There are no formalities provided by law for indemnification rights.

As mentioned above, the terms of any indemnification are provided for in a private agreement between the company and its director or may be included in the service contract itself.

The company's articles of association are not relevant in this respect.

4.3 How indemnification works

There is no formal procedure to be followed in respect of indemnification.

4.4 What cannot be indemnified

Certain rules on exclusion of liability are set out in the Civil Code. Liability for a breach of contract that might cause damage to life, physical wellbeing or health, and that has been wilfully caused by gross negligence or by a felony, cannot be validly excluded.

Unless otherwise prescribed by law, liability for breach of contract cannot be excluded or limited, unless the disadvantage incurred can be offset by adequate reduction of the consideration or by some other advantage.

The company must generally pay any fines and penalties.

In some cases the labour, tax or environmental authorities may fine the directors and officers exclusively - usually where the directors and officers do not follow and execute decisions of these authorities mentioned above. To indemnify the directors against such fines and penalties is risky from a tax point of view, since these penalties may not be deducted as operating costs. However, companies often provide indemnification in such circumstances, accepting that the director has acted in the interests of the company.

Practical advice on optimising indemnification cannot be given, as each case must be reviewed on its own facts.

The conduct and good faith of the executive officer are always relevant when considering indemnification.

5. D&O insurance

D&O insurance culture is not very developed in Hungary.

5.1 Availability of D&O insurance

In principle, there are no obstacles to the purchase of D&O insurance. However, we are not aware of any standard practice to insure directors for liabilities arising from their position as executive officers.

This is partly because in smaller companies, the officers are often shareholders. The executive officers of big international companies are usually covered by the umbrella insurance of the parent company.

5.2 Local rules on cover provided under a non-domestic D&O policy

Generally, companies are not obliged to insure their directors and officers.

It is general practice among international companies that a global policy issued by a foreign insurer shall cover the risks of an executive officer of a Hungarian subsidiary independently, whether that person is Hungarian or a foreign citizen. This is permitted as a foreign insurer outside Hungary issued the global policy and no insurance activity took place in Hungary itself.

Only domestic insurance companies and local branches of foreign insurers are entitled to pursue insurance activity in Hungary. Non-domestic, non-resident insurers are not entitled to pursue insurance activity unless they are registered in Hungary (this is possible only if there is a local branch in Hungary).

The procedure to register a non-domestic insurer is provided for in the Insurance Act (60/2003), which sets out the requirements that must be met (eg, company form, minimum share capital, risk fund requirements, business conditions).

The Hungarian Financial Supervisory Authority licenses the establishment and operation of insurance companies.

5.3 Company secretary

If permitted by the articles of association, the company's supreme body may decide to appoint one or more company secretaries to assist the executive officers in their work. Company secretaries work under the executive officers in directing the company's operations according to their instructions. Company secretaries must give priority to the interests of the company in carrying out their duties. Their activities have no impact on the liability of executive officers towards the company. The company secretaries must be employees of the company, so the Labour Code applies to the employment contract and provides the governing rules, rights and obligations and liability of the company secretary.

Israel

Norman Menachem Feder
Antal Pearl
Gad Ticho
Caspi & Co

1. Directors' duties

1.1 Nature of the duties

(a) *Duty of trust*

Under the Companies Law 1999, an officer:

- has a duty of trust towards the company;
- has an obligation of good faith in carrying out his responsibilities to the company; and
- must act for the benefit of the company.

The officer's duty of trust requires him to:

- avoid any action that involves a conflict of interest between his role in the company and other roles in his business or personal affairs;
- avoid any action which involves competition with the company's business;
- avoid exploiting a business opportunity of the company in an attempt to benefit himself or others; and
- disclose to the company any information and provide it with any documents regarding its affairs which are brought to his attention within the framework of his position in the company.

The Companies Law defines an 'officer' as including a director, general manager, chief executive officer, deputy manager and any other such executive in a company, regardless of title, including any manager who is directly subordinate to the general manager.

At the core of the duty of trust is the concept that officers in general, and directors in particular, make a commitment to the company that they will be guided in their actions by the company's welfare, and not their personal interests. To avoid abuse, the Companies Law establishes rules for corporate transactions involving officers with personal interests in company transactions – for example, decisions regarding officers' employment conditions or officers' insurance, indemnity or exemption from liability. Under these rules:

- the officer must disclose his personal issue to the company a reasonable time in advance of the anticipated meeting at which the proposed transaction will be voted on;

- an independent organ of the company - that is, an organ which has nothing to gain from the authorisation of the proposed transaction - must confirm the interested-party transaction; and
- the independent organ is limited to authorising only those transactions which it believes in good faith will benefit the company.

Under the legislation, for the prospective action to be authorised, it is sufficient that the action will not harm the company. However, the Supreme Court has heightened this standard and applies an 'entire fairness' test. Under this test, it is not sufficient that the transaction is duly approved and that the conditions of the transaction are reasonable from the perspectives of the company and its shareholders; rather, the transaction's entire fairness, including the long-term benefit to the company, is required.

(b) ***Duty of care***

Under the Companies Law, an officer also has a duty of care towards the company. In contrast to the duty of trust, which aims to prevent officers from exploiting their corporate powers for their own benefit, the duty of care aims to force officers to act reasonably and so prevent damage to the company. The duty of care should comply with certain sections of the Torts Ordinance (New Version) addressing the general prohibition on acting negligently toward any person. Additionally, the Companies Law provides that an officer should act with the level of proficiency that a reasonable officer in the same position would act with under the same circumstances. This includes taking reasonable measures to obtain information regarding the commercial sense of an action brought for authorisation, or of an action taken in the capacity as officer, and any other information pertinent to these actions. The Companies Law refers to the 'reasonable officer' as opposed to the 'reasonable person', thus heightening the duty typical under tort law.

The duty of care is personal and therefore, for example, it is imposed not merely on the entire board of directors as a whole, but rather on each director personally due to his activity on the board. As a general matter, all company officers must be able to show that they gathered the relevant information regarding the commercial sense of the action and acted upon it to enhance the company's value. Israeli case law teaches that a director's role in a company is pivotal and includes:

- being involved in the company's activities;
- knowing its business, its key players, the senior management, the internal monitoring system and its board of directors; and
- participating in board meetings.

1.2 Standards of care

An officer should act with the same level of proficiency as a reasonable officer in the same position under the same circumstances (see section 1.1(b)).

1.3 To whom duties are owed

(a) *Duty of trust*

The officer owes his duty of trust first and foremost to the company, since he controls the company and manages its affairs. It is logical that, in parallel with his power over the company, an officer should also have responsibilities towards it. However, the Companies Law explicitly notes that the duty towards the company does not preclude the existence of the same duty towards another person, such as a shareholder, employee, creditor or contract party. Case law shows that while an officer does have a duty of trust to the company, under certain circumstances he may also have a duty of trust towards a shareholder – this may occur if a special relationship has been cultivated between them or if principles of justice and good faith require this responsibility. Notwithstanding the foregoing, duties towards parties other than the company are secondary to those in respect of the company.

(b) *Duty of care*

As with the duty of trust, the officer owes his duty of care primarily to the company. By the same token, the fact that this duty is also aimed first and foremost towards the company does not preclude the existence of a duty of care in respect of other parties, such as shareholders, employees, creditors or contractual parties.

1.4 Common defences to and exemptions from liability

A company is not permitted to exempt an officer from liability stemming from breach of his duty of trust, but may exempt an officer from liability stemming from breach of his duty of care. As to the duty of care, a company is permitted to exempt an officer from all or part of his responsibility for damage caused as a result of breach of his duty of care, if this is provided for in the company's articles of association. Additionally, since the decision to exempt an officer from liability is considered a transaction with an interested party, the decision requires special authorisation pursuant to the Companies Law. For the company to grant an exemption to an officer who is not a director, this requires confirmation by the inspection committee and then the board of directors. For the company to grant an exemption to an officer who is a director, confirmation by the board of directors and then the general assembly is required. Further, in the case of a public company, confirmation by the inspection committee is also required.

Notwithstanding the above, a company is prohibited from exempting a director at the outset from responsibility stemming from negligence with respect to a distribution of dividends. This exception to the general rule that directors can be exempted from damage caused as a result of their acts of negligence aims to prevent situations in which the shareholders exempt directors from responsibility for unlawful distributions in order to promote their personal interest (eg, to increase their dividends at the expense of others, such as creditors).

Additionally, there are possibilities for indemnification and/or insurance, which are discussed in sections 4 and 5.

Officers may allege in their defence that they relied on external experts and advisers. Case law shows that for a court to accept this defence, at least the following cumulative conditions must be met:

- The officer addressed an expert who had professional knowledge and appropriate experience;
- The expert was privy to most of the facts relevant to the opinion;
- The officer acted in good faith; and
- The opinion was reasonable given the officer's skills.

Additionally, all general defences under law apply, including:

- statute of limitations;
- lack of privity between the parties; and
- the absence of a causal connection among the elements of the relevant cause of action.

2. Who can bring claims

2.1 The company (and its liquidators)

Given that it is an independent legal entity, a company has a right to bring claims against others in its own name. More specifically, this right is granted to the company's organs, including its directors.

In addition to the directors' general right to bring claims against company officers in the name of the company for breaches which have already taken place, under the Companies Law, if a director has a reasonable basis to suppose that an officer of the company is poised to breach a duty owed to the company, the director is first required promptly to convene a meeting of the board of directors to address the matter, provided that such meeting is possible under the circumstances. Next, the director may petition the district court to enforce the officer's duty or prevent the prospective act of breach. The court may issue an order preventing the action or any other remedy it deems fit under the circumstances. Notably, unless the court decides otherwise, the company will bear the expenses of a director who petitions the court in this regard. Such expenses include court and attorneys' fees.

Further, the Companies Law provides that where an officer breaches his duty of trust towards the company, the officer will be viewed as having breached his 'contract' with the company. Accordingly, general contract law will apply, including the remedies available for breach of contract, in addition to the law of tort. By reason of the fact that any person representing the company has the authority to bring claims against its officers, a successor board of directors may bring claims against its predecessor board or particular members thereof; more commonly, a company's liquidator is also entitled to bring claims. The liquidator's role, aside from managing the liquidation process, is to realise company assets and distribute the profits first between the creditors and then, if there is a surplus, between the shareholders. The liquidator essentially replaces the authorised company organs and is granted all authorities necessary to liquidate the company in the most efficient way possible. Among these authorities, the liquidator has the authority:

- held by the company directors to bring claims against the company officers, as described above; and
- to bring claims on behalf of the company against its creditors, provided that the court or company's inspection committee gives its prior consent.

2.2 Minority shareholders on behalf of the company

Despite directors' general right to bring claims against company officers, in practice, directors will frequently abstain from doing so since the claims would often need to be addressed against themselves. Due to this obvious concern, the Companies Law provides an alternative mechanism for suing officers: the derivative action brought by shareholders on behalf of the company.

Where the company organs authorised to bring claims in the name of the company due to a cause of action of the company refrain from doing so (eg, because of a conflict of interest, inability or unwillingness), a shareholder or director may do so instead in a derivative action, provided that the court gives its prior consent. A derivative action is materially different from a personal action. It is brought by a single individual or a number of persons (there is no minimum number of formal plaintiffs) on behalf of the company due to an offence against the company, whereas a personal action is brought by the direct party to the claim (ie, the injured party against the injurer). This notwithstanding, the company is the *de facto* plaintiff in the action and if the court rules in its favour, the remedy will be awarded to the company and not to the formal plaintiff.

Under the Companies Law, a prerequisite for filing a derivative action is that the prospective plaintiff first petition the company in writing and demand that the company file the action itself. The company, after receipt of the demand letter, may choose from three courses of action:

- take action to negate the cause of action or reach a decision which otherwise negates the cause of action;
- dismiss the plaintiff's demand, with an explanation; or
- file a claim.

After receipt of the company's response, the court may allow the plaintiff to file the derivative action if it is convinced that:

- *prima facie*, the action is for the benefit of the company and the plaintiff is acting in good faith;
- the action taken or the decision reached by the company to negate the cause of action failed;
- the company dismissed the plaintiff's demand to file the action; or
- the company did not respond to the plaintiff's demand or responded after the legal deadline.

Further, relevant case law indicates that a party wishing to sue on behalf of the company in a derivative action must demonstrate to the court that:

- the company's right was breached; and
- conditions exist to justify his request to wage the company's battle on its

behalf, including that his main consideration is the company's benefit and not his own.

Another prerequisite for filing a derivative action is that the plaintiff pay part of the court fees. Once the court has authorised the derivative action, the company must reimburse the plaintiff for expenses he has incurred and must pay the remaining court fees.

Notably, derivative actions cannot be brought on behalf of a company for which a liquidator has been appointed by the court.

2.3 Shareholders on their own account

In cases of minority oppression – namely, unfair distribution of resources between the company's controlling shareholders and the minority shareholders - the minority shareholders have standing to sue in order to relieve the oppression. The minority shareholders must demonstrate before the court that damage was caused to them. Recent case law shows that there is no need to demonstrate continuous oppression and even a single unlawful distribution is sufficient to raise the oppression argument. As to the damage itself to the minority shareholders, case law has developed two approaches:

- the consequential approach - damage to the shareholder is necessary and injury to a shareholder's legitimate expectations constitutes damage; and
- the intentional approach – in addition to the damage, the oppressive action was tainted with bad faith or fraud on the part of the company officer and was taken for a reason other than to benefit the company.

Additionally, a minority shareholder is entitled to file a claim when the company incurs damage and the unfairness also indirectly affects minority shareholders. Since the courts have recognised the difficulty involved in minority shareholders proving the existence of damage, the courts can apply the 'entire fairness' test in this regard, meaning that once the minority shareholder demonstrates *prima facie* evidence of oppression, the courts transfer the burden of proof to the defendants to prove the entire fairness of their actions. Likewise, there may be situations in which the shareholders, rather than the company, suffer losses, such as in case of unjust dilution of shareholders' shares. In such cases, shareholders may bring claims against directors.

Furthermore, in the event that a liquidation order is issued against the company, a shareholder, creditor, liquidator or receiver may file an action against a company officer, provided that the officer knowingly participated in fraudulent management of the company.

2.4 Third parties

A company, being a separate legal entity, can bear liability for negligence; however, the fact that a company bears liability for an action taken by a company officer does not negate the liability of the officer himself. Accordingly, the company officer is personally responsible for his actions and the company is responsible for the company officer's actions. In this regard, it is insufficient that a third-party plaintiff, such as a creditor, proves that the action was taken for the company and the company officer is a manager of the company. In contrast, to impose liability on an officer, it is necessary to show that the officer himself was the one who committed the tort, or at least participated in it, and that all elements of the tort were fulfilled with respect to him personally.

Another possible third-party plaintiff is a company employee who, for instance, is involved in a workplace accident and subsequently brings a claim against the foreman. In such case the employee would have to show that the elements of the tort of negligence were met by the foreman's acts or omissions.

Additionally, claims can be brought against directors by creditors or contracting parties in case of misrepresentation or fraud. In such cases the corporate veil may be lifted and the directors exposed to personal liability.

3. Claims culture

3.1 Litigation

Israel is a common law jurisdiction in which civil trials are conducted before a single, professional, nominated judge. There is no jury trial system. Generally, there are three levels of courts:

- at the first level are magistrates' courts;
- at the next level up are district courts; and
- at the third and highest level is the Supreme Court.

Specialised courts do exist, including family courts, labour courts, antitrust courts and small claims courts. Magistrates' courts have jurisdiction over monetary claims not exceeding NIS2.5 million (approximately $600,000) and district courts have jurisdiction over all other monetary claims. Plaintiffs who file claims in the magistrates' court have an automatic right to appeal to the district court and plaintiffs who file claims in the district court have an automatic right to appeal to the Supreme Court, which is the court of last instance. Rulings of the Supreme Court cannot be appealed.

Aside from the derivative action and the class action, actions on behalf of and against the company are filed in the same procedural manner as civil claims generally.

Claims against directors were rare in the past, but today there is a noticeable trend towards making claims against professionals in general (malpractice claims against doctors, lawyers, accountants and so on).

Often, claims against officers are brought by creditors in connection with insolvency and liquidation proceedings, and by shareholders in connection with interested-party transactions.

3.2 Ability to bring class actions

A class action is defined under the recently enacted Class Actions Law, 2006 as an action managed in the name of a group of people which did not give the representing plaintiff power of attorney to do so, and which raises substantive questions of fact or law common to all members of the group. A condition for filing a class action is that the court first gives its authorisation for the claim to be filed in the form of a class action.

For the court to authorise the filing of a class action, the plaintiff must show the existence of the following cumulative criteria:

- The action raises substantive questions of fact or law common to all members of the group;
- Based on *prima facie* evidence, there is a reasonable probability that the questions will be resolved in favour of the group;
- The class action is the most efficient and fairest way to resolve the dispute under the circumstances;
- There is a reasonable probability that the interests of the members of the group will be properly represented and managed; and
- There is a reasonable probability that the members of the group will be represented in good faith.

When class actions are brought against companies, plaintiffs commonly name the directors of the relevant company among the defendants.

3.3 Funding of claims and whether loser pays

(a) General

The court has discretion to decide whether to charge a party with payment of the attorneys' and court fees of the counterparty. Case law shows that in the absence of special circumstances that justify depriving the winning party of its expenses, it will be awarded costs. Nevertheless, the court is allowed to impose costs on a party, in favour of the counterparty or the Israeli Treasury or both, which unnecessarily prolongs the hearing by way of empty claims or otherwise, regardless of the outcome.

The costs awarded by the court are usually less than the actual legal expenses incurred. Accordingly, the risk of an adverse costs award does not materially deter claimants from bringing unmeritorious claims.

Generally, conditional and contingency fee agreements between attorneys and their clients can be made; however, payments to experts may not be made on a contingency basis.

(b) Derivative actions

As described in section 2.2, plaintiffs in derivative actions must pay an initial part of the court fees; if the action is subsequently authorised by the court, the company must reimburse the plaintiff for his expenses on behalf of the company and pay any outstanding court fees. Regarding reimbursement, the court can order the company to pay the plaintiff a certain sum for costs or to deposit a guarantee for their payment. Additionally, the court can order the company to guarantee the defendant's expected costs with a deposit.

If the defendant is awarded costs, the company must generally pay them. In exceptional cases, the court may order that the plaintiff pay the defendant's costs. Additionally, the court can order the company to pay the plaintiff's costs or order the plaintiff to pay the company's costs, depending on the circumstances.

As to attorneys' fees, the court will determine the amount of the fees to be awarded to the attorney who represented the plaintiff and such fees should generally be paid by the company. In exceptional cases, the court may determine that the plaintiff should pay the attorneys' fees.

If the court rules in favour of the company, the company will enjoy the fruit of the plaintiff's efforts. However, the court is entitled to order that the plaintiff be compensated for his efforts in filing and proving the derivative action.

(c) Class actions

A representative plaintiff seeking to file a class action based on a cause of action stemming from a connection to securities issued by the Israeli government, an option, a futures contract or securities issued to the public by a company may petition the Israeli Securities Authority (ISA) to bear his costs. If the ISA is convinced that the class action involves a public interest and there is a reasonable probability that the court will authorise it as a class action, it may take on the plaintiff's costs. If the court ultimately rules in favour of the plaintiff, it is permitted to order indemnification of the ISA for costs.

3.4 Plaintiffs' bar

There are several designated public authorities and organisations that are entitled to file class actions on behalf of large groups of people. Nonetheless, the claims are usually brought by individual lawyers.

3.5 Procedural barriers

(a) Statute of limitations

Under the Statute of Limitations Law, 1958, which deals with periods of limitations in civil actions, the limitations defence is purely an affirmative defence. If the defendant successfully raises the period of limitations defence, the court will be barred from hearing the claim, although the plaintiff's substantive right will be left unaffected. Accordingly, if the defendant does not raise a period of limitations defence within the requisite timeframe, the plaintiff can proceed with the action even if the period has lapsed. The defence should be raised at the first opportunity after the claim is filed; if later, the limitations defence will be disregarded.

The period of limitations of a civil claim that is not derived from a right to landed property is seven years. There are exceptions to this seven-year period; however, none apply to claims brought against directors and officers under the Companies Law. This seven-year period generally starts to run on the day on which the cause of action "was born". Exceptions exist - for example, in relation to the plaintiff's inability to know of the facts that gave rise to the cause of action or instances of fraud, damage etc which were revealed only later. In such cases the seven-year period will begin to run as from the plaintiff's actual or constructive discovery of the relevant facts.

(b) ***Statement of claim fails to demonstrate a cause of action***

Normally, a statement of claim must demonstrate a cause of action to proceed. If the court is of the opinion that the claim is baseless or vexing, it can 'erase' the claim – the equivalent to dismissing the claim without prejudice. Accordingly, the dismissal does not establish *res judicata* and the plaintiff can bring the claim again in the future on the same grounds.

(c) ***Failure to pay court fees***

If the plaintiff fails to pay all or part of the court fees he was required to pay, the court may erase his claim, without prejudice.

(d) ***Res judicata***

If a claim was previously filed and addressed by the court, and a judgment was issued, the same claim brought a second time will be dismissed with prejudice on the grounds of *res judicata*.

(e) ***Requisite approvals not obtained***

As mentioned in section 2.2, a shareholder or director who wishes to bring claims in the form of a derivative action must first obtain the court's consent. Similarly, a condition for filing a class action is that the court first gives its authorisation for the claim to be filed in the form of a class action.

4. Indemnification rights

4.1 When the company can indemnify

Provided that its articles of association allow it to do so, a company is permitted to indemnify an officer for money he spends or for his expenses that result from certain actions he takes in his capacity as officer. Indemnifiable costs include:

- a monetary obligation towards a third party imposed on him pursuant to a court judgment (including an arbitral award confirmed by the court and a settlement judgment handed down by the court);
- reasonable litigation costs, including attorneys' fees, which the officer expends as a result of a proceeding conducted against him which ends without filing an indictment and without charging him with monetary liability in lieu of a criminal proceeding, or a proceeding which ends without filing an indictment but with charging him with monetary liability in lieu of a criminal proceeding regarding a crime which did not require *mens rea*; and
- reasonable litigation costs, including attorneys' fees, which the officer expends or is required to pay pursuant to a court decree, in regard to a claim filed against him by the company, its representative or a third party, or with regard to a criminal charge from which he is acquitted or a criminal charge resulting in conviction for a crime which did not require *mens rea*.

In order to allow indemnification, the articles of association can include:

- a provision allowing the company *a priori* to commit to indemnify its officer, with restrictions (described below); or
- a provision allowing the company to indemnify its officers retroactively.

An *a priori* commitment to indemnify for a monetary obligation imposed on an officer pursuant to a court judgment is limited to:

- certain types of event that the board of directors thinks are foreseeable at the time the commitment to indemnify is given in light of the company's activity; and
- a certain amount of money which the board decides was reasonable under the circumstances.

In contrast, there are no predetermined limitations as to foreseeable types of event for which officers can be indemnified regarding reasonable litigation expenses.

4.2 Formalities for indemnification

As described above in section 4.1, a prerequisite for a company to be able to indemnify its officers is that its articles of association include a provision which explicitly permits it to indemnify its officers. Additionally, a decision to indemnify an officer is considered a transaction with an interested party and thus requires special authorisation pursuant to the Companies Law. For the company to commit *a priori* to indemnify an officer who is not a director, or to indemnify based on a retroactive commitment to indemnify, such decision requires confirmation by the inspection committee and then the board of directors. For the company to commit *a priori* to indemnify an officer who is a director, or to indemnify based on a retroactive commitment to indemnify, confirmation by the board of directors and then the general assembly is required. In a public company, confirmation by the inspection committee is also required.

Once the above conditions are met, the company may issue a written commitment, typically in the form of a writ of indemnification, addressed to the officer. Such commitment should specify, among other things, that the necessary company authorisations were obtained and that, within the parameters of the restrictions mentioned in section 4.1, the company *a priori* exempts such officer from potential future liability as a result of him breaching his duty of care towards the company.

4.3 How indemnification works

As mentioned in section 4.1, there are restrictions as to the types of event and the maximum sum, with regard to *a priori* commitments to indemnify for monetary obligations imposed on officers pursuant to court judgments. Additionally, all payments of indemnification moneys are subject to the particular provisions of the indemnification agreement.

4.4 What cannot be indemnified

A provision in the articles of association which permits a company to indemnify (or insure/exempt) an officer from liability will be deemed null and void if it supports any of the following:

- breach of duty of trust towards the company, unless the officer has acted in good faith and had reasonable grounds to assume that the action would not harm the welfare of the company;
- wilful or reckless breach of duty of care, as a result of negligence alone;
- action taken with an intent to produce unlawful personal gain; or
- imposition of a fine on the officer.

Additionally, a commitment to indemnify (or insure) an officer as a result of his breach of his duty of trust towards the company is deemed null and void, unless the officer acted in good faith and had reasonable grounds to assume that the action would not harm the welfare of the company. Moreover, officers themselves are explicitly prohibited from accepting such commitments and any such acceptance shall be deemed a breach of the duty of trust.

5. D&O insurance

5.1 Availability of D&O insurance

Under the Companies Law, and provided that the articles of association permit it to do so, a company can obtain insurance for an officer's liability incurred as a result of an action he takes in his capacity as an officer, with regard to each of the following:

- breach of duty of care towards the company or another person;
- breach of duty of trust towards the company, provided that he acted in good faith and had reasonable grounds to assume that the action would not harm the welfare of the company; and
- monetary liability imposed on the officer for the benefit of another person.

A company can insure its own officials, but cannot insure officials of another company; therefore, generally, a parent company cannot insure officials of subsidiaries or affiliated companies.

Additionally, the decision to obtain insurance for an officer is considered a transaction with an interested party and thus requires special authorisation pursuant to the Companies Law. For the company to obtain insurance for an officer who is not a director, confirmation by the inspection committee and then the board of directors is required. For the company to obtain insurance for an officer who is a director, confirmation by the board of directors and then the general assembly is required. In a public company, confirmation by the inspection committee is also required.

5.2 Local rules on cover provided under a non-domestic D&O policy

Under the Supervision of Financial Services (Insurance) Law, 1981, in order to engage in insurance in Israel, including the provision of D&O insurance, it is necessary to obtain an insurer's licence from the insurance supervisor. Only Israeli companies and foreign companies which are registered in Israel and engage in insurance abroad under the supervision of their home authorities are allowed to obtain such a licence. Accordingly, foreign insurers which are not licensed in Israel are not permitted to operate in Israel. That said, the Supervision of Financial Services (Insurance) Law provides an exemption for reinsurance, according to which an entity which engages primarily in insurance activity outside of Israel and does not operate in Israel, except in the field of reinsurance, will not be considered an entity that "engages in insurance" and therefore will not require a licence, unless it is a company which was incorporated in Israel.

Pursuant to the above, and as a practical matter, Israeli subsidiaries of foreign parent companies generally obtain D&O insurance from Israeli insurance companies.

Italy

Serena Triboldi
Pontecorvi Mannaerts & Triboldi

1. Directors' duties

1.1 Nature of the duties

Under Italian corporate law, company directors (of both joint stock companies and limited liability companies) are required to manage the company in compliance with the duties imposed on them both by law and by the company's articles of association (see Articles 2392(1) and 2476(1) of the Civil Code), as well as by case law.

These duties fall into two separate categories:

- specific duties, arising from the law or the company's articles of association; and
- general duties, to be fulfilled while engaging in all management activities.

In particular, directors are subject to the following specific duties, among others:

- a duty to convene a shareholders' meeting without delay in case of losses (Articles 2446 and 2447 of the Civil Code);
- a duty to assess and note in the Companies Register, without delay, the occurrence of a cause for dissolution (Article 2485(1) of the Civil Code) and a duty subsequently to limit management activity only to the preservation of corporate property (Article 2486(1) of the Civil Code);
- a duty to draft, and draft accurately, business-year balance sheets (case law);
- a duty to comply with accounting principles (case law); and
- a duty to comply with all fiscal, welfare and criminal laws (case law).

Directors' general duties are as follows:

- a duty of diligence/care (Articles 2392 and 2476 of the Civil Code); and
- a duty of loyalty - that is, a duty to pursue the interests of the corporation, avoiding conflicts of interest (Articles 2391 and 2475-*ter* of the Civil Code).

The Italian corporate law reform of 2003[1] dramatically changed the legal regime relating to directors' duties and liability, introducing more stringent measures and expanding minority shareholder protection.

1 The reform of Italian corporate law was implemented through the enactment of Decree-Law 5 of January 17 2003 and Decree-Law 6 of January 17 2003.

1.2 Standards of care

The standard of care required for directors of joint stock companies engaged in management activities is regarded as a general principle established by specific provisions of the Civil Code. It therefore needs to be elaborated by courts with regard to the particular circumstances of the case at hand. Even though there is no specific provision setting out the standard of care to be followed by directors of limited liability companies, reasons of systematic consistency lead the dominant doctrine to apply the same standard provided by the law for directors of joint stock companies.

According to the provisions of Article 2392(1) of the Civil Code, as amended by the Italian corporate law reform, "directors shall fulfil duties imposed by the law or by articles of association with the diligence required by the nature of their assignment and their specific competence". Further, directors are required to act in an informed manner (Article 2381(6) of the Civil Code) and to do whatever they can to eliminate or diminish harmful consequences, where they learn of facts which are detrimental to the company (Article 2392(2) of the Civil Code).

As a result, directors are no longer subject to the 'reasonable man' standard (the so-called 'diligence of an agent' or 'good family father' standard), but must instead be evaluated while taking into consideration the professional nature of the activity which they carry out, as provided under Article 1176(2) of the Civil Code. The activities carried out by a company director represent a professional activity that requires greater caution and attention than that ascribed to the reasonable man.

The obligation that directors act with the diligence required by their specific competence implies an evaluation of the diligence of each director on the basis of his areas of competence, which was presumably previously taken for granted upon appointment.

According to Paragraph 6.III.4 of the Report on the 2003 Law Reform,[2] the duty to employ the diligence required by the nature of the assignment "does not mean that directors must necessarily be experts in accounting, finance and every field related to the management and administration of their company, but rather, simply, that their choices must be informed and well considered, based upon their respective knowledge, and that decisions must be made based on a calculated risk, rather than an irresponsible or negligent improvisation".

Therefore, a director behaves negligently if he makes management decisions without informing himself of the issues involved or without properly weighing the attendant risks and advantages for the company.

In any case, the standard of care required by law is a general clause to be applied with regard to the unique factual circumstances of each case. Therefore, when examining a particular case to assess whether a director behaved in a way that breached his duty of care to the company or other parties, it is necessary to evaluate all aspects of the situation; such assessment is left to the judge.[3]

The factors weighed by the judge in this assessment may include:

- the kind of company involved;
- its size, field of activity, structure and financial potential;

---

2 The *Relazione Illustrativa* of November 19 2003 can be found on www.judicium.it.
3 Tribunal of Milan, December 1 1988.

- the importance and conditions of the discussed operation; and
- the timeframe available for the director to make a decision.

Directors are also subject to a general obligation to pursue the best interests of the company; but it is clear from case law that this duty is not to maximise company profits. Directors are not considered responsible for the company's economic success, and liability for breach of the duty to act in the best interests of the company can arise only from violation of a duty imposed by law or by the company's articles of association.

In fact, the courts have generally applied the business judgement rule, stating that "a judge is not allowed to decide upon the opportuneness or appropriateness of directors' management decisions, which pertain to their discretionary powers and are not subject to an *ex-post* judgment; on the contrary, a judge can only check if a decision was made without conflicts of interest and with those preventative cautions, checks and information required by ordinary professional diligence".[4]

The duty to pursue the best interests of the company is not specifically set out under any legal provision and is therefore somewhat nebulous and hard to define. Like the duty of care, it must be defined according to the factual circumstances.

However, with regard to joint stock companies, it may be indirectly inferred from Article 2391(1) of the Civil Code, under which a director must inform other members of the board of directors and the board of auditors of any interest he holds, on his own account or on account of third parties, in a specific company operation. In such situation, a managing director must also refrain from carrying out the interested operation.

In this case, a director is liable for any damage suffered by the company as a result of his act or omission. A director is also liable for any damage suffered by the company if he appropriates corporate opportunities.

A conflict of interest is presumed where a director:

- becomes a shareholder of a competing company with unlimited liability;
- carries out a competing business on his own account or that of a third party; or
- becomes director or general manager of a competing company (Article 2390 of the Civil Code).

In such case a director who acts without the authorisation of the shareholders' meeting is liable for any damage suffered by the company.

Actual examples of such actions might include:

- unauthorised withdrawals and payments; and
- intra-company operations carried out for the benefit of a parent company or other group companies which are damaging to the subsidiary company.

4 Court of Cassation, Case 3652 of April 28 1997.

1.3 To whom duties are owed

The legal provisions set out in the Civil Code identify the legal persons to whom directors owe their duties, and who are therefore entitled to bring a liability action against negligent directors.

In both joint stock companies and limited liability companies, directors' duties are owed mainly to four categories of person, as outlined below.

(a) The company

Pursuant to Article 2392(1) of the Civil Code, the members of the board of directors of a joint stock company are jointly liable to the company for damage arising from the non-fulfilment of duties imposed on them either by the law or by the company's articles of association.

The same applies to a limited liability company, as set out under Article 2476(1) of the Civil Code.

A director's liability towards the company is generally considered to be a form of contractual liability and is therefore regulated by the general principles governing contractual liability under Italian law.

(b) Shareholders

According to Article 2395 of the Civil Code, an individual shareholder of a joint stock company can bring a liability action against directors for "damages suffered as a direct result of intentional or negligent acts committed by the directors".

In this case, the damage must directly affect the assets of the individual shareholder.

As provided under Article 2476(6) of the Civil Code, an individual shareholder of a limited liability company is also entitled to bring an individual action against directors under the same conditions specified under Article 2395. An individual action brought by an individual shareholder is considered to be a tort liability action.

(c) Creditors

According to Article 2394 of the Civil Code, the directors of a joint stock company are liable towards creditors of the company "for non-fulfilment of their duties concerning the preservation of the integrity of corporate assets. Creditors can bring a liability action when the corporate assets prove insufficient to satisfy their credit".

Directors are under an obligation not to jeopardise the so-called 'creditors' guarantee', which is constituted by the corporate assets. If they breach this duty, they cause damage to the creditors by non-fulfilment of the creditors' expectation of satisfaction of their claims.

The nature of a director's liability towards company creditors is controversial; some argue that it should be regarded as contractual in nature, while others consider it to be tortious.

Since the concept of 'insufficiency of corporate assets' is considered even more serious than the notion of 'simple insolvency', this action is usually brought within the scope of a bankruptcy proceeding. In this situation, however, only the bankruptcy receiver can bring the action, and not the creditors.

(d) *Third parties*

Third parties have the same right under Article 2395 of the Civil Code as individual shareholders to bring a liability action against directors of a joint stock company. As in the case of individual shareholders, the damage must have directly affected the assets of the third party.

The same type of individual action is recognised under Article 2476(6) of the Civil Code for third parties that suffered damage as a direct result of the misconduct of directors of a limited liability company.

1.4 Common defences to and exemptions from liability

Depending on the nature of the action being brought against company directors – contractual or tort – the plaintiff must comply with different burdens of proof. Failure to do so will result in the action being rejected by the judge.

In the case of a contractual action (eg, an action brought by the company under Article 2392 or 2476(1) of the Civil Code), the burden of proof is established pursuant to the principles set out under Articles 1218 and following of the Civil Code. A claimant need only prove the following elements of the cause of action:

- The director breached a duty imposed on him by the law or the company's articles of association;
- Damage resulted; and
- A causal link exists between director's misconduct and the damage. Directors seeking exemption from liability must prove that they did not act negligently.

On the other hand, when an action is brought in tort (eg, an action brought by an individual shareholder or by a third party under Article 2395 2476(6) of the Civil Code), the burden of proof is borne by the parties according to the criteria set out under Article 2043 of the Civil Code. The plaintiff must prove all elements of the cause of action - that is, a breach of duty, intentional or negligent conduct, the damage suffered and the causal link between the misconduct and the damage.

In addition to the situation where the plaintiff fails to prove the elements of the relevant cause of action, the law sets out specific defences and exemptions.

In particular, Articles 2392(2) and 3 of the Civil Code set forth two cases of exemption from liability for the directors of a joint stock company. Directors are generally liable for the mismanagement of the company, except where:

- liability relates to specific functions which have been entrusted to an executive committee or one or more directors. However, this exemption does not exclude a director's general duty to monitor the activity of the individuals who have been entrusted with those functions. In fact, pursuant to Article 2392(2) of the Civil Code, "directors are jointly liable if, being aware of detrimental acts, they did not do whatever they were able to do in order to prevent these acts or to negate or minimise harmful consequences". Further, according to Article 2381 of the Civil Code, directors are under a duty to act in an informed manner and have an individual right to ask the delegated directors to give the board of directors information regarding the management of the company; or

- an individual director, who was not negligent, has registered his disagreement in the board of directors' meetings and resolution book (or has requested to do so), also giving immediate communication in writing to the president of the board of auditors. The request to register the director's disagreement must be promptly submitted during the meeting deciding on the specific item, before the relevant resolution becomes effective.

A similar exemption is provided under Article 2476(1) of the Civil Code with regard to limited liability companies.

Directors may also be exempted from liability to the company as a result of an express resolution by which the company waives its right to bring a liability action against its directors. Waivers by joint stock companies are regulated under Article 2393 of the Civil Code, whereas limited liability companies waive their right under Article 2476(5) of the code. The relevant procedures are dealt with in detail in section 4.

2. Who can bring claims

The legal persons to whom directors owe their duties are entitled to bring claims against the same directors.

2.1 The company (and its liquidators)

Where there is a violation of directors' duties, a solvent joint stock company can bring a liability action against the directors under Article 2393 of the Civil Code. The decision to bring the action must be resolved by the ordinary shareholders' meeting in compliance with the relevant quorum requirements set out under Article 2368; the shareholders who attend must represent at least half of the corporate capital; and the resolution must be approved by an absolute majority of the shareholders present, unless a greater majority is required by the articles of association.

The resolution can be adopted at the same meeting at which the balance sheet is discussed, even if it is not listed on the agenda, if the misconduct occurred during the fiscal year to which the balance sheet refers.

If the resolution is adopted by a group of shareholders representing one-fifth of the corporate capital, the directors against whom the action is brought are removed from office and replaced at the same shareholders' meeting.

The ordinary shareholders' meeting is also competent to approve a liability action against directors when the company is being wound up. In such case the relevant action shall be filed by the liquidator.

A corporate action can also be brought by the judicial administrator appointed by the tribunal in the course of a special proceedings started by minority shareholders under Article 2409 of the Civil Code to report the commission of serious irregularities by directors in the management of the company.

Further, according to Article 2393(3) of the Civil Code, as amended by Law 262 of December 28 2005, the corporate action can be resolved by the company's auditory body, by a majority of two-thirds of its members.

In the event of bankruptcy, compulsory winding-up or extraordinary administration, Article 2394*bis* of the Civil Code provides that the liability action is brought by the bankruptcy receiver or by the commissioner.

As mentioned above, this type of action is regarded as contractual in nature.

2.2 Minority shareholders on behalf of the company

This type of action was introduced into the Italian legal system by the 2003 corporate law reform, in order to increase the protection of minority shareholders of joint stock companies.

According to the provisions of Article 2393*bis* of the Civil Code, a liability action against a director of a joint stock company may be brought on behalf of the company by a group of shareholders representing one-fifth of the corporate capital or a different percentage as provided in the articles of association, which in any case cannot be higher than one-third.

In companies quoted on the stock exchange, the action can be brought by shareholders representing one-fortieth of the corporate capital or a lower percentage as provided in the articles of association.

Shareholders who wish to bring the action must appoint, by a resolution approved by a majority of the capital they hold, one or more common representatives who shall bring the action and carry out the subsequent actions.

The company is called in the proceedings and the summons must also be notified to the company in the name of the president of the board of auditors.

In limited liability companies, the corporate action can be brought, as provided under Article 2476(3) of the Civil Code, by any shareholder, regardless of his share participation.

In the event of a serious breach of duties, the individual shareholder can ask the judge to issue a provisional measure to remove the director from office.

The costs incurred by the shareholders in the course of the proceedings shall be refunded by the company. The nature of this type of action is also contractual.

2.3 Minority shareholders on their own account

Minority shareholders and individual shareholders can bring a liability action against directors under Articles 2395 and 2476(6) of the Civil Code for damage they suffered directly as a result of the directors' misconduct.

This in an individual action brought by an individual shareholder on his own account. As discussed in section 3.2, the Italian legal system does not accept the concept of a 'class action'.

The pendency of liability actions brought by the company, or by minority shareholders on behalf of the company, does not jeopardise an individual shareholder's right to compensation from the directors for damage directly suffered by him. This action is considered to be tortious in nature.

A typical example of liability towards an individual shareholder would arise where the directors, through the creation of a false balance sheet, led the shareholder to subscribe to shares at an unreasonable price. Further examples might include:

- the mistaken assessment of the exchange rate for shares in a merger between two companies;
- the conduct of a director who, after collecting the necessary sums from the shareholders to subscribe an increase of capital, registers the new shares in his own name; or
- the destruction by the director of bearer shares which were to be converted into nominative stocks.[5]

2.4 Third parties

Third parties are also entitled, under Articles 2395 and 2476(6) of the Civil Code, to bring a liability action against directors for damage they suffered directly as a result of the directors' misconduct.

This is also an individual action to be brought by a third party. Third parties that typically bring claims are parties to contracts with the company, such as banks, service or goods providers and consultants. This type of action is tortious in nature.

Creditors are to be considered as a special category, to which the law has reserved a specific action. According to Article 2394 of the Civil Code, they are entitled to bring a liability action against directors only when the corporate assets are insufficient to satisfy their claims, due to directors' violation of the duty to preserve the corporate assets. This is also an individual and autonomous action brought by the creditors, which are entitled to obtain an indemnification equivalent to the amount of their claim. The creditor must prove the existence of its credit right.

A waiver of the liability action against directors by the company does not prevent creditors from bringing a liability action under Article 2394 of the Civil Code.

In the event of a settlement agreed to by the company, creditors can challenge the settlement only by exercising the 'revocation action' in compliance with the relevant requirements. The nature of this action is unclear. However, the courts have usually regarded it as a contractual action.

A leading Italian case concerns directors' liability arising out of the misconduct of a director who obtained a line of credit from a bank by showing false financial statements. This caused damage to the bank, which could not obtain repayment of the sums loaned via the line of credit. Further examples would include:

- the subscription by third parties of shares at an unreasonable price, due to reliance on a false balance sheet drafted by the directors;
- directors' refusal to pay a legal bill when other creditors holding weaker claim titles had been paid; or
- the subscription by third parties of new shares pursuant to an increase of capital with a share premium which had not been resolved by a shareholders' meeting.[6]

---

5 Tribunal of Milan, March 20 1997; Tribunal of Genova, December 21 2000; Court of Cassation, Case 2055 of April 10 1979; Court of Cassation Case 1222 of February 26 1982.

6 Tribunal of Milan, December 3 1964; Court of Cassation Case 2850 of March 28 1996.

3. Claims culture

3.1 Litigation

Italy cannot be regarded as a litigation-driven society, when compared to the United States; nevertheless, there has been an increase in the number of suits brought before the Italian courts in recent years. However, these suits are mainly brought by individuals against individuals, rather than against companies.

Before the 2003 corporate law reform, civil liability actions against company directors, whether corporate or individual, were not an efficient tool in the hands of those who suffered damage as a result of directors' misconduct.

The old corporate action was rarely brought against solvent companies, since it could be filed only by majority shareholders. As a result, in light of the fact that directors are usually bound to the majority shareholders by a bond of trust, the majority would be unwilling to bring an action against their directors.

The rare cases where a corporate action was brought tended to occur in situations where majority shareholders had changed following the sale of the company's controlling stake.[7] Therefore, the corporate action was usually brought by a bankruptcy receiver or by commissioners, within the scope of a bankruptcy proceeding or a compulsory winding-up.

Article 2393*bis* of the Civil Code was introduced in order to remedy this situation, by giving minority shareholders the right to bring corporate actions on behalf of the company.

This change in the law is likely to lead to an increase in claims brought by minority shareholders, so that the Article 2393*bis* action is an important tool in the hands of minority shareholders in the event of conflict with majority shareholders.

Individual actions have thus far been quite rare and seldom successful. In particular, actions brought by creditors have generally been filed by the bankruptcy receiver, due to the fact that the circumstances in which this action can be filed imply a situation of insolvency.

3.2 Ability to bring class actions

Italy does not have a legal mechanism for US-style class actions. However, aggrieved Italian consumers have several 'quasi-class action' options available. For example, consumer associations can file claims on behalf of groups which have been damaged by corporate action. These types of claim are increasing and courts seem sympathetic – for example, a court recently allowed such a suit against banks that continued to apply compound interest on retail clients' current account overdrafts. In addition, under Article 2393*bis* of the Civil Code, 'qualified' minority shareholders are entitled to bring an action on behalf of the company to obtain compensation for damages suffered by the company. This article was added to the Civil Code pursuant to the corporate law reform of 2003 in order to protect minority and individual shareholders. However, this section contains some important restrictions; most importantly, an action under Article 2393*bis* can be brought only by minority

---

7 Court of Cassation Case 6278 of June 22 1990.

shareholders representing at least 20% of the corporate capital, or a different percentage provided in the articles of association which in any case cannot be greater than one-third (2.5% in case of listed companies). In this way, disruptive lawsuits by shareholders with marginal shareholdings are avoided.

Recently, there have been some political initiatives to institute class-action legislation similar to that of the United States. However, at the time of writing no such legislation has yet become law.

3.3 Funding of claims and whether loser pays

The general principles on funding of claims are set out in the Code of Civil Procedure.[8]

The matter is governed by two main principles:

- one provisional – the advancement of costs – to be applied from the beginning of the proceedings; and
- the other final – the condition of the losing party – to be applied upon the conclusion of the proceedings.

According to the principle of advancement of costs, each party is obliged to pay in advance the costs of the proceedings, being the costs for filing defensive deeds or requiring jurisdictional measures. In case of acts which are necessary for the proceedings (ie, ordered by the judge independently of the parties' initiative, such as technical expertise), costs are advanced by a party where the same is expressly charged by the law or the judge.[9] Therefore, the costs of the proceedings include any cost incurred by the party during the proceedings - that is, court charges, registry dues, court-appointed experts' fees and defence fees.

With regard to defence fees, the principle of advancement of costs does not apply to any fee agreed between the lawyer and the party. It refers only to those fees calculated on the basis of the 'professional fees' set out by law, which are indicated in a minimum and maximum amount, depending on the value and complexity of the case.

According to the principle of the condition of the losing party, the judge who finally rules upon a case, by the same ruling, condemns the losing party to refund the procedural costs to the winning party, and assesses and liquidates the relevant amount, which shall be inclusive of the defence fees (Article 91).

This means that, in principle, costs awards against losing parties generally reflect the costs borne by the winning party during the proceedings, subject to a few exceptions established by law. In fact, with regard to defence fees, fee liquidation included in the judicial ruling is based on the lawyers' bills and only makes reference to the professional fees set out by law. Therefore, fee agreements entered into by a party and his lawyer (eg, contingency fee agreements or conditional fee agreements) are effective only between them, and not towards third parties – not even in judicial proceedings. Hence, they cannot be included in judicial costs awards and charged to the losing party.

---

8 Book I, Title III, Section IV, entitled "Parties' liability for costs and procedural damages", Articles 90 to 98.
9 Article 90, as amended by Article 8 of Presidential Decree 115/2002.

A type of contingency/conditional fee agreement, known as *'patto di quota lite'*, was recently introduced to the Italian legal system. According to Article 45 of the Lawyers' Ethics Code, as amended by Law 223/2006 (the Bersani Decree), a lawyer is allowed to enter into fee agreements with his client whereby fees are determined in relation to the realisation of the goals pursued, provided they are proportionate to the activity carried out by the lawyer. Such agreements must be set out in writing in order to be valid; the amount of the fees can be calculated as a percentage of the value of the suit and success fees can be agreed. However, these agreements may be enforced only between the lawyer and his client, and not towards the losing party in judicial proceedings.

Further exceptions to the above-mentioned principle based on the condition of the losing party are provided by law where a strict application of the principle is likely to lead to unjust results.

Therefore, a judge can deny the winning party's right to be refunded where the costs incurred are considered excessive or superfluous; or can distribute the costs between the parties, in whole or in part, where both parties are losing parties or based on other just reasons (Article 92). As a result, in such situations it is possible that a losing party may be required to pay the winning party costs in a sum which may be lower than the costs assessed by the winning party.

In the event of a settlement, costs are divided between the parties, unless the settlement agreement provides otherwise.

A specific provision introduces the concept of 'aggrieved liability', which is intended to deter parties from bringing or defending frivolous claims. Each party can request that the judge order the losing party, which acted or defended in the proceedings with bad faith or gross negligence, not only to pay the costs of the proceeding, but also to compensate the other party for any resulting damage, which shall be liquidated by the judge in the same ruling (Article 96).

With regard to defence fees, a special payment provision is granted to the attorney who assists the winning party: he is paid directly from the settlement amount rather than by the winning party (Article 93).

3.4 Plaintiffs' bar

This issue has no significance in the Italian jurisdiction.

3.5 Procedural barriers

The procedural requirements for filing a liability action against company directors are set out in the Code of Civil Procedure. In addition, Decree-Law 5 of January 17 2003 provides a new regime for corporate proceedings. Limitation issues are also directly addressed in the Civil Code under the provisions governing each type of action.

The procedural conditions are conditions which must exist before a claim is filed for a judgment on the merits of the case. These are:

- jurisdiction;
- competence of the judge (both subject matter and territory); and
- the conditions of the action - that is, the interest in the action and the *legitimatio ad causam*.

Therefore, an action can be rejected by a procedural ruling where:

- the judge entrusted with the suit has no jurisdiction (eg, due to an arbitration clause) or competence to decide on the case;
- the claimant is not the holder of a right of action; or
- the claim is filed against a party who is not the correct defendant.

The court which has jurisdiction and competence to decide on a liability action brought against directors is the civil tribunal. If the action is started against an individual director, the competent tribunal will be the civil tribunal of the place where the director has his residence or domicile or, if this is unknown, the tribunal of the place where the claimant has his residence (Articles 9 and 18 of the Code of Civil Procedure).

If the action is brought against all members of the board of directors, it must be filed – according to the principle of plurality of defendants set out under Article 31 of the Code of Civil Procedure – before the tribunal of the place where one of the directors has his residence or domicile. In this situation, the defendant is not the board as a collective body, but rather the individual directors.

Where the action is brought by the bankruptcy receiver or by the commissioner within the scope of a bankruptcy proceeding or a compulsory winding-up proceeding, the bankruptcy tribunal shall be competent to rule on the case.

Depending on the type of liability action to be brought, the approval of corporate bodies or the court may be required by law. In the event of a corporate action under Article 2393 of the Civil Code, the *legitimatio ad causam* and legal representation in the proceedings are governed by the following rules.

The corporate action must be approved by the ordinary shareholders' meeting in compliance with the relevant quorum requirements set out under Article 2368 of the Civil Code, as described in section 2.1.

However, the persons vested with the legal and judicial representation of the company are the directors. Therefore, the action shall be brought by the new directors, if already appointed, or by the special administrator appointed by the tribunal under Article 78 of the Code of Civil Procedure. This is designed to avoid a conflict of interest where the old directors are still in office.

In the event of the winding-up of the company, the corporate action must be approved by a majority of the shareholders and will be brought by the liquidator. In case of bankruptcy, compulsory winding-up or extraordinary administration, a preliminary shareholders' resolution is not required.

However, under Article 146(2) of the Bankruptcy Law (Royal Decree 267 of March 16 1942), if the corporate action is brought within the scope of a bankruptcy proceeding, the legal representation of the company is vested with the bankruptcy receiver, subject to the prior authorisation of the judge and under the obligation to hear the creditors' committee.

In case of compulsory winding-up, the commissioner is required under Article 206 of the Bankruptcy Law to obtain prior authorisation from the authority supervising the relevant procedure.

A corporate action against directors may also be brought with the approval of:

- the qualified minority shareholders required under Article 2393*bis* of the Civil Code (in which case the action shall be brought by one or more common representatives appointed by the minority shareholders); or
- the audit board, by a two-thirds majority of its members, as provided under Article 2393(3) of the Civil Code.

The action begins with notification of the director via a writ of summons, pursuant to the terms and formalities set out by Decree-Law 5 of January 17 2003.

In addition to the procedural conditions specified above, the action can be barred due to the expiry of a statutory limitation period.

A liability action to be brought by the company under Article 2393 of the Civil Code is time barred if it is not started within five years of the date on which the relevant director was dismissed from his duties.

However, where the director's misconduct is criminal in nature (for which a longer statute of limitations applies), the civil liability action shall become time barred upon the expiry of the longer statute of limitations provided under criminal law (Article 2947(3) of the Civil Code).

In the case of an action brought by an individual shareholder or third party under Article 2395 of the Civil Code, the statute of limitations provides a five-year term starting from the occurrence of the act which damaged the claimant.

Where an action is brought by the company's creditors under Article 2394 of the Civil Code, the action is barred after the expiry of a five-year period starting from the moment at which evidence comes to light that the corporate assets will prove insufficient to satisfy the creditors' claims, as established under Article 2949(2) of the Civil Code.

4. Indemnification rights

4.1 When the company can indemnify

In order to assess whether a company is able – or even obliged – to indemnify its directors and hold them harmless from any liability or defence costs assessed by the courts, it is necessary to make a distinction based on:

- the nature of the directors' liability (contractual or tortious); and
- the type of proceedings started against them (civil, criminal or administrative).

With regard to directors' civil liability, the types of action set out by the law are grounded on acts committed as a result of wilful misconduct or negligence. Therefore, the nature of the liability is personal and rests with the individual director(s), even though the misconduct was carried out by the person acting as director of the company and undertaking management activities on behalf of the company. Therefore, the company cannot be held liable for wilful or negligent acts committed by its directors and, as a result, is under no obligation to indemnify those directors who are found guilty.

This applies where the action is brought by the company itself against its directors, since the action is based on the violation of a contractual relationship between the director and the company, arising from the appointment of the director by the shareholders. The same applies where the action is brought by individual shareholders, corporate creditors or third parties.

For the same reasons, the company is required by law neither to advance defence costs to directors who are sued for civil liability prior to a finding by a court nor to bear defence costs post-trial where a director is found guilty.

Nevertheless, the company may decide to relieve its directors from liability under specific circumstances and conditions.

It may:

- waive its right to bring a corporate action against its directors, under the terms set out in Article 2393(6) of the Civil Code; or
- advance defence costs and relieve its directors from liability where a director is found liable for acts committed without fraud or gross negligence.

Issues relating to the allocation of defence costs are to be resolved by referring to the general principles on funding of claims set out in the Code of Civil Procedure, as mentioned in section 3.3. Therefore, where the director is acquitted, defence costs will be refunded by the losing party.

Where the case is settled before trial, the defence costs shall be divided between the parties, unless the settlement agreement provides otherwise.

The company may also decide to advance defence costs to the director and refrain from asking him to refund those costs, where he is found guilty of acts committed without fraud or gross negligence.

With regard to criminal liability, companies cannot be held criminally liable for acts committed by directors, since criminal liability is personal in nature.

However, they can be subject to administrative liability for crimes committed by chief executives and employees pursuant to the provisions of Decree-Law 231 of June 8 2001. Such crimes include corruption, bribery, insider trading and misrepresentation.

According to Article 5 of Law 231/2001, a company is liable for crimes committed in its interest and to its advantage by the directors, unless they acted in their own exclusive interests or in the interest of a third party. The company can be exempted from liability by demonstrating that an adequate model of conduct was adopted and a specific compliance body was established to monitor compliance with the model of conduct. Where the company is found liable for crimes committed by its directors, it will be liable for payment of administrative penalties and costs of the proceedings. Administrative penalties imposed on the company may include fines or the temporary closure of the business.

Where the directors commit a tax law violation, Decree-Law 472 of December 18 1997 provides that the company is jointly liable for payment of the administrative penalties imposed on directors by the tax authorities. In this case, the company has the right to bring an action against its directors after paying the penalty. However, according to Article 11(6) of Decree-Law 472/1997, the company may also decide to waive its right to bring such an action and to bear the entire cost of the administrative penalty, provided that the violation was not committed with fraud or gross negligence.

4.2 Formalities for indemnification

Directors' indemnification rights for civil liability are mainly grounded on case law. In fact, under Italian law, there are no specific legal provisions compelling or allowing a company to indemnify its directors in respect of liabilities or defence costs arising from civil liability proceedings.

As mentioned above, indemnification of directors by the company is not mandatory – rather, the company can choose whether to do so based on a cost-benefit analysis.

There are two main circumstances in which indemnification by the company is permitted:

- According to Articles 2393(5) and 2476(5) of the Civil Code, the company is allowed to waive its right to bring a liability action against the directors. This provision may be construed as a sort of indemnification, provided that the company agrees to bear the economic damage resulting from the directors' misconduct, even when this results from fraud or gross negligence.
- The company can indemnify its directors in respect of liabilities which do not arise from misconduct committed by way of fraud or gross negligence. In fact, according to Article 1229 of the Civil Code, any agreement excluding or limiting a debtor's liability for fraud or gross negligence is void.

Therefore, the company may choose to grant the directors an exclusion or limitation of liability for future acts committed with little or no negligence. This may be achieved by inserting a general indemnification provision in the company's articles of associations or in the director's contract, or by adopting an insurance policy.

With regard to past acts, letters of indemnity or indemnification agreements can have the effect of a waiver of liability action by the company only when they comply with the requirements set out under Article 2393(5) of the Civil Code.

4.3 How indemnification works

As specified in section 4.2, the company may relieve directors from civil liability by waiving its right to bring an action. It does so by inserting a specific provision in the articles of association or in the director's contract, or by means of an insurance policy.

If a company decides to waive its right to bring an action, the waiver must be approved by means of a specific shareholders' resolution which sets out its content in detail (ie, referring to those management acts which were the source of liability). As a consequence, the waiver must be resolved after the occurrence of the negligent acts.

The courts have applied this principle, holding that:

- the resolution by which the shareholders approve the balance sheet and ratify the activities of a dismissed director exempting the latter from liability cannot be considered as a waiver to the corporate action;[10] and
- a general resolution adopted by the shareholders' meeting upon the dismissal of a director from his past cannot be considered as a waiver of the right to bring an action, as such a waiver must be decided upon after the director's misconduct and not before.[11]

The principles elaborated by courts have become a provision of law set out under Article 2364(1)(5), as amended by the corporate law reform. A shareholders' resolution by which an act committed by a director is authorised in advance or ratified *ex post* does not have the effect of exempting the director from liability to the company.

Therefore, a waiver to the corporate action is valid only when it is resolved by the company in compliance with the quorum requirements established by law.

According to Article 2393(5) of the Civil Code, a joint stock company can waive its right of action by way of a shareholders' resolution when it is not opposed by a minority of shareholders representing one-fifth of the corporate capital, or one-twentieth of the corporate capital in the case of a listed company (or such other percentages as are provided by the articles where the action is brought by a qualified shareholder minority under Articles 2393*bis*(1) and (2) of the Civil Code).

In the case of a limited liability company, a waiver is valid under the terms of Article 2476(5) of the Civil Code when it is approved by a shareholder majority representing two-thirds of the corporate capital and it is not opposed by a shareholder minority representing one-tenth of the corporate capital. Different percentages may be specified in the articles of association.

Likewise, the adoption of the other means available to the company to relieve the directors from liability must be approved by the shareholders' meeting. Therefore, a shareholders' resolution approving or amending the articles of association will be needed to insert a specific provision in the articles of association by which the company undertakes to indemnify the directors in the event that they are found liable by a court.

The inclusion of an indemnification clause in a director's letter of appointment shall be resolved on during the shareholders' meeting at which the director is appointed or at a subsequent shareholders' meeting.

Where criminal liability is involved, the company may be held directly liable by the courts for the administrative liability resulting from crimes committed by directors and may be penalised by administrative fines and penalties.

In the case of a tax law violation by the directors, the company may directly pay administrative penalties if the violation was not committed with fraud or gross negligence.

10 Tribunal of Termini Imerese, January 28 1993.
11 Tribunal of Milan, February 10 2000.

4.4 What cannot be indemnified

With regard to directors' civil liability, it is not clear whether a company can indemnify directors from liabilities resulting from actions brought by creditors, individual shareholders or third parties. Generally, the Italian courts have held that they cannot. However, Italian companies are starting to adopt forms of indemnification (by means of insurance policies or indemnification clauses) to protect directors from liability actions started by third parties.

As stated above, covenants entered into in advance promising to relieve directors from liability for any act or omission committed by wilful misconduct or gross negligence are void.

As regards directors' criminal liability, no indemnification right can be granted to directors, since criminal liability is personal in nature, as specified under Article 27 of the Constitutional Charter. As mentioned above, the company may be held liable only for administrative liability resulting from certain criminal acts committed by directors, as specified by Decree-Law 231/2001.

5. D&O insurance

5.1 Availability of D&O insurance

D&O insurance is a legal tool which was devised in the United States in the 1950s. The arrival of D&O insurance in Italy was relatively recent, but today it has become a common practice. In fact, the more stringent standards of liability imposed on company directors by the corporate law reform led many insurance companies to offer a wide range of D&O insurance policies.

This new practice is attractive because it satisfies the interests of both the insured director and the company; the former is relieved of the financial burden of personal liability and the latter can rely on a solvent 'debtor' - the insurance company.

Directors' and officers' civil liability is insurable under Italian law, as regards liability towards the company, company creditors, individual shareholders and third parties.

However, a distinction based on the nature of the action being brought – corporate or individual – must be made in order to determine who is charged with the obligation to pay the insurance policy premium.

If the policy covers liability towards the company, the premium should be paid by the directors and cannot be refunded by the company. Alternatively, if the policy covers liability towards company creditors, individual shareholders and third parties, the premium may be paid or refunded by the company.

The reason why the premium cannot be refunded by the company where the policy covers directors' liability towards the company itself is because to provide otherwise would jeopardise the company's right to be kept harmless from damage suffered as a result of its directors' misconduct.

On the other hand, the premium is refundable pursuant to Article 1917 of the Civil Code where the insurance covers directors' liability to individual shareholders, third parties and company creditors, because this is essentially insurance for tort liability, admitted under Italian law.

Insurance coverage can be provided for acts or omissions committed by directors as a result of negligence or gross negligence, but is excluded where the misconduct is the result of intent or fraud. However, in the most developed policies, insurance companies advance defence costs even in the case of suits based on wilful misconduct by directors. In this situation, the defence costs must be refunded by the insured if the director is found guilty by a court of intentional or fraudulent acts.

The adoption of an insurance policy in favour of the company's directors must be resolved by the ordinary shareholders' meeting. The insurance policy is taken out by the company - the contractual party - on behalf and to the advantage of the director, the insured party.

The contracting party is usually the parent company, and the policy will apply to the directors of subsidiaries and affiliates of the parent company. Domestic insurers can provide insurance policies with a worldwide reach and this therefore applies to foreign subsidiaries of an Italian resident company.

5.2 Local rules on cover provided under a non-domestic D&O policy

Non-domestic insurers may be authorised to do business in Italy under the right of establishment or the principle of freedom of services, depending on whether their head office is located in an EU/EEA state or a third state.

The authorisation is released by the Italian Supervisory Body on Private Insurance Companies (ISVAP), subject to the following conditions set out by law (Laws 174 and 175 of March 17 1995).

An EU/EEA insurance company wishing to set up a branch in Italy under the right of establishment must notify ISVAP by means of a communication with an enclosed set of documents. Within 30 days, ISVAP will inform the home supervisor of the general conditions with which the undertaking must comply as regards the contracts to be concluded and the forms of advertising adopted. Contracts are governed by Italian law, unless the parties choose a different applicable law. In such situation, Italian mandatory rules must be complied with in any case. The insurance company must provide policy holders with an information dossier pursuant to the regulations before concluding an insurance contract. A branch may be set up and start doing business as soon as the insurance company receives the consent of ISVAP or, in the event of silence, upon the expiry of a 30-day period.

An EU/EEA insurance company wishing to do business in Italy under the principle of freedom of services must notify its intention to ISVAP and submit alongside this a specific set of documents. It can begin doing business as soon as it receives notification from its home supervisor. Such company is not authorised to open a branch in Italy, but must appoint a fiscal representative in the Italian territory.

An insurance company with its head office in a third state (ie, a non-EU/EEA state) may be authorised by ISVAP to commence operations in Italy only under the right of establishment and following the issuance of an order to be published in the Italian *Official Gazette*. The company must set up a branch in Italy and appoint a legal representative resident in the Italian territory.

According to Article 29 of Law 209 of September 7 2005, persons domiciled in Italy or Italian companies are not allowed to enter into insurance contracts with insurance companies which have their seats in a third state and are doing business under the principle of freedom of services. Breach of this provision will result in the agreements being void.

A foreign insurer which is authorised under Italian law can provide policies to resident policyholders in compliance with the applicable provisions of Italian law concerning:

- the client's information obligation;
- the insurance contract; and
- advertising.

Parties are allowed to choose a different applicable law, but in such case they are also under an obligation to comply with Italian mandatory rules.

Global policies entered into by a foreign parent company and extending coverage to resident subsidiaries can be offered in Italy, provided that they comply with the applicable Italian law. They are usually structured as master policies to be combined with local policies within the scope of global insurance programmes.

Japan

Shigeru Ogiso
Yuasa and Hara

Under the Company Law, only natural persons may be appointed as company directors. Except in certain cases stipulated by law (Articles 331(1)(2) to (4)), a person is eligible for appointment as a director of a company regardless of whether he has a shareholding in the company. This chapter provides an introduction to directors' powers and responsibilities under the Company Law.

1. Directors' duties

1.1 Nature of the duties

Under the Companies Law, the position of director is based on the principle of mandate or trust, as set out in Article 643 of the Civil Code. Under the principle of mandate, a director is mandated to perform his duties with due care. Article 355 of the law stipulates that directors must faithfully perform their obligations in accordance with the provisions of laws, regulations, the company's articles of association and shareholder resolutions. Generally, if a director is in default of performance of his duty and causes the company damage, he must compensate the company for such damage based on Article 415 of the Civil Code, which sets out the defaulting director's responsibility for compensation.

Further, the Companies Law specifically stipulates the duties set out below.

(a) Loyalty to the company

Article 355 of the law requires that directors observe the provisions of laws, regulations, the company's articles of association and shareholder resolutions, and faithfully perform their duties. Some commentators interpret these provisions as setting forth a duty of loyalty similar to that required under US case law, but others maintain that this derives from the director's duty of care. This interpretation is supported by Decision 1970.6.24 of the Supreme Court, and arises naturally from the basic theory of good care, which requires that there be no conflict of interest between the director and the company.

(b) Refrain from bribery

For many years it was common practice in Japan that directors would bribe shareholders to vote in favour of proposed resolutions. In order to prevent such illegal practices, Article 120(4) of the Companies Law clearly stipulates that, irrespective of whether actual damage to the company has arisen, directors shall be obliged to compensate the company with amounts of money or benefits equivalent in value to those offered to shareholders. This legislation is an attempt to remedy the previous practice in some public companies of offering money or other benefits to placate groups of shareholders known as *sokaiya* (corporate racketeers). The provision therefore addresses the issue of corporate governance.

(c) ***Refrain from competing with the company or acting against its interests***

If the director engages in a business which competes with the company, or in any act which is contrary to the interests of the company, he will be in breach of his duty to the company (Articles 356 and 423). If such activities are backed by a resolution of the board, all directors who participated in the meeting and voted in favour of the activities will liable to compensate the company jointly and severally. If a director wishes to avoid such liability, he should be specific in expressing an objection and ensure that the secretary records his name and objection in the minutes of the board meeting.

(d) ***Loans to directors***

Where a director seeks a loan from the company, the prior approval of the general meeting (Article 356(1)(2)) or of the statutory board meeting must be obtained. If a loan is granted without the approval of the board, those directors who decided to extend the loan shall be held responsible for compensating the company, because the transaction will be deemed to be invalid (Articles 423(1) and (2)). Moreover, even if the loan is made with the prior approval of the board of directors, if the borrowing director fails to make to meet his repayment obligations, the members of the board of directors who voted for the approval may be responsible for repaying the loan, depending on the circumstances (Article 423(3)).

(e) ***Untrue disclosures***

Under the Companies Law, if a director or directors disclose untrue information about the company - for instance, by presenting falsified accounting statements, documents or records - then such director or directors shall be responsible for compensating third parties who suffer losses as a result of relying on the false information (Article 429 of the Companies Law and Article 21 of the Financial Service Commodities Law).

(f) ***Acts in violation of the law and articles of incorporation***

In principle, where any act of a director is in violation of laws or the company's articles of association and has caused damage to the company, the director must compensate the company for such damage. Any act by a director which violates applicable laws, regulations or the company's articles of association is a breach of his prime duty as a director. If such an illegal act is carried out with the cooperation of other directors, those directors will be jointly and severally responsible for compensating the company (Article 120(4)). In addition, if an illegal act is mandated by a resolution of the board, the directors who voted for the resolution will be jointly responsible for paying compensation.

(g) Illegal distribution of dividends

No distribution of profits can be made which exceeds the limits established by applicable provisions of the Companies Law. If such illegal distribution is mandated by a board resolution or by a resolution of the general meeting, the directors who made such an illegal distribution will be jointly responsible for compensating the company (Article 426(1)), unless it can be shown that there were valid reasons for it.

1.2 Standards of care

As stated in section 1.1, the Companies Law stipulates that the legal basis of the office of a director is the principle of trust or mandate, as set out in Article 644 of the Civil Code. It is expressly stipulated that a trustee must perform his duties with due care in line with the mandate. Usually, in the course of an ordinary transaction, the level of such due care is determined in accordance with the person's position, status, assignment and conditions existing at the time of the transaction. In the case of company directors, however, because of the levels of ability and responsibility required to undertake various corporate affairs, the level of due care expected is higher than that of an ordinary person (according to a 1983 Tokyo Appellate Court decision).

1.3 To whom duties are owed

(a) The company

A company director acts in the nature of a trustee and thus has a duty to perform his obligations based on the principle of mandate and trust set out in the Civil Code. A director must perform his duties in accordance with the provisions of laws, regulations and the company's articles of association. Directors' obligations are owed to the company.

(b) Third parties

Recently in Japan, the idea that companies have social responsibilities has become more commonly recognised. For instance, there is a greater understanding that companies have wider responsibilities to stakeholders such as workers and creditors, even though there is no law setting out specific responsibilities. Ecological considerations are also more widely recognised. Although directors remain primarily responsible to the company, they may also be held liable to third parties, including creditors, employees, contracting parties and any other parties who have suffered damage caused by intentional acts or acts of gross negligence made by the directors in the course of performing their duties (Articles 429(1) and 430).

1.4 Common defences to and exemptions from liability

Usually, directors conduct their defence on the following legal bases.

(a) The business judgement rule

Directors must perform their duties in accordance with the provisions of laws and regulations, the company's articles of association and shareholder resolutions. If they fail in exercising their duty of care and cause any damage to the company, they are responsible for compensating the company for such damage. The problem is judging whether they acted according to their duty of care in each case. This is determined by considering the conditions existing at the time and the ability required of the directors at the time the damage was incurred.

It goes without saying that directors will always be haunted by risk in the performance of their duties, especially in today's complex business environment. In the face of such risks, directors must exercise their professional knowledge and ability so as to honour their obligations to avoid or prevent damage to the company. As in other countries, Japanese law recognises the business judgement rule, under which sound managerial judgement will exempt directors from liability to compensate the company for any damage it suffers. However, if the judgement of directors is considered to have been flawed, they will be responsible for compensating the company for damage it suffered as a result. In this respect, the burden of proof rests with the directors.

(b) ***Exemptions***

In principle, directors' responsibilities for compensating the company may not be waived without the consent of all of shareholders (Articles 120(5) and 424). However, if a director acted in good faith and without gross negligence in the performance of his duties, a partial exemption of the director's obligation to compensate the company may be agreed by special resolution of the general meeting (Article 425). This will also apply when the articles of association authorise the board of directors partially to release the directors from such obligation (Article 369(5)). If the matter is settled before the court, the unanimous consent of all the shareholders will be replaced by a settlement agreed before the court (Article 850(4)).

(c) ***Limitation agreement***

The company may lawfully enter into a contract to limit the liability of external directors, if the articles so allow, on condition that there was no gross negligence on the part of the director in the performance of his duties (Article 427). Further, the limitation amount must be registered with the government's Commercial Registration Office.

2. Who can bring claims

2.1 The company (and its liquidators)

(a) ***Statutory auditor***

If the duties of a company director are not fulfilled, the company can sue him for damages or seek injunctive relief. The legal proceedings may be initiated by the statutory auditor (Article 386(1)) or, in the case of a company without a statutory auditor, by a person designated by the general meeting or the statutory board meeting (Articles 353 and 364). In other jurisdictions, litigation initiated by the company is commenced by writ, but no such formality is required in Japan.

In the event of company liquidation, the directors will be replaced by the liquidator, who will often be appointed by the court. When a company pursues a director for failing in his duties, the general meeting will usually nominate the liquidator to prosecute the litigation on behalf of the company.

If the company has no statutory auditor, the representative director of the company (or, if the company is in the process of liquidation, the liquidator) shall initiate proceedings and represent the company in court.

(b) ***Representative nominated by general meeting***

Anyone nominated as the representative of the company by resolution of the general meeting has the right to bring the case to court (Article 353).

(c) ***Representative nominated by the board***

Where the company's articles of association so allow, anyone nominated as the representative of the company by the board of directors shall also have the right to bring the case to court (Article 364).

2.2 Minority shareholders on behalf of the company

Under Article 847 of the Companies Law, company shareholders have the right to pursue a director in court on behalf of the company. This is because other directors may be in collusion with the director who is being pursued for his abuse of responsibility. In this regard, the meaning of the term 'responsibility' is virtually limitless, covering all direct or indirect damage inflicted on the company as far as it arises from gross negligence or an intentional act of the director. This means that such a suit may be brought against a director even after he has left office. Abuse of this right is prohibited (Article 847(1)); in order to show that the suit has been initiated in good faith, the shareholder as plaintiff may be ordered by the court to provide a security deposit at the request of the defendant director.

2.3 Minority shareholders on their own account

Under the Companies Law, certain rights are specifically vested in minority shareholders (ie, a shareholder or shareholders owning a certain percentage of all issued shares or, as the case may be, of all voting shares of the company). These rights are known as 'minority shareholder rights'. Thus, under Japanese law, the idea of a minority shareholder contrasts with that of a shareholder with one share only.

The Companies Law sets out two possibilities for minority shareholders to pursue a director for damage caused by negligence or an intentional act. First, a shareholder or shareholders holding 3% of all voting shares of the company for at least six months are entitled, as minority shareholders, to bring a case against the defaulting director for his dismissal (Articles 854(1.2) and 479(2.3)). Second, where the statutory board meeting has passed a resolution which partially exempts a director from his obligations, notice of this fact must be given to all shareholders of the company. Where this is the case, minority shareholders holding 3% of all voting shares of the company have the right to object, and such objection has the effect of invalidating the board resolution (Article 426(5)).

It is often the case in closed companies that a representative director with a substantial shareholding in the company abuses his powers and ignores the other shareholders. As a consequence, suits brought by shareholders of closed companies account for a major proportion of all suits initiated by closed companies. Where a director ignores the interests of minority shareholders and his act amounts to a tort, then aside from the remedies discussed above, such director shall be liable to pay compensation.

2.4 Third parties

(a) *Wilful conduct or gross negligence*

Where a director has caused damage to a third party as a result of a deliberate act or gross negligence, he will be responsible for compensating that party (Articles 429(1) and 430). This obligation is set out in the Companies Law in light of the importance of directors' duties and of the need to protect third parties from wilful damage or gross negligence. In such cases the director will be liable for direct and indirect damages. Some have contended that this might be considered a form of tortious liability, but a 1972 Supreme Court decision stated that it is rather a statutory responsibility arising from default of the director's duties.

(b) *Window dressing and falsified accounting documents*

Where directors have made incorrect or untrue statements in the information issued at the time of a new share issue (Articles 203(1), 242(1) and 238(1)), or have knowingly prepared incorrect accounting documents or business reports for the approval of the general meeting, any third party who has suffered damage as a result shall have the right to sue such directors for compensation, based on the theory of torts.

3. Claims culture

3.1 Litigation

(a) *General*

In recent years, shareholders have become increasingly concerned about abuses of directors' powers in the running of companies. Institutional investor activists, in particular, have become influential on the stock market and ordinary shareholders have also become active in their efforts to profit from their shareholdings. As a result of these developments, corporate suits are on the increase. These have included cases involving alleged securities fraud, illegal dividend distributions and other irregularities in which directors have been blamed for allegedly wilful acts or gross negligence, resulting in damage to the company. While the number of cases against directors brought to court by shareholders is not particularly high, the fact that institutional investors have become more vocal about the management of companies has in turn hardened the attitude of other general shareholders, who themselves have become more active in voicing their opinions at general meetings.

Thus, the number of suits against directors is expected to continue to increase, especially among public companies operating in Japan's major cities.

(b) *Recent trends*

There are various forms of litigation which may be directed against directors as defendants and it is not possible to cover them all in detail within the ambit of this chapter. However, there has been a marked increase in litigation arising from corporate takeovers and mergers and acquisitions in recent years. In such litigation, the management often takes various defensive measures, such as issuing new shares, share options and so on. The validity of these measures has always been disputed between the investors and the management of target companies. In fact, in most cases management has failed to persuade the courts in its favour and the courts have determined that the proposed defensive measures constituted unfair attempts to protect the interests of management, and not of the general shareholders. Yet many companies are still planning to set up defence measures to fend off attack from bidders who are eager to expand their businesses.

Another form of litigation which has recently been on the increase is the derivative suit. Again, directors have been attacked by shareholders for a number of reasons in this regard. As even a single shareholder is legally qualified to file a derivative suit, it is not difficult to induce frivolous litigation; but surprisingly, this legal device is rarely abused by shareholders.

3.2 Ability to bring class actions

Currently, there is no law in Japan allowing for class actions. In particular, there is no practice in Japan equivalent to the class action as it exists in the United States.

However, there are two ways to initiate similar types of action. One is a suit which is pleaded by a limited number of plaintiffs who are jointly nominated to act as the appointed plaintiff (*sentei-tojisha*). In this type of litigation, the court's decision will extend to all designated persons (Article 30 of the Civil Procedure Law). The second method is by participating as a party in the litigation. Anyone with a legal interest in the outcome of the litigation may join the suit. There are statutory requirements for such participation (Articles 38, 43 and 52 of the Civil Procedure Law).

3.3 Funding of claims and whether loser pays

In principle, costs and fees must be paid by the person who brings the suit to court. In case of litigation, a fixed legal fee is usually agreed between the law firm and its client. Otherwise, an arrangement based on hourly rates is agreed. Contingency fee arrangements are rare in Japan. The Civil Procedure Law stipulates that, in principle, costs are to be borne by the losing party; but where a partial award is made, the proportion of the costs to be borne by the losing party will be adjusted by decision of the court. Japanese law includes provisions on costs which naturally limit the amount of costs that can be claimed in practice.

In derivative suits, where the shareholder wins the case, the company will reimburse the shareholder's expenses (including attorneys' fees) (Article 852(1)).

3.4 Plaintiffs' bar

In Japan, there is no plaintiffs' bar, except in the area of labour law. There is no group of lawyers with special expertise in the handling of plaintiffs' cases, and no sign of any movement to organise such a group or association within the legal profession. This probably reflects the fact that the Japanese are not litigious and prefer to reach an amicable solution.

3.5 Procedural barriers

In Japan, the right to seek compensation from directors must be exercised within 10 years of the date on which the damage to the shareholders or the company first becomes known (Article 167(1) of the Civil Code). The idea of prescription under Japanese law differs from the statute of limitations in common law practice, in that once the period of prescription expires, the shareholder or company absolutely forfeits any right to claim, even outside legal proceedings. Further, unless a party asserts in court the expiry of the prescription period, the court will not consider the prescription defence.

In principle, any shareholder has the right to seek to pursue a director, without the authorisation of the general shareholders' meeting or any other entity or writ, if the statutory auditors fail to bring an action against the director as a corrective measure within the timeframe stipulated in the Companies Law.

4. Indemnification rights

The purpose of a lawsuit initiated by a shareholder or shareholders against a director or directors for failure to uphold their duties is to remedy the default and accordingly to protect the common interest of all shareholders. Its purpose cannot, therefore, be to pursue personal gain. In other words, the shareholders who initiate proceedings act as plaintiff on behalf of all shareholders of the company.

4.1 When the company can indemnify

From a corporate governance standpoint, the idea of assisting defendant directors by extending a loan to enable them to finance their defence costs is not desirable and should be resisted, irrespective of whether the loan is made prior to or after the commencement of legal proceedings. An exception would be for obviously frivolous cases which are without merit or cases which are motivated by a malicious intent to attack the management. For this reason, most companies will not assist a defendant director, for instance, by way of extending corporate funds to him. As a matter of pure legal interpretation, however, it cannot be ruled out that, depending on the circumstances at the time, a company may be permitted to advance defence costs to a director it is suing in order that he may defend himself. If the defence fails, those costs must be repaid to the company.

However, if the director wins the case, it would be fair for the company to reimburse a reasonable proportion of his defence costs. This is because in such cases the director's defence may reasonably be regarded as part of the performance of his duties as director, and the attendant costs may accordingly be viewed as a necessary expense in the performance of his duties. Article 650(1) of the Civil Code provides a legal basis for such reimbursement: it stipulates that a trustee shall have the right to demand that the trustor reimburse any expenses incurred in honouring his mandate, together with interest.

Regulatory penalties can be indemnified; the costs of dealing with regulatory proceedings are identifiable and may be advanced because, in most companies, regulatory matters are usually delegated to officials of inferior class. Of course, were the matter decided by the director himself, it would be a different story.

With regard to the scope of any compensation, Article 852(1) of the Companies Law stipulates that this shall be a reasonable proportion of the expenses incurred by the director, including attorneys' fees. However, as the party that wins the case can recover such fees by virtue of Article 61 of the Civil Procedure Law - which stipulates that, in principle, costs are to be borne by the losing party - these are not generally included in such expenses.

The above concerns expenses incurred by directors for their defence in legal proceedings. It also applies to the issue of whether a defaulting director can be released from responsibility for compensating the company for damage he has caused.

As regards claims brought by third parties, based on the theory of torts, whether the company advances defence expenses to the director or indemnifies those expenses will be determined in accordance with the factors described above.

As stated in section 1.4, a director may be fully exempted from compensating the company with the consent of all shareholders (Articles 120(5) and 424). If the director acted in good faith and without gross negligence, a partial exemption may be obtained by special resolution of the shareholders' meeting (Article 425), or (if the articles of association so provide) by the board of directors (Article 369(5)).

4.2 Formalities for indemnification

(a) General shareholders' meeting

Article 356(1)(2) stipulates that where a director transacts with the company on his own account, he must disclose the salient facts of the transaction to the general shareholders' meeting and obtain its approval. Requests for a loan to finance a defence to an action fall within the scope of this provision. In practice, however, the chances of such a request succeeding are very slim.

(b) Article 852(1) of the Companies Law

This provision stipulates that where a court judgment favours the director in a derivative suit, the director may request compensation for reasonable expenses incurred. In such cases, the approval of the general meeting is not required and the director has the right to demand payment.

4.3 How indemnification works

Where indemnification of costs is granted to the director, the proposal must first be presented to the general meeting for discussion by the shareholders. The salient facts of the proposed transaction (eg, a loan) must be disclosed to the meeting and approved by ordinary resolution of the majority of shares present (ie, a majority of the issued voting shares).

4.4 What cannot be indemnified

Criminal fines cannot be indemnified; nor can the costs of defending criminal proceedings be advanced by the company – although there is no law specifically prohibiting this course of action.

5. D&O insurance

5.1 Availability of D&O insurance

D&O insurance is available in Japan and is commonly availed of by many companies.

(a) *Who pays premiums*

There has been some debate within the legal profession, from the standpoint of corporate governance, as to whether insurance premiums may be borne by the company. Some hold that in performing his duties a director is always exposed to the risk of mistake or failure, and that taking out insurance cover for directors is thus part of the business of the company in order to retain capable officers. However, this point has not been definitively settled. Some companies refrain from making direct insurance payments to cover directors and instead choose to increase their remuneration by an equivalent sum. This policy may be implemented with the approval of the general shareholders' meeting.

(b) *Coverage*

D&O insurance covers:

- the director's obligation to compensate third parties and associated legal expenses;
- legal expenses incurred by the director in winning a case against the company; and
- the director's obligation to pay the company any amount ordered by the court in an action, along with legal expenses.

However, if the director has profited through his defaulting act or owes an obligation arising from a criminal act, these are not covered.

5.2 Local rules on cover provided under a non-domestic D&O policy

Under the Insurance Business Law, a foreign insurance company is permitted to do business in Japan only through a subsidiary or branch. However, if an overseas parent has global insurance, the local directors are usually covered by such foreign insurance. Accordingly, companies will usually take out insurance with domestic insurance companies, but foreign subsidiaries will be protected by global cover.

Mexico

Daniel Del Rio
Juan José López-de-Silanes
Basham, Ringe y Correa, SC

1. Directors' duties

The board of directors is the corporate body that represents the company. It has the same responsibilities as any legal representative or agent acting on behalf of a third party, plus all other liabilities that the law and the company bylaws may impose.

1.1 Nature of the duties

The management, representation and administration of a company are entrusted to a board of directors or to a sole director. The company bylaws set out the responsibilities of the board, including the powers granted to it. The board of directors is responsible for the daily management of the business of the company and is subordinate only to the general shareholders' meeting. As a result of the distribution of duties within companies, the law introduces a system of responsibilities for directors and officers, for the purpose of creating value for the company and avoiding favouring any particular shareholder or group of shareholders.

(a) Source of duties

Directors' liability is regulated by two principal laws:

- the General Corporations Law, which applies generally to all commercial companies in Mexico; and
- the Securities Law, which applies to companies whose securities are listed with the National Securities Registry.

Also, as a voluntary code, the Code of Improvement of Corporate Practices – drawn up in 1999 by the Mexican Business Coordination Council, a private business group that issues non-binding guidance on good corporate practice in Mexico - establishes guidelines for the performance of directors' duties.

The Securities Law, which became effective on June 28 2006, was intended to boost investors' confidence by introducing greater transparency and implementing mechanisms to provide adequate protection to the public. It also includes good corporate governance principles adopted by international organisations and foreign legislation, specifically the Sarbanes-Oxley Act in the United States. These principles include improvements to the board of directors to unify in a single body the responsibility for establishing the policies and overall strategy of the company, as well as the supervision of the company, leaving the day-to-day running of the company to executives and employees. To do this, the Securities Law designed one or more committees, made up of members of the board and independent directors, to supervise auditing and good corporate governance practices.

(b) *Types of duty*

(i) *Duties imposed by the Securities Law in relation to public companies*

The Securities Law introduced the concepts of diligence and loyalty with respect to directors and officers:

- The duty of diligence is a duty of care to act as if the company's business were the director's own business, and to create value or benefit for the company.
- The duty of loyalty is a duty to subordinate the director's personal interests to the interests of the shareholders and of the company, in order to achieve goals fixed by the company or to obtain benefits for the same.

The Securities Law also provides that the board of directors, as a whole, must act in good faith and in the best interests of the company. In addition, the members of the board of directors must individually discharge their duties in good faith and put the best interests of the company above their own personal interests. Directors will breach the duty of loyalty - and will thus be responsible for any damage caused to the company - when, without legitimate cause and by reason of their position, they obtain a financial benefit for themselves or a third party (including a specific shareholder or group of shareholders) that belongs to the company.

The Securities Law also provides that the members of the board of directors will breach the duty of diligence and will be responsible for damage caused to the company if:

- they do not attend a directors' meeting, with the result that the meeting cannot be held for lack of a quorum, except for justifiable cause;
- they do not disclose to the board of directors information that is necessary for the proper consideration of the matters under discussion, unless the directors in question are legally or contractually obliged to keep the information secret or confidential; or
- they violate duties imposed by law or by the company bylaws.

In addition, the members of the board of directors may not:

- misuse information that is not public knowledge;
- favour a specific shareholder in prejudice to other shareholders;
- take advantage, for their own benefit or for that of a third party, of business opportunities that belong to the company;
- vote at a board meeting on a matter in which they have a conflict of interest;
- fail to reveal a conflict of interest with respect to the company;
- take advantage of the use or enjoyment of company property in violation of the policies approved by the board of directors; or
- approve transactions to be carried out by the company without fulfilling the requirements of the Securities Law.

Pursuant to the Securities Law, the members of the board of directors are entitled to:

- request any information from the company that they consider necessary to adopt decisions;
- require the presence of the appropriate officers and other people, including external auditors, who may contribute to the decisions of the board;
- postpone a board of directors' meeting if one of the directors was not given notice of the meeting or was not given timely notice, or if all members of the board did not receive the same information concerning the agenda for the meeting; and
- discuss and adopt decisions in a meeting at which only board members are present.

(ii) *Duties imposed by the General Corporations Law in relation to all companies*

Directors bear the liabilities inherent in their office and the obligations imposed on them by law and the company bylaws. Directors are thus under a general duty to act in accordance with the company bylaws and applicable law, and to fulfil their duties without conflicts of interest. Otherwise, they can be held responsible for any damage or lost profits incurred by the company.

Directors will be deemed responsible for any such damage and lost profits incurred through breach of the law, negligence or misconduct. Any director with an interest in a transaction that is in conflict with the interests of the company must inform the other directors and refrain from voting on any such matter. If a director contravenes this requirement, he is personally liable for any resulting damages suffered by the company.

The General Corporations Law sets up the following additional specific cases in which directors may be liable for damages and lost profits:

- Directors are individually liable when they default on the proper distribution of the company's dividends.
- Directors are jointly liable with the other members of the board for faulty or deficient keeping of accounts, files, records and registration systems of the company.
- Directors are jointly liable with the other members of the board for failure to account for capital contributions of the company.
- Directors are jointly and severally liable, together with their predecessors, for any irregularities in which the latter may have been involved if, on becoming aware of them, the new directors fail to report them in writing to the statutory auditors.
- Directors are individually liable where they fail to carry out the resolutions adopted by the shareholders' meeting.
- Directors are jointly liable with the other members of the board for any delay in presenting the annual report regarding the business and operations of the company to the corresponding ordinary shareholders' meeting.

Directors may also be jointly and severally liable to the company, and also to third parties, for not creating a 'legal reserve' in accordance with the General Corporations Law.

The company bylaws may include an obligation for the directors to post security for the faithful discharge of their duties. The law imposes liability upon directors and the bylaws of the company may impose additional liability.

While a company is under threat of dissolution, it may not engage in any new business. The directors will be personally, jointly and severally liable to third parties for any new business undertaken.

The General Corporations Law provides that if a new company is not registered in the Public Commercial Register, it will be considered as an irregular company. As a result, any director acting on behalf of the company, as its legal representative, will be jointly and severally liable for any loss or damage caused to third parties.

The General Corporations Law establishes that the administration of a company is entrusted to one or more directors whose appointments are temporary and revocable. The position of member of the board is a personal responsibility and cannot be carried out by a legal representative to whom discharge of the office is delegated. From a tax point of view, directors are jointly and severally liable with the company for any taxes the company fails to pay or withhold, or where the company's assets are insufficient to pay these amounts.

1.2 Standards of care

Pursuant to the Securities Law, directors should manage a public company with the same care that they would exercise in their own personal business.

The Code for the Improvement of Corporate applies to all companies and provides non-binding guidelines concerning the standards of care and conduct expected of directors. Directors should:

- notify the chairman and the other members of the board of directors if a conflict of interest exists, and not participate in any board meetings that consider issues pertaining to the conflict of interest;
- use the assets or services of the company only to fulfil corporate objectives. The company should have clear policies that allow assets to be used for personal matters in exceptional circumstances;
- dedicate the necessary time and attention to their function, attending at least 70% of board meetings;
- keep confidential all information received as a result of their position, especially deliberations that take place during board meetings;
- be informed of any matters discussed at board meetings; and
- assist the board with opinions regarding the analysis of the company's business – all decisions adopted should be duly sustained.

1.3 To whom duties are owed

As a general rule, the directors' duties - and therefore their liability for any wrongful acts – are almost always to the company and its shareholders, except where the law expressly states that a third party injured by such wrongful acts may also be entitled to sue for damages (mainly creditors, employees and the tax authorities).

1.4 Common defences to and exemptions from liability

The Securities Law establishes exemptions from liability as a result of breach of a director's duties of diligence and loyalty. Directors are not personally liable for damages that might result from a decision made in good faith with respect to certain matters, such as:

- carrying out requirements of law or the company bylaws;
- acting on information provided by management, external auditors, independent experts or the corporate practices and audit committee;
- choosing the most appropriate course of action which does not have an adverse impact on the company according to the information available at the time; or
- implementing a decision of a shareholders' meeting that does not break the law.

For the purposes of establishing liability, a distinction is made between conduct arising from poor management and conduct resulting in a personal benefit or a benefit to third parties. If the claimant cannot prove that the director has failed to meet the required standard of conduct, the director is not liable. The Securities Law enshrines the business judgement rule, which provides that directors will not be liable for loss or damage caused to the company as a result of their conduct or decisions when acting in good faith, based on all the information available when they made their decision

The Securities Law also provides that the general shareholders' meeting may limit the liability of directors and officers for breach of their duty of diligence, as long as the conduct in question is not fraudulent, in bad faith or against the law. However, the Securities Law does not allow provisions that exempt the members of the board from liability to be included in the company bylaws. On the other hand, the General Corporations Law provides that directors shall be exempt from liability if they disagreed with a resolution taken by the rest of the board at the time of voting.

2. Who can bring claims

2.1 The company (and its liquidators)

The General Corporations Law provides that a company can file actions against its directors only with the approval of the shareholders' meeting. The shareholders must designate the person who will submit the formal claim against the directors.

The Securities Law provides that a company may bring a claim for damages against a director as a result of a breach of the duty of diligence or loyalty, and that the procedure for bringing actions against a director as a result of a breach of his duties is identical to that established under the General Corporations Law.

Pursuant to commercial insolvency law, if a company becomes bankrupt because of the acts or omissions of its directors, they will be liable and can be sued.

2.2 Minority shareholders on behalf of the company

Pursuant to the General Corporations Law, shareholders holding at least 33% of the share capital of a company may directly bring a civil action against the directors for damages suffered by the company arising from the actions of the directors in question, provided that:

- the action is brought on behalf of the company for the total liability incurred, not just individual shareholder interests; and
- the claimants have not approved a resolution at a shareholders' meeting releasing the directors from liability.

Any proceeds from this action will belong to the company.

On the other hand, the Securities Law provides that shareholders holding at least 15% of the capital stock of a public company may also bring a civil action for damages against directors in accordance with the provisions of the General Corporations Law.

In addition, shareholders may challenge in court resolutions adopted by the shareholders' meeting on matters over which they have a right to vote if they hold 20% of the shares, either individually or in a group.

2.3 Minority shareholders on their own account

The Securities Law provides that shareholders holding 5% or more of the shares with a right to vote, either individually or in a group, including shares with restricted or limited voting rights, may directly bring a civil action against a director within five years for damages they have suffered on their own account as a result of the director's misconduct.

Shareholders may bring an action at any time against the directors, with the prior approval of the general shareholders' meeting and in accordance with the provisions established in the Securities Law or the General Corporations Law, for damages the shareholders have suffered on their own account as a result of the directors' misconduct.

2.4 Third parties

Any third parties which have suffered damage as a result of the directors' misconduct may bring a civil action. The Federal Code of Civil Procedure establishes the procedure for filing an action against directors, or against a company where the directors will be jointly liable.

The tax authorities may also file an action against the directors and the individuals who signed tax records, tax returns and/or other tax-related documents. The violation of tax law may result in criminal liability and/or financial penalties. Pursuant to the Federal Tax Code, directors may be liable if the company:

- has not paid its taxes;
- has not registered as a taxpayer with the Federal Taxpayers Registry;
- has changed its tax domicile without notifying the tax authorities once a tax audit had begun; or
- has not maintained the accounting records required by law, or has hidden or destroyed such records.

Third parties may bring a civil action against directors for any damages and lost profits if the directors acted outside the power of attorney granted to them by the company. Directors may also be criminally liable for acts or omissions carried out on their own account or on behalf the company, as companies are not subject to criminal liability. This type of liability applies only to individuals.

3. Claims culture

3.1 Litigation

In general terms, Mexico does not have as strong a culture of litigation as exists in many other countries, such as the United States, particularly with respect to tort liability (as opposed to liability for breach of contract). This latter concept does exist in Mexico, but is not well developed in practice, and those who have suffered a wrong rarely resort to court proceedings. In addition, where court proceedings in tort are brought, the damages awarded are much lower than those awarded in many other countries. As a result, litigation against directors and executives for breach of their duties is highly unlikely, unless it involves criminal responsibility. There are alternative dispute resolution methods that can be used to avoid litigation, such as negotiation, conciliation, mediation and arbitration.

3.2 Ability to bring class actions

Class actions are not recognised in Mexico.

3.3 Funding of claims and whether loser pays

In litigation, each party generally assumes his own costs and fees. However, when a party litigates in bad faith or without right, he may be asked to pay the attorneys' fees incurred by the other party. Also, the Federal Code of Civil Procedure provides that the losing party must pay the costs, attorneys' fees and legal and miscellaneous expenses of the other party. The judge will determine these.

The Securities Law also provides that the parties in a director's liability action may arrange for payment of the damages incurred by the director, subject to approval by the board. In Mexico, it is possible to enter into a conditional and contingency fee agreement, executed on an equitable basis.

3.4 Plaintiffs' bar

A plaintiff's bar does not exist in Mexico, probably because class actions are not possible.

3.5 Procedural barriers

Pursuant to Article 255 of the Federal Code of Civil Procedure, litigation documentation must include the following information:

- the court where the claim will be submitted;
- the plaintiff's name and domicile;
- the defendant's name and domicile;
- the object claimed;

- a statement of facts in which the plaintiff states his case; and
- the signature of the plaintiff or of a legal representative who has the authority to act on behalf of the plaintiff.

The plaintiff does not require court approval to initiate a civil action against a director.

The Civil Code provides that the statute of limitations for an action for damages is 10 years.

The Securities Law provides that shareholders representing 5% or more of the shares with a right to vote may directly bring a civil action as a result of the directors' misconduct within a period of five years.

4. Indemnification rights

4.1 When the company can indemnify

The Securities Law allows directors to be indemnified against liability for misconduct. There are no specific provisions in the General Corporations Law regarding indemnification for directors.

In fact, the issue of indemnification of company directors is not a common one in Mexico, since in general terms, directors are not normally sued with respect to their conduct.

4.2 Formalities for indemnification

Indemnification of directors is permitted, but no specific regulations govern it. Any provisions concerning indemnification and formalities for the indemnification of directors are set out in the company bylaws. Indemnification agreements as such do not exist, although insurance is possible (see section 5).

4.3 How indemnification works

There are no specific regulations regarding indemnification in Mexico.

4.4 What cannot be indemnified

Directors cannot be indemnified in the event of gross negligence, wilful misconduct, criminal behaviour, conflict of interest or liability to the company itself.

5. D&O insurance

Pursuant to Article 33 of the Securities Law, companies may obtain directors' liability insurance or bonds for members of the board of directors and the general manager to cover the monetary damages or harm they may cause to the company, unless the damage or harm was caused by fraud or the bad faith of the directors or the general manager, or was against the law. The General Corporations Law imposes no restrictions on insurance policies for directors.

5.1 Availability of D&O insurance

A company may purchase insurance for its directors for any loss or damage they may cause.

5.2 Local rules on cover provided under a non-domestic D&O policy

There are no specific rules on non-domestic D&O policies. Thus, there are no restrictions on non-domestic D&O policies or global policies, whereby a parent company obtains a global policy to cover all its directors, including those of any domestic subsidiaries.

Netherlands

Berth Brouwer
Jan ter Meer
Frits van der Woude
Boekel De Nerée

The issue of the personal liability of directors of Dutch companies is a growing concern for directors. Case law in which directors have been found liable has increased in recent decades, as a result of new legislation imposing liability for mismanagement on the part of directors. This legislation, which incorporates the contents of the relevant EU directives, is part of Book 2 of the Civil Code.

This chapter focuses on the liability of directors of companies that are established in the form of a *naamloze vennootschap*[1] (NV) or *besloten vennootschap met beperkte aansprakelijkheid*[2] (BV). The relevant statutory rules are included in Title 1 (which applies to all Dutch legal entities),[3] Title 4 (NV) and Title 5 (BV) of Book 2 of the Civil Code. The statutory duties of the directors of NVs and BVs are almost identical.

In the Netherlands, a distinction is made between managing directors and supervisory directors. Insofar as it is possible to compare these concepts with the relevant the Anglo-Saxon terms, managing directors are the Dutch equivalent of the executive members of the board and supervisory directors may be compared with non-executive members, albeit that the managing directors and supervisory directors each make up a separate body within the company (ie, a two-tier structure). Although supervisory directors are also accountable for their acts and any failure to act in respect of their supervisory duties, this chapter concentrates on the position of managing directors.

Section 2:11 of the Civil Code makes clear that legal entities can be managing directors and, as such, can be found liable. If a legal entity is found liable in its capacity as managing director, all managing directors of this legal entity (at the time liability is incurred) are jointly and severally liable.

1. Directors' duties

1.1 Nature of the duties

(a) Proper performance of management duties

Section 2:9 of the Civil Code states, in general, that each managing director[4] shall

1 Comparable to the English public limited company.
2 Comparable to the English private company limited by shares.
3 New legislation is expected to come into force in 2007 on general partnerships and limited partnerships. This will provide the possibility of opting for corporate personality.
4 According to Sections 2:151 (NV) and 2:261 (BV) of the Civil Code, a supervisory director who performs acts of management pursuant to a provision of the articles of association or a resolution of the general shareholders' meeting shall be liable as if he were a managing director.
5 Including the NV and the BV.

properly perform the duties assigned to him by the legal entity.[5] The duties and liabilities under Section 2:9 of the Civil Code are, in principle, collective. If a matter falls within the scope of responsibility of two or more managing directors, each shall be jointly and severally liable for any shortcoming, unless a director can prove that it was not attributable to him and that he was not negligent in acting to prevent the consequences.

Violating the statutory provisions of the articles of association of the company which are designed to protect the company will, in principle, establish the managing director's liability.[6] This may be the case, for instance, when a managing director represents the company beyond his representative powers or without having obtained the required prior consent.

(b) *Reasonableness and fairness (good faith)*

As with any other person within the organisation of the company, the managing director is obliged to conduct himself in accordance with the requirements of reasonableness and fairness towards the company and those who are involved in the organisation of the company pursuant to statutory law and its articles of association (Section 2:8 of the Civil Code). Resolutions adopted by a management board without observing these good-faith requirements may be annulled, and these may subsequently establish the liability of the managing directors.

(c) *Duties towards third parties; tort*

In principle, a managing director acting on behalf of the company binds only the company and cannot be held personally liable for the fulfilment of the company's obligations.

However, there are important exceptions to this rule. Under Dutch law, anyone who violates the rights of another person, or who acts or fails to act contrary to a statutory duty or a rule of unwritten law pertaining to proper social conduct, can be held liable for the damage suffered by the other person.[7] This also applies to managing directors in relation to third parties.

Important case law in this respect has been established by the Supreme Court. Under certain circumstances the non-fulfilment of obligations of the company towards third parties may constitute a tortious act by the managing director.

In several cases, the Supreme Court has held managing directors liable towards a creditor of the company for non-fulfilment of the obligations of the company. According to this case law, a condition for such liability is that it can be shown that at the time the company entered into the respective agreement, the managing director knew or should have been aware that the company would be unable to fulfil its obligations and would not have the means to pay damages. Even if the managing director in such case did not seek personal advantage, this will not necessarily exempt him from personal liability.

Case law has further shown that a managing director may be liable in person towards a creditor if he prohibits the company from performing an existing

---

6 Dutch Supreme Court, November 29 2002, NJ 2003, 455 (*Schwandt v Berghuizer Papierfabriek*).
7 Section 6:162 of the Civil Code.

obligation. A condition for such liability to exist is that the managing director is personally involved and the default is 'seriously imputable'.

(d) *Specific duties and liabilities in the case of bankruptcy*

Where the company becomes bankrupt, each managing director – and indeed any other person who acted as if he were a managing director[8] – shall be jointly and severally liable for the liabilities of the company to the extent that these cannot be satisfied out of the liquidation of the assets, if:

- the management of the company has been manifestly improper; and
- it is plausible that this was an important cause of the bankruptcy.[9]

The burden of proof is on the trustee.

If there is no proper bookkeeping or if the company has not deposited its annual accounts with the Trade Registry of the Chamber of Commerce in accordance with relevant time limits, then the managing directors are considered to have performed their duties in a manifestly improper way and this (non-)performance is presumed to be an important cause of the bankruptcy of the company.[10] The managing directors must then prove that the (non-)performance did not cause the bankruptcy.

An action may be instituted on the grounds of improper performance of duties only in respect of the duties performed in the three years preceding the bankruptcy.

The bankruptcy trustee also has the power to institute an action on the grounds of a (management) agreement with the managing director or on the grounds of Section 2:9 of the Civil Code.

According to Sections 2:149 (NV) and 2:259 (BV) of the Civil Code, the provisions of Sections 2:138 and 2:248 of the Civil Code apply, *mutatis mutandis*, in respect of the performance of the duties of the supervisory board.

(e) *Non-payment of taxes and social security premiums and pension premiums*

According to Dutch statutory law, a managing director – or any other person who has acted as if he were a managing director – can be held liable for non-payment of certain taxes, social security premiums and pension premiums if the non-payment is due to manifestly improper management by the managing director.[11]

If the financial deficit of the company leading to the non-payment is reported to the appropriate fiscal, social security and pension authorities within 14 days of the failure to pay, the authorities bear the burden of proving manifestly improper management. If, however, the failure to pay is not reported within the requisite timeframe, or is otherwise improperly reported or not reported at all to the authorities, it is presumed that the non-payment is the consequence of manifestly improper management which is imputable to every managing director for a period of three years, with effect from the moment the company defaulted.

---

8 Sections 2:138 sub 7 (NV) and 2:248 sub 7 (BV) of the Civil Code.
9 Sections 2:138 (NV) and 2:248 (BV) of the Civil Code.
10 Sections 2:138 sub 2 (NV) and 2:248 sub 2 (BV) of the Civil Code.
11 Section 36 of the Act on the Collection of Taxes 1990; Section 16 of the Act on Social Security Coordination; Section 23 of the Act on Compulsory Participation in an Industry Level Pension Fund 2000.

(f) Misleading accounts

If third parties sustain any loss by publication of annual accounts, interim figures or annual reports, the managing directors shall be jointly and severally liable towards these third parties to the extent that the accounts, figures or reports misrepresent the condition of the company.[12]

(g) Incorporation of the company

Unless explicitly agreed otherwise, any person acting on behalf of a company in the process of incorporation is jointly and severally liable towards third parties for transactions performed on behalf of the company in the period prior to the passing of the notarial deed of incorporation, until the company has ratified such transaction after its incorporation.[13] Ratification by the company may take place explicitly or implicitly.

If, after ratification, the corporation fails to perform such obligations, the persons who acted on behalf of the company are jointly and severally liable if they knew or ought to have known that the company would be unable to comply with these obligations. Knowledge of the company's inability to comply will be implied if the company is declared bankrupt within one year of incorporation.

Ratification on behalf of the company after its incorporation is usually done by the managing directors. If a managing director is not sufficiently diligent when ratifying pre-incorporation transactions, he may be held liable by the company, the trustee or third parties.[14]

(h) Prior to registration/capital payments

The managing directors shall be jointly and severally liable for legal acts binding the company until:

- the company is duly registered with the Trade Registry of the Chamber of Commerce;[15]
- an amount equal to at least the minimum capital is paid up;[16] and
- at least one-quarter of the nominal value of the share capital issued at incorporation is paid up.[17]

(i) Acquisition by the company of its own shares

The acquisition by the company of its own shares is strictly limited. For instance, an NV or a BV may not acquire for consideration more than 10% or 50% respectively of the issued shares of its share capital. An acquisition in breach of these rules can lead to the managing directors being jointly and severally liable towards a *bona fide* transferor who sustains a loss as a result of the nullity of such transaction.[18]

12 Sections 2:139 (NV) 2:249 (BV) of the Civil Code.
13 Sections 2:93 and 2:203 (BV) of the Civil Code.
14 In accordance with Section 2:9, Sections 2:138 (NV) and 2:248 (BV) respectively, and Section 6:162 of the Civil Code.
15 For this reason, ratification of pre-incorporation transactions should take place only after these requirements have been fulfilled.
16 Currently, €45,000 for an NV and €18,000 for a BV.
17 Sections 2:69 sub 2 (NV) and 2:180 sub 2 (BV) of the Civil Code.
18 Sections 2:97a (NV) and 2:207a (BV) of the Civil Code.

(j) Acquisition or holding of shares in a parent company

The acquisition or holding of shares by a company in its parent company is limited under Dutch law. Managing directors can be held jointly and severally liable in case of breach of the respective provisions.[19]

(k) Criminal offences

Both a company and its managing director(s) can commit criminal offences. A criminal offence committed by a company can also impose criminal liability on the managing director who ordered the respective act or who was in fact in charge of this act.[20] The concept of 'being in charge of committing the criminal offences by the company' has been extended in Dutch case law. Not only does the giving of instructions or orders to commit offences impose a criminal liability on the managing director, but also the fact of being aware of the offences without interfering or stopping them.

1.2 Standards of care

In principle, all duties imposed on a managing director of a company are based on statutory provisions,[21] the company's articles of association and its bylaws and resolutions. Some of the statutory duties are precisely defined (see under sections 1.1(g) to 1.1(j)); most are further defined in case law (eg, duties indicated under sections 1.1(a) to 1.1(f)).

It is generally accepted in legal commentaries and in case law that a managing director can be held liable by the company only if his conduct is considered to constitute a 'seriously imputable' default with respect to the performance of his duties under Section 9 of the Civil Code. When considering the question of a 'seriously imputable default', the court will take into account all relevant circumstances of the matter, in view of the insight and care one may expect from a diligent acting managing director who has the skills required for his task.[22]

Mistakes or misjudgements by a managing director do not necessarily give rise to liability to third parties based on tort (see section 1.1(c)). Case law indicates that liability to third parties requires that the conduct of the managing director be sufficiently (ie, seriously) imputable.

If a company is bankrupt, managing directors may be held liable if manifestly improper management has been established (see under sections 1.1(d) and (e)). Although there is no statutory definition of 'manifestly improper management', the following examples (given by the minister of justice on the occasion of the parliamentary hearing on the respective statutory rules) may be mentioned:

- wilful default;
- gross negligence; and
- wilful neglect of essential management duties - for example, duties of bookkeeping and administration.

---

19 Sections 2:98d (NV) and 2:207d (BV) of the Civil Code.
20 Section 51 of the Criminal Code.
21 See the statutory sections indicated under section 1.1.
22 Supreme Court, January 10 1997, NJ 1997, 360 (*Staleman v Van der Ven*).

A Supreme Court ruling states that improper management exists only if "no reasonably thinking director would have acted in this way under the same circumstances".[23]

The duties referred to under sections 1.1(f) and 1.1(h) to 1.1(i) are in general to be considered as duties of care. Acting contrary to these duties implies negligence.

1.3 To whom the duties are owed

The duties referred to under section 1.1(a) (proper performance of management duties) are owed to the company. Duties mentioned under section 1.1(b) (good faith) are owed to the company and any other person within its organisation. A managing director must observe duties mentioned under sections 1.1(c) (tort), 1.1(f) (misleading accounts), 1.1(g) (incorporation), 1.1(h) (acts prior to registration/capital contribution) and 1.1(i) (acquisition of shares) towards third parties. The duties and liabilities included under section 1.1(d) (bankruptcy) are owed to the joint creditors. Duties mentioned under section 1.1(e) (non-payment of taxes and premiums) are to be observed towards the respective tax, social security and pension authorities.

1.4 Common defences to and exemptions from liability

A defence generally applied by managing directors against whom claims are instituted aims to prove that, taking all circumstances into account, their conduct was not negligent or imputable to the extent required to establish liability. Obviously, the level of damage claimed and the causal relation between the breach of duty and the damage incurred are usually disputed.

It is apparent from statutory and case law that there are specific exemptions for certain duties.

In respect of claims based on (manifestly) improper management (see under sections 1.1(c) and (d)), the managing director can escape liability if he proves that the improper performance by the management board is not attributable to him and that he was not negligent in acting to prevent the consequences thereof.[24]

It is possible for the general shareholders' meeting to absolve the managing director of his responsibility towards the company. Such a *décharge* will, if explicitly given, in principle prevent the managing director from being held liable towards the company. However, a *décharge* is of relevance only for matters that are apparent from the (relevant) annual accounts or the minutes of the general shareholders' meeting in the relevant period. A *décharge* can be declared null and void by the court if its granting is in violation of the principles of reasonableness and fairness. An action based on manifestly improper management (see section 1.1(d)) shall not be barred by a discharge granted to a director.[25]

The amount for which the managing directors can be held liable for manifestly improper management (see section 1.1(d)) can be reduced by the court, taking into account the seriousness of the manifestly improper performance of his duties by the

---

23 Supreme Court, June 7 1996, NJ 1996, 695 (*Drankenhandel Van Zoolingen*) and Supreme Court January 10 1997, NJ 1997/360.

24 Section 2:9, respectively 2:138 sub 3 (NV) and 2:248 sub 3 (BV) of the Civil Code.

25 Sections 2:138 sub 6 (NV) and 2:248 sub 6 (BV) of the Civil Code.

managing director.[26]

If a managing director is held liable by the competent tax, social security or pension authorities in the event that a failure to pay has not been reported in time (see section 1.1(e)), rebuttal will be possible only if he can persuasively argue that the company's failure to notify the authorities is not attributable to him. As a rule, this is difficult to prove.

A managing director is not liable for a misleading presentation of annual accounts or interim figures (see section 1.1(f)), if he can prove that the misrepresentation is not attributable to him - for example, because he refused to sign the accounts. It is not sufficient for the managing director simply to state that he relied on the opinion of an accountant or another adviser with regard to the respective documents.

2. Who can bring claims

2.1 The company (and its trustee in bankruptcy)

As a main rule, a company may be represented towards third parties or in court proceedings by its management board or, subject to the articles of association, by one or more managing directors. If a managing director is (possibly) liable towards the company, it is obvious that the interests of the managing director are contrary to those of the company.

In this situation, there are several possibilities for instituting proceedings against the managing director. These apply regardless of the nature of the claim.

The most obvious approach is to dismiss the managing director. Subsequently, the remaining (or newly appointed) managing board can institute an action against the dismissed managing director. A resolution backed by the requisite majority in favour of such dismissal must be achieved at the general shareholders' meeting.[27] Further, there must be no conflict of interest between the company and the remaining/newly appointed managing board members when instituting an action against the dismissed managing director. The same applies, *mutatis mutandis*, for suspending the managing director.

If the company has a supervisory board,[28] another approach is for the supervisory directors to institute proceedings on behalf of the company against the managing director under fire. The power to represent the company follows from the inherent conflict of interest between the company and the managing director involved.[29]

In any event, the general shareholders' meeting is entitled to designate one or more persons to institute proceedings on behalf of the company.[30] Obviously, adopting a resolution to this end requires the requisite majority of votes at the general shareholders' meeting. If such majority is available, it is usually possible to

26 Sections 2:138 sub 4 (NV) and 2:248 sub 4 (BV) of the Civil Code.

27 In large companies, the supervisory board is entitled to dismiss the managing director after consultation with the general shareholders' meeting.

28 Dutch private companies must have a management board. A supervisory board is mandatory for large companies and optional for other companies.

29 Sections 2:146 (NV) and 2:256 (BV) of the Civil Code.

30 Sections 2:146 (NV) and 2:256 (BV) of the Civil Code.

dismiss the managing director as well.

In the event of bankruptcy, the trustee is entitled to start legal proceedings against a managing director on behalf of the company or the joint creditors.

2.2 Minority shareholders on behalf of the company

Individual shareholders cannot institute an action on behalf of the company against a managing director. An exception to this rule is the appointment of one or more minority shareholders by the general shareholders' meeting (see section 2.1).

Under certain conditions, one or more minority shareholders (and holders of depositary receipts) are entitled to request the Enterprise Chamber of the Amsterdam Court of Appeal to order an inquiry against the company. This appears to be a useful alternative if the division of (voting) power prevents the company from instituting proceedings against a managing director (see section 2.4).

2.3 Shareholders on their own account

It follows from a Supreme Court decision of December 2 1994 (*Poot/ABP*)[31] that if a third party causes damage to a company, only the company is allowed to claim compensation, and not its shareholders. This applies for both minority and majority shareholders. It is assumed that this case law also applies if the third party is a managing director. Therefore, shareholders have no claim for a decrease in the value of their shares. Even the fact that the company does not recover damages does not imply that a shareholder can claim from the managing director. An exception to this rule may be allowed if the managing director's negligence violated the interest of a particular shareholder. This may be the case when a managing director's unlawful act against the company intentionally aims to harm a particular shareholder.

2.4 Right of inquiry

Dutch statutory law[32] provides that, upon the request of those authorised to do so, the Enterprise Chamber of the Amsterdam Court of Appeal may appoint one or more persons to undertake an inquiry into the policy and conduct of business of a legal person, either as a whole or in respect of a part thereof, or in respect of a specific period.[33] Those who are authorised are, in the case of an NV or a BV:

- one or more holders of shares or depositary receipts issued for shares who, solely or jointly, represent at least 10% of the issued share capital, or who are entitled to an amount in shares, or depositary receipts issued therefore, with a nominal value of at least €225,000 or such lesser amount as is provided by the company's articles of association;[34]
- those authorised to do so by the company's articles of association or under an agreement with the company;[35] or
- an association of employees which has among its members persons working

31 Supreme Court, December 2 1994, NJ 1995, 288.
32 Sections 2:345 *et seq.* of the Civil Code.
33 The policy and conduct of business of a legal person shall include the policy and conduct of business of a limited partnership, or a general partnership of which the legal person is a fully liable partner.
34 Section 2:346 sub b of the Civil Code.

for the enterprise and which has had full legal capacity for at least two years, provided that its object under its articles of association is to promote the interests of its members as employees and it is active in such capacity in the sector of business or in the enterprise.[36]

The public prosecutor of the Amsterdam Court of Appeal is also authorised to file a request where it believes the public interest is at stake.

The Enterprise Chamber will grant the request only if there appear well-founded reasons to doubt the appropriateness of the policy and conduct of business of the company.[37] Where this is the case, the Enterprise Chamber will nominate one or more persons to carry out the investigation as it is ordered. The persons appointed by the Enterprise Chamber will be entitled to examine such books and records of the company as they consider necessary for the proper performance of their duties. The assets of the company must be shown to them upon request. The managing director(s), the members of the supervisory board, if any, and the employees of the company shall, on request, be obliged to provide all such information as is necessary to carry out the inquiry. The same duty shall be owed by persons who were managing directors or members of the supervisory board of the legal person or partnership, or who were employees thereof during the period to which the inquiry relates.[38]

The Enterprise Chamber can forcefully intervene in the affairs of a company by means of a relatively quick procedure. For instance, if the Enterprise Chamber is of the opinion that there are sound reasons to doubt whether the company's policy has been appropriate, it can in principle impose any immediate provisional measure it deems necessary in view of the company's (poor) situation.[39] Such immediate measures may include:

- suspension of managing directors or supervisory directors;
- temporary appointment of a supervisory director with special powers;
- suspension of voting rights;
- suspension of pre-emptive rights;
- order of a standstill;
- suspension of resolutions of the management board; and
- prohibition against entering into new agreements.

If, on the conclusion of the inquiry, misconduct or mismanagement is deemed to have taken place, the Enterprise Chamber may, upon request of the initial applicants, issue any one or more orders.[40] These might include:

- the suspension or annulment of a resolution of the managing directors, the supervisory board, the general meeting of shareholders or of any other constituent body of the company;
- the suspension or dismissal of one or more directors or supervisory board

35 Section 2:346 sub c of the Civil Code.
36 Section 2:347 of the Civil Code.
37 Section 2:350 of the Civil Code.
38 Section 2:351 of the Civil Code.
39 Section 2:249a of the Civil Code.
40 Section 2:355 of the Civil Code.

members;

- the temporary appointment of one or more directors or supervisory board members; or
- the temporary derogation from such provisions in the articles of association of the company as shall be specified by the Enterprise Chamber.[41]

A conclusion that misconduct or mismanagement has occurred does not imply or establish the liability of the managing director or the supervisory board members; but a judgment that mismanagement has taken place on the part of the company is binding on those who were represented in the inquiry proceedings. The Supreme Court[42] has ruled that the facts established during inquiry proceedings are not binding in any subsequent proceedings regarding the liability of managing directors or supervisory board members. However, a judgment of the Enterprise Chamber establishing misconduct or mismanagement may be used as evidence in the court which then has to pass judgment as to liability.

2.5 Third parties

An action against a managing director by a third party is possible. This applies especially in those circumstances set out under sections 1.1(c) (tort), 1.1(f) (misleading accounts), 1.1(g) (incorporation), 1.1(h) (acts prior to registration/capital contribution) and 1.1(j) (acquisition of shares).

In addition, a third party has the right to institute inquiry proceedings (see above) if this right is granted to him by the company.

3. Claims culture

3.1 Litigation

The Netherlands does not have a litigation culture in the traditional sense, compared with the United States, for example. In the last decade or so, however, there has been an increasing tendency to demand financial compensation in the form of damages. This tendency is strengthened by discussions regarding corporate governance and has been influenced by Enron, World Online, Ahold and other high-profile corporate scandals. Shareholder activism seems to have increased in recent years, not least because of hedge funds' optimal use of their shareholders' rights. These developments have also had an impact in the area of directors' liability. The courts are more willing to accept liability than before, but are still reluctant to award immense amounts of compensation.

3.2 Ability to bring class actions

(a) Class action

Dutch procedural law does not recognise the concept of a 'class action' as known in

41 Section 2:356 of the Civil Code.
42 Supreme Court, April 8 2005, NJ 2006, 443.

the United States, where damages can be claimed by a group of similarly situated parties in class action proceedings.

(b) *Collective action*

A collective action[43] may be brought by an association or a foundation, but limited to the protection of the interest of other persons as described in the bylaws of these entities. The action must have the aim of protecting groups of persons who have a common interest. An action instituted by an association or a foundation cannot include a demand for financial compensation for damage incurred. It is only the individual claimant who can do so, mainly because of the particulars of the individual claim. A person who does not wish to be bound by the decision of the court can oppose the effect of the decision, unless the nature of the decision implies that its effect cannot be excluded. Since its introduction into Dutch law, an increasing number of high-profile cases have been brought before the courts using the collective action facility.

(c) *Settlement agreements declared binding on third parties*

A contract for compensation for damage caused by an event or events, which is entered into by a foundation or association with one or more other parties who undertake thereby to compensate this damage, may, upon the joint request of the parties to the contract, be declared binding by the court in favour of persons to whom the damage has been caused, provided that the foundation or association, by virtue of its articles of association, represents the interests of such persons.[44] The contract must[45] include:

- a description of the group or groups of persons in whose favour the contract has been entered into, according to the nature and the seriousness of their damage;
- a description (which must be as accurate as possible) of the number of persons belonging to the group or groups; and
- the level of compensation to be awarded to the members of the group or groups.

The main reason[46] for the court to disallow the request is that the amount of compensation awarded is not reasonable, taking into account the extent of the damage, the ease and speed with which the compensation may be obtained and the possible causes of the damage. It may also be disallowed on the grounds that the foundation or association that entered into the agreement is not sufficiently representative of the interests of those in whose favour the contract has been concluded, or because the group of persons in whose favour the contract has been concluded is not sufficiently large to justify a declaration to make the contract binding.

As soon as the request to declare the contract binding has been irrevocably

---

43 Section 3:305a of the Civil Code.
44 Section 7:907 sub 1 of the Civil Code.
45 Section 7:907 sub 2 of the Civil Code.
46 Section 7:907 sub 3 of the Civil Code.

granted, the contract shall have, as between the parties and those entitled to compensation, the effects of a contract of settlement, to which each of those so entitled shall be deemed to be a party.[47] The declaration shall have no effect upon a person entitled to compensation who, within a period to be determined by the court, has given notification that he does not intend to be bound.[48] A person entitled to compensation who, upon the announcement of the contract being binding, could not be aware of the damage is not bound by the declaration if, after the damage has become known, he has given notification that he does not intend to be bound.[49]

3.3 Funding of claims and whether the loser pays

The bringing of claims is usually funded by the litigating party itself. Insurance to cover legal fees is possible. Legal assistance insurance always covers legal costs and most policies allow a lawyer chosen by the insured party. There is no legal proscription which prohibits third parties from funding litigation.

As a general rule, a plaintiff must be represented by a lawyer in court proceedings. Dutch lawyers generally submit bills based on hourly rates in commercial litigation. It is possible to agree fee arrangements tailored to the particular case, such as a conditional fee arrangement or a contingency fee arrangement, but not for the entire amount of the fee. The court fees to be paid by plaintiffs and defendants amount to approximately €6,000 at the maximum.

The losing party does not pay the other party's legal costs in full, but only a limited and fixed amount. The legal costs to be paid consist of a small part of the attorneys' fee and disbursements such as court fees, bailiff's costs and disbursed costs of witnesses or experts. With respect to attorneys' fees, the court will award an amount based on a 'liquidation tariff', which varies from approximately €400 to €3,500 depending on the monetary value of the case. The costs of court-appointed experts are usually borne by the losing party.

In some cases, the court can also decide to compensate legal costs wholly or partially between the parties, which means that the court decides that each party must bear its own costs, or that the unsuccessful party need only pay a smaller part of the legal costs of the other party than indicated above. This depends on the extent to which a party has won the case, in the opinion of the court.

3.4 Plaintiffs' bar

In the Netherlands, the concept of a plaintiffs' bar is unknown. Sometimes a law firm advertises with respect to a particular case to bring together a number of claimants for collective action. In general, law firms in the Netherlands represent claimants as well as defendants.

3.5 Procedural barriers

The procedural barriers to the bringing of claims are low, especially since the losing party pays only a limited part of the winning party's legal costs. In general,

47 Section 7:908 sub 1 of the Civil Code.
48 Section 7:908 sub 2 of the Civil Code.
49 Section 7:908 sub 3 of the Civil Code.

representation by a lawyer is mandatory. Court approval is not required.

The initiation of proceedings by a company against its managing director generally requires the involvement of the general shareholders' meeting and/or the supervisory directors (see section 2.1). The articles of association may include additional conditions.

The law on limitation periods is set out in the Civil Code. For most claims, the limitation period is five years from the date of inception of the cause of action.[50] Generally, a claim expires after 20 years.[51]

4. Indemnification rights

4.1 When the company can indemnify

It is generally assumed that Dutch law allows the company to indemnify the managing director for claims brought against him by third parties, taking into account certain limitations (see section 4.4). In respect of claims by the company, the company may undertake to indemnify the (legal) costs of defending the claim, albeit that if the claim is awarded the costs are to be borne by the managing director himself and repayment must take place (see section 4.4).

4.2 Formalities for indemnification

There are no statutory provisions or court rulings on whether a company may indemnify its managing director from claims. Indemnification rights can be part of the agreement between the company and the managing director, can be agreed under a separate agreement or may follow from the company bylaws.

4.3 How indemnification works

If a claim is instituted against a managing director which falls within the scope of the indemnity, the managing director can claim against the company in accordance with the terms of the indemnity. If the company does not voluntarily perform its obligations, the managing director can begin legal proceedings to enforce performance. In that case, the managing director must fund both proceedings upfront, in spite of the indemnity.

4.4 What cannot be indemnified

It seems that there is a common understanding in the legal literature that upfront indemnification of the managing director by the company is not possible for liability towards the company resulting from 'seriously imputable defaults'. Such indemnity would contravene compulsory statutory law on managing directors' duties towards the company.[52] An indemnity for less serious default is of no use, since under those circumstances a managing director is not liable towards the company. An indemnity afterwards (*décharge*) is possible. Case law shows, however, that a *décharge* cannot always be upheld.[53]

---

50 Sections 3:307 to 3:310 of the Civil Code.
51 Section 3:306 of the Civil Code.
52 Section 2:9 of the Civil Code, see under section 1.1(a).

In general, the indemnification relates to damages payable to third parties and defence costs resulting from (alleged) acts or omissions in the execution of his duties. If the acts resulting in liability towards third parties also constitute a seriously imputable default towards the company, then in principle the managing director will not benefit from the indemnity.

Dutch law provides that a third party, like a shareholder, can provide the managing director with an indemnity regarding claims from the company or third parties. However, an indemnity cannot protect a managing director for damage caused deliberately or by gross negligence. If, for instance, a fine or penalty is imposed which is attributable to the managing director's intent, then indemnification is not possible.

5. D&O insurance

5.1 Availability of D&O insurance

D&O insurance is widely available in the Netherlands and is offered by national and international operating insurers. Dutch law sets out no particular rules on D&O insurance or rules that apply to non-domestic policies. The rules governing this form of insurance are the general civil rules and those on insurance contracts (part of Book 7 of Title 17 of the Civil Code).

Almost all Dutch insurers provide coverage for internal liability (claims from the company), as well as for third-party claims (external liability). There are substantial limits available covering losses as well as defence costs, and a deductible is not usually applicable.

5.2 Local rules on cover provided under a non-domestic D&O policy

On January 1 2007 the Financial Supervision Act came into force and replaced the Act on the Supervision of the Insurance Industry 1993. The Netherlands Bank (DNB) has statutory powers to intervene in relation to insurers that are not in compliance with the Financial Supervision Act.

Non-domestic insurers are, in general, not allowed to provide D&O policies to Dutch companies covering the liability of directors and officers without the prior consent of the DNB. The general rule is that if the insurer is domiciled in an EU member state and has permission from its supervisory authority, it must notify its supervisory authority of its intention to provide policies in another member state. The domestic supervisory authority of the insurer will notify the DNB, which will subsequently contact the insurer.[54] Where the insurer is not domiciled in an EU member state, it must notify the DNB. That insurer must also comply with Dutch regulatory rules, such as with regard to the solvency of the insurer.[55]

If the D&O risk is located in the Netherlands and coverage is provided under a policy by a non-domestic insurer, Dutch regulatory rules will apply. Where, for instance, the parent company of a Dutch subsidiary obtains a global policy from a

---

53 See section 1.4 on *décharge*.
54 Section 2:34 of the Financial Supervision Act.
55 Section 2:45 of the Financial Supervision Act.

non-domestic insurer covering the Dutch subsidiary, a notification to the DNB or compliance with Dutch regulatory rules will be applicable, as mentioned above.

Poland

Michał Barłowski
Wardyński & Partners spk

1. Directors' duties

1.1 Nature of the duties

The management board is the compulsory executive body of a company. Its responsibilities include the day-to-day internal management and organisation of the company. It is also entitled to act externally on the company's behalf, including making statements in the name of the company. As a result, the board has both an organisational and a representative capacity. The rule that specifically describes the board's position in relation to the company's other official bodies is set out in the Commercial Companies Code, in Article 201(1) for limited liability companies and Article 368(1) for joint stock companies. The board must act and represent the company in accordance with the code.

The running of a company by the management board involves all legal and non-legal matters pursued with the aim of realising the company's goals. There is no limit to the scope of company business that may be undertaken by the management board, including atypical activities when the need arises. The activities of the management board relating to the administration and running of a company's affairs are regulated by Article 208 of the code. However, the provisions of this article may be modified without restriction in the company's articles of association. In accordance with this provision, each management board member can, without prior resolution, conduct matters that are within the scope of the company's ordinary affairs. However, if prior to the conclusion of any such matter at least one of the remaining members of the management board raises an objection, a resolution of the management board is required to continue the activity. A resolution is also required where the matter falls outside the scope of the company's ordinary business activity.

Management board resolutions are adopted by absolute majority of votes, regardless of the number of board members actually present, but on the condition that all board members have been duly notified of the meeting. Different provisions apply to proxies. The appointment of a proxy requires the consent of all management board members, although the proxy can be dismissed by any single board member acting independently.

Any action effected by the management board that requires the prior consent of the appropriate body of the company is regulated by Article 17 of the code. This stipulates that if the law requires a resolution of the shareholders or of the supervisory board, any action effected without such resolution shall be invalid. Consent may be given before or after the company makes a representation, but no later than two months from the date on which the representation was made. The confirmation shall be retrospective as at the date of the action.

Where no consent is required by law, the consequences are different in the case of acts effected without the consent of the company's appropriate body. However, if consent is required under the articles of association or the company statute, the act shall be valid; this does not exclude the liability of members of the management board towards the company for breaches of the articles of association or statute.

The authority of the management board members to represent the company depends on the company's individual arrangements. If a board has a number of members, its representation is defined in the articles of association. Otherwise, in order to make statements on the company's behalf, two board members must act jointly; or alternatively one member and a proxy must act jointly (Article 205(l) of the code). However, for day-to-day representations, such as the acceptance by the company of various statements, declarations and other representations addressed to it, it is enough to serve a written communication or to serve the representation on a single member of the management board or on a proxy (Articles 205(2) and 373(2) of the code).

The rights of a member of the management board to act on behalf of the company and to represent it are extensive and concern all matters relating to court proceedings, as well as other matters. This right cannot lawfully be restricted with respect to third parties (Articles 204 and 372 of the code).

Management board members are obliged to act with due care and in good faith, demonstrating trust, honesty and loyalty in relation to the company. A provision in the code stipulates that a board member cannot, without the company's consent:

- engage in competitive business or participate in a competing company;
- serve as a member of a governing body of a competing company; or
- participate in another legal entity as a member of its governing board.

This ban also applies to participating in a competing company in which the board member holds at least 10% of that company's shares or has the right to appoint one or more members to its management board.

In Polish capital companies, alongside a management board it is also common to have a supervisory board. It is not compulsory for a Polish limited liability company to set up a supervisory board. However, Article 213(2) of the code states that a supervisory body should be instituted if the capital of the limited liability company exceeds PLN500,000 and there are more than 25 shareholders.

A supervisory board is obligatory in a Polish joint stock company.

The liability of supervisory board members is not regulated by separate legal regulations. In particular, there are no provisions on this matter in the Commercial Companies Code. However, it should not be inferred that a supervisory board has no liabilities for actions undertaken in the company. All cases are considered on their individual merits, since Polish case law on the question of the liability of supervisory board members is still in its infancy.

1.2 Standards of care

There are no provisions in the Commercial Companies Code or in other legislation stating that a director is required to meet particular standards in terms of diligence, skill or expertise in order to carry out the duties of a director.

Customarily, Polish companies have high requirements of candidates for management positions, in terms of education, managerial experience and success achieved. However, this results only from the code of good corporate practices in capital companies. The issue of the requirements demanded of managers continues to be neglected by the Polish legislature. Nevertheless, an urgent need to resolve this problem has been identified by organisations operating in Poland, with the aim of promoting high standards of corporate governance, as well as high ethical and moral standards among entrepreneurs, directors, shareholders and supervisory board members.

1.3 To whom duties are owed

The most significant issue for management board members is that their duties are owed to the company. Under Polish law and general principles of good commercial practice, they are required to act in the company's best interest and represent the company. Board members must not directly represent any shareholder or influence the company on any individual shareholder's behalf. Rather, they should act in the interests of all shareholders by ensuring that the business makes the highest profits possible.

Furthermore, the new Article 375 of the Commercial Companies Code, which relates to joint stock companies, definitively excludes the shareholders' meeting from issuing binding orders to the management board. On one hand, this provision is intended to ensure the independence of the management board in conducting the company's affairs; on the other, it makes it more practical to assign liability for certain actions (or for failure to act).

However, the fact that board members act on behalf of and represent the company does not permit them to cause harm to the company's creditors, employees or business partners on the pretext of acting in the company's best interest.

1.4 Common defences to and exemptions from liability

The most important issues relating to the liability of management board members are regulated by Articles 291, 292, 293, 299, 479, 480 and 483 of the Commercial Companies Code.

Management board members must provide a statement to the registration court that contributions have been fully made. Articles 291 and 479 concern the liability of management board members towards a company's creditors in cases where they have provided false statements regarding contributions to cover share capital.

Three conditions must be satisfied for liability under Articles 291 and 479 to apply. The first, basic condition for liability is that board members have given false statements – for example, stating that all contributions have been made when the share capital is not actually fully paid up. The second condition is that the actions of the management board are culpable. Liability may arise both from intentional actions and from inadvertent actions, such as negligence. A third condition for liability relates to the three-year limitation period from registration of the company or registration of an increase in its share capital at the registration court; that is, creditors must raise claims within three years of the registration date, which is defined as the day on which data is submitted to the court's IT system.

Polish case law takes the firm view that the responsibility of management board members for making false statements is not a compensatory liability.

Articles 292 and 480 of the code concern the liability of management board members to the company for damage caused by illegal actions taken while setting up the company. This liability is compensatory, which means that establishing the occurrence of harm is a precondition for the company raising a claim and the magnitude of the harm determines the size of the claim.

What is remarkable is that this provision can be used to bring claims against persons other than the management board members who directly participated in setting up the company.

The management board member's culpable actions (acts or omissions of duty which are contrary to the law or the company's articles of association) and the associated damage to the company are the basis of the member's liability. This matter is regulated in Articles 293(1) and 48 of the code. Once again, the occurrence of damage is a prerequisite of liability and also a measure of its size. Since it presumes guilt, the above provision means that particular persons are burdened with having to prove their innocence, while the company, apart from the duty of disclosing the damage, is also obliged to prove a causal relationship between that individual's actions and the harm incurred. This responsibility is joint and several where a number of persons are involved in the occurrence of the damage.

Article 299 of the code regulates the liability of management board members for the company's obligations when it is not possible to enforce claims from the company's assets. Naturally, the impossibility of satisfying creditors' claims from the capital of the company causes harm to the creditors. Therefore, it is crucial, with regard to the extent of the liability of the person who is not a debtor (the debtor is the company and not the management board member), to define the circumstances that allow a claim to be pursued against them. According to the code, there are three such circumstances:

- the existence of an unsatisfied claim against the company;
- the impossibility of enforcing claims from the company's assets (ie, from the debtor's assets); and
- the person's status as a management board member.

The creditor need prove only these circumstances. A separate issue is that the management board member can extricate himself from liability by proving – according to Article 299(2) – that the petition for a declaration of bankruptcy was filed or arrangement proceedings were instituted within the proper time.

Pursuant to Article 296 of the code, a management board member is not released from responsibility, even when a shareholders' meeting has exonerated him. This provision excludes the possibility of protecting persons who are responsible for causing damage to the firm by means of a resolution granting exoneration, as well as of abandoning claims for compensation, in two cases:

- the initiation of a suit by a shareholder on the basis of Article 295 of the code (a situation described in section 2.3); and
- the firm's bankruptcy (or, more formally, the declaration of bankruptcy by a court).

Conversely, one can draw the conclusion that in all other cases, it is possible to defend a director effectively by means of exoneration or if the company abandons its claims. This will concern all situations in which the firm itself raises compensatory claims.

2. Who can bring claims

2.1 The company (and its liquidators)

If a management board member illegally breaks company formation regulations and thereby causes the company harm, the company will normally bring claims against that person by way of a decision of the management board. The offending person is then obliged to repair the harm caused to the company. However, the company must first prove the existence of circumstances from which the damage arose.

A company may also make claims against a board member who caused harm to the company during its activities by acts which are contrary either to law or to the company's articles of association/statute. Here again we are faced with liability of a compensatory nature for harm caused which the board member is obliged to repair. Again, however, the company must demonstrate a causal relationship between the board member's actions and the existence of the harm.

A company may also sue any individual (including a board member) who obtains, for himself or for third parties, opportunities for excessive benefits in connection with the formation of the company or an increase in share capital. This may take the form of receiving excessive payments for in-kind contributions, for the acquisition of property or for remuneration that is disproportionate to the services provided.

In principle, the same provisions of the Commercial Companies Code concerning management board members apply to liquidators. In view of this, a liquidator representing the firm may lay claims against the firm's board members on the basis described above.

2.2 Minority shareholders on behalf of the company

A company operates with the assistance of its management board, whose members need not be selected from among the shareholders. A management board member (and not a shareholder) representing the firm must file any claims raised in relation to persons who have caused damage to the company – even if the offending person is a member of the same management board. A shareholder may exercise his right to initiate claims (and thereby to realise the interests of the firm indirectly) in the situation described below.

2.3 Minority shareholders on their own account

The provisions of the Commercial Companies Code on claims initiated by shareholders do not distinguish between majority or minority shareholders. Each shareholder is entitled to pursue claims to repair harm caused against anyone who caused such harm, even if that person is a management board member. A shareholder can exercise this right if, within one year of the time at which the action causing the harm was disclosed, the company has not initiated a suit to seek reparation for the harm. In such case the shareholder avails of his own rights and acts not as a representative of the company, but rather as a party to the proceedings. Even though the company has not initiated a suit within the required period, it is not denied the opportunity to take part in the proceedings: it can join the proceedings on the basis of a subsidiary intervention if it demonstrates an unassailable legal interest for the resolution of the proceedings in the interest of the shareholder. The specific nature of this situation is such that the shareholder, in exercising his rights, despite not being a representative of the company, is in fact acting in its interests. This is because the judgment, when pronounced, will have direct effect between the company and the party sued by the shareholder of the company.

2.4 Third parties

The nature of claims of third parties that may be raised against the management board member is, above all, compensatory.

As stated above, a creditor may, on the basis of Article 291 of the Commercial Companies Code, summons to appear before the court those members of the board who have unintentionally or through carelessness made false declarations concerning the cover for contributions. The persons mentioned in the provision – that is, the company and members of its management board - may be summoned jointly and severally. If the creditor decides to summon only one person – the company or a member of the management board – it is not possible to obtain an enforcement clause against the remaining responsible persons on the basis of an enforcement warrant issued against that person. However, in the case of seeking claims jointly and severally against all sides responsible, the court will issue as many titles of execution as there are debtors against whom the claims have been judged.

Article 484 of the code gives specific rights to third parties to seek compensation for the harm caused. This provision applies also to a member of the management board, as well as other persons. A management board member who has cooperated in the issue by the company of shares, bonds or other instruments giving an entitlement to participation in profits, and has published false information in advertisements or other announcements relating to the issue, is obliged to repair the harm caused to third parties. Third parties can raise claims to repair the harm caused against a member of the management board who took part in concealing significant information required by law on the financial condition of the company.

3. Claims culture

3.1 Litigation

The Civil Procedure Code was not significantly amended following the collapse of communism in Poland. However, rapid commercial growth and progress introduced major changes to the way in which the Polish courts implement the law relating to commercial entities. The process of settling commercial disputes and proceedings has been accelerated.

Court demands with regard to the fulfilment of formal procedural requirements have significantly increased in relation to commercial entities, their attorneys and proxies. This means that the Polish courts often do not settle cases on their merit, but tend to reject proceedings as a result of initial procedural errors.

There has been a noticeable increase in the number of cases brought against company board members. This is doubtless the result of the greater awareness of people participating in commercial activities (in the wider sense) regarding the sort of responsibilities that fall on parties who operate in the name of the firm.

The results of such cases depend on the character of the individual and the court's assessment; thus, it is impossible to state unequivocally whether claims against directors are generally successful.

3.2 Ability to bring class actions

Under the Civil Procedure Code, a number of persons can act as claimants in a single case if the subject matter of the litigation:

- relates to rights and duties which are common to them;
- is based on the same factual and legal grounds (substantive joint participation); or
- constitutes claims or obligations of one type based on the same factual and legal grounds.

Nevertheless, each joint participant takes part in the litigation in his own name.

The Ministry of Justice is working on amendments to the Civil Procedure Code which will allow class actions to be brought. The completion of this work and entry of the amendments into law are expected by the end of 2007.

3.3 Funding of claims and whether loser pays

The generally accepted rule in Poland is that court fees are paid by the party which takes the matter to court. However, to prevent situations in which citizens are deprived of access to justice through lack of funds, the legislature allows costs to be waived in certain circumstances. Anyone who cannot afford to initiate civil proceedings may submit a suitable declaration to the court, together with a request for waiver of the court fees. After examining the financial condition of the applicant, the court may accept the request and decide not to charge fees.

Another accepted rule in Poland is that there are no conditional or contingency fees or success fees.

Even if court fees are not waived, they are usually recoverable, at least in part. The rule in contested cases is that the losing side pays. Thus, if the court finds in your favour, your costs will be charged to your opponent. However, it is important to request the reimbursement of costs in writing by no later than the closure of proceedings, just before the pronouncement of judgment. The principle that costs are borne by the losing party covers not only court fees, but also costs of legal representation, as well as the costs of travelling to court to attend hearings at which attendance is obligatory. Where a party loses only a certain part of a case, the court is free to apportion the costs between the parties to the dispute.

Court fees may also be partially recovered when a party is instrumental in shortening the duration of proceedings. The court usually refunds three-quarters of the court fees if, during proceedings, settlement is reached before a mediator, and one-half of the fees if a party withdraws its claim before the start of the hearing and makes a court settlement.

3.4 Plaintiffs' bar

There is no plaintiffs' bar in Poland. There are, of course, entrepreneurs' organisations and bodies representing group interests that are active in specific commercial sectors. However, such entities cooperate primarily for commercial reasons, rather than to provide support in court. The principle in court proceedings is that everyone represents his own interests.

3.5 Procedural barriers

The principal limitation to bringing a claim is the relatively high cost of proceedings, in the form of a court fee, which must be transferred to the court's bank account before proceedings commence. The court fee may be as high as 5% of the value of the subject of the dispute (to a maximum of PLN100,000).

To speed up proceedings in commercial cases, the claimant is required (under Articles 479(12) and 479(14) of the Civil Procedure Code) to present all allegations and supporting evidence in the statement of claims; meanwhile, the defendant must provide in response to this statement all counter-allegations, objections and supporting evidence, on pain of losing the right to refer to this information during proceedings.

Polish law does not regulate the need to obtain corporate consent in order to bring claims against a management board member. This matter is rather governed by the company's internal regulations.

If claims are brought, this is normally done by the management board in the name of the company. It can also take place, for example, on a motion from the supervisory board as the result of an inspection.

Generally, a company should file a claim within one year of discovery of an action that causes harm. If the company does not initiate proceedings within one year, a shareholder can exercise his right to initiate proceedings by the method described in section 2.3.

4. Indemnification rights

4.1 When the company can indemnify

The Labour Code is a collection of provisions regulating relations between employer and employee, who is engaged on the basis of an employment contract. It provides no guidance on the underwriting or guaranteeing of the various types of court costs which a management board member may have to meet.

However, in most Polish companies, members of the management boards operate on the basis of so-called 'management contracts'. These are governed by the Civil Code, and in particular by Article 353(1) on the freedom to conclude agreements. This provides that parties may arrange their contractual agreements in whatever way they wish, as long as this does not conflict with general rules of social order and the Civil Code. These types of contract, apart from regulating matters between the parties, accord all sorts of benefits to directors.

In general, there are no legal impediments preventing a company from defraying or guaranteeing the costs of proceedings undertaken against a board member or that require his participation. The type of proceeding (civil, criminal or regulatory) is irrelevant. These costs may also include expenses relating to legal representation. Issues relating to court and legal assistance costs may be settled in a number of different ways. In general, a company can cover a management board member's legal costs in their entirety or limit his share of such costs to a set amount, or refund the costs of proceedings and legal representation to the board member, only once he has been cleared of responsibility by the court. However, it is also possible to cover court fees, legal representation and any compensation which a director may be ordered to pay when he is at fault, provided that this is stated in his management contract.

4.2 Formalities for indemnification

The formalities for indemnification rights may be defined in the company's internal regulations or the contract between the company and management board member. Responsibility for drafting such rules is sometimes given to the company's supervisory body, in order to avoid the possibility of the management board choosing to draft solutions that are most convenient for its own members.

4.3 How indemnification works

There are no specific procedures to be followed in respect of indemnification under Polish law.

4.4 What cannot be indemnified

Clearly, it would be illogical for a company to refund the legal costs of a management board member against whom it had launched proceedings.

It is not possible to exempt a management board member from liability for damage caused to the company if the action is brought by a shareholder (and the company has not brought an action within one year of the offending act). Also, under Article 296 of the Commercial Companies Code, a responsible management board member may not be released from such responsibility, even if a meeting of shareholders has previously exonerated him by agreeing that the member carried out his obligations in a proper manner during his time in office. A company cannot provide guarantees to a management board member that he will not be held responsible in such situation.

The law is silent on whether a company can cover fines imposed against a management board member. If the parties so agree, there is thus nothing to prevent the company from paying fines that are imposed on a management board member in connection with the conduct of his prescribed functions in the company. However, this does lead to certain tax implications for the member concerned.

5. D&O insurance

5.1 Availability of D&O insurance

Increasing numbers of specialised insurance products are becoming available to Polish managers. Third-party insurance for managers helps them give their full concentration to business decisions and substantially improves the company's image of reliability on the market. The need for such products also arises from Poland's ongoing adaptation to the requirements of EU membership.

D&O insurance is aimed at management board members, chief executives and directors, and provides cover against civil responsibility for damage caused to the company or to third parties. This form of insurance only recently obtained separate product status in Poland. Previously, it was part of a general corporate insurance package offered to clients.

The major concerns of Polish managers include:

- their liability for damage done to the company or to third parties;
- the covering of costs incurred while preventing greater damage;
- insurance against wrongful decisions;
- the covering of defence costs in court proceedings against them; and
- the covering of defence costs in court actions initiated by the insurer or with its consent.

Despite generally low levels of legal awareness, managers appreciate the advantages that D&O insurance protection affords under Polish business conditions and the reduction in civil liability which it provides.

A key area of concern for managers interested in D&O insurance is that of protection from the risks involved in making poor business decisions. If problems arise as a result of bad decisions, a management board member may be personally liable. However, D&O insurance allows board members to take bold decisions despite the associated high levels of risk. Many Polish managers mention that the fear of making a mistake, combined with the stress of their role and ever-increasing competition, is magnified by Poland's economic instability and the continually changing legal environment.

Although D&O insurance is quite well known, fewer than 20% of Polish managers are covered by it. According to statements from the insurance companies themselves, those managers who do have D&O insurance are rarely aware of what risks are covered by their policies and some do not even know which insurance company provides their cover – although this may be because the insurance is provided for them by their companies.

In Poland, several insurance firms already offer such insurance for managers. This type of insurance has a bright future in Poland, because of the growing awareness of the need for protection and because such protection improves the company's image on the market.

5.2 Local rules on cover provided under a non-domestic D&O policy

Different insurance firms have different terms for providing cover. The agreement is concluded for the company as a whole (as the insured party), and usually covers all members of its management board. In order to obtain terms for the insurance contract, it is sufficient to present the company's balance sheet and profit and loss account.

Insurers are more willing to provide cover for companies that do not operate in the financial sector and have been operating in Poland for at least three years. In Poland, any company that may be exposed to claims from other countries (with the exception of the United States, unless that country is specifically included in the general terms of insurance) can be insured. In order to obtain cover, companies must usually present:

- detailed financial reports;
- the articles of association;
- information on whether the company has issued or intends to issue any shares; and
- information on planned changes in the list of shareholders and any mergers.

It is also important to identify the sector in which the company operates, as well as the amount of insurance cover required. The minimum amount insured is PLN500,000 and there is no upper limit.

The insurance premium depends on at least three factors:

- the company's financial situation;
- the sector in which it operates; and
- the amount of cover provided.

Premiums range from several thousand zloty annually to several hundred thousand zloty (an increase in the amount covered does not lead to a proportionate increase in premiums), and usually represent several percentage points of the sum insured. Some insurance firms stipulate an excess (an amount which the insured must contribute) to any claim. Usually, D&O insurance is taken out for one year and is renewable annually, although terms may differ if the financial situation of the company has changed or if a claim has been raised against the management.

It is also possible for the parent company of a Polish subsidiary to obtain a global D&O policy from a non-domestic insurer to cover the subsidiary and its operations. Several insurers provide this kind of service.

Foreign insurance firms are permitted to conduct insurance activity in Poland on the basis of the Insurance Activity Act of May 22 2003.

Foreign insurance firms operating in Poland are under the supervision of the Financial Supervision Commission. A firm requires a permit to conduct insurance activity in Poland, regardless of whether its registered office is located in an EU member state or outside the European Union. The Financial Supervision Commission is responsible for issuing these permits. A permit will be issued as long as the foreign firm holds the appropriate permits to conduct insurance activity in the state in which its registered office is located. Insurance activity in Poland may be conducted through either a joint stock company or a mutual insurance society, although the second form is less common. The requirement as to corporate form does not apply to foreign entities whose registered office is in a state which is a member of the World Trade Organisation.

Russia

Anastasiya V Khruleva
Konstantin I Krasnokutskiy
Alexander V Mednikov
Jurinflot

Before reviewing the issue of directors' liabilities under Russian law, it is necessary to examine the structure of management bodies in commercial companies in Russia.

Russian law provides for two principal types of commercial company with limited liability:

- the *obscshestvo s ogranichennoy otvetstvennostyu* – a limited liability company; and
- the *akzionernoye obscshestvo*, a form of joint stock company, which may be open or closed.

The principal difference between the two types of company is that limited liability companies do not issue shares; instead, their charter capital is divided into 'participatory interests' whose nominal values are specified in the constitutional documents of the company. The charter capital of joint stock companies, on the other hand, comprises the nominal values of shares issued. Closed joint stock companies, unlike open joint stock companies, may not offer their shares to the public. Neither limited liability companies nor closed joint stock companies can have more than 50 participants or shareholders.

The structure of the managing bodies is similar in both types of company; however, each has certain important distinguishing features. The supreme corporate body is the general meeting of shareholders (or participants), whose competence extends to issues including:

- reorganisation and liquidation of the company;
- amendment of the company's constituent documents;
- appointment of members to other corporate bodies;
- increases and reductions in the charter capital;
- issuance of securities;
- distribution of profits; and
- approval of certain transactions.

In limited liability companies, the general meeting has more direct influence over the affairs of the company than in joint stock companies.

The role of the board of directors in the Russian corporate system is different from that played in some other countries since, in accordance with Russian law, the board of directors (also called the 'supervisory board') is more of a supervisory body. (In accordance with the Law on Joint Stock Companies, the board of directors exercises "general governance of the company's business".) Its competence normally extends to issues such as:

- setting the principal guidelines for the development of the company;
- convening the general meeting and approving its agenda;
- approving the company's internal documents;
- approving certain types of transaction; and
- appointing and dismissing executive bodies.

In limited liability companies, a board of directors may be set up, but in most cases it is not. In contrast, joint stock companies must, as a rule, have a board of directors. In joint stock companies with 50 or fewer shareholders, the functions of the board of directors may be exercised by the general meeting. Members of boards of directors are not called 'directors' in Russia. They are elected by the general meeting. Limited liability companies are free to determine the number of board members. In joint stock companies, there must be at least five board members; this figure rises to seven for companies with over 1,000 shareholders and to nine for companies with over 10,000 shareholders.

The everyday management of the company's affairs is exercised by the executive bodies of the company. Both limited liability companies and joint stock companies may opt to have either a sole executive body only (comprising a single chief executive officer (CEO)), or both a sole and a collective executive body (comprising a number of persons). The sole executive body is responsible for all management matters which do not fall within the competence of other corporate bodies (ie, the general meeting, the board of directors and the collective executive body (if such exists)). Among other things, the sole executive body:

- acts in the name of the company without a power of attorney;
- effects transactions in the name of the company;
- hires and dismisses personnel; and
- issues orders which are mandatory for company employees.

The collective executive body, if there is one, exercises the powers vested in it by its constitutional documents (eg, it might approve transactions in excess of a stipulated amount, approve the appointment or dismissal of particular officers etc). The sole executive body of the company is also, *ex officio*, the president of the collective executive body, where one exists. Both the sole executive body and the members of the collective executive body are appointed and dismissed by the general meeting (or sometimes by the board of directors). It is the officers acting as the sole executive body who are normally known as 'directors' in Russian practice. (The law additionally allows the sole executive body of a joint stock company to be given the official title of 'general director', and of a limited liability company to be known as 'president', in addition to 'director' and 'general director'.) The authority of the sole executive body of the company may be vested in a manager (either a management company or a sole entrepreneur), by resolution of the general meeting. That person will then perform the functions of the sole executive body of the company pursuant to a contract with the company.

There are important differences between the sole executive body, members of the collective executive body and members of the board of directors. Members of the executive bodies – with a few exceptions – are company employees. As such, their relations with the company and the extent of their rights, obligations and duties towards the company are governed not only by corporate legislation, but also by labour law.

Except where the contrary is specifically stated, this chapter deals with the duties and responsibilities of members of sole executive and collective executive bodies.

1. Directors' duties

1.1 Nature of the duties

The law provides the main basis for the duties and responsibilities of a corporate executive officer in Russia. The chief principle that informs the duties owed by a person acting in the name of a company towards the company is formulated by Article 53(3) of the Civil Code: "A person which, pursuant to the law or to the constitutional documents of the legal entity acts in its name, must act in the interests of the legal entity which it represents in good faith and reasonably."

A similar provision is included in Article 44(1) of the Law on Limited Liability Companies. This obliges members of the board of directors, the sole executive body, members of a collective executive body and external managers to act in the interests of the company, reasonably and in good faith. Article 71(1) of the Law on Joint Stock Companies extends this obligation, beyond these parties, to temporary executive bodies of the company which are appointed in the event of the early termination of authority of the regular executive bodies.

Article 53(3) of the Civil Code further provides that a person acting in the name of the legal entity must "upon demand of founders (participants) of the legal entity, if the law or a contract does not provide otherwise, compensate damages which it caused to the legal entity". The relevant provisions of the Law on Joint Stock Companies and the Law on Limited Liability Companies additionally clarify that relevant persons (ie, members of the board of directors, CEOs and members of a company's collective executive body) are liable to the company for damage caused by their culpable acts or omissions. (As in criminal law, both intentional and negligent guilt is taken into account in such cases, but unlike in criminal law, in the event of a violation/breach, the absence of guilt must be proven by the person who is alleged to have committed a violation/breach of duty). This implies that a person appointed to a certain position in the company must exercise his powers in the best interests of the company, acting reasonably and honestly. Further, he must act in such a way as to avoid damage to the company which may arise from intentional acts, negligent omissions or even mistakes.

As noted above, relations between the company and its officers occupying positions on the sole executive body or the collective executive body are governed by the legislation on legal entities (the Civil Code, the Law on Joint Stock Companies, the Law on Limited Liability Companies and so on) and, with few exceptions (eg, when the CEO of the company is also its sole participant/shareholder), also by labour legislation (the Labour Code). This means that certain additional duties of such company officers are provided for under the labour legislation. The principal responsibilities of company officers who are also its employees are:

- to fulfil in good faith employment functions and responsibilities pertaining to a specified position;
- to comply with internal labour regulations; and
- to take proper care of the company's property.

The Labour Code also provides specific grounds for the termination of employment of the CEO or other managing officers, such as in case of "a singular gross violation of duties of employment" or "a poorly justified decision that caused damage to the employer". The Labour Code also sets out special rules on responsibility for damage caused to the company by the officer's actions. (Article 277 stipulates that a CEO will be deemed fully responsible for any damage caused to the company by his culpable actions.)

In addition to the duties imposed by corporate and labour legislation, executive officers (especially the CEO) have a number of other duties. These include the 'public' or 'external' duties of the company itself (and at the same time, the duty owed to the company for proper fulfilment thereof). The executive body, as the instrument through which the corporation fulfils its obligations and exercises its rights, is ultimately responsible for the proper fulfilment of all obligations imposed on the company by law, including:

- proper bookkeeping;
- compliance with licensing terms (if the company engages in any licensed activities);
- compliance with safety regulations; and
- payment of taxes.

If such obligations are neglected or are not exercised properly, penalties may be applied; and in some cases, such as certain administrative offences (eg, non-filing of antitrust notices on due dates), both the company and the responsible company officers (usually executives) will be fined. The principal basis for this kind of duty is the law. In many cases, however, the proper fulfilment of such duties may be viewed as an example of the fulfilment of the overarching duty to act in the interests of the company reasonably and in good faith.

Certain duties of company officers, including the sole executive body, members of the collective executive body and of the board of directors, may also be stipulated by the company's internal documents, such as provisions adopted by resolution of the competent corporate body (the general meeting or the board of directors). Generally, however, such internal documents interpret and specify the requirements of law.

1.2 Standards of care

While the principal source for the standards of care owed by directors is the law, this is by no means the only source. In practice, court judgments (especially of the higher courts) and practice overviews of the Supreme Court and the Higher Arbitration

Court carry significant weight as regards the interpretation of the law. They also set out practical modes of application of the law. The company's internal documents might also set out specific standards and requirements for company officers, and are important in determining the nature of the duties owed to the company.

In accordance with the principles described earlier, the general standard of care set by the law is very wide, obliging executive officers to act in the interests of the company, reasonably and in good faith. In conjunction with the obligation to compensate the company for damage caused as a result of the acts or omissions of any officer, the standard of responsibility for an executive officer is essentially to do his best as a manager and head of the company, and at all times to achieve the best possible results for the company. In other cases (relating to the fulfilment of a special duty required by the law, such as filing a debtor's application in insolvency proceedings), the standard of care may be understood as the requirement to do what is required by the law and within the stipulated timeframes. This requirement is much too general and may be easily applied in only the most straightforward cases – which are the exception, rather than the norm. The main practical obstacle in applying this principle is proving that damage suffered by the company has occurred as a result of a breach of duty by the company officer. At present, this obstacle is exacerbated by the lack of legislative interpretation as to what is understood by the idea of acting in the interests of the company 'reasonably and in good faith'.

The corporate law (in particular, Article 71 of the Law on Joint Stock Companies) also provides that in establishing the basis of guilt and the extent of the liability of company officers, the normal terms of business and other facts relevant to the particular situation must be taken into account. Thus, the claimant will need to prove, among other things, that the officer's actions and their consequences deviated significantly from those that would be expected in the normal course of business dealings in the particular sphere of business and under the relevant conditions.

1.3 To whom the duties are owed

Both the Law on Limited Liability Companies and the Law on Joint Stock Companies view the principal duty of a company officer (ie, to act in the interests of the company, in good faith and reasonably) as owed directly to the company. Other duties referred to in section 1.1 may be considered to be owed to society or to the state; but the damage incurred as a result of a failure to fulfil such duties - including fines imposed on the company as penalties for particular violations - may be viewed as a violation of the principal duty of care. Such damage may therefore be actionable on behalf of the company itself. With regard to the specific duty incumbent on executives and other company officers to comply with the provisions of Russian insolvency law (in particular, to file an application for the commencement of insolvency proceedings under the circumstances specified by law), there is a responsibility for any liability which may arise due to a violation of such obligations. Therefore, this duty is owed to any party which may incur damage as a result of such violations (first and foremost, the creditors); and any such party may claim for the relevant default.

Normally, claims relating to any breach of the principal duty of the directors may be brought by the company itself and by its participants or shareholders. In joint stock companies, only shareholders holding more than 1% of the ordinary shares of the company can exercise this right.

1.4 Common defences to and exemptions from liability

Company officers may be held liable for damage incurred by the company only if:

- the damage is incurred as a result of acts or omissions which comprise a breach of duty of the particular officers (here the burden of proof rests with the claimant); and
- such acts or omissions were committed deliberately or as a result of negligence (here the burden of proof rests with the defendant).

The second element indicates that an act or omission which leads to damage must also comprise a violation of officers' duties, and, first and foremost, of the duty to act in the interests of the company, in good faith and reasonably. Since the procedural legislation requires any party to the judicial dispute to prove the facts and circumstances to which it refers as the grounds for its demands and statements, the claimant must prove the violation of a duty and the existence of causation. If it fails to do so, its claims will be dismissed. Therefore, the defendant will have a sound defence if it can prove the absence of a causal link between his acts or omissions and the damage suffered, or the absence of guilt in any form.

Article 71 of the Law on Joint Stock Companies and Article 44 of the Law on Limited Liability Companies also provide that where damage has arisen as a result of a decision of a collective corporate body (a governing board or a board of directors), those members of such body who voted against a particular resolution or did not participate in the vote will be exempt from liability. As in cases where a group of persons are held liable for a single cause, their liability is considered joint and the company can require any one of such persons to cover the full amount payable; this will be a defence from being required to make any further payments.

On the other hand, Article 277 of the Labour Code does not require that direct damage incurred by a company have been caused by culpable acts or omissions of an officer. Thus, strictly speaking, in labour relations only a causal link between acts or omissions and the damage suffered need be proven. In practice, however, the view of the authors is that such a claim is unlikely to be satisfied if the claimant cannot prove a breach of duty.

Where a breach of duty also comprises an administrative or criminal violation, the exemptions provided for by the relevant laws (eg, the Code on Administrative Violations, the Criminal Code) may be applied. Such exemptions would include duress, the minor nature of any breach and so on.

2. Who can bring claims

2.1 The company (and its liquidators)

A solvent company may bring a claim if it has suffered damage due to the culpable acts or omissions of the officers or corporate bodies of the company. The most obvious form of claim is for compensation for damage suffered as a result of acts or omissions on the part of company officers. Damage can be incurred in a number of ways, including:

- intentional breach of a duty;
- management error;
- unauthorised disclosure of classified information;
- failure to exercise obligations; and
- violation of legal requirements which result in harm to the company (eg, fines, business closure, revocation of licences and permits).

Depending on the circumstances, claims may be addressed to both acting or dismissed officers and members of corporate bodies. Usually, the interests of the company are represented by its CEO who, unless the constitutional or internal documents require otherwise, is authorised to decide on the filing of a claim and to sign submissions of claim (either personally or by issuing a power of attorney to a representative). Therefore, if a claim is to be brought against a CEO for alleged breach, the authorised body of the company (ie, the general meeting or board of directors) will need to dismiss or at least suspend the CEO in question and appoint a new or temporary CEO, who will then be able to file a claim on behalf of the company. The issue of deciding on whether to institute court proceedings may be transferred to the competence of a different corporate body. A resolution of that body will then be required to file a claim. Other formalities required for the successful filing of a claim include:

- payment of a specified amount of state duty; and
- submission of a properly drafted and executed submission of claim with appropriate attachments within specified timeframes.

At certain stages of the insolvency procedure (ie, external administration and competition administration), arbitration administrators (and, in the latter case, the *de facto* liquidator) are entitled to bring claims in order to secure the company's property. These include claims against company officers and/or members of the corporate bodies for damage suffered by the company as a result of their acts or omissions both prior to and during insolvency proceedings, as well as for damage suffered as a result of their violation or neglect of specific responsibilities imposed on them by the Law on Insolvency. In such cases, the external administrator or competition administrator signs and files the submission of claims.

2.2 Minority shareholders on behalf of the company

Minority shareholders or participants may file a claim against a company officer or a member of a corporate body in the same way as described at section 2.1, if the company has sustained damage as a result of the acts or omissions of the defendant. Such claim will be filed in the name of the shareholder or participant, but for the benefit of the company. Consequently, depending on whether the shareholder or participant is a legal entity or a physical person, corresponding formalities, similar to those described above, must be observed.

In the case of limited liability companies, any participant may bring a claim, regardless of how small his participatory interest may be. In joint stock companies, such right is limited to shareholders holding at least 1% of the ordinary shares of the company.

2.3 Minority shareholders on their own account

Participants in limited liability companies are entitled to demand that the court of resolutions invalidate resolutions made by corporate bodies which violate their rights. Shareholders in open joint stock companies are also entitled to claim compensation for damage suffered due to non-fulfilment or improper fulfilment by corporate bodies of their duties in connection with the purchase by a single person or entity of 30% or more of the company's shares. (Such obligations include serving corresponding notices on shareholders, making recommendations on the details of the offer to purchase shares and so on.) Since minority shareholders or participants may, as with other categories of person, incur damage due to non-fulfilment or improper fulfilment by the company officers and corporate bodies of obligations imposed on them by the Law on Insolvency, they are also entitled to claim compensation for such loss.

The formalities for filing a claim in such cases are similar to those mentioned in section 2.1.

2.4 Third parties

Since the principal duty of a company officer or a member of a corporate body is owed to the company, there are few options for third parties to claim against such persons for breach of their duties in their capacity as company officers. Claims for most wrongdoings committed by company officers that have caused damage to third parties are therefore brought against defendants in their personal capacity. The principal exception is the abovementioned example of claims for compensation for damage incurred as a result of breach of obligations imposed on officers and members of corporate bodies by the Law on Insolvency. Formalities required in such cases are generally the same as those described above, and the parties entitled to compensation include various persons and entities which have suffered damage as a result of any violation, including contractual counterparties, debenture holders, employees and those whose health or life has been threatened.

We do not deal here with claims brought against company officers by state authorities for breach of legal obligations and duties towards the public, because the types of duty and the procedures for applying penalties are completely different.

3. Claims culture

3.1 Litigation

Conflicts between participants or shareholders of companies and their management are common in Russia and often proceed to the courts. However (and the following is just an evaluation based on observation, since no publicly available unified statistical data is available), they do not represent a large proportion of corporate disputes in general. At the same time, the number of such cases is growing and will continue to do so, mostly due to current trends in corporate management. At present, a large percentage of privately owned businesses are run by their owners. Such people have nobody else to blame for any losses caused by malpractice or mismanagement. However, more and more companies are passing into the hands of specialists; company ownership is also changing hands; and M&A transactions are also becoming increasingly frequent. All these developments will probably lead to an increase in the number of claims against company management, and the law and judicial practice are likely to become more sophisticated due to increased public demand.

Most claims (again, this is just an observation based on a review of a certain number of published judgments) are made by the shareholders or participants of the company, many of which hold less than the blocking percentage in the company (ie, 25%+1 in joint stock companies, one-third+1 in limited liability companies). The most widespread basis for claims is damage caused to the company (eg, loss of property or lost profits) as a result of breaches of duty (caused deliberately or by negligence) by the company officers. A large number of claims are satisfied, but many are rejected or not satisfied in full. The claims most likely to succeed are probably those arising from the most obvious violations of management duties, such as deliberate acts or omissions intended for personal gain.

3.2 Ability to bring class actions

Russian procedural law allows for the submission of joint claims by more than one claimant, particularly if:

- the common rights of claimants are the basis of the claim;
- the rights of different claimants have a single basis; or
- similar rights underlie the claim.

In some cases, it is also possible to submit a claim for the protection of the rights of third parties (at their request), and for the protection of the rights of an indefinite circle of persons. This may be done by:

- physical persons;
- legal entities;
- municipal bodies;
- bodies of a state authority; and
- the Prosecutor's Office.

Every claimant acts in the course of a procedure as a separate party; but it is possible to authorise one or more particular co-claimants to represent the interests of all co-claimants before the court.

The procedure for bringing class actions does not differ significantly from that for bringing an ordinary claim. Certain forms for such claims are exempt from the obligation to pay state duty. Claims for the protection of the rights of third parties (though not of an indefinite circle) may be filed where the relevant parties are unable to take measures to protect their own rights (by prosecutors) or on obtaining the consent of such persons (all other cases).

Class actions are quite common. In addition to the forms of class action discussed above, parties whose rights and obligations may be influenced by a court judgment in a given matter may join the procedure as third parties. It is also possible to regard as a form of group protection the right to demand invalidation by the court of resolutions passed by corporate bodies in certain instances, as a result of the fact that persons other than the claimant may be influenced by the judgment of the court.

3.3 Funding of claims and whether loser pays

The claims are funded by the claimant. The losing party will be ordered to pay the court expenses of the winning party (eg, state duties; sums payable to experts, interpreters and other external participants; postage and travel expenses; expenses for legal representation). If the claim has been satisfied in part, the parties are awarded costs in measures proportionate to the satisfied and rejected portions of the claimed amounts. Expenses for legal representation are awarded in 'reasonable' amounts, which do not always reflect the actual expenses of the relevant party. In the event of an amicable settlement, the distribution of expenses must be dealt with by the parties. Conditional and contingency fee agreements are generally not favoured, but are sometimes applied. If the claimant loses, it may be ordered to cover the defendant's expenses; in addition, a claimant who files an unmeritorious claim may be ordered by the court to compensate the defendant for loss of time.

At present, the issue of costs does not seem to have a significant influence on the decision as to whether to initiate claims against company officers. In general, however, costs do influence the situation, with the company itself more likely to file such a claim than, for example, a minority shareholder. Where companies bring claims, however, such claims are usually filed with the approval or on the initiative of the major shareholders.

3.4 Plaintiffs' bar

The concept of a plaintiffs' bar is not known in Russia. There are separate lawyers and firms in Russia that specialise in different kinds of claim, and for some, legal claims relating to company officers and directors - or, more properly, corporate disputes in general - comprise the major part of their practice. However, there is no tradition of using contingency fees for such matters.

3.5 Procedural barriers

For most types of claim, the general time bar of three years will apply. However, in some cases (eg, when an application is made to invalidate decisions of corporate bodies), a special time bar will apply (ie, two months from the date when the claimant became aware or should have become aware of such decision).

Procedural barriers and formalities for filing claims against company officers by various categories of claimant are discussed in sections 2.1 to 2.4.

4. Indemnification rights

4.1 When the company can indemnify

Indemnification of company officers is not widespread in Russia. Technically, a company may indemnify its executive officers in respect of amounts which they may be required to pay in compensation as a result of a breach of their obligations and damage suffered by other parties as a result. However, since under current Russian law the company and its participants or shareholders are the principal potential claimants against any officer in breach of his duty, such indemnification is unlikely. This is because, at least where general indemnification is concerned, such indemnification clauses could give *carte blanche* for violations of all kinds by officers. In many companies, the structure of ownership and executive management would practically rule out such possibilities (eg, when a company CEO is one of the owners, especially one of few owners; or where a company with one or a small number of owners hires an outside CEO). However, limited indemnification in respect of certain kinds of liability may be agreed - in particular, in relation to administrative fines, damages and other costs which the officer may be required to pay the state or third parties in connection with violations of legal requirements, or in connection with certain damage to third parties. Strictly speaking, there are no legal limits on the types of liability in respect of which company officers may be indemnified. The relevant procedures, scope and amount of indemnification would need to be agreed on between the company and the officer who is being indemnified. Indemnification advances may be made prior to any proceedings. If the officer is acquitted, most expenses will be refundable from the claimant and the treatment of such amounts may also be regulated by the indemnification agreement as between the company and the officer. Whether any repayments are due to the company in the event that the company officer is found guilty will also be set out in the agreement.

4.2 Formalities for indemnification

There is no specific legislation governing issues relating to the indemnification of company officers. Therefore, the law does not explicitly state when indemnification is allowed or prohibited. As noted in the previous paragraph, existing legislation views the company and its owners (participants or shareholders) as the parties most likely to suffer from officers' violation of their duties, whether by mistake or intentional misconduct. For those parties, damage may be suffered:

- directly (eg, through loss or damage of company property, or improper spending of funds); or
- indirectly (eg, through loss of reputation or market share, or by being required to pay damages to third parties or fines to the state due to improper acts or omissions of the officer).

Therefore, any indemnification to be granted by the company to its officer will need to be provided for in an explicit agreement to this effect. This may take the form of a separate agreement or a special clause in the principal agreement between the company and the officer in question. In most cases, since the company officer will be the beneficiary under such an agreement, the law will regard it as a transaction with an interested party. As such, the approval of a competent corporate body (eg, the general meeting or the board of directors, depending on the law and the company's constituent documents) will be required for such transaction. Lack of such approval may lead to the agreement being declared invalid by the court at the request of the company, or its shareholders or participants.

4.3 How indemnification works

Indemnification must be agreed upon in principle between the company and the officer in question. The agreement must include the main parameters of indemnification (ie, the kinds of liability to which it extends, the amounts agreed and procedures for invoking the indemnity). The agreed terms must be set out in a written agreement signed by the parties. From the company's side, the agreement must be approved by the competent corporate body – the general meeting or the board of directors – as a transaction with an interested party. Such approval may be granted before or after the agreement is signed, but is necessary in any event because otherwise the agreement may be invalidated by the court.

4.4 What cannot be indemnified

Since, as stated above, Russian law does not currently regulate issues relating to the indemnification of company officers, there are no prohibitions on indemnification in relation to any proceedings whatsoever - even those concerning gross negligence, wilful misconduct or criminal behaviour. However, as the company and its owners will normally be the parties against which such actions will be aimed and which will suffer damage in the first place, it is unlikely that indemnification in respect of liability arising out of gross negligence, wilful misconduct or criminal behaviour will be offered.

On the other hand, in the normal course of business, it is often difficult to avoid minor administrative violations. For example, recent anti-monopoly legislation requires parties that already occupy positions on the executive or supervisory body of one company to notify the anti-monopoly authorities within a specified timeframe if they are appointed to a position on the executive or supervisory body of another company. This requirement was not as well known to many corporate managers as it should have been. In such cases, fines paid by the company officer and expenses incurred in the course of proceedings would be more or less acceptable for compensation by the company.

In such circumstances, the only practical advice which is viable to give in order to maximise the possibility for indemnification would be for the prospective manager to assess the principal risks which he would face in the proposed position and negotiate terms and conditions of indemnification with the company.

5. D&O insurance

5.1 Availability of D&O insurance

D&O insurance is still the exception rather than the norm for the majority of Russian companies. According to some estimates, in 2006 the entire domestic D&O insurance market did not exceed $25 million, and the total number of policies covering such risks measured only in the tens. As a result, the terms and conditions of insurance are not particularly sophisticated and premiums are high, often reaching 2% or more of the maximum insured liability amount, thus making this kind of insurance prohibitively expensive for smaller companies. Nevertheless, the leading insurers are striving to develop their share of this market. The biggest national companies also prefer to have D&O coverage. All this reflects a general trend towards increasing insurance coverage for various sorts of professional liability.

5.2 Local rules on cover provided under a non-domestic D&O policy

In accordance with current legislation, insurance (except reinsurance) of interests in the territory of the Russia may be exercised only by insurers which are licensed to conduct insurance activities in Russia. Therefore, at present, non-resident insurers may not insure the interests of Russian legal entities and individuals as relating to their activities in Russia. This does not exclude the possibility of Russian companies and individuals obtaining policies from non-resident insurers in connection with their activities abroad. Therefore, there are no specific local rules as such on foreign insurance of a resident policyholder or on global insurance obtained by the parent company of a resident subsidiary. Exercise and enforcement would need to be sought abroad, with necessary Russian proceedings (enforcement of foreign judgments and so on) being performed in the ordinary manner, just as in any other case.

Until recently, foreign insurers wishing to do business in Russia were required to create a local subsidiary in order to qualify for a Russian insurance licence. Where this course of action is taken, the parent company must have at least 15 years' experience as an insurer in its home country and at least two years' experience of participating in Russian insurance companies (ie, with a stake of under 49%). In general, foreign investment in insurance companies registered in the Russian Federation is capped at 25%. Insurance companies must obtain prior official authorisation of foreign investment in their share capital and of the sale of shares/participatory interests to foreign parties.

Insurance companies with a foreign capital stake in excess of 49% are not permitted to provide certain kinds of personal insurance, obligatory insurance, insurance of state and municipal organisations and so on. Such companies must also obtain special permits in order to open branches or to participate in other insurance companies in Russia. The CEO and the chief accountant of an insurance company with foreign investment must be temporarily resident in Russia (as is the case with any other insurance company).

Most of the abovementioned limitations for insurance companies with foreign capital do not extend to companies with a stake in excess of 49% owned by insurers domiciled in EU member states which are party to the agreement on partnership and cooperation concluded on June 24 1994 between Russia and the European Union.

However, major changes to this legislative framework are on the way, as the terms and conditions of Russia's accession to the World Trade Organisation provide for liberalisation of the Russian insurance sector. In particular, foreign insurers will eventually be allowed to do business in Russia through branches and not only through subsidiaries. At present, however, the exact terms of such changes are not fully known.

South Africa

Michael Hart
John Neaves
Deneys Reitz, Inc

Company law in South Africa is regulated by the Companies Act 1973. This act predates a period of fundamental change in South Africa, in particular changes in the political, social and economic environment and the implementation of a constitutional dispensation with the passage of the South African Constitution in 1996.

The first King Report on Corporate Governance in South Africa (King I) was published in 1994, followed by the second King Report on Corporate Governance in South Africa (King II) in 2002. These reports made wide recommendations for the reform of corporate law. Both reports are non-legislated codes and have been accepted as binding by all companies listed on the JSE securities exchange.

In May 2004 the Department of Trade and Industry (DTI) published a policy paper entitled "Company Law for the 21st Century", which aimed to:

- review and modernise South African company law;
- bring it into line with international trends; and
- reflect and accommodate the changing environment for business in South Africa.

In February 2007 the DTI issued the Companies Bill 2007. It is envisaged that the bill will be passed into law at the end of 2007. It will replace the Companies Act. Some observations of the bill and comment on likely changes to the law as it relates to directors' liabilities and indemnification are included at the end of this chapter.

1. Directors' duties

1.1 Nature of the duties

King II sets out the role and functions of the board of directors in the current South African environment and states that all companies should be headed by an effective board which can both lead and control the company. The company should have executive and non-executive directors (including independent directors), to the extent appropriate. The most common board structure in South Africa is a unitary board, consisting of executive directors and non-executive directors. The board has collective responsibility for providing effective corporate governance involving the relationships between the management of the company, its board, the shareholders and other relevant stakeholders.

King II sets some general guidelines for directors. These include the following:

- All directors, both executive and non-executive, are bound by fiduciary duties and duties of care and skill;
- Directors must exercise the utmost good faith, honesty and integrity in all their dealings with or on behalf of the company, and must act independently of any outside fetter or instruction;
- Directors must exercise the care and skill any reasonable person would be expected to show in looking after his own affairs, as well as having regard to their actual knowledge and experience;
- Directors must act in the best interests of the company; and
- Directors must never permit a conflict of duties and interests, and must disclose potential conflicts at the earliest possibly opportunity.

Directors' duties arise in a number of ways and may be found in separate contractual undertakings given by the director, in the memorandum and articles of association, and under common law or statute. Contractual duties and duties contained in the memorandum and articles of the particular company are company specific.

(a) Common law duties

The core duty of the director under common law is the duty to show good faith to the company in respect of which he has been appointed. Directors' duties rest on the director individually and not on the board of directors. Directors are required to comply with the duties personally and failure to do so may attract personal liability. Directors' duties at common law include the following.

(i) Fiduciary duties

These include:

- the duty to avoid conflicts with regard to a director's personal interests;
- the duty not to exceed his powers;
- the duty to exercise independent and unfettered discretion; and
- the duty to exercise powers for proper purpose.

(ii) Duty of care and skill

Directors must exercise their powers for the benefit of the company and must exercise the required degree of care and skill. The standard of care and skill is dealt with below.

(b) Statutory rights and duties

The statutory rights and duties of directors are mainly found in the Companies Act. The act contains numerous administrative and regulatory duties. Chapter VIII of the Companies Act deals generally with directors and contains the following provisions relating to the activities of directors:

- Section 221 restricts the power of directors to issue share capital. This can be done with the prior approval of the company in general meeting. A director who knowingly takes part in an issue of shares in contravention of this section may be liable to compensate the company for loss or damage that the company may sustain.

- Section 222 restricts the issue of shares and debentures to directors unless such issue has been specifically approved by the company in general meeting. Contravention of this section by a director could lead to a criminal conviction and personal liability to the company.
- Section 223 restricts share option plans where directors are involved unless authorised by special resolution of the company.
- Section 225 prohibits tax-free payments to directors.
- Section 226 prohibits loans to directors unless with the prior consent of all of members of the company or by special resolution. Contravention of this section could lead to a criminal conviction or personal liability to the company.
- Section 227 prohibits unauthorised payments to directors for loss of office or in connection with arrangements or takeover schemes, unless full particulars with respect to the proposed payment, benefit or advantage have been disclosed to members and approved by special resolution of the company.
- Section 234 requires that directors disclose their interests in contacts. Failure to do so may lead to a criminal conviction.

There are many other statutes imposing duties on directors, including:

- the Mineral and Petroleum Resources Development Act 2002;
- the Occupational Health and Safety Act 1993; and
- environmental statutes including the National Water Act 1998, the Environment Conservation Act 1989 and the National Environmental Management Act (107/1998).

For example, the Mineral and Petroleum Resources Development Act provides that the directors of a company are jointly and severally liable for any unacceptable negative impact on the environment, including damage, degradation or pollution, advertently or inadvertently caused by the company they represent or represented. This is a form of strict liability.

1.2 Standards of care

A director must perform his duties with the same degree of care and skill that a reasonable person would display in the conduct of his own affairs, and with the degree of skill which may reasonably be expected of a person with his knowledge and experience. The test is the objective test of negligence. A breach may give rise to personal liability for damages.

A director may also incur personal liability if he carries on the business of the company recklessly or with intent to defraud (see Section 424 of the Companies Act, which is dealt with more fully below).

In *Fisheries Development Corporation of SA Ltd v Jorgensen* 1980 (4) SA 156 (W) at 165, the court summarised the principles governing the duty of care and skill relevant to the conduct of directors as follows:

- The extent of a director's duty of care and skill depends to a considerable degree on the nature of the company's business and on any particular obligations assumed by or assigned to him.
- The director is not required to have special business acumen or expertise, or singular ability or intelligence, or even experience in the business of the company.
- The director is expected to exercise the care which may reasonably be expected of a person with his knowledge and experience.
- The director is not liable for mere errors of judgement.
- In respect of all duties that may properly be left to some other official, a director is, in the absence of grounds for suspicion, justified in trusting that official to perform such duties honestly. He is entitled to accept and rely on the judgement, information and advice of the management, unless there are proper reasons to query this.
- A director exercising reasonable care would not accept information and advice blindly. He may accept it and is entitled to rely on it, but he must give it due consideration and exercise his own judgement in light thereof.

1.3 To whom duties are owed

As a general rule, a director's duties are owed to the company - that is, the general body of shareholders - and not to individual shareholders, creditors or any third parties.

A director may, by agreement or conduct, be placed in a position where he owes one or more shareholders a fiduciary duty. A director could constitute himself as an agent for members to carry out particular transactions, thereby accepting special fiduciary duties to those members.

By the same token, a director is not, as director, usually liable as such to creditors of a company or third parties, but he may assume special duties to creditors or third parties, for example, in supplying information to the creditor. Where the business of a company is being carried on recklessly or with an intent to defraud creditors, a director may become personally liable to creditors or any other persons for the debts or liabilities of the company. Section 424 of the Companies Act provides as follows:

> *When it appears, whether it be in a winding-up, judicial management or otherwise, that any business of the company was or is being carried on recklessly or with intent to defraud creditors of the company or creditors of any other person or for any fraudulent purpose, the Court may, on the application of the Master, the liquidator, the judicial manager, any creditor or member or contributory of the company, declare that any person who was knowingly a party to the carrying on of the business in the manner aforesaid, shall be personally responsible, without any limitation of liability, for all or any of the debts or other liabilities of the company as the Court may direct.*

Section 424 establishes a punitive remedy in which a director can be held personally liable for all liabilities of the company without proof of any causal link between his conduct and those liabilities.

A director will not, as director, owe special duties to employees, but directors may assume individual liabilities to employees.

1.4 Common defences to and exemptions from liability

The most common defence by directors to claims against them is to deny the breach of contract, the duty of care or negligence, and to demonstrate that they have acted diligently and with due care in the conduct of the affairs of the company.

The Companies Act prevents a company from exempting or indemnifying directors from their legal liability to the company for negligence, default or breach of duty, or breach of trust. The company may, however, take out insurance as indemnification against liability of directors towards the company and may indemnify such directors against costs incurred in defending any related proceedings, provided that they are successful in such defence. Section 247 of the Companies Act provides as follows:

(1) Subject to the provisions of subsection (2), any provision, whether contained in the articles of a company or in any contract with a company, and whether expressed or implied, which purports to exempt any director or officer or the auditors of the company from any liability which by law would otherwise attach to him in respect of any negligence, default, breach of duty or breach of trust of which he may be guilty in relation to the company or to indemnify him against any such liability, shall be void: Provided that this subsection shall not be applicable to insurance taken out and kept by the company as indemnification against any liability of any director or officer towards the company in respect of any negligence, default, breach of duty or breach of trust.

(2) The provisions of subsection (1) shall not be construed as prohibiting a company from indemnifying any director, officer or auditor in respect of any liability incurred by him in defending any proceedings, whether civil or criminal, in which judgment is given in his favour or in which he is acquitted or in respect of any such proceedings which are abandoned or in connection with any application under section 248 in which relief is granted to him by the Court.

Section 247(1) of the Companies Act was amended in 1998 in order to provide clarity on the insurance provisions, the intention being to allow the company to effect insurance for directors at company expense and thereby provide a form of indemnity to directors. Unfortunately, the amendment did not clarify the position and, despite the provisions permitting the company to take out insurance on its own behalf, directors remain exposed.

Section 248 of the Companies Act provides as follows:

(1) If in any proceedings for negligence, default, breach of duty or breach of trust against any director, officer or auditor of a company it appears to the Court that the person concerned is or may be liable in respect of the negligence, default, breach of duty or breach of trust, but that he has acted honestly and reasonably, and that,

having regard to all the circumstances of the case, including those connected with his appointment, he ought fairly to be excused for the negligence, default, breach of duty or breach of trust, the Court may relieve him, either wholly or partly, from his liability on such terms as the Court may think fit.

(2) Any such director, officer or auditor who has reason to apprehend that any claim will be made against him in respect of any negligence, default, breach of duty or breach of trust, may apply to the Court for relief, and the Court shall on any such application have the same powers to grant relief as are by subsection (1) conferred upon it with reference to proceedings referred to in that subsection.

It will be seen from the above that directors may be given relief against claims by the company or by third parties even where they may be liable in respect of negligence, default or breach of duty or breach of trust, but where they have acted reasonably or honestly.

2. Who can bring claims

2.1 The company (and its liquidators)

The most likely claims against a director - whether for breach of contract, breach of duties under the memorandum or articles of the company, or breach of common law or statutory duties - would be in the form of claims by the company itself.

In addition to normal claims for loss or damage suffered by the company for breach of contract, breach of duties or negligence, a number of statutes provide for personal liability. These include circumstances where:

- a director permits unauthorised loans to be made to a holding or a fellow subsidiary;
- there has not been proper disclosure or use of the company's name;
- the director is guilty of insider trading; or
- the director has knowingly been party to the carrying on of the business recklessly or fraudulently.

There are no specific procedures required for a company to sue a director other than a resolution of the board. A director can be removed from office by ordinary resolution of the members at a general meeting.

On the winding-up of a company, a liquidator may, in the name of the company in liquidation, pursue any claims that the company may have had against a director. In this regard, we refer to Sections 423 and 424 of the Companies Act.

2.2 Minority shareholders on behalf of the company

Generally, where a company suffers damage as a result of the wrongful acts of a director, the company must claim from the director and the member or shareholder cannot sue the director for loss of value of his shares. In very limited circumstances a member or shareholder may sue for such loss.

A member or shareholder may bring what is known as a 'derivative action'. A shareholder has such a remedy where loss or damage is caused by controlling shareholders or directors who use their control to prevent an action by the company against them. A group of controlling shareholders or directors may block a resolution authorising the company to sue members of the group. The minority shareholders may in such circumstances, and in terms of this procedure, institute an action to claim damages on the company's behalf.

This common law remedy has been recognised in the Companies Act. Section 266 provides as follows:

> *(1) Where a company has suffered damages or loss or has been deprived of any benefit as a result of any wrong, breach of trust or breach of faith committed by any director or officer of that company or by any past director or officer while he was a director or officer of that company and the company has not instituted proceedings for the recovery of such damages, loss or benefit, any member of the company may initiate proceedings on behalf of the company against such director or officer or past director or officer in the manner prescribed by this section notwithstanding that the company has in any way ratified or condoned any such wrong, breach of trust or breach of faith or any act or omission relating thereto.*

2.3 Shareholders on their own account

Members or shareholders may also bring an action against a director personally to restore property, repay money or contribute to compensation where it appears, in the course of a winding-up or judicial management, that the director has misapplied, retained or become liable for money or property of the company, or has been guilty of a breach of faith or trust in relation to the company. In this regard we refer to Section 423 of the Companies Act.

Finally, a member or shareholder may apply to court for an order compelling a director who is personally liable for the debt of a company where the director was knowingly party to the carrying on of the business recklessly or fraudulently. In this regard, reference should be made to Section 424 of the Companies Act.

2.4 Third parties

(a) Master, liquidator, judicial manager, creditor, member or contributory

Directors are generally not liable for the obligations or liabilities of their companies. There are exceptions to the rule.

The following exceptions are contained in the Companies Act:

- In terms of Section 423 of the Companies Act, where in the winding-up or judicial management it appears that the director has misapplied or retained or become liable or accountable for any money of the company, or has been guilty of any breach of faith or trust in relation to the company, the court may, on application of the master, the liquidator, any creditor member or contributory of the company, inquire into the conduct of the director, and may order him to repay or restore the money or property or to pay compensation.

- In terms of Section 424 of the Companies Act, the court may, at any time - whether during winding-up, judicial management or otherwise - on application of the master, the liquidator, any creditor, member or contributory, declare that any person including a director who was knowingly party to the carrying on of the business recklessly or with intent to defraud creditors, or for any fraudulent purpose, be personally responsible for the debts or other liabilities of the company.

These sections empower the courts to inquire into the conduct of directors and to make appropriate orders. The sections create no new rights, but provide a summary procedure for enforcement of rights which the company already has. Ordinary causes of action in contract or delict do not fall within these sections. When ordering an inquiry, the court will define the matters about which the inquiry is to take place and will give appropriate procedural directions for discovery, the calling of witnesses and the like.

(b) ***Generally***

A director may be sued by any third party, including shareholders, creditors or employees of the company, for any personal wrongs committed by the director to those parties. This kind of action is an action against the director not in his capacity as a director, but rather in his personal capacity for personal wrongs he may have committed. However, such actions may arise out of acts committed by the director in the performance of his duties.

3. Claims culture

3.1 Litigation

Historically, South Africa has not had a litigious culture.

There are no published statistics and very little reported case law reflecting the frequency of claims against directors in South Africa. In the last two years, however, there have been a number of high-profile actions against well-known directors of companies following liquidation and investigatory proceedings. The most high-profile of these follows the failures of the Leisurenet Group, in which claims running into hundreds of millions of rands were made by the liquidators against the non-executive directors. The claims were ultimately settled for an amount reportedly in the vicinity of R20 million. This was the limit of the directors' insurance cover.

This kind of action will become more prevalent in South Africa.

The regulatory framework dealing with the monitoring and control of financial institutions has been significantly strengthened over the past few years. Intervention by the banking and financial service regulators is now a common occurrence. These interventions are frequently accompanied by inspection processes which attract significant publicity, particularly in the case of savings and loans failures. They often focus on the role played by the directors. The use of the interrogatory procedures set out in Section 417 of the Companies Act has led to increased public awareness of the rights of creditors, shareholders and investors, and this carries with it an increased willingness to enforce those rights by way of litigation.

Section 417(1) provides as follows:

(1) *In any winding-up of a company unable to pay its debts, the Master or the Court may, at any time after a winding-up order has been made, summon before him or it any director or officer of the company or person known or suspected to have in his possession any property of the company or believed to be indebted to the company, or any person whom the Master or the Court deems capable of giving information concerning the trade, dealings, affairs or property of the company.*

Shareholder activism is increasingly a feature at meetings of listed companies. Hostile questioning of company directors draws significant media coverage, which in turn stimulates the environment in which litigation is discussed in public circles.

3.2 Ability to bring class actions

There is no current process in South African civil procedure for the bringing of class actions, although this area of procedure is likely to develop fairly rapidly in the future. Section 38 of the Constitution introduces the concept of a class action in matters in which it is contended that a right in terms of the Bill of Rights has been infringed or threatened. The procedure envisaged in this section would not generally apply to civil litigation between persons or corporations, but the introduction of this remedy in respect of constitutional causes of action may well represent a step in the development of general class actions.

The prospects of collective action by groups of claimants are increased by the introduction of terminology in recent amendments to the Companies Act and by the terms of the Auditing Profession Act 2005. These include definitions expressly recognising the rights of a category of users of financial reports which is wider than the traditional concept of members or shareholders. The Companies Act provides a definition of ‘user’ to include “a shareholder, prospective shareholder, creditor, regulator or any person who relies on information contained in the report”. The Auditing Profession Act 2005 defines ‘reportable irregularities’ as including unlawful acts or omissions which have caused loss or are likely to cause material financial loss to a wide group of parties, including “the entity or to any partner, member, shareholder, creditor or investor of the entity”.

It would be reasonable to expect that the recognition of these groupings may lead to collective actions by them in the future.

3.3 Funding of claims and whether loser pays

The general rule in civil litigation is that the unsuccessful party pays the successful party’s costs. These costs are determined in accordance with the tariff of the court in which the matter is heard. Costs are normally awarded on the scale as between party and party. The court has the discretion to award costs on the higher scale as between attorney and client. While the system does not necessarily allow the successful party to recover all costs that it has incurred, it does mean that the loser bears the risk of having to make a significant cost payment to the winner in addition to funding its own costs. This has the effect of reducing frivolous litigation, but may also serve as an obstacle to a legitimate but impecunious claimant.

Contingency fee arrangements are permissible in terms of the Contingency Fees Act 1997. The contingency fee allowed is not to exceed the amount of fees normally charged by more than 100%, provided that, in the case of claims sounding in money, the total of any such success fee payable is not to exceed 25% of the total amount awarded, excluding any costs. A written contingency fee agreement is required to be entered into containing essential allegations set out in the statute. A settlement of a matter subject to a contingency fee arrangement may be accepted only after the legal practitioner has filed an affidavit in court (if the matter is before court), or with the professional controlling body justifying the recommendation in regard to settlement. The introduction of this contingency fee (or conditional fee arrangement, as it is known in other jurisdictions) has not significantly increased the number of cases relating to directors' and officers' liability.

South Africa has a system for providing legal aid to impecunious plaintiffs. The system is administered by the Legal Aid Board, which provides financial support at an agreed tariff for persons who are indigent or regarded as such on the basis of a means test established by the board. The threshold level of the test is so low that cases covered by legal aid are not a significant feature in litigation involving directors. Legal aid does not cover the costs awarded against an unsuccessful litigant.

3.4 Plaintiffs' bar

There is no formal plaintiffs' bar in the South African legal system. However, a number of practitioners specialise in handling commercial litigation flowing from corporate failures. These teams of attorneys and advocates are well versed in the advantages to be derived from participation in the regulatory investigation process and in the interrogation procedures available in cases involving liquidations and insolvency. The standard of service offered by them to their client base (generally institutions which have provided finance to the failed corporation) is sophisticated and well supported by forensic services typically provided by divisions of the major international accounting practices.

3.5 Procedural barriers

Directors of listed and private companies enjoy no procedural protections restricting the institution of action against them by the company or third parties, based upon any alleged breach of duty owed by them to the company or such third parties. The director incurs no liability for the debts owed by a limited liability company, but remains responsible for any action based upon the director's own personal breach of duty in circumstances where such an action is recognised.

In terms of the Prescription Act, claims against directors must be brought within three years of the date on which the debt giving rise to the claim becomes due. The legislation contains provisions dealing with the interruption of the running of the time bar similar to enactments found in other common law jurisdictions (eg, incapacity of the creditor, insolvency of the debtor, absence of the debtor from the country). Prescription is also interrupted where the creditor is a legal person (which includes a company) and the debtor is a member of the management board of such entity. Prescription does not run where the debtor expressly acknowledges liability for the debt.

A debt is not deemed to be due until the creditor has knowledge of the identity of the debtor and of the facts giving rise to the debt. A creditor is deemed to have such knowledge if it could have been acquired through the exercise of reasonable care.

4. Indemnification rights

4.1 When the company can indemnify

Section 247 of the Companies Act renders void any provision, whether contained in the articles of the company or in any contract with the company, which purports to exempt any director from any liability which by law would otherwise attach to him in respect of any negligence, default, breach of duty or breach of trust of which he may be guilty in relation to the company, or to permit the company to indemnify him against any such liability.

This prohibition is subject to two qualifications. First, the company is permitted to indemnify the director for the costs incurred in defending himself in civil or criminal proceedings in which judgment is given in his favour or in respect of which he is acquitted. Second, the prohibition is not applicable to insurance which is taken out and kept by the company as indemnification against any liability of the director towards the company in respect of any negligence, default, breach of duty or breach of trust. Despite the convoluted wording of the section, this has been taken by the insurance market in South Africa as authority for the company to acquire and fund directors' indemnity insurance both for its own exposure and on behalf of such directors.

Section 248 of the Companies Act authorises a court, in any proceedings for breach of duty against a director or officer, to relieve him, either wholly or partly, of any liability if it is satisfied that the director has acted honestly and reasonably and that, having regard to the circumstances of the case, he ought fairly to be so excused. The matter may be raised by the court of its own accord or upon application to it by a director or officer.

4.2 Formalities for indemnification

No particular formalities are required for the provision of indemnities in circumstances where these can legitimately be provided by the company. It would obviously be prudent for the fact of the indemnity and its extent to be properly recorded in the articles of the company, or in any letter of appointment or service contract between the company and the director.

Where the indemnity is by way of a liability insurance policy purchased on behalf of the director by the employer company, then such indemnity should be set out in writing in an appropriate policy document which will record the terms and conditions upon which the indemnity is provided.

4.3 How indemnification works

There are no specified procedures for the process of indemnification. Indemnification will be sought and enforced under the ordinary civil procedure litigation process.

4.4 What cannot be indemnified

At common law, the director cannot personally be indemnified against the consequences of fraud or wilful misconduct. There is no statutory prohibition against the insurance of fines or penalties levied upon directors or officers, but the common law holds that it is against public policy to indemnify a party against fines or penalties flowing from criminal or regulatory breaches. There is no relevant case precedent dealing specifically with regulatory or criminal fines. This coverage is not offered in the policies currently underwritten in the local market.

5. D&O insurance

5.1 Availability of D&O insurance

D&O insurance is freely available in the South African market. It is underwritten by the local licensed and registered offices of multinational insurance companies, and by domestic short-term insurers. Lloyds underwriting syndicates are also licensed to write this form of business in South Africa and several of them are active in the local market. Rates have been keen, as would be expected in a market in its developmental stage, but the advent of claims made and payable in the last few years has brought about some re-rating of the cost of the product. The coverage is freely available and generally marketed through the offices of the insurance broking community.

5.2 Local rules on cover provided under a non-domestic D&O policy

An insurance contract between a non-domestic insurer and a South African resident is not *per se* unlawful. However, South African insurance/exchange-control legislation is structured in such a way that the practical implementation of an insurance programme involving a non-domestic insurer will require specific approval. This is generally provided against a written acknowledgement by the insured of the fact that it recognises that it is entering into a contract with a party not subject to the jurisdiction of the local regulator, and that it will therefore not be in a position to look to the regulator for assistance in the event of a dispute in regard to the policy. Requisite exchange-control approval to remit premiums to a non-domestic insurer will generally be given by the banking authorities only against confirmation from the insurance regulator that it has given its approval in this way.

Global policies issued by non-domestic insurers offering protection without direct cost to a local South African subsidiary are not unlawful. The payment of any claim under such a global policy will generally require the local bank, as agent of the South African Reserve Bank, to be satisfied that this is a *bona fide* policy indemnity payment and not the introduction of capital or loan funds for the local subsidiary. Global policies by non-domestic insurers which require premium payments by the local subsidiary are subject to the same approval requirements as other non-domestic policies, as set out above.

There are no specific rules restricting territories from which insurance may be obtained, but the local regulator is in close contact with worldwide regulatory bodies and is unlikely to grant approval if there are concerns as to the origin of the non-domestic insurer.

6. Postscript – the Companies Bill 2007

The Companies Bill 2007 was issued in February 2007 and will replace the Companies Act. It constitutes a complete revamp of South African company law. It does away with the concepts of 'private companies' and 'public companies'. A distinction is drawn between 'for-profit' and 'not-for-profit' companies. For-profit companies are then further distinguished between 'widely held companies' and 'closely held companies'. There is also a group of companies described as 'public interest companies'.

Sections 85 to 94 deal with directors; of particular relevance is Section 91, which provides for the codification of standards of directors' conduct. This codification does not exclude the common law duties of directors, but does extract from the common law the director's duty to exercise care, skill and diligence, and the fiduciary duties to act honestly, in good faith and in the best interests and for the benefit of the company. The section provides that a director, in discharging his duties, may rely on the performance of others, including employees or outside professionals, as well as on information reports and financial data prepared or presented by them.

Section 92 provides for conflicting interests and requires that the director act in the interest of the company and not for his personal financial interest. The director may not gain advantage for himself or cause detriment to the company. The director must declare any conflicting interest.

Section 93 deals with the liability of directors and renders void any provisions purporting to relieve a director of liability for:

- gross negligence, wilful misconduct or breach of trust;
- signing or consenting to the publication of financial statements which are false or misleading;
- knowingly being a party to the reckless carrying on of the company business; or
- any act or omission by the company calculated to defraud a creditor, employee or security holder of the company, or with other fraudulent purpose.

The bill provides that the company may advance expenses to a director to defend litigation arising out of the director's service to the company, and that it may indemnify a director for expenses so advanced or for liability arising out of the director's service to the company. This does not apply to liability for gross negligence, wilful misconduct or breach of trust, unless the proceedings exculpate the director or are abandoned before judgment.

The company may purchase insurance to protect the company or the director against liability or expenses incurred in defending litigation in any proceedings, provided that it does not arise from reckless trading, gross negligence, wilful misconduct or breach of trust.

Finally, the court may, in any proceedings against a director, other than for gross negligence, wilful misconduct or breach of trust, relieve the director from liability if the court is of the view that, although liable, he has acted honestly and reasonably. A director who has reason to apprehend a claim against him other than on the grounds of negligence, wilful misconduct or breach of trust may anticipate the claim and apply to court for the necessary relief.

The bill then makes provision in Sections 162 to 166 for a number of rights to seek specific remedies.

The first of these provides for an application to court by a shareholder for a declaratory order determining any rights that the shareholder may have in terms of the company's memorandum of incorporation or any rules of the company.

The second is new in South African law and provides for an application by any one or more of a group of persons - including the company, a shareholder, a director, a company secretary or other officer of the company; a registered trade union or other representative of the employees of a company, or the Commission or Takeover Regulation Panel - to apply to court for an order to declare a director delinquent or under probation. There are a number of grounds for such an order, including gross abuse of the position of a director, the taking of personal advantage or opportunity, and intentionally or grossly negligently inflicting harm on the company. If a director is declared delinquent, the order may prohibit him from holding a directorship for a lengthy period and, in certain circumstances, for his lifetime.

The third provides for relief to shareholders, creditors or directors of companies for oppressive and prejudicial conduct of the business of the company.

Section 165 provides for dissent in shareholders' appraisal rights, in terms of which a dissenting shareholder can in certain circumstances require the company to acquire his shares at fair value.

Finally, Section 166 provides for the shareholders' derivative action. The bill provides for the abolishment of the common law derivative action and sets out the basis for a derivative action. The bill sets out the procedures which may be adopted by a shareholder, director or trade union if that person requires the company to commence or continue with legal proceedings to protect the interests of the company.

The Companies Bill 2007 introduces wide-ranging changes to the company law in South Africa and anyone interested in company law in South Africa should consider the Companies Bill and the new Companies Act when the bill is passed into law.

Spain

Ignacio Figuerol
Davies Arnold Cooper

---

1. Directors' duties

1.1 Nature of the duties

The general duties of directors are established in Section 127 of the Companies Act. Section 127 was extensively amended by the Transparency Act of July 2003, which implemented the recommendations of the Aldama Report on the Corporate Governance of Listed Companies (January 8 2003). Section 127 sets out the following obligations and duties of directors.

(a) General duties

(i) Duty of diligent management

Section 127.1 provides that directors must act with the diligence of a prudent businessperson and a loyal representative. Under Section 127.1(2), each director must diligently acquaint himself with the running of the company.

(ii) Duty of faithfulness

Section 127*bis* establishes that, in complying with their duties, directors must at all times be faithful to the corporate interest (ie, the interest of the company).

Traditionally, the 'corporate interest' has been deemed to be the common interest of the shareholders. However, the 'corporate interest' is now defined as the interest of the company. This may give rise to debate, since it leads one to wonder whether the interest of the company is different from the shareholders' common interest. Apparently, the intent of Section 127*bis* is that the directors of a company, when making any decision, take into account not only the interest of the shareholders, but also the interests of other stakeholders (eg, employees, suppliers, creditors).

(iii) Duty of loyalty

Section 127*ter* sets out four specific duties:

- A director shall not use the name of the company or his position as a director of the company to carry out any personal transaction.
- A director cannot carry out any investment or transaction linked to company assets which he became aware of due to his position as director if the investment or transaction was offered to the company or the company is

interested in the same, unless the company has rejected this business opportunity without the influence of the director concerned.

- The directors must report any direct or indirect conflict of interest they may face to the board. In the case of a conflict of interest, the director concerned may not participate in the transaction in question. All conflicts of interest are published in the company's annual report on corporate governance.
- The directors must communicate their participation in the share capital of other companies engaged in the same or similar business, as well as the positions they hold in any of those other companies.

In respect of these duties, the persons affected are not only the directors themselves, but also their relatives, companies in which they participate and so on.

(iv) Duty of confidentiality

Under Section 127*quarter*, directors, even after their resignation, must not disclose any confidential information of the company. In this respect, it is expressly stated that the directors must not disclose any details, reports or facts that might damage the company. The directors are exempt from this duty only where a piece of legislation specifically authorises them to do so.

(b) Other duties

In addition to the above general duties, the Companies Act provides for a number of specific duties of directors, such as formulating annual accounts, convening general shareholders' meetings and so on.

The Aldama Report included several non-binding recommendations on what directors' duties should include. A director should:

- follow with dedication and the necessary diligence the issues affecting the management of the company;
- attend and actively participate in board and committee meetings;
- oppose resolutions that are contrary to law, to the memorandum and articles of association, and to the company's interest;
- request that board meetings be convened when required; and
- request and obtain the necessary information to understand the business and management of the company to enable him to fulfil his mission.

In turn, the Conthe Report on the Corporate Governance of Listed Companies (of May 19 2006) advised that one of the core functions of the board of directors should be to approve corporate strategy and ensure that the management of the company meets the objectives set for the company's interests and corporate purpose.

1.2 Standards of care

Pursuant to Section 127.1 of the Companies Act, directors must act with the diligence of a business executive and a loyal representative. This requires that the directors comply with any duties established for them in the law and in the company's articles of association. This is understood to mean that they should apply the same level of care, dedication, prudence, professionalism and ability to the company's assets as they would to their own. In this context, factors such as the size of the company, whether the post is remunerated and so on are deemed to bear an influence.

1.3 To whom duties are owed

Section 133 of the Companies Act states that directors shall be liable to the company and its shareholders and creditors for any damage that they cause.

1.4 Common defences to and exemptions from liability

Directors can avoid liability only if they prove that:

- they did not participate in the adoption or implementation of the relevant resolution and had no knowledge of it;
- on becoming aware of the resolution, they took all practicable steps to avoid the damage being suffered; or
- they expressly opposed the relevant resolution.

The Companies Act expressly provides that the fact that an agreement is subseuently ratified by the general shareholders' meeting does not release the directors from liability.

The business judgement rule is not recognised as such by Spanish law. However, the Conthe Report recommended that the regulations on the liability of directors for breach of trust be tightened, but expressly stated that such a recommendation should not apply to claims for mere negligence.

2. Who can bring claims

The Companies Act distinguishes between various types of action against directors on the basis of the nature of the damage claimed, rather than the type of claimant. On this basis, the Companies Act provides for the following actions.

2.1 The company (and its liquidators)

Under Section 134 of the Companies Act, where damage is allegedly caused to the company, the company can bring an action against its directors. This is known as a 'corporate liability action'. To do this, a majority of the shareholders must pass a resolution to this effect at a general shareholders' meeting.

In respect of liability in insolvency situations, the Insolvency Act, which came into force in September 2004, established a specific liability of directors (including *de facto* directors) where companies have entered into insolvency proceedings.

If there is no creditors' agreement, such liability of directors may be attached only if the insolvency is classified as 'negligent' (ie, where there has been bad faith or gross negligence on the part of the directors of the company which resulted in the company's insolvency). The Insolvency Act provides certain guidelines in this respect.

In accordance with Section 164 of the Insolvency Act, the insolvency will always be considered negligent where:

- the company is legally obliged to keep accounts but substantially fails to do so, keeps double accounts or commits an irregularity relevant to the understanding of the financial situation for which it is supposed to keep accounts;
- there are serious inaccuracies in any of the documents accompanying the declaration of insolvency, or the company submits or presents false documents during the proceedings;
- liquidation commences as a consequence of breach of a creditors' agreement which is attributable to the company;
- the company absconds with the whole or part of its assets, causing harm to its creditors, or realises any act which delays, causes difficulty to or impedes the effectiveness of a seizure of property in any class of execution initiated or
- in the two years prior to the declaration of insolvency, rights or assets from the company were fraudulently transferred elsewhere; or
- before the declaration of insolvency the company carried out any legal act in order to feign a financially fictitious situation.

In addition, pursuant to Section 165 of the Insolvency Act, there is a rebuttable presumption that the directors acted in bad faith or were guilty of gross negligence where they:

- failed to apply for a declaration of insolvency within the required timeframe (two months);
- failed to comply with the duty to cooperate with the judge dealing with the insolvency proceedings or with the administrators;
- did not make the necessary information available to investigate the insolvency or did not attend a creditors' meeting, either personally or through an agent; or
- did not fulfil their legal obligation to produce the annual accounts or subject them to audit, or did not deposit them in Companies House in any of the three financial years before the declaration of insolvency.

Where, on the basis of the above grounds, the insolvency is classified as negligent, the judge may (but is not obliged to) order any directors who held this position in the two years prior to the declaration of insolvency to pay, in whole or in part, the shortfall between the amount of their credit and the sum they received in the liquidation of the rights and assets. In other words, the directors may have to cover the financial deficit of the company.

The requirement of bad faith or gross negligence on the part of the directors in the generation or aggravation of the state of insolvency is a peculiarity of the Insolvency Act with respect to liability under the Companies Act. Here, negligence (as opposed to gross negligence) suffices.

The liability as described above will be established in the judgment to be issued following the insolvency proceedings. This notwithstanding, the Insolvency Act provides for an interim guarantee measure while the insolvency proceedings are ongoing. From the commencement of proceedings, the judge may order the seizure of the assets of the directors (including those who held this position in the two years prior to the declaration of insolvency), if there are indications that the insolvency may be classified as negligent and that the assets of the company will be insufficient to satisfy all claims.

A seizure order may be replaced by a guarantee from a credit institution.

2.2 Minority shareholders on behalf of the company (derivative actions)

Those shareholders representing at least 5% of the share capital of the company are entitled to request that a general shareholders' meeting be convened to discuss bringing the action. If the directors fail to convene a meeting when requested, or if the company fails to bring the action within one month of the date of the agreement to do so (or if the general shareholders' meeting decides not to bring an action), these minority shareholders will be entitled to bring the action themselves.

2.3 Minority shareholders on their own account

Under Section 135 of the Companies Act, any shareholder is entitled to bring a liability action against the directors who caused direct damage to them. This is known as an 'individual liability' action. For this type of action to succeed, it is essential that the claimant can provide evidence that the alleged damage is a direct result of a specific wrongful act by the defendant director(s).

2.4 Third parties

Company creditors can also bring a corporate liability action against the directors, but only if the company or shareholders have failed to bring it, and provided that the assets of the company are insufficient to meet its liabilities. In addition, under Section 135 of the Companies Act, any third party is also entitled to bring an individual liability action against the directors who caused direct damage to such a third party.

The Companies Act also establishes an action to allow a claim against directors for the company's debts where certain dissolution causes occur.

Under Section 260.1 of the Companies Act, a company shall be dissolved, among other things, where:

- it is manifestly impossible to carry out its corporate purpose;
- losses reduce its net equity to less than half of its stock capital, unless the stock capital is then increased or reduced in a sufficient manner and insolvency proceedings are not appropriate;
- the corporate capital is reduced below the legal minimum; or
- a cause for dissolution established in the articles of association takes place.

If any of the above occurs, the dissolution of the company requires a resolution of the general shareholders' meeting. To this end, the directors must convene the meeting within two months of the adoption of a resolution to dissolve the company or carry out an act to remedy the cause for dissolution. Alternatively, the directors may apply for a declaration of insolvency if the company was in an insolvency situation.

In addition, the directors are required to apply within two months for the judicial dissolution of the company if the resolution is against dissolution or where no resolution is adopted.

The directors shall become jointly and severally liable for the company's debts and obligations if they fail to comply with the requirement:

- to convene the general shareholders' meeting within two months;
- to pass a resolution to dissolve the company; or
- to apply for the judicial dissolution of the company or, if appropriate, for the commencement of insolvency proceedings within two months of the date set for a meeting that was not held, or from the date of the meeting that passed a resolution against dissolution.

However following a reform of the Companies Act in November 2005, directors shall now be liable for debts that occur subsequent to the dissolution clause. The act provides that debts are presumed to be subsequent to the dissolution clause unless the directors provide evidence to the contrary.

3. Claims culture

3.1 Litigation

Litigation involving directors' and officers' liability is on the rise. Our recent survey has provided some valuable information about trends and the number of claims against company directors. However, the results cannot be used as a proper and accurate statistical study.

(a) Supreme Court judgments in civil proceedings against directors from 1999 to 2005

(i) Types of action brought

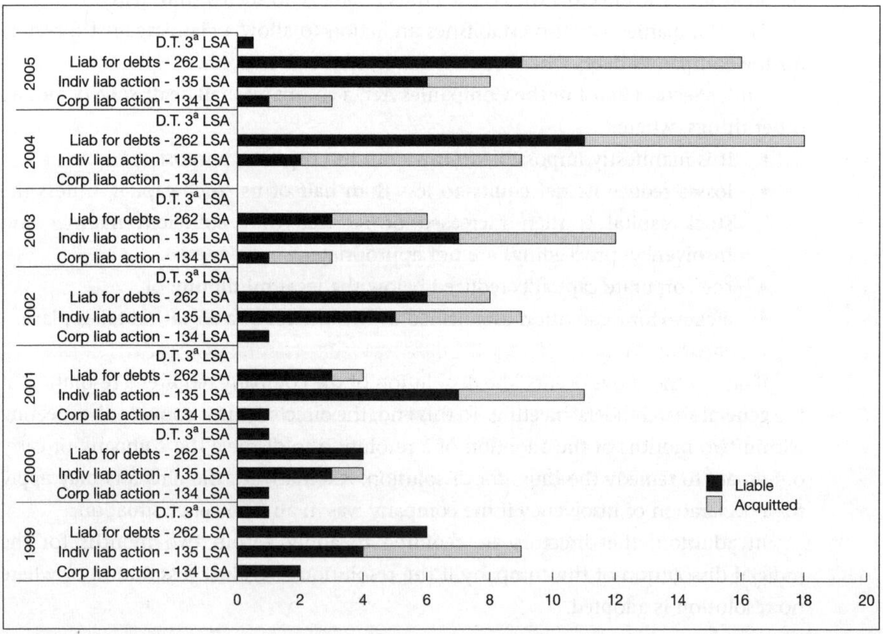

- Corporate liability action – a claim against the directors by the company, shareholders or creditors for damage caused to the company;
- Individual liability action – a claim against the directors by a shareholder or third party for damages caused to such shareholder or third party; and
- Liability for debts – a claim against the directors for joint and several liability for the company's debts.

(ii) Quantum of claims and/or damages awarded

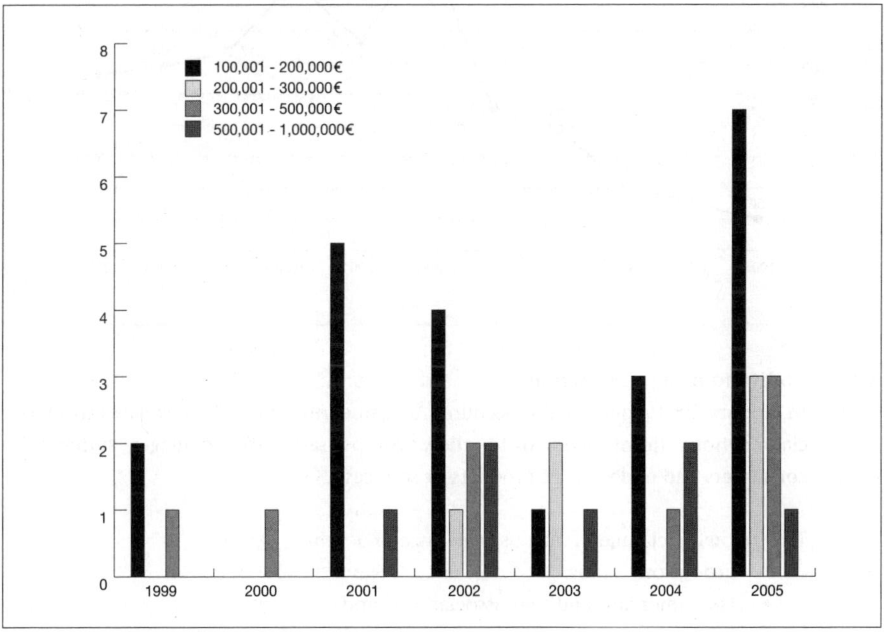

The following conclusions may be reached:

- The number of matters heard by the Supreme Court has increased over the years. Claims against directors are thus more frequent.
- Corporate liability actions are the least frequently brought action against directors. In addition, they rarely succeed.

Individual liability actions and actions for liability for debts are by far the most frequent actions. They are usually brought by creditors and employees of companies in financial difficulties.

In respect of actions for liability for debts, between 1999 and 2002 the majority of judgments went against the defendant directors. However, from 2003, the number of judgments finding directors liable and acquitting them has increased, due to a change in the interpretation criteria of Section 262 of the Companies Act.

The amounts claimed and/or awarded have increased significantly. Most claims and/or awards tend to range between €50,000 and €200,000.

(iii) *Appeal court judgments in civil proceedings against directors from 1995 to 2005*
Supreme Court judgments provide information on trends, but do not allow us to form a view about the actual frequency of claims in Spain. However, the number of judgments issued by the various courts of appeal may give a clearer picture.

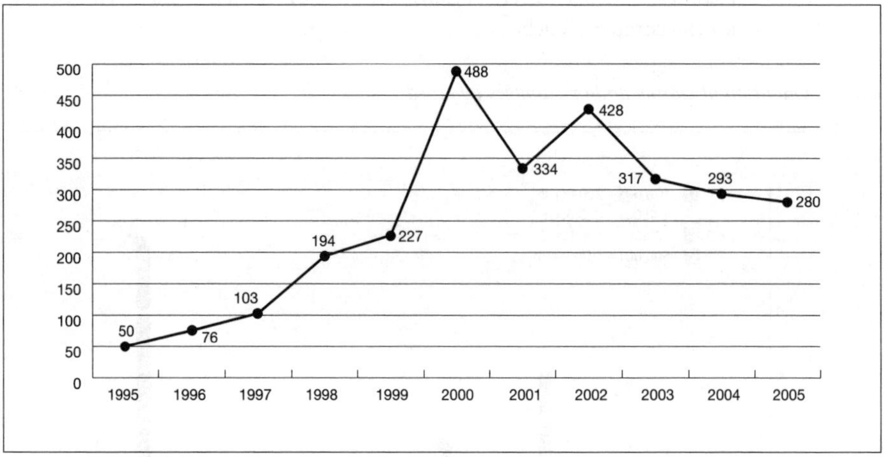

3.2 Ability to bring class actions

In January 2001 a new Civil Procedures Act came into force. The new law introduced class actions (joint actions) to allow compensation for damages suffered by consumers and end users of products or services.

The following claimants may use this type of action:

- groups of victims;
- consumer and end user associations; and
- bodies that are legally incorporated for the protection of consumers and end users.

An association must advertise its intention to claim in advance. It is required to notify its members and any other victims whom it regards as identifiable of its intention to bring a claim or the terms under which it intends to seek to claim. This notice must be given by 'appropriate means'. If this notice has not been given, the judge must not admit the claim, even if this is an error that can be rectified.

Having given the required advance notice, the claim is submitted together with any appropriate documentation – certificates, medical reports, expert reports and so on. Once the claim has been submitted, the court will call all those prejudiced parties who may have an interest in joining as claimants to the proceedings.

In the event that potential prejudiced parties cannot be readily identified (where the general interest is being defended), the judge will suspend the proceedings for a maximum of two months in order to allow prejudiced parties to appear. Both the call to the proceedings and the prior notice must be given in writing or by computerised means which are capable of covering the territory where victims may be located.

If the potential prejudiced parties can be easily identified, the proceedings will not be suspended and prejudiced parties may join the proceedings at any time. In this event they may pursue individual actions within the same proceedings or ask the association to represent them.

The content of the judgment varies according to the type of person affected. When an action is brought with the intention of defending a collective interest - that is, the persons affected are known and are on record as individuals - the judge will be required to assess each individual who is entitled to receive a benefit when making his judgment. However, if a class action is brought for the benefit of consumers in general (in defence of the general interest), the judge must take particular care when making his judgment, as he will be required to determine the detailed characteristics of the victims and to establish the criteria which they must satisfy to benefit from it. If they meet those criteria, victims may approach the court directly to seek enforcement of the judgment and obtain the benefit.

Once the judgment has been given, prejudiced parties have a period of five years to seek enforcement of the judgment. In cases where an association acts in defence of collective or general interests, if the prejudiced party does not seek to be involved in the proceedings or does not seek enforcement of the judgment within the five-year period allowed, he will not be allowed to bring a new action (at that point, the matter will be final and binding).

3.3 Funding of claims and whether loser pays

Firms in Spain usually charge as per the guidance rules provided by their local law society. These rules, which are not mandatory, are based on a tariff system, in proportion to the amount of the claim, and usually establish billing timeframes (eg, 50% of the fees to be billed upon submission of the lawsuit, 20% after the preliminary hearing and the outstanding 30% after the trial). However, firms usually require an upfront payment on account, which may be substantial.

Pursuant to Section 394 of the Civil Procedures Act, a cost order shall be given against the losing party (ie, the party whose claims are rejected in full), unless the case presented reasonable doubts. If the claim partially succeeds, each party must bear its own costs.

The costs recoverable under a costs order may not be all the expenses actually incurred, since they are limited to the amounts set out in the tariff system. In this respect, if the amount at stake is high, the costs recoverable will be significantly less than the actual amount incurred.

A crucial factor in criminal proceedings is that, in practice, costs orders do not exist. Therefore, claimants usually bring criminal complaints and, at the same time, claim for damages. (Under Spanish law, a civil and a criminal action can be brought together, and both actions are heard by the criminal court with little or no risk of facing an adverse costs order.)

'No win, no fee' agreements are not allowed. Additionally, it is not allowed to agree, before the completion of the case, that the client shall pay only a percentage of the amount obtained. In turn, a success fee may be agreed, but it is not recoverable from the losing party.

3.4 Plaintiffs' bar

There is no equivalent in Spain.

3.5 Procedural barriers

Spanish law provides no specific barriers to the bringing of claims.

The Conthe Report recommended that the regulations governing the liability of directors for breach of trust be tightened, but that at the same time a leave to proceed filter should be established so that judges could reject any cases constituting an abuse of process. This recommendation has not been implemented.

On the contrary, Spanish law makes it easy to bring claims. By way of example, one procedural peculiarity in Spain is that where criminal proceedings are brought, the plaintiff (ie, the prejudiced party) is entitled to claim for damages within the criminal proceedings. In addition, third parties are entitled to bring proceedings directly against liability insurers since, under Spanish law, insured and liability insurer are deemed to be jointly and severally liable to third parties.

4. Indemnification rights

4.1 When the company can indemnify

Spanish law does not regulate the indemnification of directors – indemnification is neither expressly allowed nor forbidden.

In the absence of specific regulation, Section 10 of the Companies Act provides that the company's articles of association may include any agreement that is not contrary to the act or to the legal principles that shape limited companies.

On this general basis, some legal commentators maintain that indemnification agreements are not legal, since they would:

- amount to an exemption of liability for directors beyond that permitted in the Companies Act;
- render the regulation of liability of directors (which is of a mandatory nature) void; or
- be detrimental to companies and for the exclusive benefit of directors.

Other legal commentators conclude that indemnification is legal. To this end, they rely on the application by analogy of Section 1893 of the Civil Code which, in respect of the so-called '*negotiorum gestio*' (management of third-party business), establishes the obligation to indemnify to the manager the necessary and useful expenses incurred and the prejudices caused in the performance of the task.

On these grounds, it is argued that indemnities and defence costs could, or even should, be legally indemnified by companies where the defendant directors have not breached any of their duties, provided the claimant is not the company itself. Where the defendant directors have breached their duties, there is more debate, but some commentators still believe that indemnification would be legal with few exceptions (ie, save in certain cases). For instance, companies should not indemnify where:

- the damage has been caused to the company itself;

- the director concerned carried out a wrongful act in breach of fiduciary or loyalty duties to the company; or
- a criminal offence or dishonest act has been committed.

4.2 Formalities for indemnification

No specific formalities are required.

4.3 How indemnification works

In the absence of specific regulation, indemnification should work as follows:

- If the defendant director is found guilty in respect of any of the conduct referred to in section 4.4, the company cannot be required or permitted to indemnify him in any respect (for damages or defence costs).
- If the defendant director is acquitted, the company is permitted to indemnity defence costs. If the acquittal is based on the fact that the defendant director did not breach any duty, the company is required to indemnify defence costs.
- Companies arguably do not have an obligation to advance defence costs, but are permitted to do so.

However, in Spain, indemnification is not an issue since it is not regulated and individual agreements are not that common. In practice, therefore, directors' and officers' liability (D&O) claims in Spain, under Spanish policies, are always handled under Side A.

4.4 What cannot be indemnified

In the absence of specific regulation, pursuant to general legal principles as indicated above, companies arguably cannot indemnify the following:

- damage caused to the company itself, or where the director concerned carried out a wrongful act in breach of fiduciary or loyalty duties to the company;
- damage arising from a criminal offence or dishonest act; and
- fines and penalties.

5. D&O insurance

5.1 Availability of D&O insurance

Spanish companies are not restricted in their ability to take out D&O insurance from any licensed insurer.

5.2 Local rules on cover provided under a non-domestic D&O policy

Where a D&O policy is taken out by a non-resident policyholder from a non-domestic insurer, in principle, the only requirements to be met from the Spanish insurance regulatory perspective relate to licensing (see below) and taxation (insurance premium tax and certain surcharges). Domestic policyholders can take out insurance only from insurers authorised in Spain (whether domestic or non-domestic).

In order to provide insurance business in Spain, a non-domestic insurer must set up a subsidiary. This requires the full incorporation of a new Spanish insurance company and compliance with all the legal and capacity requirements in accordance with Spanish law, not only from an insurance, but also from a corporate point of view.

(a) *EU-based insurers*

An EU-based insurer may set up a branch. Under EU directives, this is the freedom of establishment system. Opening a branch means that the EU-based insurer has a permanent presence in Spain, without losing its nationality. The branch shares the legal personality of the insurer, its assets and its structure.

It is necessary to submit an application to the regulator of the insurer's member state, which will notify the Spanish regulator of the fact that the insurer wishes to open a branch in Spain. Once the Spanish regulator has received the notification, it will have two months to indicate to the regulator of the insurer's member state any conditions under which, for public policy reasons, the applicant would not be entitled to carry out insurance in Spain. If the two-month period elapses and no such indication has been received, the applicant will be entitled to start insurance operations in Spain. The operations of the branch are subject to the supervision of the regulator of the insurer's member state.

Alternatively, EU-based insurers can write insurance on a freedom of services basis. 'Freedom of services' means the direct sale from any EU member state without any permanent presence in Spain. The application process is similar to that described above. A fiscal representative must be appointed to ensure that Spanish tax obligations are met.

(b) *Global policies*

In respect of global or master policies taken out by a non-resident policyholder with a subsidiary in Spain, under the Insurance Regulation and Supervision Act, in the case of liability insurance, the risk is deemed to be located in the state in which the policyholder is domiciled. However, risks affecting a branch are deemed to be located where the branch is domiciled. The consequence is that the insurer issuing a policy that covers the directors and officers of the resident branch must be authorised to do business in Spain. Insurance premium tax must be paid in Spain for the part of the premium corresponding to the risks of the branch.

In addition, non-domestic insurers should note that under Spanish law, third parties are entitled to bring a direct action against liability insurers. Hence, even if the insurance policy may be validly subject to a foreign law, which may not recognise such direct action, there is the risk that a claimant which brings proceedings in Spain may successfully join D&O insurers as a co-defendant.

5.3 Peculiarities of D&O insurance in Spain

(a) *Dishonest acts by the insured*

Section 19 of the Insurance Contracts Act provides that the insurer shall be obliged to pay the indemnity, except where the loss has been caused in bad faith by the insured. In turn, however, Section 117 of the Criminal Code provides that insurers covering liabilities arising from goods, business or any other activity shall be liable, even where the loss constitutes a criminal offence, without prejudice to their right to recover from the insured. Section 76 of the Insurance Contracts Act provides similarly.

On the basis of the above provisions, the Supreme Court has issued a number of judgments which establish that, while it is not legally acceptable for the insured to obtain cover in respect of its fraudulent or dishonest acts, victims must be protected even where the loss is caused by fraudulent acts of the insured. In other words, where the loss arises from a fraudulent, deliberate or dishonest act of the insured, the insurer can deny payment of the loss to the insured, but not to the prejudiced party if the latter brings a direct action against the insurer. Insurers have the right to recover from the insured on payment to the prejudiced party.

(b) *Claiming for damages in criminal proceedings*

Where an act or omission amounts to a criminal offence, the prejudiced party is entitled to bring criminal proceedings. In addition, the prejudiced party is entitled to claim for damages within the criminal proceedings. That is, under Spanish law, civil and criminal actions can be brought together and both actions will be heard by the criminal court. If the court finds that a criminal offence was committed following the trial, damages can be awarded by the criminal court (ie, the criminal court is not allowed to award damages if it finds that no criminal offence was committed). If the defendant is acquitted, the claimant will be entitled to bring civil proceedings.

As indicated above, prejudiced parties are entitled to bring direct action against liability insurers. Consequently, prejudiced parties that bring a criminal complaint against the perpetrator of the facts may claim for damages against the accused person and also against its liability insurer. Thus, liability insurers may become a party to criminal proceedings.

(c) *Bonds*

In criminal proceedings, a judge may impose two different kinds of bond:

- Bail bond – this is a surety required by a judge or court to guarantee the presence of the defendant at the trial while the court is investigating the circumstances surrounding the alleged commission of a crime.
- Civil bond – this is a surety required to secure the payment of damages which may arise from a crime being committed in case the accused persons are found guilty following the trial.

The manner in which bonds should be deposited is left to the discretion of the judge. In practice, the bonds, which can be deposited either by the defendant or by a third party, are paid into the court in one of the following ways:

- in cash;
- by means of a real guarantee (ie, a charge, mortgage or pledge over the assets of the defendant or a third party);
- a bank guarantee; or
- a so-called 'insurer guarantee' (ie, a letter signed by a representative of the insurer securing the payment of the relevant amount, similar to a bank guarantee).

D&O policies usually indicate the extent to which the insurer will contribute to the deposit of the bonds. In practice, the possibilities are as follows:

- The insurer will provide the bond (insurer guarantee). In this case, no cost will be incurred initially by the insurer. However, if the accused director is found guilty of the alleged crime and is ordered to indemnify damages, the bond provided by the insurer will be executed. The insurer will therefore be in a situation in which it must pay a claim to the prejudiced party that arose as a result of a dishonest act of the insured and then attempt to recover from the latter.
- The insurer will run not with the cost of the amount of the bond, but with the financial cost of keeping a bank surety. In practice, this will mean that once the court imposes the bond, the insured defendant will have to attempt to obtain a surety from a bank, which will then be deposited at the court. The insured will be required by the bank to offer a counter-guarantee or comfort letter. He will be able to do this only if he has sufficient assets. Thus, if the bond is for a substantial amount, the insured may not be able to offer such a counter-guarantee and will be unable to obtain the bank surety, so the coverage will be of no use.

However, the Criminal Procedures Act provides that a civil bond may be imposed not only on the accused person (ie, on the person who allegedly committed the criminal offence), but also on any 'liable person' (ie, any person or entity that could be liable for the damage allegedly caused by the accused person). Liability insurers fall within the concept of 'liable persons'. So, for the mere fact of having issued a liability policy, insurers may be directly ordered by the courts to post a civil bond where criminal proceedings are brought against its insured, whether or not the policy provides this kind of cover, as in this case the bond is imposed on the insurer.

(d) Late notification

Late notification of a claim by the insured merely entitles the insurer to seek to recover from the insured, if he can prove it, any damage he may have suffered as a result of the late notification.

This rule is the same regardless of whether prompt notification is stated to be a condition precedent – the condition precedent part of the notification clause will be declared null and void by a Spanish court.

(e) Non-disclosure and misrepresentation

In the event of non-disclosure or misrepresentation of material information, Section 10 of the Insurance Contracts Act allows insurers to rescind the policy within one month or, if the claim has already taken place, to reduce the indemnity by the same proportion as it would have increased the premium had the insurer been aware of the non-disclosed circumstance.

To comply with the duty to disclose all circumstances that may influence the evaluation of the risk, the policyholder need only provide the information that is specifically requested in the proposal form or questionnaire prepared by the insurer.

If the insurer fails to ask about a particular issue, then it cannot at a later stage allege non-disclosure.

Non-disclosure or misrepresentation, save in respect of fraud, gives rise not to avoidance, but merely to rescission. The difference is relevant because avoidance renders the policy invalid *ab initio* (ie, *ex tunc*), while rescission renders the policy invalid from the time rescission is made, but not before (ie, *ex nunc*).

(f) *Claims made*

Following the implementation of EU directives in November 1995, the Spanish Insurance Contracts Act was amended to allow 'claims-made' clauses in insurance policies. At present, a claims-made clause is stated to be a limitation and, as such, is not permitted unless either:

- the contract provides at least one year's retroactive cover; or
- the contract provides at least one year's discovery period.

Therefore, if the claims-made policy contains at least one of these clauses, it will be enforceable. However, claims made and reported provisions are not valid.

Sweden

Susanna Norelid
Advokatfirman NorelidHolm

This chapter focuses solely on the joint stock company. The joint stock company is governed primarily by the Companies Act 2005, in force since January 1 2006, and by the company's articles of association. Since 2005, there has been a Business Code in use among the major companies on the Swedish stock market. This code is a result of self-regulation and contains, among other things, recommendations on the work, composition and tasks of the board of directors. There are no regulations on remedies in the code.

The governing powers of a company are divided between the shareholders' meeting, the board of directors and the managing director, which stand in a strictly hierarchical relationship to each other. The board of directors has the right to appoint a managing director; but there is an obligation to do so only in public companies. The Companies Act also contains provisions on a fourth company body, the auditors.

The shareholders' meeting is the company's supreme governing body and can decide on almost all matters relating to the company. Among other things, it is responsible for:

- adoption of the profit and loss account and the balance sheet;
- allocation of the company's losses and profits;
- discharge from liability of members of the board and the managing director;
- election of members of the board and of the auditors;
- amendment of the articles of association;
- new issues and bonus issues;
- reduction of share capital;
- winding-up; and
- dissolution.

In companies with no managing director, the board is responsible for all matters that are not dealt with at the shareholders' meeting (ie, the organisation and general management of the company). Where a managing director is appointed, his duties are the day-to-day management of the company. This is discussed below.

1. Directors' duties

1.1 Nature of the duties

As mentioned above, in companies with no managing director, the board is responsible for all matters that are not dealt with at the shareholders' meeting. This includes:

- establishing long-term goals for the company;
- setting up the budget;
- preparing the annual report;
- providing the company with an effective organisation; and
- ensuring the organisation of company records and the management of company funds.

The board must also follow orders and directions given by the shareholders' meeting, provided that such orders do not infringe the Companies Act or the articles of association, and are not so far reaching that the board loses its actual power to manage the company.

The board may delegate some of its responsibilities to certain directors or other parties, but cannot delegate ultimate responsibility for:

- the organisation and general management of the company;
- control of the company's bookkeeping; or
- the continuous economic assessment of the administration of the company's assets and financial situation.

As the board is responsible for the long-term goals of the company, the managing director is in charge of the day-to-day business. The scope of this responsibility extends to all measures which are not exceptional or of major importance, considering the scope and nature of the company's operations. Typically, this includes matters such as responsibility for:

- the company's business and its staff;
- ensuring control of the company's bookkeeping; and
- the continuous economic assessment of the administration of the company's assets and financial situation.

The managing director's duties also include an obligation to prepare matters for decision by the board and to keep the directors informed on all matters that are necessary for them to fulfil their duties.

Since the question of what comprises day-to-day management often differs from company to company, depending on size and operations, it is sometimes difficult to determine where the responsibilities of the board end and those of the managing director begin. For the sake of clarity, the board is obliged to set out written instructions for the managing director, as well as procedural rules for its own operation.

In urgent cases, the managing director can act beyond the scope of day-to-day management, but he must notify the board of his actions at the earliest possible opportunity. The board also has the right to empower the managing director to act beyond the scope of day-to-day management, although this can never be allowed to limit the board's status as the superior company organ.

It is possible to select one or several deputy managing directors, but not to select several managing directors and prescribe joint decision-making powers or to divide responsibility among them.

1.2 Standards of care

Members of the board and the managing director are liable for damage caused within the scope of their responsibilities. Such liability is regulated by the Companies Act.

There is no collective liability for the board. An individual assessment is always made regarding the acts of every director. Under the Companies Act, members of the board and the managing director may be liable for pure financial loss (ie, if they intentionally or negligently cause such loss to the company when performing their duties). Damage caused by directors outside the scope of their duties in the company is governed by the Tort Liability Act and general principles on tort. Liability towards shareholders and third parties arises where the financial loss is caused by an act which violates the Companies Act, the Law on Annual Accounts or the company's articles of association.

The evaluation of whether an act was caused by neglect is made by comparing it to the normal standard of care that may be expected in the business or the company. The starting point is the Companies Act, the company's articles of association and any other regulation or guidance for directors used in the company. A director's personal knowledge or lack of experience is rarely seen as providing an exemption from liability, although the evaluation of what is negligent behaviour is stricter for a director specifically appointed for his skills or knowledge.

Where a director or managing director is liable for damages, these may be adjusted in accordance with what is reasonable, taking into consideration the nature of the act, the extent of the damages and the general circumstances of the case. Where several persons are deemed liable for the same damage, they are jointly and severally liable.

Officers and other company employees who are not directors are not covered by the regulations on damages in the Companies Act. Their responsibility towards third parties relating to actions within the scope of their employment is regulated by the Tort Liability Act. It is the company, and not the employee personally, which is responsible for personal or property damage caused by errors or neglect, as well as for financial loss, if the act or omission constitutes a criminal act. In order for the company to be responsible, the act must have been taken by the employee within the scope of his employment. An employee can be personally responsible only in exceptional cases; an assessment is made of the nature of the act, the employee's position in the company, the interest of the injured party and all other circumstances. Examples are cases where the employer is the injured party, where the damage was caused intentionally or where the employee was employed due to his special knowledge or had a special position in the company. Liability towards the company can be imposed on officers and other employees only for financial losses caused by a criminal act.

1.3 To whom duties are owed

(a) *The company and the shareholders*

Directors and officers are expected to act in the best interest of the company (ie, in a way that does not harm the company). Directors may be liable to pay damages to the company where they cause financial loss to the company intentionally or as a result of negligence. In severe cases of damage, directors can also be sentenced for disloyalty. When making business decisions, there is always a risk that the decision may prove to be wrong and that the company will suffer losses. The directors and the managing director are expected to identify and minimise risks; but a certain degree of risk will always be accepted and will not be seen as arising as a result of negligence, provided that the act itself does not violate the Companies Act or the articles of association. The degree of accepted risk taking varies from business to business, but overall, directors are always entitled to take business risks without being held liable for losses by such decisions. This is known as the business judgement rule.

In cases where the company must pay damages to shareholders and third parties and the damage was caused by a director's negligence, but without any violation of the Companies Act, the Law on Annual Accounts or the articles of association, the company in turn may claim against the director for the loss it suffered.

The board is never obliged to perform legal acts or take other steps which are intended to provide undue advantage to a shareholder or other person to the disadvantage of the company or other shareholders.

(b) *In case of insolvency*

Immediately upon determining that there is reason to believe that the share capital of the company is less than one-half of the registered share capital, the board is obliged to prepare and present a control balance sheet to the auditors. If this balance sheet confirms the suspicion, the board shall, as soon as possible, present the matter of winding up the company to the shareholders' meeting. The shareholders must, within eight months, either approve a balance sheet approved by the auditors showing that the share capital is restored or, if it is not restored, decide to wind up the company. If the capital is not restored and a decision on winding-up is not made, the directors must make a submission to the court to wind up the company. If the board or directors fail to fulfil these duties, they will be held jointly and severally liable for any obligation incurred by the company.

(c) *Tax, labour and environmental legislation*

The board of directors and the managing director may be held personally liable to pay taxes where the company fails to pay its taxes or does not withhold tax in due time, according to the Tax Payment Act. A director who has filed incorrect information leading to the company being credited with excess input of value added tax is – along with the company – liable to repay the relevant amount.

As it is the company, and not the board, which is seen as the employer, the directors or officers are not held personally responsible for any violation of employment legislation, such as wrongful termination of contracts carried out by the company. It is always the company that is liable for such acts.

(d) *Criminal liability*

(i) *General*

According to Swedish law, a legal entity cannot commit a crime. When a crime is committed, it is therefore always a physical person who will be held liable according to law.

(ii) *Penal Code and tax, labour and environmental legislation*

Examples of crimes in the Penal Code for which a director, manager or officer may be held liable relating to his duties in the company include disloyalty, fraud and various kinds of economic crime. Violations of the Occupational Safety and Health Act and other violations relating to employee protection can also be prosecuted.

(iii) *Companies Act*

According to the Companies Act, fines or terms of imprisonment not exceeding one year shall be imposed on any person who violates certain regulations of the act. This applies mainly to any person who intentionally attempts to sell shares or offer securities for subscription or sale to a wide range of people or on an organised marketplace (investor fraud), and to other related minor misdemeanours.

A fine can be imposed on a board member who intentionally contributes to the election of a managing director who has no intention to participate in the management of the company, if the purpose of such action is to conceal the identity of the person who is actually in control of the company.

1.4 Common defences to and exemptions from liability

As previously mentioned, the act or omission causing the damage must have been caused within the director's scope of responsibility in order for the damage to be regulated by the Companies Act. The act or omission itself must have been done negligently or intentionally, and must in itself have caused the damage. If the damage would have occurred anyway or was caused by factors other than the act or omission, the director is not held liable.

In cases where the work and responsibilities of the board members or the managing director are strictly regulated by the shareholders' meeting, or where the managing director is closely monitored by the board, and duties are imposed on the directors according to law, the director is not held liable for damage caused. Thus, for a director to face personal liability for damage, he must have had scope to act with a degree of freedom within the capacity given to him by the Companies Act. Otherwise, liability will lie with the organ holding the real power.

At the shareholders' meeting, the shareholders shall, when confirming the balance sheet, decide whether to discharge the board of directors and the managing director from liability towards the company. This decision is made regarding each individual director and not the board as a whole. The decision granting discharge from liability constitutes confirmation by the shareholders that the duty was duly performed and that the company does not intend to initiate any legal proceedings regarding damages. For exemptions, see section 3.5.

2. Who can bring claims

2.1 The company (and its liquidators)

A claim for financial loss on behalf of the company may be brought against the directors if a majority of the shareholders, or a minority representing 10% of the shares, decides at the shareholders' meeting either to raise a claim or not to discharge the directors from liability towards the company. The claim is then brought on behalf of the company by one of the company's bodies – normally, the board of directors.

The liquidator and the administrator in bankruptcy may also bring proceedings regarding damages against directors, on behalf of the bankrupt estate.

A matter can be settled by a majority of shareholders, unless a minority holding a minimum of 10% of the shares votes against it.

2.2 Minority shareholders on behalf of the company

A minority of the shareholders representing at least 10% of the shares also has the right to claim damages on behalf of the company.

2.3 Shareholders on their own account

Minority shareholders are in this case seen as regular third parties (see section 2.4).

2.4 Third parties

As previously stated, liability towards individual shareholders and third parties presupposes that the directors in question have violated the Companies Act, the Law on Annual Accounts or the articles of association, or that the injury was caused by a criminal act. Due to these prerequisites, directors cannot be held directly liable for breach of contract.

A creditor may secure its rights against the company through an action for damages made through the receiver in bankruptcy or can bring proceedings for damage against the directors directly.

Where an omission or decision made by a director or managing director constitutes a criminal act, the injured person may also invoke liability in tort in cases involving financial loss.

3. Claims culture

3.1 Litigation

The Swedish judicial system is divided between:

- courts with civil and criminal jurisdiction; and
- special administrative courts with jurisdiction regarding the public and the government.

Swedish law is codified. The two court systems consist of civil and administrative district and appellate courts, as well as one Supreme Court and one Supreme Administrative Court.

Court proceedings and all documents submitted are public. The courts are also obliged to provide access to their files.

In civil proceedings, the burden of proof rests with the person making a claim. Remuneration for physical damage and personal injury is restricted according to Swedish tradition. Under general principles on tort, it is possible to bring an action only for financial loss caused by a criminal act.

The most common situations where a claim is made against board members or directors are in case of bankruptcy, claims relating to taxes or in regard to M&A transactions. Most of these cases are settled by arbitration. In recent years, increasing numbers of claims have been brought in Sweden, although case law is still lacking.

3.2 Ability to bring class actions

It is possible to bring class actions in Sweden. Generally, such actions are brought in consumer-related matters and in case of environmental damage. The major pieces of legislation in this area are the Law on Class Actions, the Environmental Code and the Code of Judicial Procedure.

The system of class actions is based on an opt-in model. Only persons who have given written notification to the court within a specified timeframe will be allowed to participate. Members of the class in Sweden do not become parties to the proceedings and are not required actively to participate in the proceedings. The court's judgment is binding.

Three types of action are allowed:

- private class actions, where any person may initiate an action as long as that person is part of the class;
- organisational class actions, where certain non-profit making consumer and labour organisations may initiate actions without having a claim of their own. Generally, these claims must concern disputes between consumers and providers of goods or services; and
- public class actions, where an authority appointed by the government may bring an action if the public interest so requires.

Only six claims have been brought since the act entered into force in January 2003. This compares with assumptions made before the act was enacted of about 15 to 20 cases annually. This can be explained by the restrictive opt-in system, as compared with the US opt-out system.

3.3 Funding of claims and whether loser pays

According to the Code of Judicial Procedure, litigation costs claimed by a party in a civil procedure shall fully cover the cost of preparing the case and bringing it to trial.

According to the Code of Judicial Procedure, the losing party, including the party whose claim is dismissed, is liable to pay the other party's legal costs (this is known as the 'English rule'). The exceptions are certain criminal cases and matters regarding family law.

The regulation of litigation costs differs somewhat where a class action is brought, as a member of the group bringing a class action is normally not responsible for paying the plaintiffs' litigation costs himself. In general, passive class members have no obligation to compensate a successful defendant for any legal costs.

In class actions, the plaintiff may adopt a contingency fee arrangement, making the fee dependent on the outcome of the case. Such agreements are not yet allowed in any other type of case according to the ethical rules of the Swedish Bar Association.

3.4 Plaintiffs' bar

There is no such thing as a plaintiffs' bar in the Swedish legal system

3.5 Procedural barriers

A claim for financial loss on behalf of the company may be brought against the directors if a majority of the shareholders, or a minority holding at least 10% of the shares at a shareholders' meeting, decides either to raise a claim or not to discharge the directors from liability towards the company. The decision on whether to discharge the board and the managing director from liability is made regarding each director individually. In cases where a director is not discharged from liability, proceedings on behalf of the company for damages as a consequence of decisions or measures taken during the financial year must be brought not later than one year from the date on which the annual report and the auditors' report for that financial year were presented to the shareholders' meeting.

Where a shareholders' meeting has discharged the directors from liability or the statute of limitations has expired, an action may nonetheless be brought if the decision was based on a faulty report. The formal discharge from liability is thus of minor legal importance in reality. Having said that, no claim for damages - unless it is based on criminal acts - may be brought against directors if five years have elapsed since the expiry of the financial year in which the act on which the legal action is based was adopted or taken. Special time bars apply in relation to criminal acts. As regards liability for tax, the prescription period is a maximum of five years from the expiry of the year of assessment in which the recovery process was initiated.

If the company is declared bankrupt pursuant to a petition filed before this five-year period has expired, the bankruptcy estate may bring proceedings regarding damages, notwithstanding that the directors were discharged from liability by the shareholders' meeting, the matter was settled or the one-year period mentioned above has expired. Following the expiry of the five-year period, such proceedings may not be brought later than six months after the date of the hearing in respect of administration of oaths.

4. Indemnification rights

4.1 When the company can indemnify

The company can indemnify its directors under Swedish law for damages they are obliged to pay when acting on behalf of the company, as well as for defence costs. The company also has the right to advance defence costs and to indemnify if the claim is settled before trial. This can be arranged either through a D&O insurance or by paying from its own funds. All of this is covered by D&O insurance. The form of proceeding is irrelevant as regards indemnification, since it is the act itself that determines whether the director can be indemnified (but see section 4.4 on criminal acts).

4.2 Formalities for indemnification

There are no statues or other legislative sources regulating indemnification. The issue is governed by the insurance policy or by the company's articles of association. This can also be regulated between the company and the members of the board, or by the director in a special agreement.

4.3 How indemnification works

There is no special procedure to be followed in respect of indemnification and the parties therefore decide how this should be carried out.

4.4 What cannot be indemnified

The director of a board is liable for acts within his duties as a member of the board. Only such acts can be indemnified; these can include minor criminal violations of special legislation.

5. D&O insurance

5.1 Availability of D&O insurance

The shareholders' meeting decides whether the company will purchase D&O insurance. The decision is formally granted to the board within certain economic limits. D&O insurance is very common in Sweden.

D&O insurance, domestic or foreign, states that the law of the country where the damage was caused (*lex loci delicti*) regulates the amount of the remunerable damage and the amount paid under the insurance. Damage that occurs in Sweden is therefore governed by Swedish law - that is, by the Insurance Contract Act. The act covers both domestic and non-domestic insurance. It sets minimum standards that may be departed from only if this is to the benefit of the insured; but the act also contains many rules that can be set aside by the contracting parties.

The insurer is free from liability if a loss is caused by an insured intentionally. Where an insured has failed to comply with a safety regulation issued by the insurer, the insurer is free from liability only if the failure has a causal link to the damage.

The only directors regulated in Swedish company law are the members of the board of directors and the managing director. The company's auditors, although a corporate 'body', are not considered as officers or directors of the company. The position of chief financial officer is not legally defined in Swedish company law.

5.2 Local rules on cover provided under a non-domestic D&O policy

An insurer that is authorised to operate as an insurer in its home country within the European Union is automatically authorised to act in all other EU countries, including Sweden. An insurer from a non-EU country wishing to act in Sweden must establish a branch or a subsidiary company in Sweden. The insurer establishing a subsidiary in Sweden may automatically act through that subsidiary throughout the European Union, but a company establishing only a branch office is allowed to act only in the country where the branch is established.

In Sweden, an insurance licence is granted by the Financial Supervisory Authority, which is the regulating body for the financial markets. The company must deposit a security to a value of about Skr12 million (January 2007) before a licence can be granted.

There are no special local rules where the parent company of a Swedish subsidiary obtains a global policy from a non-EU insurer and this covers the resident subsidiary. The parties are free to decide on the rules to apply to this situation. Most commonly in Sweden, the law of the country where the damage was caused (*lex loci delicti*) is chosen as applicable law when determining liability as such, the size of the remunerable damage and the possibility for any recovery of paid amounts. It is common among Scandinavian multinationals to obtain master policies with global scope from insurers located outside the European Union and to add local sub-policies based entirely on local law for subsidiaries in selected countries.

5.3 Statute of limitations

The insurer may order an insured to present his claim for damages within six months of first becoming aware of the claim. In addition, the person who has a claim must bring a legal action against the insurer within three years of becoming aware of the claim and not later than 10 years from the time the claim could first be made. If the claim is presented within the appropriate timeframes, a legal action must be brought by the insured within six months if the insurer finally denies the claim.

5.4 Availability of D&O insurance (Scandinavia)

(a) Denmark

According to the Danish Insurance Act, the regulations on penalties for late premium payments are mandatory. Where the insured has caused the loss through gross negligence, the indemnification is reduced in accordance with what is reasonable. Agreements under which the insurer is freed from liability in cases of non-gross negligence are forbidden, although the amount of indemnification can be reduced by a maximum of 5% in such cases.

A claim is time barred if it is not presented to the insurer within two years of the calendar year in which the injured party becomes aware of both the existence of claim and the fact that it is due, or at the latest five years after the claim becomes due. The insurer also bears the burden of proving that the insured did not follow safety regulations. The Danish regulations are being reviewed at the time of writing.

(b) *Finland*

Agreements executed under the Finnish Insurance Act and which derogate from the act to the disadvantage of a party other than the policy holder, such as another insured or other person entitled to compensation, are not allowed Where the insurer uses misleading or inaccurate information in its marketing, the insurance agreement may be regarded as including the content which the insured had reason to believe was contained therein as a result of the information he received. The same applies to information provided during the insurance period.

The Finnish act contains mandatory provisions on when and how an insurer may terminate the insurance. In cases where the insured does not fulfil the obligation to provide information, or deliberately or negligently provides inaccurate information, the insurer can refuse to pay all or part of the indemnification and has the right to terminate the insurance or change its conditions. Similar rules apply for risk increases. The insurer is free from liability where the insured has intentionally caused the damage; and the indemnification may be refused or reduced in case of gross negligence. The same applies where the insured negligently fails to comply with a safety regulation.

The Finnish Act also contains provisions on late payment of insurance premiums; and there are limitations regarding the indemnification of goods where the insurance amount exceeds the value of the goods insured. A third party can in some cases (eg, bankruptcy) demand indemnification directly from the insurer.

A claim is time barred if it is not presented to the insurer within one year of the insured finding out that such a claim could be made or at the latest 10 years after the damage has occurred. In addition, a person who receives a decision regarding the insurance must bring a legal action against the insurer within three years of the decision.

(c) *Norway*

As a fundamental principle, the Norwegian Insurance Act has mandatory application in favour of the policy holder or the insured. Application of the law is largely non-mandatory in relation to some insurance with foreign links and company insurance for bigger enterprises - that is, companies that fulfil two of the following criteria:

- more than 250 employees;
- a turnover of at least Nkr100 million; or
- property of a value of at least Nkr50 million.

Fulfilment of the information duties of insurers is governed by the Norwegian supervisory authority. If the company fails to fulfil these duties, it is obliged to pay damages. The Norwegian act also includes regulations on:

- how an insurance agreement can be entered into;
- the period during which insurance companies can be held liable for losses;
- termination and changes of insurance;

- issues of premiums;
- termination of insurance for late payment of premiums;
- amounts of indemnification;
- third-party rights;
- prescription rules;
- the handling of claims by national boards; and
- certain time limits.

It further sets out the duties of the insured, such as:
- the information duty of the insured;
- the duty to apply safety regulations;
- how to act when the risk of a loss has increased;
- the duty to minimise damage;
- the duty to report damage; and
- cases where damage is caused intentionally or by gross neglect.

If these rules are not followed, the indemnification is reduced in accordance with what is reasonable. In certain cases, the insurer may be freed from liability.

Switzerland

Philipp Känzig
Staiger Schwald & Partner

1. Directors' duties

1.1 Nature of the duties

This chapter focuses on the duties and liabilities of directors of Swiss companies limited by shares. Many of the rules relating to the duties and, in particular, the liability of directors also apply to other executive bodies of a company, such as the liquidators, the auditors and, in particular, the officers of the company to whom the directors have delegated some of their duties. Also, although the company limited by shares is by far the most popular corporate structure in Switzerland, similar rules apply to the executive bodies of other legal entities such as a limited liability partnership and a cooperative.

(a) *Source of duties*

The primary source of the duties of the directors of a company limited by shares is Section 26 (Articles 620 to 763) of the Federal Code of Obligations, in particular Articles 716 and 717. The fundamental provisions on the liability of directors, auditors, liquidators, founders and officers of companies limited by shares can be found in Articles 752 to 760 of the Federal Code of Obligations. Apart from these fundamental rules, various other laws and regulations impose duties on executive bodies of companies and deal with the possible consequences of a violation of these duties. Most notably, the Federal Code on Stock Exchanges and Securities Trading imposes duties on the officers and directors of listed companies, particularly in the context of public offerings. The Federal Code on Debt Collection and Bankruptcy provides for the assignment of liability claims to the creditors of a bankrupt company if the receiver is not inclined to pursue these claims itself.

(b) *Types of duty*

The two principal duties of the directors of a company are the duty of due care and the duty of loyalty. Article 717 of the Federal Code of Obligations expressly mentions only these two duties and the duty to treat all shareholders equally in comparable circumstances (Article 717(2)). All other duties (eg, the duty of confidentiality, good faith) are generally allocated to one or both of the two principal duties.

(c) *Delegation*

Article 716 of the Federal Code of Obligations expressly provides that the board of directors is actively in charge of running the company's day-to-day business to the extent that it has not delegated these duties. By law, the board of directors is responsible not only for strategic decisions and the supervision of company officers, but also for the day-to-day running of the company's business. However, Article 716b of the Federal Code of Obligations allows the board of directors to delegate the running of the company's business to company officers if the power to delegate is explicitly provided for in the articles of association. Where the articles of association allow delegation, the board of directors must enact written bylaws for management. However, there is a list of fundamental duties that cannot be delegated and will remain the exclusive responsibility of the board of directors. According to Article 716a, this applies to:

- the overall executive responsibility for the company;
- the definition and implementation of the organisational structure of the company;
- the implementation of correct bookkeeping procedures, financial planning and financial control;
- the appointment and removal of officers;
- supervision of the officers of the company;
- preparation for, and reporting to, the general shareholders' meeting;
- implementation of resolutions of the general shareholders' meeting; and
- notification of the competent court in the event of insolvency.

The board at all times remains fully responsible and liable for the careful and loyal execution of these duties. Delegation of these fundamental duties will not be effective, even if the articles of association were to allow for it. These duties also define the areas in which the board should not tolerate interference from the shareholders. To the extent that the board of directors has exercised its right to delegate duties in compliance with the formal and material requirements for delegation, the members of the board of directors are released from their obligation to carry out these duties themselves. However, the board of directors remains responsible for the diligent selection, instruction and supervision of the officers to whom these duties have been delegated. As mentioned above, Article 716a provides that the board of directors must supervise the officers of the company.

A formal and materially correct delegation could also prevent criminal prosecution. In a recent revision of the Penal Code, provisions were introduced which make it possible to punish a company (with heavy fines) if a criminal offence is committed within the company and it is not possible to attribute the criminal act to an individual. This is an additional reason why the board of directors should take great care in implementing organisational bylaws that not only delegate certain duties, but also carefully define responsibilities. Failure to do so would be a breach of the duty to exercise due care and can, in the event that the company is fined, lead to the personal liability of the members of the board of directors.

(d) *Scope of the law*

Article 717 of the Federal Code of Obligations provides for a duty of care and loyalty, not only of the directors but also of any other individuals entrusted with the management of a company. These duties apply to all executive bodies of the company who are expressly empowered to make material decisions on behalf of the company, such as the officers and directors who are registered in the Commercial Register. However, these duties also apply to those who exercise corporate powers without being formally registered. This is of particular importance for creditors, who could be tempted to get involved in management decisions in a restructuring scenario.

The rules relating to the duties of the board of directors are addressed not only to the board of directors as a corporate body, but also to every individual member of this corporate body.

The scope of application of the rules on liability is even broader. These rules apply not only to the directors, but also to the founders, the authors of any prospectus, the auditors and all individuals who are in charge of running the company. Again, it is not the formal position that counts, but rather the functions a person undertakes. The Federal Supreme Court has applied the rules of liability to all those who have a substantial influence on the policy of a company and who actually take decisions that should be taken by the company's officers or directors. Banks and other major creditors of companies in financial distress which have been unable to withstand the temptation to exercise influence have, in the past, found themselves in the position of defendants, responding to claims based on the concept of 'factual corporate body'.

The duties mentioned above and the rules on liability do not extend to a shareholder of a company, even if the shareholder holds a majority interest. Again, it is important that the shareholder does not involve himself in the management of the company by taking decisions that by law, or in accordance with the company's articles of association, are reserved for the board of directors. If a shareholder limits himself to casting his vote at the general shareholders' meeting, he cannot be held liable. A majority shareholder may therefore influence the policy of a company without incurring liability. This can make the position of the board of directors difficult, particularly if the general shareholders' meeting gives directions that the board of directors cannot implement without violating its duties. In such case the directors can avoid personal liability only by resigning. They cannot hide behind the decisions of a majority shareholder.

1.2 Standards of care

(a) *Source of required standard of care*

As mentioned above, Article 717 of the Federal Code of Obligations states that a member of the board of directors is required to exercise due care (and to be loyal to the company). The guidelines given in Article 99 of the Federal Code of Obligations deal with liability resulting from the violation of legal obligations. In addition, two regulations have recently been enacted which attempt to define standards of corporate governance for listed companies. The SWX Guidelines regarding Information on Corporate Governance were enacted based on Articles 8(2) and (3) of the Stock Exchange Act and contain rules for transactions with related parties, in particular with officers and directors. The second document is the Swiss Code of Best Practice for Corporate Governance, published by economiesuisse, an important private association of Swiss industry. As economiesuisse has no legislative powers, the code contains only recommendations. However, with time, these recommendations can be used to define the standard in industry.

(b) Standard of care required

The standard of care required from a member of the board of directors is measured in an objective manner. Every member of the board must act in the manner that may reasonably be expected of an 'ordinary person' in the same situation. According to the established jurisprudence of the Federal Supreme Court, the law requires that a person should accept a position on a board of directors only if he is capable of assuming the duties of that position and of spending the time necessary to comply with them. Therefore, a member of a board of directors cannot excuse himself by claiming a subjective lack of knowledge or lack of time.

Basically, the law provides for liability even for slight negligence, the real test being whether the person in question acted in a manner that could objectively be expected from a person in his position.

Recently, there has been a tendency to depart from the commonsense approach historically applied and to use the business judgement rule in defining the objective level of care required. This rule tends to put an emphasis on compliance with correct procedure in reaching a decision, rather than the material soundness of the decision as such. In other words, the decision-taking process is placed under scrutiny. According to Swiss law, it is not permitted to limit this investigation solely to formal aspects. At the very least, a procedurally correct decision must also be reached based on a reasonable analysis of adequate information. Also, the decision of the directors must be lawful. An unlawful decision, even if reached through a formally correct procedure, remains a violation of the duty of due care.

(c) Duty of loyalty

It is not always easy to distinguish between the duty of due care and the duty of loyalty. According to Article 717, the members of the board of directors have a duty of loyalty and must act in the interests of the company to the best of their ability. The Federal Supreme Court has, in a long series of decisions, defined some principal duties that must be observed in this respect:

- The directors and officers of a company are required to keep any business secrets of the company strictly confidential and not to use personally or divulge any insider information.
- The members of the board of directors and the officers of a company are not allowed to compete with the company.
- The members of the board of directors must always put the interests of the company first. Although it is not illegal for a member of the board to enter

into a contractual relationship with the company, the transaction is required to be at arm's length in all respects. The members of the board of directors must also put the interests of the company before the interests of its shareholders. This can be a problem in the – quite common – case that the director is a nominee. Such members of the board of directors can easily find themselves with a conflict of interest. Although it has been argued that different rules should apply for members of the board of directors in groups of companies (appointed by the parent company to serve as member of the board of a subsidiary company), the Swiss courts have not accepted a different standard thus far. Individual members of the board of such companies remain personally liable if they put the interests of the parent company before the interests of the company itself.

- The duty of equal treatment of shareholders is also considered to be part of the directors' duty of loyalty. Unequal treatment is not prohibited *per se*, but must always be motivated by objective reasons and be in the interest of the company.
- Finally, in the event of a conflict of interest, a member of the board of directors should resign in order to avoid liability, and if this is not possible, must not involve himself in any manner whatsoever in the process by which a decision is reached.

1.3 To whom duties are owed

As mentioned above, the primary duty of a director is always owed to the company. Nevertheless, the Federal Supreme Court has distinguished between rules that were established – at least in part – for the protection of creditors and rules that are significant only to the relationship between the company and its directors. This distinction is significant in the context of the right of creditors to bring claims. The most notable rules intended for the protection of creditors are as follows:

- The board of directors must immediately notify the bankruptcy judge if the company is over-indebted. If the members of the board delay notification, they can become liable for any increase in damages suffered by the creditors from the point of time the judge should have been notified.
- The board must act if assets no longer cover less than half of the share capital and legal reserves of the company. In this event, the board is required immediately to convene a general shareholders' meeting and propose financial restructuring measures.
- The law restricts the possibility of the company legally to acquire its own shares. Various other provisions of the law are designed to preserve the share capital and legal reserves of the company as potential security for the claims of creditors. Any violation of these provisions by the board of directors would constitute a serious breach of duty.
- An important provision is also addressed to the auditors of the company. In accordance with Article 729b of the Federal Code of Obligations, the auditors are legally required to notify the bankruptcy judge if the company is over-indebted and the board of directors does not itself notify the judge. Failure to comply with the duty can lead to the liability of the auditors of the company.

Other duties are owed to the shareholders. Most notable among these is the duty, already mentioned above, to treat shareholders equally. The shareholder also has a right of information and supervision. Article 696 of the Federal Code of Obligations provides that the board of directors has a duty to provide the shareholders with the information necessary to exercise shareholders' rights in the general shareholders' meeting. Article 697 further provides for a right of the shareholder to direct enquiries to the board of directors and the auditors of the company. The board and the auditors must provide information to the extent that this is necessary for the shareholder to exercise shareholders' rights. However, business secrets do not have to be disclosed. According to Article 752 of the Federal Code of Obligations, subscribers of securities issued by a company have a cause of action against anyone, including the directors of the company, who was involved in the subscription procedure and made or disseminated incorrect, misleading or incomplete statements.

No specific separate duties are owed to employees. However, they frequently form an important group of (preferred) creditors in an insolvency scenario. The payment of social security contributions often becomes an issue if a company is declared bankrupt. The members of the board of directors can be made personally liable if these contributions were not fully paid up to the date of bankruptcy.

1.4 Common defences to and exemptions from liability

(a) Failure to establish elements of relevant cause of action

As with most claims for liability, the cause of action for directors' liability requires four elements:

- a breach of duty;
- specific quantifiable damages;
- an adequate causal link between the breach of duty and the damages incurred; and
- negligence.

A breach of duty is assumed if the director acts in violation of a duty stated by the law or by the articles of incorporation. As mentioned above, the principal duties are the duty of due care and the duty of loyalty. An objective test is applied in order to determine whether such a duty has been violated (see section 1.2).

'Damages' are defined as the difference between the actual current financial situation of the company and the situation the company would be in if no violation of duty had taken place. A distinction is made between direct and indirect damages. This distinction is extremely important with respect to the right of shareholders and creditors to bring claims. If damages are suffered directly by shareholders or creditors, they are entitled to proceed directly against the responsible directors. If not, the company has a cause of action and creditors and shareholders may have derivative actions.

A violation of a duty complies with the test of 'adequate causal link' if, according to the normal course of events and the general experience of life, it is likely to result in the damages effectively incurred. The Federal Supreme Court has consistently applied this formula.

Negligence is rarely a difficult element to prove if a breach of duty has objectively been determined. As mentioned above, even slight negligence is sufficient.

(b) *Specific defences*

(i) *General*

The board of directors has a number of duties it cannot delegate and for which it is always directly responsible (see section 1.1). If a violation of such a duty results (in an adequate causal manner) in damages, there is very little the director can use as a defence apart from purely formal objections (eg, statute of limitations, formal discharge). Outside of the scope of these core duties, however, a director can defend himself by showing that the duty in question was delegated to the management of the company in a formally correct manner and that he complied with his duties of carefully choosing, instructing and supervising management.

(ii) *Discharge*

The law provides for the possibility that the annual general shareholders' meeting gives discharge to the members of the board of directors. The effects of such a discharge are described in Article 758 of the Federal Code of Obligations. With respect to any facts disclosed to the shareholders, the discharge has the effect that both the company and the shareholders that voted in favour of the discharge or that acquired shares subsequently with knowledge of the resolution are barred from bringing an action against the board of directors. The right of all other shareholders to bring an action against the members of the board of directors expires six months after the discharge was granted. The discharge of the board of directors is therefore regularly on the agenda of the annual general shareholders' meetings of Swiss companies limited by shares. Frequently, however, it does not serve to protect the directors, as the facts that later lead to a claim for liability are regularly not disclosed to the shareholders.

2. Who can bring claims

2.1 The company (and its liquidators)

(a) *Solvent company*

The company itself is the principal party authorised to bring a claim for damages against the directors and officers for losses due to their negligent acts. As indicated above (see section 1.4), the company is able to make its directors liable only to the extent that they have not been given a valid discharge by the general shareholders' meeting. In theory, the board of directors of a company would be the appropriate corporate body to resolve formally to bring an action against a member of the board of directors or an officer. If the board does not act on its own initiative, Article 693 of the Federal Code of Obligations gives the shareholders the right to pass a resolution to bring the action, by a majority of the share capital represented at the general shareholders' meeting (and not, as is normally the case, by a majority of votes).

(b) ***Insolvent company***

Where a company has become insolvent and a receiver has been appointed, the right to bring an action for damages incurred by the company passes to the receiver. In Switzerland, this is generally the official receiver of the community or canton in question. However, in large and complicated bankruptcies, the creditors regularly appoint an extraordinary receiver. This is also the case in the event of a forced reorganisation or liquidation process. The decision on whether to bring an action normally lies with the second creditors' meeting that takes place at a rather late stage of the bankruptcy procedure. If a creditors' committee was elected at the first creditors' meeting, the approval of this committee is required. Court approval is not necessary.

2.2 Minority shareholders on behalf of the company (derivative action)

The law does not distinguish between majority and minority shareholders in this respect. All shareholders enjoy the same rights.

Where the company is still solvent, the company enjoys the primary right to bring an action against its officers and/or directors. As mentioned above (see section 1.4), shareholders that discharge the board at the annual general shareholders' meeting are not authorised to sue if the basis of the claim was disclosed to the shareholders. The other shareholders are authorised to bring an action in place of the company where the company itself has decided not to bring a claim for damages against its directors. Damages obtained as a result of this type of action are paid directly to the company. The shareholder is entitled only to demand the direct payment of damages he himself incurred as a direct result of the negligent act. For this reason, derivate actions of shareholders outside of bankruptcy are extremely rare.

Derivate actions of shareholders remain the exception even after the company has been declared bankrupt. In principle, the same rules apply as for the derivate claims of creditors (described in more detail in section 2.4). Derivate actions of shareholders remain rare, as the participating creditors have a primary right to compensation and must be fully satisfied before any participating shareholders receive anything at all.

2.3 Minority shareholders on their own account

The law does not distinguish between minority and majority shareholders in this respect. Any shareholder is entitled to bring a claim if he has directly suffered damages as a result of a negligent breach of duty by an officer or director. In a recent leading case, the Federal Supreme Court specified that the distinction between direct and indirect damages is to be made based on ownership of the affected assets. If the shareholder owns the assets, the shareholder suffers direct damages. If the company owns them, the shareholder suffers only indirect damages (if any). The reduced value of the shareholder's shares falls into the second category of indirect damages, so shareholders can bring a derivative action (on behalf of the solvent company and under the further restrictions applying to such actions) only to obtain a remedy against such a loss in value.

2.4 Third parties

Third parties entitled to bring claims are primarily the creditors of the company (including preferred creditors such as employees and social security institutions) and the subscribers of securities issued by the company (see section 1.3).

The same distinction between direct and indirect damages applies to the creditors of a company. A creditor that has suffered direct damages due to a negligent breach of duty by an officer or director has a direct cause of action against this officer or director.

A creditor of the company can also suffer indirect damages if the company becomes insolvent. In this case, the competent bankruptcy court will appoint a receiver and the receiver will have the primary right to bring an action against the officers, directors and auditors of the company, claiming compensation for the damages suffered by the company.

To the extent that the receiver decides not to enforce itself the claims against the directors, Article 260 of the Federal Code on Debt Collection and Bankruptcy provides the creditors with the right to request an assignment of these claims and then to proceed against the directors in their own name. In the event of such an assignment, the proceeds of the legal action against the directors serve to satisfy the claims of those creditors which initiated the action and took the associated financial risk. Any surplus is then used to satisfy the shareholders that did participate in the action (see section 2.2), then the remaining creditors and finally the remaining shareholders. As mentioned above, it is extremely rare for shareholders to participate in such actions. Creditors that do assume the risk of the legal procedure are usually inclined to settle for an amount that is equivalent to their own claims. Therefore, in practice, a surplus is rarely achieved.

Creditors (or shareholders) that sue the directors can claim for the entire loss suffered by the company, irrespective of the amount of their own losses. Sometimes, creditors will sue for more than their own claim to have room for settlement negotiations. However, this can be expensive due to the rules concerning costs (see section 3.3). Any defences available to the directors in the context of their relationship with the company or with individual creditors cannot be used as a defence against a derivate action initiated by the creditors.

Finally, direct actions based on direct claims can be brought irrespective of either direct actions filed by the receiver or derivate actions filed by the creditors based on an assignment.

3. Claims culture

3.1 Litigation

(a) Increase in claims in recent years

A certain increase in claims over the past decade may be observed. The major contributing factor is an increasing awareness among creditors and shareholders of their rights under the law. Also, recent bankruptcies (eg, Biber, swissair) have resulted in increased awareness of the principles of corporate governance and the duty of the officers and directors of a company to implement correct procedures. These two developments also seem to have had an effect on the courts, which appear to be applying stricter standards today than they did two or three decades ago.

(b) ***Most common types of claimant and claim***

As mentioned above (see section 2), the most frequent claims brought against officers and directors are either direct claims brought by the receiver of an insolvent company or derivate claims brought by the creditors of such a company. The company itself generally brings claims against the directors of a solvent company. The tendency here is clearly to sue directors and officers only for serious breaches of their duties. As long as the company remains solvent, it is frequently difficult to prove damages and a feeling of loyalty between employer and employee (respectively, company and director) will, except in the most grievous circumstances, prevent a direct action by a solvent company. Direct or indirect actions by creditors or shareholders of a solvent company are almost unheard of, as in most cases the creditors will also have a claim against the company itself and consider the company to be more solvent. Shareholders of a solvent company can make derivate claims only for payment of damages to the company and the associated risks (costs) are generally disproportionate to the potential benefits for an individual shareholder.

(c) ***Nature of claims most likely to succeed***

As a general rule, the claims most likely to succeed are either direct claims of the receiver of an insolvent company or derivate claims of the creditors of such a company for damages resulting from the negligent violation of duties of directors. Except for very specific claims based on specific provable acts, the most frequent violation of duties asserted is the failure to inform the bankruptcy judge in a timely manner of the fact that the company is over-indebted or that the company is insolvent (see section 1.3).

(d) ***Chances of success***

In general, it is impossible to comment on the chances of success of claims against the directors and officers of a solvent company. This will depend on the circumstances of the specific case. The claimant must prove all four elements mentioned in section 1.4. In an insolvency scenario, it is usually possible to prove a violation of duties – the difficulty lies in proving the actual damage that resulted from this breach of duty. Creditors contemplating a claim must therefore be willing to accept substantial costs for a professional review of the books and records of the company. If this is done seriously and it can be shown that the over-indebtedness of the company increased due to the director's failure to notify the bankruptcy judge in a timely manner, actions are frequently successful, as it is then usually not difficult to prove the adequate causal connection and negligence.

3.2 Ability to bring class actions

Swiss law does not provide for the possibility of bringing class actions. However, a group of shareholders or creditors that have all suffered damages are entitled to initiate a joint action. With respect to derivate claims, the creditors are not only entitled, but also required, to bring a joint action. In a leading case that has just recently been confirmed, the Federal Supreme Court held, some 15 years ago, that all persons that have obtained an assignment of a claim from the receiver may bring an action only if they act collectively. The legal profession has criticised this decision as directors are often creditors of the company and may also have good relationships with other creditors or shareholders. The position of the Federal Supreme Court gives directors the possibility of blocking, or at least delaying, legal proceedings by – indirectly – participating on both sides. In the same decision, the court also held that the right to sue based on a claim assigned by the company may not be misused. However, this jurisprudence effectively makes it much more difficult validly to introduce a claim.

3.3 Funding of claims and whether loser pays

(a) General

In the past, the risks associated with bringing an action have frequently prevented creditors and shareholders from pursuing claims. Article 756(2) of the Federal Code of Obligations now provides that the court may order the company to pay all or part of the costs of an action brought by a shareholder where the shareholder was justified, in light of the facts available to him, in bringing the claim. However, this does not apply to creditors.

(b) Allocation of court costs and attorneys' fees

By law, the losing party pays the court costs. These are determined in accordance with the respective cantonal tariff and usually depend on the amount of the claim. The losing party, in accordance with cantonal procedural law, is also required to indemnify the winning party, either partially or entirely, for its attorneys' fees. Usually, court costs and legal fees are allocated depending on the extent to which one party has prevailed. As an example, if a claim is brought for Sfr1 million and an award is rendered in the amount of Sfr250,000, the plaintiff will be required to pay 75% of the court fees and 50% of an indemnity for attorneys' fees (calculated in accordance with the cantonal tariff). This system gives the claimant a strong incentive to determine the amount of his claim carefully and not to over-claim. It is also an effective deterrent against unmeritorious claims.

As mentioned above, the cantons have legislative power with respect to procedural law and the tariff applicable to court costs and attorneys' fees. This makes it very difficult to make a general statement on whether the indemnity payable by the losing party adequately compensates the winning party. As also mentioned above, responsibility claims are frequently expensive, as an accountant is required to calculate damages. So as a rule, it may be said that the indemnity awarded to the winning party rarely covers its attorneys' fees in full. In general, the plaintiff is fully indemnified only if the amount in dispute is very high.

(c) *Contingency fee arrangements*

Historically, contingency fee arrangements were prohibited in most cantons as a matter of cantonal law. This also applies to similar fee arrangements such as conditional fees. The new Article 12(e) of the Federal Code on the Provision of Legal Services, which came into force on January 1 2007, prohibits contingency fee (and conditional fee) agreements concluded prior to the end of a legal dispute. The interpretation of this provision is such that a partial contingency fee arrangement is permissible even prior to the conclusion of a legal dispute if it is agreed that the client will pay a low basic rate sufficient to cover the attorneys' costs irrespective of the outcome of the dispute. As a rule, however, the fees of the major law firms with the necessary resources and knowledge to bring and defend such actions successfully are calculated on an hourly basis.

3.4 Plaintiffs' bar

A plaintiffs' bar does not exist in Switzerland. There is a Federal Bar Association and a bar association in each canton. Attorneys (even large firms) generally act on behalf of both plaintiffs and defendants.

3.5 Procedural barriers

(a) *General*

Responsibility claims can be brought either at the domicile of the company or at the place of residence of the defendant. In general, the claimant must first apply to the justice of the peace, who then attempts to mediate between the parties. In responsibility claims, the mediation is rarely successful, as the parties will generally have exhausted the possibilities of reaching a settlement. The procedure before the justice of peace is therefore reduced to a mere formality, with the claimant insisting on his claim and the defendant denying the claim. The justice of the peace is then required to issue a writ that authorises the claimant to bring the claim before the ordinary court.

(b) *No action by company/receiver*

As described above, the company, or the receiver of an insolvent company, has the primary right to bring a claim against officers and directors. Derivate claims are possible only if the company, or receiver, does not bring the claim. In a bankruptcy scenario, the receiver will, after deciding not to initiate the claim itself, offer an assignment to all creditors. Those creditors which have requested an assignment then receive a document formally confirming their right of action.

(c) *Limitation issues*

Responsibility claims become time-barred after a period of five years from the date on which the plaintiff becomes aware of the loss and the identity of the person who has caused this loss. An absolute limitation period of 10 years applies from the date on which the damaging action took place. In the event that the claim is based on the commission of a criminal offence, the statute of limitations applies to the crime in question and also applies to any resulting civil actions.

4. Indemnification rights

4.1 When the company can indemnify

(a) *General*

An indemnification of the officers and directors of a company is not provided for in law. The question is rather whether the company is entitled to agree to indemnify its officers and directors against claims. A company purchasing D&O coverage generally avoids this issue. Agreements between companies and their officers and directors to indemnify these officers and directors against liability claims are practically unknown.

(b) *Indemnification against costs*

Swiss legal authorities unanimously take the position that a company is not entitled to indemnify its officers and directors against the costs of procedures in the event that the officer or director is guilty of gross negligence or wilful misconduct. This is considered to be a violation of Article 678 of the Federal Code of Obligations. There are different opinions about whether slight negligence also excludes indemnification. However, it is accepted that the company can agree to indemnify officers and directors for the cost of procedures when no blame can be attributed to the individuals in question. Legal authorities propose that this be done by granting loans to the officers and directors who are at the receiving end of a legal action. This will be repaid in the event that the court affirms liability based on gross negligence or wilful misconduct (according to some authorities, even if the court affirms liability based on slight negligence). If the defendant prevails, he is required to pay back only such an amount of the loan as is not covered by the indemnity awarded to him by the court.

(c) *Indemnity for liability*

The same principles with respect to costs also apply to the question of whether the company can legally agree to indemnify its directors and officers for potential liability incurred in their official function. According to most authorities, an agreement to indemnify officers and directors is legally possible if the liability is not incurred as a result of gross negligence or wilful misconduct. Some legal authorities maintain that even an agreement to indemnify a director for slight negligence would violate the principles set out in Article 678 of the Federal Code of Obligations.

(d) *Indemnification by the shareholder*

A large number of Swiss companies have nominee directors, nominated either by the parent company or by shareholders domiciled abroad. It is a common practice in Switzerland for such nominee directors to enter into an agreement with their principal which provides full indemnification for costs and liability. In most cases the agreement excludes indemnification in the event of gross negligence or wilful misconduct. A legal barrier, however, exists only in Article 20 of the Federal Code of Obligations. This provides that a contract whose contents are either illegal or immoral is null and void, and would make a claim for indemnification unenforceable if liability were incurred through a criminal act.

4.2 Formalities for indemnification

As mentioned above, there is no legal provision that requires a company to indemnify its officers and directors against liability claims, the theory being that the plaintiff will indemnify the defendant for his costs if the claim is not justified.

4.3 How indemnification works

As outlined in section 4.1, Swiss companies, in particular large Swiss companies, frequently purchase D&O coverage for their officers and directors. Also, nominee directors usually have a contractual right of indemnification against their principals. According to legal literature, the company is, in theory, entitled to indemnify its officers and directors against costs and liability, but only if the directors are not guilty of gross negligence or wilful misconduct. Some legal authorities maintain that an indemnification is invalid even in the event of slight negligence.

4.4 What cannot be indemnified

As outlined above, the company cannot indemnify costs and liabilities resulting from gross negligence or wilful misconduct

5. D&O insurance

5.1 Availability of D&O insurance

D&O insurance for directors of Swiss companies is available both on the domestic market and on the London market.

5.2 Local rules on cover provided under non-domestic D&O policy

The Federal Law on Insurance Supervision strongly restricts the ability of non-domestic insurers to provide cover to resident policyholders. Regulatory approval from the Federal Private Insurance Office is required and can be obtained only if it is applied for by a subsidiary of the non-domestic insurer or by an authorised representative of the foreign insurer domiciled in Switzerland. This also applies where the parent company of a resident subsidiary obtains a global policy from a non-domestic insurer that also covers the resident subsidiary. Under the Federal Insurance Supervision Law, this is possible only if the insurer has a subsidiary or a duly licensed resident representative in Switzerland. Violations of the Federal Insurance Supervision Law are subject to fines of up to Sfr1 million.

United Kingdom

Edward Smerdon
Reynolds Porter Chamberlain LLP

1. Directors' duties

1.1 Nature of the duties

In the United Kingdom, directors owe fiduciary duties and a duty of care to their companies. Until 2007, these duties were derived primarily from case law and judicial interpretation of statutes. This meant there was room for uncertainty as to their precise nature and scope. The Companies Act 2006 has, for the first time, set out directors' duties in one place and has sought to define them clearly. The government has stated that with one exception – a new duty – the duties are intended to reflect the existing law. Further, the new statutory provisions are to be interpreted according to the existing common law and equitable principles (Section 170(4) of the Companies Act 2006).

In the past there has been confusion regarding to whom directors owe their duties. Section 170(1) of the Companies Act 2006 makes it clear that the duties are owed to the company. The duties are owed by all directors, whether elected and registered, *de facto* or shadow directors.

The Companies Act 2006 sets out the directors' general duties in seven provisions, Sections 171 to 177, as follows.

(a) Duty to act within powers

A director must act in accordance with the constitution of the company (memorandum and articles of association), and exercise the powers vested in him only for the purposes for which they are conferred (Section 171). This is an existing fiduciary duty and is already fully established in law.

(b) Duty to promote the success of the company

A director must act in a way which he considers, in good faith, would be most likely to promote the success of the company for the benefit of its members as a whole (Section 172). In doing so, he must have regard to the following, among other things:

- the likely long-term consequences of any decision;
- the interests of employees;
- the need to foster relationships with suppliers, customers and others;
- the impact of the company's operations on the community and environment;

- the desirability of the company maintaining a reputation for high standards of business conduct; and
- the need to act fairly between shareholders.

This is the new duty, which has been the subject of much anticipation. As to how it may be applied, the first important consideration is that it is fiduciary in nature and therefore is regarded as part of the package of duties requiring that the directors act in good faith and with loyalty towards the company at all times. It is therefore not subject to any objective standard – if a director acts in a way he considers is in the best interests of the company (as long as that was in good faith), a court will not penalise him, even if the relevant course of conduct turned out to be ill advised (see, however, Section 174 of the Companies Act 2006).

This approach is likely to be reinforced by the courts' reluctance to reopen business decisions of boards – a court need only ascertain whether the directors, in good faith, considered they were promoting the success of the company by their actions. They will also need to show they took the list of six factors above into account.

It is important to bear in mind that the factors do not override the duty itself, but are subordinate to the duty, and no factor has greater weight than any other. However, in given situations, certain factors will be more obviously relevant than others. For example, the directors deciding that it is in the best interests of the company to embark upon a redundancy programme will need to have particular regard to the interests of employees and the impact of the decision on the community. The duty anticipates that this is more than simply a reference in the relevant board minutes, requiring that steps be taken to weigh up those factors before the decision is finally taken. The more that is done, the less likely the directors' decision will be questioned.

(c) ***Duty to exercise independent judgement***

The directors must exercise their powers on behalf of the company independently of influence from other parties, unless authorised by the company's constitution (Section 173). This is an existing fiduciary duty and is already fully established in law.

(d) ***Duty to exercise reasonable skill, care and diligence***

A director must exercise reasonable skill, care and diligence (Section 174). This is the skill, care and diligence of a reasonably diligent person with:

- the general knowledge, skill and experience that may reasonably be expected of a person carrying out the functions carried out by the director concerned (eg, as finance director, chief executive, sales director etc); and
- the general knowledge, skill and experience that the director has (eg, the number of years' actual experience, qualifications and training actually received).

This duty was originally contained within the restrictive confines of Section 214 of the Insolvency Act 1986, but in the last 15 years has been interpreted by courts to apply more generally to directors' conduct. This is now confirmed by Section 174 of the Companies Act 2006. It is not a fiduciary duty and so contains an objective element (the first limb of the standard).

A director is to be judged partly by the standard reasonably to be expected of a director occupying his post. Unlike the standard applied in the United Kingdom to professionals, however, a court shall also take into account the director's actual circumstances before deciding whether he has failed to act with reasonable skill, care and diligence (the second limb of the standard). For less experienced or less educated directors, this may result in more relaxed treatment by the courts, but where directors are very experienced or highly qualified they may well find this results in a tougher stance taken towards their conduct.

If the factors listed in relation to the Section 172 duty to promote the success of the company are not properly taken into account by boards when making important decisions, where those decisions later turn out to be flawed, this could lead to allegations that the directors failed to exercise reasonable skill, care and diligence, so as to find them in breach of this Section 174 duty (irrespective of a breach of the Section 172 duty).

(e) Duty to avoid conflicts of interest

A director of a company must avoid a situation in which he could have a direct or indirect interest that conflicts with the interests of the company (Section 175). This is an existing fiduciary duty and is already fully established in law. However, the provision does simplify the rules, making it clear that the duty applies to the exploitation of any property, information or opportunity. Further, the duty is not breached when the company, by its board, has 'authorised' the conflict in a vote that did not include the affected director, as long as it is permitted to do so by its constitution.

(f) Duty not to accept benefits from third parties

A director must not accept a benefit from a third party by reason of his being a director or his doing (or not doing) anything as a director (Section 176). This is an existing fiduciary duty and is already fully established in law. A breach of this duty is not capable of being 'authorised' by the company; however, the provision makes it clear that the duty is not breached if a benefit is received that cannot reasonably be expected to place the director in conflict of interest with the company.

(g) Duty to declare interest in a proposed transaction or arrangement

Where a director has a direct or indirect interest in a proposed transaction or arrangement, he must declare the nature and extent of that interest to the other directors (Section 177). This is an existing fiduciary duty and is already fully established in law, although the new provision alters the position slightly, in that shareholder approval is now not required, unless the constitution says otherwise.

1.2 Standards of care

The majority of the above duties are specific and absolute – they do not depend on standards to determine whether they have been breached.

The duty to promote the success of the company is clearly to be applied subjectively, in the sense that the court will need to decide not whether a director's decision making was reasonable, but only whether as a matter of fact he thought in good faith that it would promote the success of the company, with regard to the factors.

However, as discussed above, the duty to exercise reasonable care, skill and diligence is expressly subject to a two-stage objective/subjective standard due to the general nature of the duty. In this respect, the intention is to ensure that a minimum standard of conduct is required of all directors.

1.3 To whom the duties are owed

As stated above, Section 170(1) of the Companies Act 2006 confirms that the duties are owed to the company. Duties are not owed to individual shareholders or individual creditors, although with regard to the latter, where a company is trading while insolvent, the directors must consider or act in the interests of creditors of the company as a whole.

The factors listed in the duty to promote the success of the company refer to various groups of people whose interests should be taken into account, but the factors do not mean the duty is owed to such groups. The duty is owed only to the company and only the company can enforce it.

Other duties may be owed to third parties – these are dealt with under section 2.

1.4 Common defences to and exemptions from liability

A director can seek to circumvent a possible claim by asking the company to ratify his breach of duty under Section 239 of the Companies Act 2006. Ratification is not new, but the act makes it clear that it can be granted only by a shareholder resolution, in which the director concerned and any connected person cannot participate. Once ratified, the conduct which was the subject matter of the ratification cannot be the subject of a claim brought by the company (either on its own behalf or by way of a shareholder derivative action). The procedure is not commonly used and if it is, it tends to be in smaller companies, but it may become more prevalent in large companies as a result of the new shareholder derivative action rights.

In respect of claims for breach of a fiduciary duty, factual matters may very well be in dispute and so much will depend on the findings of fact by the court. Then the question whether the relevant conduct amounted to a breach of the duty will need to be addressed. In respect of the duty to promote the success of the company, the directors will defend on the basis they did consider, by reference to the factors, that they were promoting the success of the company. Evidence will be crucial; it will assist such a defence if board minutes and other internal documents can be produced to show that the issues really were considered.

In respect of the duty to exercise reasonable skill, care and diligence, the director will need to show he met the two-stage standard of care. Even if the duty was breached, the question of whether the loss complained of was caused by such breach may be complex, particularly in cases of corporate collapse.

Even where directors are found to have been in breach of duty, or they anticipate a claim may be brought for breach of duty, they may ask the court to relieve them from liability under what used to be Section 727 of the Companies Act 1985, but is now Section 1157 of the Companies Act 2006. This provides that if the court considers that a director may be liable but acted honestly and reasonably, and having regard to all the circumstances of the case he ought fairly to be excused, the court may relieve him in whole or in part from liability. There appears to be an inherent conflict between this relief and the duty to exercise reasonable skill, care and diligence, as for the duty to have been breached the court must find the director had not acted 'reasonably', and so the relief could never apply. What is probably intended is that where directors are found to have been in breach of the duty to exercise reasonable skill, care and diligence in relation to a specific issue, they may nevertheless still be relieved if their general conduct as a director was honest and reasonable, taking into account the particular circumstances of the company (eg, whether the director was operating under very difficult conditions), against which the negligence occurred. What is clear from the cases on the relief is that the court has significant discretion and each case is likely to turn on its own facts.

These defences relate only to claims brought by the company for breach of duties. Other defences will be applicable to claims by third parties/liquidators on behalf of creditors (see below).

2. Who can bring claims

This topic is closely related to the issue of to whom the directors owe their duties (ie, the company). However, there are additional categories of claimant who can bring claims for breach of other duties.

2.1 The company (solvent)

As identified above, the duties are owed to the company and so the primary source of claims for breach of duty is the company. However, in the United Kingdom, claims are rarely brought by companies against their directors. This is because in a unitary board system, directors are unlikely to recommend to the company that a claim be brought against themselves. What is more common is that the company brings a claim against directors who have already retired from the board or have been dismissed. New directors are much more likely to bring a claim against their previous incumbents, particularly if it underscores the fact that they themselves inherited a problem rather than caused it. The famous recent case of *Equitable Life* was an example of a new board pursuing members of an old one.

The process for deciding whether to bring a claim against a director is ultimately determined by the constitution of the company (ie, the articles of association). It may be left to the directors to decide or a shareholder resolution may be required.

2.2 The company's liquidators

Liquidators of insolvent companies are a significant potential source of claims against the former directors. The Insolvency Act 1986 contains three causes of action that may be exercised by the liquidators, as follows:

- Section 212 – this enables administrators or liquidators to bring a claim for breach of any duty to the company, as if brought by the company. In other words, it simply enables insolvency practitioners to bring the company's claim as if it were still solvent.
- Section 213 – this enables the liquidators to bring a claim for fraudulent trading, whereby the business of the company is carried on with the intent to defraud creditors, or for any other fraudulent purpose, in the directors' full knowledge. The remedy is for the directors to contribute to the assets of the company available for distribution to creditors. In practice, it is rarely used because 'wrongful trading' (see below) is easier to establish.
- Section 214 – this enables the liquidators to bring a claim for wrongful trading, whereby the company continues to trade beyond the point where the directors knew, or ought to have known, there was no reasonable prospect of avoiding liquidation. The standard of care applicable to the directors' conduct is the same as the two-limb standard for the duty to exercise reasonable skill, care and diligence. The remedy is for the directors to contribute to the assets of the company available for distribution to creditors and effectively represents the additional debts incurred after the point when they should have ceased trading. Establishing where such a point occurred can be a complex exercise requiring expert accountancy input.

Liquidators have broad powers to investigate the circumstances surrounding the liquidation and the directors' conduct. Often, prior to bringing a claim, a liquidator will summon the directors for an interview pursuant to Section 236 of the Insolvency Act. There are few legitimate grounds on which a director may refuse to attend, and the liquidators can obtain a court order requiring their attendance. In practice, directors negotiate the terms on which the directors voluntarily attend such meetings, but they may be recorded and a transcript produced.

2.3 Minority shareholders on behalf of the company

The principle of 'majority rule' among shareholders is fundamental in English company law. Therefore, if a majority of shareholders do not support the company bringing a claim against the directors, it cannot usually proceed. Reflecting this, until the introduction of the Companies Act 2006, minority shareholders had only limited rights to bring claims on behalf of the company against the directors. Such limited rights were developed, and ultimately constrained, by case law. The claims, known as 'shareholder derivative actions', could generally be brought only where two situations existed at the same time:

- The directors against whom the claim was to be brought by the company controlled a majority of the shares in the company, so as to prevent the company ever bringing a claim on its own behalf. This requirement is often referred to as 'wrongdoer control'; and
- The conduct of the directors complained of was of an egregious nature, such as dishonesty, breach of fiduciary duty or acting in bad faith towards the company. Negligence was not sufficient.

Cases in which both of the above could be demonstrated were rare and this resulted in courts dismissing most at an early stage, which discouraged further development of the right on behalf of minority shareholders. However, the Companies Act 2006 has, at least in theory, widened the scope for such actions to be brought.

Under Section 260 of the act, any shareholder may bring a claim against directors on behalf of the company, for negligence, default, breach of duty or breach of trust. Immediately the second historic restriction has been removed, as it is now clear mere negligence is sufficient to mount a claim. The claim may be brought by a shareholder in respect of a matter which pre-dated his becoming a member or in anticipation of a situation. There is no mention of 'wrongdoer control', so the first historical restriction has also been removed. Claims may be brought against former directors as well as present directors.

The government has stated that the provision is about process and is not intended greatly to alter the substantive right to bring a derivative action. However, it is difficult to separate the substantive right from the process, and the process has been made simpler and easier. Is this likely to give rise to a significant increase in derivative claims? First, derivative claims are brought for the benefit of the company and so, if successful, the shareholder does not benefit personally (at least in any direct sense). This is likely to reduce the propensity for claims to be brought. Second, and crucially, Section 261 of the act provides that a shareholder must apply to the court for permission to continue the action, once issued.

At the hearing for permission - which will involve the shareholder bringing the action, the company and the proposed defendant directors - the court may:

- refuse permission to continue and dismiss the proceedings;
- give permission for the claim to continue on such terms as it considers appropriate; or
- adjourn the proceedings for further evidence.

Permission will be refused where the court is satisfied that:

- a person promoting the success of the company would not seek to continue the claim; or
- the company has already ratified the alleged wrongdoing (see above).

Directors facing an unwanted shareholder derivative action can seek a ratification in order to stop it from proceeding beyond the permission hearing. Assuming there has been no ratification, the court will not automatically dismiss the claim but shall consider:

- whether the shareholder is bringing the action in good faith;
- the importance that a person promoting the success of the company would attach to continuing the action;
- the likelihood the company could still ratify the conduct complained of;
- whether the company has decided not to pursue a claim; and
- whether the shareholder could obtain redress by bringing an action in his own right.

In doing so, the court may seek evidence from other shareholders who are not connected with the matter as to whether the action should be allowed to continue.

The substantive merits of the claim are not expressly relevant to the granting of permission, although they are likely to affect the court's attitude to factors such as whether someone promoting the success of the company would continue it and the likelihood of a ratification. Any action obviously brought to make mischief or a 'political' point is likely to fail the 'good faith' test and not be allowed to continue.

If leave to continue the action is given, the court is likely to order, among other things, that the company indemnify the shareholder who has brought the action on its behalf, in respect of the past and future costs incurred.

It is anticipated that from October 2007 there will be shareholder derivative actions brought based on the duties set out in Sections 171 to 177 of the Companies Act 2006, the majority of which will be refused permission to continue; but some of these cases will go to the higher courts, which will be obliged to consider the factors and lay down judicial guidelines. Subsequently, the number of actions will be materially higher than under the old rules, but they will still be relatively infrequent.

2.4 Shareholders on their own account

As stated above, directors owe their duties to the company and not to any individual shareholder. A shareholder bringing an action against the directors for breach of duty other than as a derivative action is likely to face an application to strike out the claim for disclosing no cause of action.

Where a minority shareholder considers his rights have been unfairly prejudiced by the company, he may petition the court under Section 994 of the Companies Act 2006 (formerly Section 459 of the Companies Act 1985) for an appropriate order restraining the company from conducting itself in such a manner, or some other direction, such that the shareholder shall have his shares bought by other shareholders or the company at a price to be decided. Directors may find themselves party to such actions, either in their capacity as officers of the company or because they are also shareholders themselves, but not in respect of any alleged breach of their duties as directors.

Shareholders are potentially able to bring claims against the directors in their capacity as investors who bought their shares based on misleading information. This is considered in section 2.5(c).

2.5 Third parties

Generally, when directors deal with third parties such as trading partners, suppliers and customers, they do so as officers of the company and it is the company against which any cause of action arises from such dealings. This is due to the principle that the company is a separate legal person and third parties should not be able to pierce the 'corporate veil' unless there are exceptional circumstances. Where a company is insolvent or has no assets and there are aggrieved third parties, there is a greater likelihood of claims which allegedly fall within one of the exceptions.

(a) ***Fraud***

Where a director, who is also the principal shareholder, has used the corporate entity to commit fraud against a third party, a court will allow the third party to pierce the corporate veil to recover from that director.

(b) ***Assumption of personal responsibility***

Where, in making a misstatement to a third party, a director has assumed a 'personal responsibility' to the third party, he may be liable. The scope for third parties to establish this is limited; in other words, courts require a very clear indication that a personal assumption of risk by a director was anticipated. This goes beyond any ordinary dealings as a director and would require, for example, the use of personal stationery or oral statements that made it clear they were on behalf of the director himself and not the company.

(c) ***Investors who are mis-sold shares***

Directors may be liable, together with the company, to investors who suffer losses as a result of a misleading statement or non-disclosure in the company's share offering documentation. The liability position varies depending on the type of offering involved.

Public offerings of shares on a market regulated by the Financial Services Authority (FSA), such as the London Stock Exchange, are governed by the Financial Services and Markets Act 2000. Under Section 90 of the act, the company and the directors may be liable to investors who suffer loss as a result of any misleading statement in the offering prospectus. Schedule 10 of the act contains a defence that the directors shall not be liable if they show they reasonably believed, having made such enquiries as were reasonable, that the statement was true and not misleading.

Public offerings of shares on a non-regulated market, such as AIM, are not governed by the Financial Services and Markets Act 2000 and so liability for misleading statements in the offering documentation is governed by common law. There are few cases involving such liability, but it is arguable that the company would be liable to investors who suffer loss as a result of a misstatement, particularly where the identities of the investors were known to the company and the investors could show they relied upon the misleading statement. Whether the directors are liable would depend on their having assumed personal responsibility, as outlined above. The AIM rules require the directors to verify, in writing, the accuracy of the statements in the offering documentation. This arguably amounts to a personal assumption of responsibility, but the position has never been ruled upon by a court.

Private sales of shares are likely to follow similar considerations as for non-regulated market offerings, except that liability for misstatements is more likely under common law given that the particular purchasers of the shares will be known to the company, creating an obvious duty of care. Again, the directors' liability will depend upon a personal assumption of responsibility; in practice, this is secured via personal guarantees as to the accuracy of the information given.

Liability for misleading statements in the company's reports is subject to a different regime, which has recently changed. The common law has not recognised a duty owed to prospective investors who rely on statements in company reports because their identities and motives are not known to the company, and so cannot be the subject of an assumption of responsibility. However, Section 1270 of the Companies Act 2006 has introduced a new provision to Section 90A of the Financial Services and Markets Act 2000 to reflect the EU Transparency Directive, which provides that the company (only) can be liable to investors who buy shares in reliance upon a misleading statement or non-disclosure in a report if a director knew such statement was misleading. This creates an exception to the general position where a director dishonestly allows a misleading statement or non-disclosure to be made. The director himself cannot be liable to the third-party investors. By virtue of Section 463 of the Companies Act 2006, he can be liable only to the company.

3. Claims culture

3.1 Litigation

Despite an increase in the amount of governmental regulation in the United Kingdom in recent years, there is an increased 'blame culture'. But for the limitations of the United Kingdom's litigation rules, there would be a lot more civil compensation claims generally. Other factors contributing to a relatively benign claims culture include the fact that cases are decided by judges, not juries, and the following.

(a) *'Deep pocket' factor*

In the past, directors have rarely been sued by their companies unless there has been a catastrophic collapse or insolvency once they have left the company. Even then, auditors have far more often been the primary target of litigation, as they were perceived to be easier liability targets with deeper pockets.

In what could prove to be a significant change to this attitude, auditors are permitted, by Section 534 of the Companies Act 2006, to enter liability limitation agreements with the companies they audit. The agreements, which must be approved by the shareholders, can limit the liability of auditors for breach of duty. How such liability is limited is not defined and the parties are free to decide, as long as in any given claim the court considers it has reduced the auditor's liability only to a level that is fair and reasonable. If the court decides the limitation is excessive, it may limit the liability of the auditor to the level it considers is fair and reasonable in the circumstances.

In conjunction with auditors limiting their liability, D&O insurance limits have been steadily increasing. Whereas in the past auditors were obviously the deeper pocket, this is less true now, with companies buying limits that make D&O more than simply a directors' defence costs fund.

(b) *Financial need to sue*

The machinery in Section 90 of the Financial Services and Markets Act 2000 for investors to bring claims for the mis-selling of shares is six years old and has hardly been used (indeed, it is largely a repeat of the provisions of the even older Financial

Services Act 1985, which themselves were seldom used). There need to be falling market conditions for the machinery to be attractive. There is some evidence to suggest that institutional investors will look more closely at the remedies available should they lose significant sums next time the markets fall significantly. In the past, they have been at pains to state that the most appropriate way to address companies' performance issues is through pressure for better corporate governance, not litigation; but a need to meet their obligations to their own members may necessitate a tougher stance in the future.

3.2 Ability to bring class actions

Class actions, as recognised in the United States, are not available as such in the United Kingdom. However, in 2000, a procedure was introduced by the UK Civil Procedure Rules in the form of group litigation orders (GLOs). In contrast to the US model, this is an opt-in procedure covering only claimants who have taken deliberate steps to participate. Further, it is a tool for managing large numbers of claims, as opposed to a tool for facilitating the bringing of large numbers of claims.

A GLO may be made where there are, or are likely to be, a number of claims giving rise to common or related issues of fact or law (these are known as 'GLO issues'). It will provide for the management of claims which give rise to GLO issues in a coordinated way. A register must be set up on which all claims managed under the GLO will be entered, specify the GLO issues and identify the court, known as the 'management court', which will manage the claims on the GLO register.

Importantly, and in contrast to the United States, the GLO simply 'bundles' the individual claims together; it does not rationalise them into one proceeding. Therefore, all claimants must settle pleadings and initiate proceedings to take part, which creates logistical hurdles for claimants thinking of joining. The GLO simply rationalises the common issues.

A managing judge will be appointed to assume responsibility for the management of the GLO claims and to hear the trial of all GLO issues. The management court is free to decide how GLO claims should be managed and may:

- vary the GLO issues;
- provide for one or more claims to proceed as test claims; and
- appoint the lawyer of one or more parties to be the lead lawyer for the claimants or defendants.

As mentioned above, in a GLO situation, only claimants entered on the register will be bound by a judgment given. In a US class action, all members of the class are bound by the judgment, unless they have expressly opted out.

Since the procedure was adopted in 2000, fewer than 60 GLOs have been made. Most have been made in relation to personal injury and product liability actions. A GLO could, however, be made in the context of claims against directors, for example for actions under Section 90 of the Financial Services and Markets Act 2000.

3.3 Funding of claims and whether loser pays

English civil proceedings generally operate on a 'loser pays' basis, so that an unsuccessful claimant pays the successful defendant's costs. Unlike some jurisdictions where this can be a token amount, the successful party can usually expect to recover 70% to 80% of his costs. This provides a significant deterrent to the bringing of vexatious or hopeless claims.

Claims are generally funded by the claimant paying for the litigation privately, occasionally by public funding (unlikely to be available for claims against directors) or by conditional fee arrangements. Contingency fee agreements - where the claimant agrees to pay the lawyer a proportion of his damages if he is successful - are not permitted under English law.

A conditional fee arrangement is an agreement whereby the lawyer agrees not to charge the claimant in the event that his claim is not successful. In the event that his claim is successful, the claimant agrees to pay the lawyer his normal fees plus, in most cases, although not necessarily, a success fee, which is calculated as a percentage of the lawyer's actual fees. Both the actual fees and any success fee may be recovered from the losing party under general costs principles. The success fee is based on the merits of the case and may not exceed 100% of the actual fees.

If the claimant is unsuccessful, he will still be liable for the winning party's costs and, potentially, any disbursements incurred on his behalf by his own lawyers. To cover these costs, the claimant may purchase 'after-the-event' insurance. The premium for the after-the-event insurance is recoverable from the losing party in the same way as the lawyer's actual fees and success fee. A claimant who does not want to enter into a conditional fee arrangement may still obtain after-the-event insurance. In addition to covering the other side's costs, the after-the-event insurance may also cover his own legal costs.

3.4 Plaintiffs' bar

There is no organised group of lawyers who specialise in the bringing of claims against directors in the United Kingdom. This is to a large extent a reflection of the other factors outlined above in relation to claims culture. Whether this will change is likely to depend on the courts' initial handling of shareholder derivative cases and any future significant falls in the financial markets. That said, for claims that have a US aspect to them, it is potentially more lucrative for UK shareholders to join their US counterparts in US proceedings, despite the significant jurisdictional hurdles that may exist.

3.5 Procedural barriers

Except in relation to shareholder derivative actions, where the court's permission is needed to pursue such claims, there are no special procedural requirements for claims against directors.

The limitation period for claims against directors varies, depending upon the type of duty alleged to have been breached. Under the Limitation Act 1980, negligence-based causes of actions, such as a breach of the duty to act with reasonable skill, care and diligence, have a limitation period of six years from the date of loss, with a possible further three years from the date of discovery that a loss had been suffered, subject to a 15-year long-stop.

Breach of fiduciary duty, on the other hand, has no statutory limitation period and, depending on the nature of the breach, the courts may either apply a six-year period where the breach may be analogous to a tort or breach of contract, or prescribe no limitation period at all.

4. Indemnification rights

Until April 2005, UK law largely prohibited indemnification, except to the extent that a director had successfully defeated a claim and had unrecovered costs and expenses. Since April 6 2005, UK companies have been permitted to indemnify their directors in certain situations. The Companies Act 2006 does not substantively alter this law, which is now contained in Section 234.

4.1 When the company can indemnify

Under Section 234 of the Companies Act, a company's indemnification arrangements must fall within the scope of a "qualifying third party indemnification provision". The rules apply equally where a company agrees to indemnify its own directors or where a group/parent company agrees to indemnify the directors of another group (or the parent) company. The criteria for a qualifying third party indemnification provision are a list of categories of claim for which a company may agree to indemnify its directors, on certain terms.

(a) *Claims by the company*

As stated above, claims by the company are theoretically the most likely under English law, as it is to the company that directors primarily owe their duties. Apart from claims instigated by the company, shareholder derivative actions are also claims by the company. Under Section 234 of the Companies Act 2006, a liability to the company cannot be indemnified – so any payment made by a director to the company by way of a judgment or settlement (including damages and claimants' costs) is not indemnifiable.

The company is permitted to advance defence costs to directors it is suing so they may defend themselves effectively; however, where a final judgment (after appeals) is given against the director, those costs must be repaid. Such a clawback does not appear to apply to settlements where the director agrees to make a payment to the company.

(b) *Criminal proceedings*

Criminal fines cannot be indemnified. The costs of defending criminal proceedings are indemnifiable and may be advanced by the company. However, if the director is convicted (after appeals), the costs must be repaid, regardless of the precise nature of the offence.

(c) *Regulatory proceedings*

Regulatory fines or penalties cannot be indemnified. The costs of dealing with regulatory proceedings are indemnifiable and may be advanced. There is no clawback of costs if the director is found liable (unless the director is found to have acted dishonestly).

(d) ***Claims by third parties***

As stated above, claims by parties outside the company are quite rare because of the protection given to directors by the corporate veil; however, and importantly, 'third parties' for the purposes of this definition include any person who purchased shares in the company based upon allegedly misleading information. Apart from the UK risk, directors of UK companies with US listings are vulnerable to US shareholder lawsuits and indemnification is vital in such situations.

The Companies Act 2006 imposes no restrictions on indemnification of such claims (assuming no dishonesty on the part of the directors), and so damages are indemnifiable and there is no clawback of advanced defence costs in the event the director settles or is found liable to the third party.

(e) ***Advancement of costs and claw-back mechanisms***

As mentioned above, the company may advance defence costs to a director in all cases, but in respect of claims by the company and criminal proceedings those costs must be repaid on a final judgment (after appeals) against the director, and in any claim where the court finds the director acted dishonestly. The advancement of costs by the company is therefore regarded as a loan to the director, to be repaid in the event of such outcomes. Loans by the company to the directors are prohibited by Section 197 of the Companies Act 2006; however, the advancement of defence costs is an exception, as long as the qualifying third party indemnification provision requires the advanced costs to be repaid in the event of an adverse final judgment.

(f) ***Formalities for indemnification***

The overriding source of indemnification rights comes from Section 234 of the Companies Act 2006. The law permits indemnification in the situations identified above. Under Section 232 of the act, any indemnification provision that is broader than what is permitted by Section 234 is void in its entirety (not merely to the extent that it is broader). The law is permissive in that it does not oblige companies to indemnify their directors.

(g) ***Articles of association***

Notwithstanding that the law now permits indemnification of directors, a company is not permitted to indemnify its directors unless the shareholders have granted such permission, in line with Section 234 of the Companies Act 2006. This is provided via the articles of association, one of the constitutional agreements of the company. It is an agreement between the shareholders themselves and with the company, but not the directors (in their capacity as directors). The articles of association therefore dictate whether the company has the power to indemnify and to what extent, as long as it is no broader than is provided by Section 234. It is therefore possible that the power to indemnify created by the articles may be more restrictive than is permitted under Section 234.

(h) *Indemnification agreements*

The directors, who are the beneficiaries of the indemnity but who are not party to the articles of association, have no direct enforceable right to be indemnified to the extent permitted by the articles of association, even if they state that the company will indemnify the directors. The Contracts (Rights of Third Parties) Act 1999 allows some third-party beneficiaries under a contract to enforce its terms, but Section 6 expressly precludes the application of such rights to companies' articles of association. Therefore, without a separate indemnification agreement between the company and the directors conveying the indemnity, the company may have the power to indemnify, but is not obliged to do so, and therefore indemnification is entirely discretionary.

The indemnification agreements can take different forms, but are usually designed to operate separately from the directors' service contracts, in order that they survive the retirement of the directors and remain enduringly enforceable. Often the indemnity is conveyed formally in a 'deed of indemnity' or, if the articles contain a mandatory right of indemnification, by a letter confirming that such mandatory right is directly enforceable by the director.

As with the articles, indemnification agreements can provide more restrictive indemnification than that allowed by Section 234 of the Companies Act 2006.

4.2 How indemnification works

Please see above comments. Once indemnification agreements are in place, the directors need do nothing unless or until a claim is made, following which they will notify the claim to the company and invoke the right to be indemnified. Companies often require in return that they control the directors' defence (unless they are the claimants).

4.3 What cannot be indemnified

Please see above, but in summary, the following cannot be indemnified:

- criminal fines and criminal defence costs, where convicted;
- regulatory fines;
- settlements and damages paid to the company;
- costs of defending company claims where found liable; and
- any claims where dishonesty is established.

5. D&O insurance

5.1 Ability to purchase D&O insurance

D&O insurance is widely available and there is considerable capacity to provide it in the London insurance market. This is both for UK companies and for companies based in other countries (subject, of course, to any regulatory requirements of those jurisdictions).

5.2 Local rules on cover provided under a non-domestic D&O policy

There are restrictions as to where a UK company can buy its D&O insurance from. The rules vary depending on whether the proposed D&O insurer is based inside or outside the European Union.

(a) EU-based insurers

The insurer need not be authorised by the UK regulator, the FSA, but can be passported into the UK by its own local regulator. The type of passport required depends on whether the insurer has an agent or an office in the United Kingdom, in which case it will require a right of establishment passport, or whether it is offering products without an agent or an office (cross-border services), in which case it will require a freedom of services passport. The processes involved in obtaining such passports are relatively straightforward, and once the insurer has the relevant passport there are no restrictions on their offering D&O insurance to UK companies.

(b) Non-EU insurers

The insurer may need to be authorised by the FSA, depending on where the activity takes place. Authorisation by the FSA is needed if the insurer is carrying on 'regulated activities' in the United Kingdom by way of business. Effecting and carrying out (ie, providing) insurance contracts are 'regulated activities' under Section 10 of the Financial Services and Markets Act 2000 (Regulated Activities) Order 2001. The non-EU insurer is clearly carrying out a regulated activity, but the issue arises as to where the activities are taking place.

A non-EU insurer with a branch office in the United Kingdom would need FSA approval to offer D&O insurance from that office. An insurer based outside the United Kingdom could still be regarded as carrying on activities in the United Kingdom, even if it does not have a place of business in the United Kingdom. For example, if someone (ie, either an agent or an employee of the non-EU insurer) in the United Kingdom were able to bind the non-EU insurer and accept risks on its behalf, the effecting of the insurance contract would take place in the United Kingdom. The insurer in this situation would need to be regulated in the United Kingdom by the FSA, and until then would not be permitted to offer D&O insurance to UK companies. If, on the other hand, the insurance contract were bound in the non-EU state and the policy documentation were issued from that state, the non-EU insurer would not be carrying on activities in the United Kingdom. In the latter case the non-EU insurer would not need authorisation by the FSA and (subject to its own jurisdiction's rules) would be free to offer D&O insurance to UK companies.

(c) Global policies

These rules apply equally where non-UK companies, with global insurance programmes written outside the United Kingdom, have UK subsidiaries.

5.3 D&O and indemnification

Directors should seek as broad an indemnity from their companies as the companies are permitted to provide pursuant to Section 234 of the Companies Act 2006.

Indemnification may be available where D&O insurance is not. For instance, D&O insurance may exclude certain types of loss that would be covered by indemnification. Conversely, directors will be without indemnification in the following instances:

- where the company is insolvent or otherwise financially unable to pay the indemnification; claims by a company's liquidators are obviously non-indemnifiable for this reason and liquidators (see above) represent a potent source of claims for small/medium-sized companies (and, occasionally, large companies);
- where the law does not permit the company to indemnify. The most obvious gap in the indemnification protection is where the director is liable to the company (see above);
- in instances where the clawback machinery applies following an adverse final judgment; and
- where the company otherwise refuses to indemnify. This may be because the relevant indemnification agreement is more restrictive than the law permits or because, for some other reason, the company does not honour its obligations under the indemnification agreement.

These potentially significant gaps can be filled by D&O insurance, either via the traditional D&O policy or via a cheaper 'Side A only' D&O policy, which is specifically designed to fit around the indemnification and plug gaps.

indemnification may be extended where D&O insurance cover is inadequate. These exemptions may exclude certain types of liability that [illegible] or [illegible] indemnification [illegible] directors will be [illegible] in the following instances:

- where the company is insolvent or otherwise financially unable to pay the indemnification (this is [illegible] ... indemnities of this reason and [illegible] above) represent a [illegible] concern for small and medium-sized companies (and [illegible] large companies);
- where the law does not permit the company to indemnify the director or [illegible] in the indemnification agreement [illegible] where the director is [illegible] to the company (see above);
- in instances where the law [illegible] an adverse final judgement; and
- where the company [illegible] to indemnify [illegible] the relevant director [illegible] because, for some other reason, the company [illegible] under the indemnification agreement.

These potentially significant gaps can be filled by D&O insurance cover [illegible] Side A only D&O [illegible] designed [illegible] (see p. [illegible]).

United States

Dan A Bailey
Darius N Kandawalla
Bailey Cavalieri LLC

This chapter provides an overview of the legal duties and liability exposure of directors and officers of US corporations.

1. Directors' duties

1.1 Nature of the duties

The standards of conduct imposed on directors and officers of US corporations are defined by two sources. First, statutes, regulations and court decisions of the state in which a corporation is chartered impose certain fiduciary duties and otherwise define important parameters affecting the responsibilities and liability exposure of directors and officers. Those standards are largely consistent from state to state, although some important variations exist. Second, a variety of federal statutes impose duties upon, and can be the basis of important liability exposure for, directors and officers, regardless of what state law otherwise applies. The most prominent of these federal laws are the federal securities laws, which generally require directors and officers to disclose punctually, honestly and fully all material information about their company and its publicly held securities. Other federal statutes that create liability exposure for corporate directors and officers include the Employee Retirement Income Security Act (ERISA) and numerous pollution, employment, antitrust and intellectual property statutes. Many of these federal statutes are discussed in sections 2.3 and 2.4.

In virtually all states, directors and officers owe their corporations, their shareholders and certain third parties fiduciary duties of diligence and loyalty. These basic fiduciary duties are discussed below.

(a) Duty of diligence

Directors and officers must discharge their duties as corporate fiduciaries:

- in good faith;
- in a manner they reasonably believe to be in the best interests of the corporation; and
- with the care an ordinarily prudent person in a like position would exercise under similar circumstances.

The duty of diligence encompasses an implicit or, in some states, explicit duty of reasonable inquiry. Directors and officers must maintain an awareness of corporate developments, monitor corporate affairs and policies and investigate events and developments when circumstances would warn a reasonable director or officer of the need to do so.[1] Ignorance of corporate affairs, whether because of inexperience or inattention, will generally expose a director or officer to the same potential liability as a director or officer who has actual knowledge of adverse circumstances but fails to act.[2]

(b) *Duty of loyalty*

The duty of loyalty requires that directors and officers:

- scrupulously protect the interests of their corporation;
- refrain from personal activities that could injure the corporation; and
- subordinate their personal interests to the interests of their corporation, its shareholders and other constituents.[3]

Directors and officers may not:

- take advantage of the corporation or its shareholders;
- realise a secret profit;
- compete with the corporation to the corporation's detriment; or
- usurp an opportunity belonging to the corporation.[4]

The duty of loyalty is premised on the notion that directors and officers are required to put the interests of their corporation and its constituents ahead of their own interests. As such, directors and officers may not engage in activities or make decisions that further their own interests at the expense of the corporation or its shareholders. A director or officer who engages in self-dealing transactions, insider trading or other actions that take advantage of his position with the corporation to its detriment is in clear breach of the duty of loyalty.

When a director's or officer's interests are potentially in conflict with the corporation's interests, the director or officer must fully disclose to all other decision makers the existence of the conflict and abstain from any discussion or vote on the matter at issue. Candour is an elementary principle of fair dealing, and the law imposes an unwavering obligation on directors and officers to disclose to other corporate fiduciaries information they obtain in the course of representing corporate interests.[5] When a director or officer approves a transaction in which he has a conflict of interest, he will usually be required to establish that the transaction was entirely fair and in the best interests of the corporation as a whole in order to escape liability.

The duty of loyalty is not limited to instances of classic self-dealing or fiduciary conflicts of interest. Rather, it encompasses a broader requirement that directors and

1 *Smith v Van Gorkom*, 488 A2d 858 (Del 1985); *Hanson Trust PLC v ML SCM Acquisition, Inc*, 781 F 2d 264, 274 (2d Cir 1986).

2 *Doyle v Union Ins Co*, 277 N W 2d 35 (Neb 1979); *In re The Walt Disney Co Derivative Litig*, 906 A 2d 27 (Del 2006).

3 *Cede & Co v Technicolor, Inc*, 634 A2d 345 (Del 1993).

4 *United States v Byrum*, 408 US 125 (1972)).

5 *In re Allegheny Int'l, Inc*, 954 F 2d 167 (3d Cir 1992).

officers act in good faith.[6] Sometimes regarded as a separate fiduciary duty, the duty of good faith is breached where, among other things, "the fiduciary intentionally acts with a purpose other than that of advancing the best interests of the corporation, where the fiduciary acts with the intent to violate applicable positive law, or where the fiduciary intentionally fails to act in the face of a known duty to act, demonstrating a conscious disregard for his duties".[7]

1.2 Standards of care

In scrutinising directors' and officers' decisions, simple negligence is generally not enough to impose liability. For instance, under Delaware law, a plaintiff would normally be required to prove that the conduct at issue rose to the level of 'gross negligence', which is generally defined as a reckless indifference or deliberate disregard for the corporation's or its shareholders' interests or a gross abuse of the director's or officer's discretion.

However, the standard of care expected of directors and officers varies with each director and officer, based upon his personal expertise, training, knowledge and experience. In other words, directors and officers are expected to utilise in full all of their skills in performing their jobs and will be accountable if they fail to make informed decisions. The standard of care also varies depending on the nature of the transaction and the importance of the decision to the corporation. For example, greater diligence and investigation generally will be required when deciding whether to approve a takeover proposal than when overseeing the election of a junior officer.[8] Similarly, decisions involving financially troubled corporations, responses to shareholder demands and distributions to shareholders may all be subject to heightened scrutiny due to the increased vulnerability of the constituents involved.

Ultimately, however, directors and officers are not guarantors of the success of their business decisions. Courts do not second-guess the quality of directors' and officers' decisions, but only critique the process used to reach the decision.[9] This important defence is called the 'business judgement rule' and generally insulates directors, and sometimes officers, from liability for business decisions as long as they acted on an informed basis, in good faith and in the honest belief that their decisions were in the best interests of the corporation and its shareholders.[10]

1.3 To whom the duties are owed

Directors and officers generally owe their fiduciary duties to their corporation and their corporation's shareholders. Normally, directors and officers do not owe any

---

6 *Stone v Ritter*, 911 A 2d 362 (Del 2006); *In re Walt Disney Co Derivative Litig*, 906 A 2d 27 (Del 2006); *Blake v Friendly Ice Cream Corp*, 21 Mass L Rep 610 (Mass 2006).

7 *Disney*, 906 A 2d at 67, quoting *In re Walt Disney Co Derivative Litig*, 907 A 2d 693 (Del Ch 2005).

8 *Anadarko Petroleum Corp v Panhandle Eastern Corp*, 545 A 2d 1171 (Del 1988).

9 *Aronson v Lewis*, 473 A 2d 805, 812 (Del 1984); *Paramount Communications, Inc v Time, Inc*, 571 A 2d 1140 (Del 1989).

10 *In re Caremark International Derivative Litig*, 698 A 2d 959 (Del Ch 1996): "[W]hether a judge or jury, considering the matter after the fact believes a decision substantively wrong, or degrees of wrong extending through 'stupid' or 'egregious' or 'irrational,' provides no ground for director liability as long as the court determines that the process employed was either rational or employed in a good faith effort to advance corporate interests."

independent duties to the corporation's creditors, customers or other third parties. The relationship between a corporation and its creditors and other third parties is usually contractual in nature; thus, any claims by third parties are often limited to the corporate entity.[11]

However, directors and officers may owe duties to, and subject themselves to liability from, creditors and other constituents in certain circumstances, including the following.

(a) *Piercing the corporate veil*

When corporate formalities are not followed or when a director or officer has commingled his personal assets with the corporation's assets, the corporate veil may be pierced, subjecting the director or officer to personal liability for the corporation's debts as the 'alter ego' of the corporation.

(b) *Statutory duties*

Federal and state statutes specifically impose duties on directors and officers that may be enforced by third parties. For instance, directors and officers may be liable for their violations of certain antitrust, anti-discrimination and environmental statutes, and various provisions of ERISA, the Racketeer Influenced and Corrupt Organizations Act (RICO), the False Claims Act and other federal statutes. Some state statutes also impose personal liability on directors and officers for certain corporate misconduct, including:

- the improper management or disposition of corporate assets;
- the improvident distribution of a corporate dividend; and
- the issuance of knowingly false documents, statements or reports.

(c) *Insolvency and bankruptcy*

When a corporation is in the vicinity of insolvency or near bankruptcy, many states have held that the directors' and officers' fiduciary duties shift from the corporation and its shareholders to the corporation's creditors, because the creditors are the true stakeholders of the corporation in that situation. In such circumstances, directors and officers may face liability for, among other things, management decisions that unreasonably harm the interests of creditors or asset transfers for less than fair consideration.

(d) *Tortious misconduct*

Directors and officers may be liable to third parties for their own participation in tortious conduct. For example, while directors and officers are generally not liable for their corporation's contractual obligations, they may be liable for causing the corporation to breach its contractual obligations or for interfering with the corporation's contractual relationships with third parties. Directors and officers may also be liable for:

- their own misrepresentations;
- concealment of material facts;

11 *United States v Van Diviner*, 822 F 2d 960 (10th Cir 1987); *Birbara v Locke*, 99 F 3d 1233 (1st Cir 1996).

- failure to make adequate disclosures to creditors and customers; or
- conversion of property, including money, that belongs to third parties for their own use or for the benefit of their corporation.

(e) *Patent and copyright infringement*

In some jurisdictions, courts have imposed liability on directors and officers for their corporation's infringement of other's intellectual property when they have approved, participated in or failed to prevent such infringement.

1.4 Common defences to and exemptions from liability

The best defence to any claim of wrongdoing is that the corporate fiduciary complied with his duties of diligence and loyalty. To establish such performance, a director will frequently need documentation or other proof of what was done, considered, reviewed or rejected. The careful, accurate and complete preparation of corporate minutes for meetings of the board and its committees may be critical to successfully establishing defences against liability.

The following sets forth the most common affirmative defences generally available to directors and, sometimes, officers.

(a) *Business judgement rule*

The business judgement rule is "a presumption that in making a business decision the directors of a corporation acted on an informed basis, in good faith in the honest belief that the action taken was in the best interests of the company".[12] While the application, contours and scope of the business judgement rule differ from state to state, there are five prerequisites that must generally be present before the rule will apply:

- The directors made a business decision. The rule does not apply when a director fails to act or abdicates his responsibilities;
- The directors were 'disinterested' in the transaction or subject matter at issue;
- The directors were informed in making their decision;
- The directors acted in good faith; and
- The directors' conduct was not an abuse of discretion.

A plaintiff challenging a director's decision bears the burden of proving that at least one of those elements is not present. If a plaintiff is able to do so, the burden shifts to the director to prove the 'entire fairness' of the transaction.[13] This standard can be a very high burden because the director must establish his utmost good faith and the most scrupulous inherent fairness of the transaction, in terms of both fair dealing and fair price.[14] A director's subjective belief as to the fairness of a transaction is not sufficient for this purpose.[15]

12 *Aronson v Lewis*, 473 A 2d 805, 812 (Del 1984).
13 *Grobow v Perot*, 539 A 2d 180 (Del 1988).
14 *Cede & Co v Technicolor, Inc*, 634 A 2d 345 (Del 1993).
15 *AC Acquisitions Corp v Anderson, Clayton & Co*, 519 A 2d 103 (Del Ch 1986).

(b) *Dissent*

A director may avoid liability for certain board decisions by establishing that he did not vote for the challenged decision. Accordingly, if a director does not support a board decision, he should affirmatively dissent and should be sure the dissent is recorded in the board minutes by name. A director's failure to vote, because of either his absence from the meeting or his decision to abstain from the vote, is not usually a defence.

(c) *Reliance*

Reliance upon qualified persons, such as officers, experts, board committees and attorneys, may be a defence to liability if the reliance is in good faith and with the proper degree of care. In performing their duties, directors may rely on information, opinions, reports or statements, including financial statements and other financial data prepared or presented by officers or employees of the corporation, legal counsel, public accountants, other professionals or a committee of the board, provided the information or advice relied upon is within the expertise or qualifications of the source. Directors will be unable to utilise this defence if they have knowledge that would cause their reliance to be unwarranted. Moreover, although directors may delegate certain responsibilities to others, they may not abdicate their responsibilities by completely ignoring the matter being delegated.

(d) *Ratification*

Ratification of board decisions by shareholders, if made with full disclosure, may constitute a defence to an action against the directors. Such ratification must be the free, voluntary and informed act of the shareholders. For a complete defence, ratification by 100% of the shareholders following full disclosure of all material facts may be necessary.

(e) *Liability relief statutes*

Most states have enacted statutes intended to provide relief from some of the burdens of liability imposed on corporate directors. While the level of protection varies from state to state, the statutes generally provide limited protection and most do not relieve the following types of liability:

- breach of the duty of loyalty;
- acts not in good faith;
- liability to third parties other than the corporation and its shareholders;
- non-monetary relief;
- liability under federal statutes;
- liability in an officer capacity; or
- liability for defence costs.

2. Who can bring claims

Claims against directors and officers can be made by a variety of parties, including the company, shareholders and, in certain situations, third parties.

2.1 **The company**

A corporation may bring a direct action against current or, more often, former directors and officers for breaching duties to the corporation or its shareholders. The corporation's board of directors generally has the power to determine whether such a lawsuit should be filed against the corporation's directors and officers and, if it is filed, controls all strategic decisions regarding the litigation.

When a corporation is insolvent or bankrupt, an entity that 'stands in the shoes' of the corporation, such as a trustee, receiver or liquidator, may also initiate a claim directly against current or former directors or officers of the corporation. The plaintiffs in those cases will often allege that the directors and officers fraudulently transferred or misappropriated funds, or engaged in gross mismanagement, causing the corporation's insolvency or bankruptcy.

2.2 **Shareholders on behalf of the company**

A derivative action may be brought by one or more shareholders on behalf and for the benefit of the corporation to recover losses or damages suffered by the corporation. If harm or loss is suffered directly by the corporation, thereby reducing the value of the corporation's assets, shareholders are usually required to bring a derivative lawsuit, rather than a direct lawsuit.

Derivative lawsuits are frequently brought against incumbent directors who, because of their own self-interest, elect not to authorise such an action by the corporation against themselves or other directors and officers. Recovery in a derivative lawsuit is paid to the corporation, not to the shareholders who brought the action, although the fees and expenses of the shareholders' attorneys are usually paid if a favourable settlement or judgment is obtained.

Because a derivative action is brought on behalf of the corporation, and because directors are normally entitled to deference in their corporate decisions (including the decision as to whether to pursue legal action), a shareholder seeking to bring a derivative claim must usually first either demand that the board authorise the company to prosecute the claim directly or demonstrate the futility of making such a demand.[16] The primary exception to the demand requirement is where a demand would be useless or futile because the directors are "incapable of reaching an impartial decision to pursue litigation".[17]

In the face of a derivative lawsuit, directors will often appoint a special litigation committee comprised of disinterested directors to conduct an independent evaluation as to whether pursuing the proposed litigation is in the best interests of the corporation. Generally, if the committee is independent in both its investigation and conclusions, a court will defer to the committee's decisions on whether continuing or terminating the litigation is in the best interest of the corporation.[18]

---

16 *Kamen v Kemper Fin Servs, Inc*, 500 US 90 (1991); *Levner v Saud*, 903 F Supp 452 (SDNY 1994), *aff'd*, 61 F 3d 8 (2d Cir 1995).

17 *Alabama By-Products Corp v Cede & Co*, 657 A 2d 254 (Del 1995); *Aronson v Lewis*, 473 A 2d 805, 811-12 (Del 1984).

18 *Kaplan v Wyatt*, 499 A 2d 1184 (Del 1985).

2.3 Shareholders on their own account

Shareholders have standing, individually or in class actions, to sue directors and officers in a variety of situations where direct harm results to one or more, but not all, of the shareholders.

Most commonly, shareholders will bring class action lawsuits against directors and officers for misrepresentations or omissions of material information about the corporation or its financial performance, condition or prospects. Two federal securities statutes – the Securities Act of 1933, which regulates the issuance of securities, and the Securities Exchange Act of 1934, which pertains to subsequent trading and reporting activities – generate the greatest and most severe source of securities claims against directors and officers of public corporations. In addition, change of control situations often lead to additional sources of claims by shareholders.

(a) The Securities Act of 1933

The Securities Act governs the conduct of issuers, underwriters and dealers in connection with the issuance of securities by the corporation. The sections of the act most often giving rise to civil liability of directors and officers include Sections 11, 12 and 15.

Section 11 imposes civil joint and several liability against a corporation, its directors and officers, and others for material misrepresentations or omissions in a company's registration statement filed with the Securities and Exchange Commission (SEC) in connection with a public offering of securities by the corporation. Most commonly, a Section 11 claim is brought by and on behalf of investors who purchased securities in a public offering and who allege that the purchase price of those securities was artificially inflated due to misrepresentations of material facts in the registration statement. In order to establish a *prima facie* case under Section 11, a plaintiff need not allege intentional fraud or even negligent conduct on the part of the defendants. Rather, the statute imposes liability if the registration statement contains a misrepresentation or omission of material facts, subject to certain defences. Once a plaintiff satisfies the relatively low pleading burden under Section 11, the director and officer defendants may attempt to rebut liability by establishing one of the following affirmative defences, among others:

- They exercised due diligence by conducting a reasonable inquiry into the truthfulness of the registration statement; or
- The plaintiff knew of the misstated or omitted facts when he purchased the securities.

Section 12(2) imposes liability on any person who offers or sells securities by using a prospectus or other disclosure containing a materially false statement or omission of fact. While a plaintiff must establish privity of contract with the issuer of the security, he need not allege fraud or negligence in order to plead a cognisable claim under Section 12(2).

Section 15 of the Securities Act imposes 'controlling person' liability on anyone (including a director) who does not directly violate Section 11 or 12, but who controls a direct violator.

(b) *The Securities Exchange Act of 1934*

Section 10(b) of the Securities Exchange Act, and Rule 10b-5, broadly prohibit the use of any manipulative or deceptive device, the making of any misrepresentation or omission of any material fact, and the commission of any practice that operates as a fraud or deceit upon any other person in connection with the purchase or sale of securities. Section 20(a) of the act imposes liability upon any person who directly or indirectly controls a person who has committed that underlying violation. These 'catch-all' anti-fraud provisions apply to the purchase or sale of securities in the open market (eg, on a securities exchange) when the company or its directors and officers issued false or misleading information that artificially increases or decreases the market price of the securities. These statutes are designed to ensure that all market participants have access to the same information when making investment decisions and are pleaded in nearly every securities class action lawsuit.

In order to establish a claim under Section 10(b), a plaintiff must allege that:

- he is a purchaser or seller of securities;
- the defendant made a misrepresentation or omission of a material fact;
- the defendant acted with scienter (ie, an intent to defraud or a reckless disregard for truthfulness);
- the plaintiff justifiably relied on the defendant's misrepresentation or omission (although this reliance is presumed if the securities transaction occurred on an efficient securities exchange); and
- the defendant's misrepresentation or omission proximately caused the plaintiff's damages.

(c) *Change of control situations*

The susceptibility and frequency of litigation against directors materially increase following a company's involvement in a merger or acquisition. Directors are the central figures in change of control contests and generally have an inherent conflict between and among:

- their duty to shareholders to ensure that they receive a fair and maximum price for their shares;
- their duty to the corporation to protect its best interests as a corporate entity; and
- their self-serving interest of preserving their own personal jobs and security.

In case of a sale of control, directors are under an obligation to act reasonably to seek the transaction offering the best value reasonably available to the shareholders. However, given the inherent conflicts, virtually any decision reached by corporate managers involving a change of control situation may be subject to attack as an alleged violation of the fiduciary duties of the directors.

By definition, directors of the target company are intimately involved in any takeover. They analyse and respond to the takeover proposal on behalf of the corporation and its shareholders. Accordingly, they frequently become the focus of litigation when someone becomes dissatisfied with the directors' response to a proposal. Depending on the nature of the proposal and the board's response to it, shareholders of the corporation, the persons or entity making the proposal, creditors and regulatory agencies may each be potential plaintiffs.

The primary claims against directors, and sometimes officers, in change of control situations include the following.

(i) *Resistance to hostile takeovers*

Directors of a target company who resist a hostile takeover attempt can be vulnerable to disgruntled shareholders who allege that they were deprived of the opportunity to sell their shares at a higher offering price. While courts have given significant deference to directors when deciding an appropriate response to a hostile takeover bid, such claims are not uncommon and settlements or at least a plaintiff attorneys' fee award in such litigation can be material.

(ii) *Approval of friendly takeovers*

The directors of a target company who approve an acquisition of their company are also frequently sued by shareholders who allege that the directors failed to make an informed decision regarding the adequacy of the purchase price or that they failed to 'shop' the company or otherwise failed to get the best terms. These cases are typically less severe than the hostile takeover case, since the potential recoverable damages are usually much lower. Shareholders in this type of litigation frequently seek a 'bump-up' in the purchase price, as opposed to the entire acquisition premium. These types of case usually either settle for a relatively modest amount or are eventually dismissed for lack of merit.

(iii) *Pre-acquisition mismanagement*

After a company is acquired, the new owners and their appointed managers may determine that the directors and officers of the acquired company mismanaged the company prior to the acquisition. These claims are not common because the acquiring company typically conducts a thorough due diligence investigation before agreeing to purchase the company. However, this type of claim can be particularly problematic for the defendant directors and officers since they no longer control the company or its indemnification or insurance programmes.

(iv) *Failure to disclose*

Change of control activity frequently results in class action securities lawsuits against the directors and officers of the target company, alleging that they did not accurately, completely or timely disclose the existence of their negotiations or other related material information about the transaction. Courts have refused to articulate a bright-line test for determining when such negotiations must be publicly disclosed. Directors and officers are thus placed in a dilemma of not wanting to disclose the existence and terms of the negotiations either prematurely or delinquently. If disclosure is too early and the transaction does not occur as disclosed, shareholders who purchased stock after the disclosure will allege they were injured because the defendants artificially inflated the stock price by the premature disclosure. If disclosure is too late, shareholders who sold their stock prior to the disclosure will allege that they were injured because they sold their stock prior to the large price increase following the merger announcement. This disclosure exposure exists with respect to directors and officers of both the target company and the acquiring company. In addition, the exposure exists not only with respect to the timing of voluntary disclosures, but also with respect to the directors' and officers' response to inquiries from analysts or reporters regarding rumoured negotiations.

(v) *Mismanagement*

Directors and officers of the acquiring company can also incur liability exposure in connection with the management of the acquired company or the disclosure of the likely effects or actual results of the transaction. This exposure has proven particularly problematic when the acquisition is part of a diversification programme of the acquiring company, as directors and officers of the acquiring company frequently have little experience with respect to the management of a company in a completely new industry or market.

2.4 Third parties

As set out in section 1.3, creditors, customers, contractors and competitors of the corporation may initiate claims against directors and officers in certain circumstances. Directors and officers may also be the subject of claims brought by company employees, participants in and beneficiaries of the company's employee benefits plans, and government regulators, among others. The most common forms of these third-party claims are summarised below.

(a) *Employee claims*

The most common types of employment-related claim involve discrimination and wrongful termination under Title VII of the Civil Rights Act of 1964, as amended by the Civil Rights Act of 1991, the Age Discrimination in Employment Act and the Americans with Disabilities Act. While those legislative schemes create liability for statutorily defined 'employers', most courts have held that liability does not exist under those statutes for directors, officers and other individuals. Accordingly, except in some exceptional circumstances, the primary employment-related liability exposure for directors and officers is under state and common law for wrongful discharge, retaliation, workplace harassment, defamation, infliction of emotional distress, invasion of privacy and negligent hiring, training or supervision. Because these types of claim are typically unique to an individual claimant, they are rarely the basis of a class action and thus generally present a relatively low severity of liability exposure for directors and officers. However, employment claims brought by senior officers with high compensation or involving lucrative stock options can be difficult and expensive to defend. In addition, directors face potential liability and far more significant potential exposure when their board decisions are perceived to have impacted negatively on a class of employees, such as with large-scale reductions in force.

(b) *Employee benefits claims*

Typically, individual directors are not named as defendants in claims brought by members of a company's employee benefits plan involving a plan participant's alleged loss or denial of benefits, although officers who are also plan fiduciaries are frequently named as defendants. Both directors and officers can face potential liability exposure under ERISA when they:

- function as fiduciaries of those plans;
- serve on committees that oversee or monitor the plans; or
- issue statements that may influence a plan participant's decisions with respect to the plan.

In recent years there has been a marked increase in the frequency and severity of class-action litigation against plan fiduciaries (including directors and officers) following a significant drop in the company's stock price. These class-action lawsuits are filed by and on behalf of participants and beneficiaries of a company's retirement plan if the plan owns company stock and there is an allegation that the defendants breached their fiduciary duties under ERISA by:

- allowing the plan or its participants to purchase, or authorise the plan's purchase of, company stock as an investment option when they knew or should have known that the stock was not a prudent investment; or
- misrepresenting or failing to disclose to the plan participants material information about the company.

(c) *Government regulators*

State and federal regulators have broad enforcement powers over corporate directors and officers. Amid the widespread corporate scandals in recent years, the SEC, the US Department of Justice and corresponding state regulators have been especially active in their investigation and prosecution of directors and officers involved in corporate misconduct and securities fraud. In several high-profile cases, directors and officers have been:

- liable for significant fines and penalties;
- forced to disgorge illegally obtained profits;
- barred from serving as directors or officers of any public company; and
- increasingly, sentenced to substantial prison terms.

The Sarbanes-Oxley Act of 2002 was enacted by Congress to address several areas of national concern regarding corporate accounting and auditing, fraud and officer liability, and corporate transparency. The most notable provisions include:

- the creation of an independent accounting board to oversee corporate accounting and auditing practices;
- a requirement that chief executive officers (CEOs) and chief financial officers (CFOs) of public companies participate in the preparation of financial statements and personally certify the accuracy of such statements;
- a requirement that an 'internal control report' be included in a public

company's annual report, and that the company's public accountant attest to management's assessment of the company's internal control structures;
- a ban on corporate loans to directors and officers, except in certain limited circumstances;
- the accelerated reporting of insider trades;
- a requirement that audit committees be composed entirely of 'independent' directors; and
- the forfeiture of bonus and equity compensation for CEOs and CFOs in the event of a material restatement of a company's financial statements.

Sarbanes-Oxley imposes meaningful deterrents to promote compliance with both the act and pre-existing corporate obligations. Among other things, Sarbanes-Oxley establishes:
- substantial monetary penalties and prison sentences for officers who falsely certify financial statements;
- criminal charges for the wrongful destruction of documents or for failure to maintain audit records;
- an extension of the statute of limitations for private securities fraud lawsuits; and
- criminal charges for certain federal securities law violations.

3. Claims culture

3.1 Litigation

The United States is a highly litigious society in which the court system is easily and readily accessible to any aggrieved party. Most civil lawsuits are filed by plaintiffs motivated by the prospect of monetary compensation, although some civil lawsuits and most criminal and regulatory proceedings are designed to punish wrongdoing, deter future misconduct and recoup ill-gotten gains.

Securities class-action litigation under the federal securities laws is the source of the most significant monetary exposure for directors and officers of public companies. These lawsuits are filed against corporations and their directors and officers almost reflexively following a sudden drop in the company's stock price immediately following the announcement of disappointing financial results or other negative news. According to one recent report, the average public corporation (and inevitably its directors and officers) faces a 7.8% likelihood of experiencing at least one shareholder class-action lawsuit over a five-year period.[19] However, both the frequency and severity of claims against directors and officers increase depending on:
- the size of the corporate entity (larger corporations are more susceptible to larger and multiple claims);
- whether the corporation has been engaged in merger, acquisition or divestiture activity; and
- whether the corporation is thriving or bordering on insolvency.

19 See Todd Foster, *et al*, *Recent Trends in Shareholder Class Action Litigation: Filings Plummet, Settlements Soar* (NERA January 2007) at 3.

The price of settling these securities class actions has increased dramatically in recent years, primarily due to the size of investor losses and the magnitude of the corporate wrongdoing involved in recent claims. Over the last few years, the average securities class-action settlement was between $20 million and $35 million and, during that period, seven securities class actions settled for over $1 billion.[20] While nearly all securities class-action settlements are funded by either the corporation or its D&O insurers, a few recent settlements have included significant personal contributions from directors' personal assets. For instance, the outside directors of Enron paid a total of $13 million and the directors of Worldcom paid a total of $24.7 million out of their own assets to settle securities class action lawsuits. While that unprecedented level of personal exposure may be justified by the magnitude and severity of the fraud at issue in those cases, the directors who contributed their personal assets toward those settlements were not 'masterminds' of the fraudulent misconduct, let alone 'active' participants in the wrongdoing. Rather, their liability was largely based on their failure to maintain an awareness of corporate developments, to monitor corporate affairs and policies, and to investigate events and developments. In other cases, lead plaintiffs are settling with only some of the individual defendants for the entire amount of the available insurance, thereby leaving the remaining defendants uninsured. When combined with the explosion in the size of securities settlements, these developments are alarming for even the most scrupulous director or officer.

3.2 Ability to bring class actions

The vast majority of securities lawsuits are filed on behalf of a class of investors who purchased company stock while the market price was artificially inflated due to alleged misrepresentations or omissions by the defendants. Federal Rule of Civil Procedure 23(a) and comparable state rules and statutes, set out four prerequisites for a shareholder to prosecute a lawsuit on behalf of a class of injured parties:

- Numerosity - the aggregate of potential claimants similarly situated must be so numerous that their prosecution of an action as individual plaintiffs would be impracticable. Class status has been sustained in cases involving as few as 18 claimants[21] and as many as 6 million.[22]
- Commonality - there must be questions of law or fact common to the class. Minor differences between class members will not usually defeat a showing of commonality, but claimants should be generally similarly situated, united in a common interest and pursuing the same claim for relief.
- Typicality - the claims of the named plaintiffs as representatives of the class must be typical of the claims of those being represented to ensure that the interests of some of the class members will not be neglected. If a named plaintiff's interests are in conflict with other class members' interests, the court may decline to certify a class.

---

20 Foster at 5, 6.

21 *Cypress v Newport News Gen & Nonsectarian Hosp Ass'n*, 375 F 2d 648 (4th Cir 1967).

22 *Eisen v Carlisle & Jacquelin*, 479 F 2d 1005, 1008 (2d Cir 1973), vacated on other grounds, 417 US 156 (1974).

- Adequate representation - the named plaintiff must be a member of the class he represents and must "be able to show injury to himself in order to entitle him to seek judicial relief".[23] The class representative must be able to discharge his fiduciary obligation to protect fairly and adequately the interests of the class.

These prerequisites usually exist in securities class actions. The Securities Litigation Uniform Standards Act generally provides that federal, and not state, courts have exclusive jurisdiction over securities fraud class action lawsuits. As class actions are generally much more lucrative to plaintiffs' counsel than individual shareholder lawsuits, the vast majority of securities suits are filed in federal court on behalf of a putative class.

With respect to shareholder derivative lawsuits on behalf of the corporation, only shareholders who own corporate securities are usually entitled to prosecute derivative suits, as former shareholders no longer have an interest in acting in the best interests of the corporation.

3.3 Funding of claims and whether loser pays

Except in some limited circumstances, each party bears its own attorneys' fees and expenses in prosecuting and defending claims, regardless of the result. Rarely, a losing party may be ordered by a court to pay the other party's attorneys' fees, but only when actions taken by the party or its counsel are unreasonable or in bad faith. Certain federal and state statutory schemes also contain fee-shifting provisions, whereby a culpable party may be liable for the other party's attorneys' fees and expenses, but such circumstances are also relatively rare.

Sections 10(b) and 20(a) of the Securities Exchange Act and Sections 11, 12 and 15 of the Securities Act do not contain fee-shifting provisions. Defence counsel for the defendants is traditionally compensated on an hourly rate basis, with those costs typically paid by the corporation, its directors and officers, or their D&O insurers. Plaintiffs' counsel is generally compensated on a contingency fee basis and, unless the claim is dismissed, their fees and expenses are paid as a percentage of any settlement or judgment recovery. This contingency fee structure allows individual shareholders to bring claims directly against directors and officers without the burden of funding a costly investigation and litigation, while at the same time motivating plaintiffs' counsel to file and aggressively prosecute cases on the shareholder's behalf. Given the size of settlements in securities class action lawsuits, coupled with the enormous fee awards often granted to plaintiffs' counsel, the contingency fee structure is the driving force behind the high number of securities class-action lawsuits filed against directors and officers.

Because plaintiffs' counsel has a direct financial stake in the success of the litigation and the size of any settlement or judgment, the Federal Rules of Civil Procedure provide that a class action may not be settled without approval of the court and without notice to all members of the class. Moreover, the court must

---

23 *Kansas City v Williams*, 205 F 2d 47, 51 (8th Cir 1953).

review and approve any fees awarded to class counsel. Plaintiffs' counsel will generally request between 20% and 35% of the settlement amount in attorneys' fees and, depending on the nature, size and complexity of the litigation, the court will often approve attorneys' fees in that range. Settlements and plaintiff-counsel fees in derivative lawsuits must also be approved by the court.

3.4 Plaintiffs' bar

While there is an abundance of entrepreneurial lawyers with the incentive to pursue securities class-action lawsuits, the largest securities cases are generally dominated by a relatively small group of sophisticated plaintiffs' firms which have the resources successfully to investigate and prosecute these expensive claims on a contingency fee basis.

Lead counsel in a securities class action is generally selected by the lead plaintiff, subject to the court's approval. While courts traditionally deferred to lead plaintiffs' choice of counsel, they have employed more scrutiny in recent years. Some courts have instituted a bidding process whereby competing law firms submit sealed bids setting forth:

- the firm's experience in securities class action litigation;
- its ability to complete the work necessary to represent the class;
- its insurance coverage for malpractice;
- evidence that it has evaluated the case; and
- perhaps most importantly, a detailed description of the proposed fee structure.

While some courts have suggested that an 'auction' for lead counsel is inappropriate, courts typically review only the counsel proposed by the lead plaintiff to ensure that the class receives quality representation at a fair price.

3.5 Procedural barriers

The following are the most significant limitations on plaintiffs' ability to file and maintain securities class action lawsuits.

(a) Private Securities Litigation Reform Act of 1995

The Private Securities Litigation Reform Act of 1995 was passed by Congress in an effort to eliminate many of the abusive practices utilised by the plaintiffs' bar. The primary changes implemented by the act include the following.

(i) Heightened pleading standard

Congress sought to encourage the dismissal of meritless claims early in the litigation with minimal cost to the defendants. To that end, the Private Securities Litigation Reform Act codified for the first time a pleading standard for securities class-action lawsuits under the Securities Exchange Act. In order to survive dismissal, a complaint alleging securities fraud must specify:

- each statement alleged to have been misleading;
- the reason or reasons why the statement is misleading; and

- if an allegation regarding the statement or omission is made on information and belief, all the facts on which the belief is formed.

In order sufficiently to allege scienter, the complaint must further "state with particularity facts giving rise to a strong inference that the defendant acted with the requisite state of mind".

(ii) *Stay of discovery*

To prevent 'fishing expeditions', the Private Securities Litigation Reform Act requires courts to stay all discovery in the lawsuit pending a ruling on the defendant's motion to dismiss. Courts may, under exceptional circumstances, permit particularised discovery if necessary to preserve evidence or to prevent undue prejudice to a party. Coupled with the heightened pleading standard discussed above, this discovery limitation is designed to protect defendants from the time and expense of discovery in response to frivolous suits.

(iii) *Lead plaintiff selection*

The Private Securities Litigation Reform Act contains various procedural requirements intended to increase the likelihood that the lead plaintiff who prosecutes the securities class action will adequately represent the interests of the class and will diligently oversee and control counsel for the class. In theory, the act precludes "professional plaintiffs" from serving as lead plaintiff by limiting a person from serving in that capacity more than five times in three years, without special court approval. In actuality, the act has resulted in more institutional investors taking an active role in the litigation, which has generally contributed to an increase in the cost of settlement.

(iv) *Elimination of joint and several liability*

With certain limited exceptions, defendants are liable to pay only that portion of a judgment that is apportioned to each defendant based upon its "percentage of responsibility", measured as a percentage of the total fault of all persons who caused or contributed to the loss. In determining that percentage, the court must examine the nature of the conduct of each person, and the nature and extent of the causal relationship between the conduct of each person and the damages incurred by the plaintiffs.

(v) *Safe harbour for forward-looking statements*

The Private Securities Litigation Reform Act creates a safe harbour to protect directors and officers when making written or oral forward-looking statements that are identified as forward looking and are accompanied by meaningful cautionary statements. A person making a written or oral forward-looking statement will not be liable for that statement unless a plaintiff proves that the person made the statement with actual knowledge that it was false or misleading. The safe harbour does not apply to all forward-looking statements. For instance, it does not apply to forward-looking statements:

- contained in financial statements prepared in accordance with generally accepted accounting principles;
- contained in an initial public offering registration statement;
- made in connection with a tender offer;
- made in connection with a partnership or certain partnership transactions;
- made in certain change of control disclosure statements filed with the SEC;
- made in connection with a going-private transaction; or
- made by a non-SEC reporting company.

(vi) Ninety-day look-back period

The Private Securities Litigation Reform Act provides that plaintiffs' damages be calculated based upon the difference between the value of the security on the date the plaintiffs originally bought or sold the security and the average value of the security during the 90-day period after dissemination of information to the market which corrects the misleading statement or omission.

(b) Dura Pharmaceuticals

On April 19 2005 the US Supreme Court issued an important decision concerning plaintiffs' burden of proving "loss causation".[24] In a unanimous decision, the court rejected the plaintiffs' attempts to sustain a securities fraud case based on the mere allegation that a company's stock price at the time of the plaintiffs' purchase was "inflated". Rather, the court held that plaintiffs must establish a causal link between a defendant's alleged misrepresentations and the plaintiffs' economic loss. While the court did not specify how plaintiffs could establish that link, its decision essentially requires plaintiffs to plead and prove that the corrective disclosure of misrepresented information directly caused the company's stock price to drop.

The *Dura* decision has led to somewhat fewer securities cases being filed, as plaintiffs' counsel have seemingly refrained from filing securities class action lawsuits in the absence of a significant stock drop immediately following a corrective disclosure. The decision has also resulted in somewhat more dismissals of securities fraud complaints, especially in those jurisdictions that, prior to the decision, imposed a more lax pleading standard for loss causation. In addition, the decision has given defendants increased ammunition in challenging plaintiffs' claimed damages, which plaintiffs traditionally base on a company's total market capitalisation loss, as opposed to that portion of any loss that is even arguably attributable to any alleged fraud.

(c) Statute of limitations

Prior to Congress's enactment of the Sarbanes-Oxley Act, claims under Section 10(b) of the Securities Exchange Act had to be brought within the earlier of one year from the plaintiffs' discovery of facts constituting the alleged violation or three years after the alleged violation. However, the Sarbanes-Oxley Act substantially expanded the time in which plaintiffs can file a lawsuit under the Securities Exchange Act.

24 *Dura Pharmaceuticals, Inc v Broudo*, 161 L Ed 2d 577, 125 S Ct 1627 (2005).

Plaintiffs now have two years from the discovery of facts constituting the alleged violation and five years after the alleged violation, whichever is earlier, to commence an action for "fraud, deceit, manipulation or contrivance".

Because Section 11 claims under the Securities Act are based on strict liability or negligence, as opposed to a theory of fraud, most courts have held that the longer statute of limitations period set forth in Sarbanes-Oxley does not apply to those actions. Accordingly, claims based on a company's stock offering under Section 11 of the Securities Act generally must be brought within three years of the offering.

Other claims, such as causes of action based on a director's or officer's alleged breach of fiduciary duties, generally arise under state law. Therefore, the applicable statute of limitations will be prescribed by the laws of the state that govern the action. Most frequently, a four-year statute of limitations applies to claims for breach of fiduciary duty, although that four-year period does not typically begin until a plaintiff could reasonably have discovered the alleged wrongdoing.

4. Indemnification rights

Indemnification rights are governed by the law of the state in which a corporation is chartered. Each state has enacted indemnification statutes that govern when a director or officer may be indemnified by the corporation and the procedures for obtaining indemnification.

4.1 When the company can indemnify

Under most state indemnification statutes, a corporation is permitted to indemnify directors and officers for loss incurred in connection with a lawsuit or proceeding, or threatened lawsuit or proceeding, related to their role, position or status as directors or officers of the corporation.

Except as explained below, this permissive indemnification applies to any defence costs, settlement or judgment for which the director or officer is legally obligated to pay on account of an indemnifiable claim. In most states, though, a corporation may not indemnify settlements and judgments in claims by or on behalf of the corporation (including shareholder derivative lawsuits), as any such indemnification would result in the corporation returning to the director or officer the amount paid to the corporation in the settlement or judgment.

To avoid protecting a director or officer against self-dealing or egregious wrongdoing, the state indemnification statutes permit indemnification of a director or officer only if the director or officer satisfied a defined standard of conduct. Typically, state indemnification statutes require as a condition for indemnification that the director or officer acted in good faith and in a manner he reasonably believed to be in, or not opposed to, the best interests of the corporation. With respect to criminal proceedings, the statutes usually require that the director or officer also had no reasonable cause to believe that his conduct was unlawful.

State statutes also permit the corporation to advance expenses incurred by its directors or officers before the corporation can determine whether the standard of conduct was satisfied and, thus, whether indemnification is permitted. As a condition to such advancement, each director or officer must enter into a written undertaking to repay any advanced sums if it is ultimately determined that he is not entitled to the indemnification. A director's or officer's right to advancement of expenses may be broader than his right to indemnification and is available in some circumstances where indemnification clearly will not be permitted ultimately.

These state indemnification statutes permit, but do not require, indemnification unless a director or officer successfully defends the claim. To qualify for this statutory mandatory indemnification, a director or officer typically must obtain a final judgment in his favour. Dismissal of an action against a director or officer generally is regarded as success on the merits.[25] In addition, most courts have held that a settlement in which the director or officer is not obligated to pay or assume any liability constitutes success and triggers the corporation's mandatory indemnification obligations. However, other courts have held that a settlement, as opposed to a successful judgment, would not necessarily entitle the director or officer to mandatory indemnification.

4.2 Formalities for indemnification

The vast majority of the indemnification protections set out in most states' indemnification statutes are permissive in nature. Therefore, aside from the relatively narrow scope of mandatory indemnification discussed above, a corporation is not required to indemnify a director or officer unless the corporation's articles of incorporation, bylaws or other corporate documents specifically mandate such indemnification. Virtually all public corporations have adopted broad, mandatory indemnification provisions to enhance the financial protection for their directors and officers.

A corporation which aims to put in place the broadest scope of indemnification for its directors and officers should include the following features in its internal indemnification provision:

- providing for indemnification "to the fullest extent permitted by law";
- requiring indemnification, rather than merely permitting the corporation to indemnify;
- requiring the advancement of defence expenses, subject only to an unsecured obligation to repay the expenses if a court subsequently determines the indemnification was not permitted;
- shifting the burden of proof to the corporation to prove that the director or officer is not entitled to the requested indemnification;
- requiring the corporation to reimburse the director or officer for any expenses incurred in a claim against the corporation for such indemnification if the director or officer is successful in whole or in part;
- providing that the director or officer has a right to an appeal or an independent *de novo* determination as to indemnification entitlement;
- expressly stating that the indemnification rights constitute a contract, are intended to be retroactive to events occurring prior to their adoption and

25 *Waltuch v Conticommodity Servs*, 88 F 3d 87 (2d Cir 1996: "Whatever the impetus for the plaintiffs' dismissal of their claims against [the director], he still walked away without liability and without making a payment. This constitutes a success that is untarnished by the process that achieved it").

shall continue to exist after the rescission or restrictive modification of the provision with respect to events occurring prior to that rescission or modification. Alternatively, a separate indemnification contract could be executed by the corporation and the director or officer;

- expressly stating that any director or officer who serves on behalf of a subsidiary of the corporation or any employee benefit plan of the corporation or such subsidiary is deemed to be providing such service at the request of the corporation. Thus, a director or officer of a subsidiary will be entitled to indemnification from both the subsidiary and the parent company; and
- requiring indemnification of expenses incurred by a director or officer as a plaintiff in a suit only if the board of directors approves prosecution of the suit by the director or officer.

4.3 How indemnification works

In the absence of mandatory indemnification because the claim was successfully defended, indemnification is not automatic but must be authorised case by case, based on whether the applicable standards of conduct were satisfied. Under most state statutes, the determination as to whether indemnification is authorised may be made by one of the following:

- the board of directors, by a majority vote of directors who are not parties to the proceeding;
- independent legal counsel in a written opinion;
- a majority of all shareholders; or
- a court.

The determination of whether the standard of conduct was satisfied need not await termination of the underlying proceeding and the right to indemnification is not generally contingent on the result of the proceeding. Even if charges made against a director or officer in the underlying action are true, most states permit indemnification provided the director or officer acted in good faith and in the reasonable belief he was acting in the corporation's best interests.

If a corporation denies a request for indemnification, the director or officer may seek judicially to enforce the indemnification rights by asserting a claim against the corporation. A court will then make an independent determination as to whether the director or officer is entitled to the indemnification. If a court determines that indemnification or advancement was improperly denied, some courts have allowed the director or officer to recover the reasonable fees and expenses he incurred in enforcing his indemnification rights.

4.4 What cannot be indemnified

Even if a corporation agrees to indemnify its directors and officers to the fullest extent permitted by law, the directors and officers still face the risk of personal, non-indemnifiable exposure. The circumstances under which indemnification is either legally not permitted or otherwise unavailable differ slightly from state to state, but generally include the following.

(a) ***Derivative lawsuits***

Most state indemnification statutes prohibit indemnification of settlements and judgments in claims by or on behalf of the corporation, including shareholder derivative lawsuits. Because a shareholder instigates and prosecutes the claim against the directors and officers on behalf of the corporation and any recovery obtained in that litigation is paid into the corporation, this limitation is intended to avoid the circularity which would result if funds received by the corporation in the litigation were simply returned to the defendant director or officer in the form of indemnification. Even with respect to defence costs incurred in this type of claim, indemnification is not permitted under most state statutes if the director or officer is adjudged liable to the corporation, unless and only to the extent that a court determines that the defendant director is fairly and reasonably entitled to indemnification for the expenses.

(b) ***Standards of care***

Most state indemnification statutes permit indemnification only if the director's or officer's conduct was in good faith and he reasonably believed that the conduct was in the best interests of the corporation, or at least not opposed to the corporation's best interests. In the case of criminal proceedings, the director or officer must have had no reasonable cause to believe the conduct was unlawful. Conduct violating these standards may not be indemnified.

(c) ***Violations of certain statutes***

Indemnification for violations of the federal securities laws may be precluded by public policy or by constitutional pre-emption principles. The longstanding view of the SEC is that such indemnification is against public policy and unenforceable.[26] In the view of the SEC, indemnification of federal securities law violations would defeat the deterrent effect intended by those laws and therefore should not be permitted. This same reasoning is potentially applicable to indemnification under other federal statutes, such as RICO, antitrust laws and the Foreign Corrupt Practices Act of 1977.

(d) ***Financial inability to pay***

Even if indemnification is legally permissible, a corporation may be financially unable to fund the indemnification, either because it is insolvent or because of cash-flow constraints. Not only does a corporation in bankruptcy have limited, if any, ability to indemnify, but even solvent corporations may have difficulty funding the magnitude of losses often incurred in suits against directors and officers without materially impairing the corporation's business activities.

26 See, for example, 17 CFR Paragraphs 229.510 and 229.512(h).

(e) ***Regulated companies***

Various federal and state statutes applicable to certain types of regulated company, such as banks, savings and loans and mutual funds, limit or prohibit indemnification in certain circumstances.

5. D&O insurance

5.1 Availability of D&O insurance

State indemnification statutes permit a corporation to purchase D&O insurance, which covers both loss indemnifiable by the corporation and loss not indemnifiable by the corporation. As a result, virtually all publicly held corporations and many privately held corporations maintain D&O insurance. According to a recent survey of approximately 2,700 companies, 99% of the participants reported having D&O insurance and all participants reported that they were able to obtain D&O coverage.[27]

5.2 Local rules on cover provided under a non-domestic D&O policy

The D&O insurance market in the United States is generally accessible by non-domestic insurers. In order to avoid negative US tax and jurisdictional consequences, some non-domestic insurers conduct all business with US insureds solely outside the United States through foreign brokers, who then transact with US brokers. These non-domestic insurers monitor and control claims through US attorneys, who can act on the non-domestic insurer's behalf without subjecting the insurer to the jurisdiction of the US courts.

D&O policies that are sold in the United States can be issued on either an 'admitted' or 'non-admitted' basis. To be an 'admitted' policy, the insurer must be licensed, and satisfy various regulatory requirements, in the state in which the policy is sold, and the regulator must approve the policy form and the insurer's rate schedule. Insureds have numerous regulatory protections if they purchase an admitted policy from a licensed insurer and insureds thus strongly prefer that type of policy.

A 'non-admitted' policy need not comply with many of those regulatory requirements, but the insureds do not have many of the regulatory protections associated with the admitted policies. Even insurers selling non-admitted policies, though, are required to make certain filings with, and pay certain taxes to, the respective state and are subject to certain regulatory restrictions.

No US law specifically prohibits or restricts a multinational company from purchasing a global D&O policy for itself and its US subsidiaries. Accordingly, a non-domestic corporation normally may insure both itself and its US subsidiaries under the same policy, whether issued by a US or foreign insurer. Moreover, D&O policies issued in the United States are typically written to provide worldwide coverage, subject only to the limitations imposed by any other more restrictive country.

---

27 See Tillinghaust-Towers Perrin, *Directors and Officers Liability, 2005 Survey on Claims and Insurance Purchasing Trends* at 18.

Venezuela

Francisco M Castillo
Hoet Peláez Castillo & Duque

1. Directors' duties

The term 'director' usually refers to members of a board of directors of a company, but in Venezuela, except in rare cases, the law does not require companies to have a board of directors. A company can be incorporated as long as it has a shareholders' assembly, a comptroller and a representative, to whom the law refers as 'administrator'.

The shareholders have the supreme power over decisions concerning the company and the law reserves certain matters to their decision. The administrator or administrators are empowered to represent the company in:

- its dealings with third parties, and as regards decisions on all matters not reserved to, or previously decided by the shareholders;
- the administration of the company; and
- the running of its business.

The existence of a board of directors means that the powers of the administrator are shared between two different company organs – the executive officers and the directors - but both are usually considered by law to form a unique body of administrators to whom the law assigns duties and responsibilities. Therefore, every director is legally also an administrator.

Although for the sake of consistency we have followed the structure and terminology of the other chapters in this book, it may be useful to remember that in Latin countries a difference exists between:

- 'duties', which are imposed by law and result in penalties if not performed; and
- 'obligations', which are owed towards one or more parties and which result in liability for reparation if not performed.

Breach of duties, in this sense, may occasionally cause damage to third parties and damage caused by such breach will create an obligation to remedy it. Duties are owed not to anyone in particular, but to the state or society or some other body - in our case, the shareholders of the company; whereas every obligation has a creditor.

1.1 Nature of the duties

The first and most fundamental legal duty of any person is not to cause damage to any other person or entity, either deliberately or through negligence, imprudence or failure to observe any laws and regulations pertaining to the act. This is a personal general duty and applies individually to directors in their personal or corporate acts. Breach of this duty creates an obligation to repair the damage caused, except in rare cases. This is the main source of tort liability and the foundation of the liability of the directors towards individual shareholders and third parties.

As in Venezuela, directors are legally grouped with representatives of the company as 'administrators', duties are shared. The directors are empowered to make decisions on particular matters and the representatives act to implement those decisions.

The general duties of the administrators issue from:

- laws;
- the company's act of incorporation and bylaws;
- decisions of the shareholders; and
- internal decisions of the board of directors.

Although the Commercial Code in one instance refers to the 'mandate' of the administrators, the general understanding is that they are not attorneys in fact or agents of the company, but rather officers with specific functions. In this sense, the law and legal commentators refer to them as 'direction employees' and include them as benefiting from labour laws. The company's relationship with a director is similar to that of a public entity with a public office holder, in the sense that the director partially creates the will of the company and is not an external agent. In this sense, when the law speaks of 'mandate', it should be taken as meaning 'function'.

From the point of view of the company, directors collectively are an 'organ', which is to say that they have a predetermined function in the process of creating the collective will of the company, as a legally recognised person with separate rights, duties and obligations.

(a) Implied duties

Neither the law nor, usually, the bylaws include any general description of directors' duties. The bylaws generally state the matters which are reserved to the board of directors, the number and the manner of appointment and duration of office of the directors.

Nor do legal commentators generally make special mention of directors' duties, as they are generally understood to be implicit in the standard of behaviour that is expected and their classification or expression leads to no different standards of behaviour or different consequences in the event of any breach.

Nevertheless, it is clear from their functions and legal obligations that the directors have a duty to:

- attend all board meetings and ensure that they are adequately reported in the minutes;
- decide all company matters within their function with good faith, diligence, prudence and in accordance with the law, the bylaws and decisions of the shareholders;

- implement and ensure that all decisions of shareholders' meetings are carried out fully;
- abstain from divulging confidential company matters or acting on them to the detriment of the company or its shareholders; and
- oversee all company activity and ensure that accurate records, accounting and company documents are properly kept.

Directors are not held to any standard of skill and knowledge in their decisions relating to company affairs, but are chosen by the shareholders for their personal characteristics. Their failure to appraise a situation or take appropriate decisions has no other consequence than to discredit them before the shareholders.

(b) ***Legal obligations***

The Commercial Code (Article 266) makes all administrators jointly and severally liable towards the company, individual shareholders and third parties for damage caused as a result of failure to comply with:

- the effective receipt by the company of amounts that are declared to have been paid by the shareholders. This includes not only the payment of capital, but also any other amounts that the company states it has received from the shareholders which have been or are to be used in the company's business;
- the 'real existence' of the dividends decreed. This refers to the reality of earnings which by law can be used to pay dividends (Article 307 of the Commercial Code), which limits such dividends to liquid earnings (ie, that really exist in cash form and have been fully received by the company before decreeing the dividend). This sets an upper limit on dividends for all companies; but companies whose shares are quoted on the Caracas Stock Exchange also have a lower limit established by law (ie, 50% of the earnings that could be distributed as dividends to shareholders in any given year);
- the due performance and execution of decisions made at shareholders' meetings; and
- the 'exact performance' of all duties attributed to them in the law and the company bylaws (which include the articles of incorporation).

Duties expressly attributed in the law to all administrators are as follows:

- to have a number of shares deposited in the company vaults as a guarantee against possible liabilities. This is an individual obligation of each administrator and they are jointly obligated to see that it is performed by all;
- to ensure that accounting books required by law are maintained by all those dedicated to commerce (diaries, ledgers and inventory books) and other books specially required by law for companies (shareholders' meetings, directors' meetings, shareholders' register), are properly and legally maintained, and are up to date;
- to ensure that shareholders have access to the shareholders' register and that the comptroller has access to all books;

- to have a summary balance sheet drawn up every six months and provided to the comptroller;
- to see that the company accounts are prepared according to the law and general rules of accounting, and to vouch for the veracity of the amounts expressed therein and in any supporting documents;
- to have an inventory made of the company assets and a general balance made at the end of each commercial period (yearly). The inventory and balance must be presented to the comptroller at least 30 days before the date of the general shareholders' meeting at which it is to be examined;
- to give notice to the other directors of the company whenever the director has an interest contrary to that of the company, and to abstain from voting in meetings when the administrator has a conflict of interest with the company in the matter discussed;
- to abstain from voting their shares or having them voted in matters pertaining to the approval of balances, approval of the administration or the administrator's responsibility towards the company;
- to give the general shareholders' meeting an account of the administration of the past year;
- to convene the annual general shareholders' meeting each year and other shareholders' meetings whenever necessary, or when 20% or more of the shareholders so request;
- to convene a shareholders' meeting whenever the capital is eroded by one-third, to decide whether the shareholders will repay the lost capital or reduce the capital to the existing sum;
- to stop all company business and proceed to liquidation if the capital diminishes to less than one-third of its statutory amount, convening a shareholders' meeting to decide on whether to continue the liquidation or restart the company;
- to ensure that there are no avoidable hazards in the workplace for employees by overseeing and implementing the rules deriving from the pertinent law and regulations;
- to ensure that no environmental degradation results from the company's actions by complying with the pertinent law and its regulations;
- to ensure that all applicable taxes are declared (eg, income tax, value added tax, municipal taxes); and
- to abstain from falsely asserting that subscription money has been received or outside persons are a part of the company, or announcing false earnings or subscriptions to obtain shares or place company obligations or change their value in the market.

For certain types of company, such as publicly traded companies, the law imposes special duties on administrators. These include duties:

- to report certain events;

- to make public declarations and file reports of certain business;
- to pay special taxes; and
- not to use insider knowledge for personal profit.

In addition to the normal duties of the administrator, some specific legal duties derive from the nature of the activities carried out by the company and are set out in commercial law, banking law, insurance law, mining law, the law of warehouses, the law regulating capital markets, the law regulating accidents in the workplace, fiscal and tax laws, environmental laws and others.

1.2 Standards of care

The general standard of care for fulfilment of the administrator's duties is the same as for the performance of normal obligations, and each administrator must proceed like a *bonus pater familiae* - that is, he must proceed with the same care, diligence, prudence, goodwill and respect to the law as a good, law-abiding and responsible citizen.

As discussed in detail in section 1.1(b), the law establishes duties for all administrators and directors must take the decisions necessary to enable the executive officers to perform them. As directors are jointly liable together with other administrators for the fulfilment of legal duties, they must also oversee the performance of all legal and statutory duties, even if the corresponding matter is not within the immediate scope of their responsibilities. Further to this, they may oppose any actions that may eventually make them liable. Therefore, company directorships under Venezuelan law carry liabilities which are avoidable only through the presence and diligence of the director himself.

Breach of their duties, whether by acts of negligence, imprudence, wrongful misconduct or disregard of the laws and regulations applicable to the company's actions, will make them liable not for the obligations of the company, but for the damage such wrongful actions cause. Such liability will give rise to obligations to indemnify the damage caused.

Generally, directors do not, by virtue of the exercise of their management responsibilities, assume personal liability regarding the business of the company. They are not liable for company debts, unless:

- they have acted representing a foreign or national company that has not complied with the requirements of the Mercantile Registry;
- they have carried out business after the company should legally have been in liquidation; or
- they have entered into branches of business outside the scope of the objects indicated in the bylaws.

In this sense, Article 243 of the Commercial Code states: "The administrators respond only for the execution of the mandate and for the obligations imposed by law, and do not assume by reason of their administration any personal obligation for the business of the company." However, it also states an exception: "They cannot perform other operations than those expressly established in the articles of incorporation and bylaws, and in case of transgression, they are personally liable to third parties as well as to the corporation."

In Venezuela, there is no doctrine of *ultra vires* invalidating any actions of the representatives of the company that are beyond the business scope set out in the company's act of incorporation or bylaws. However, Article 243 makes such acts a breach of duty on the part of the administrators and creates for them a personal liability not only towards the company itself, but to all third parties.

This responsibility apparently does not entail a personal liability for the obligations thus incurred in the name of the company (as do those set out in first two bullets listed above), but only for damage caused. In the first two instances listed above, the administrators purport to act for a company which does not have a legal existence or right to act, whereas in the third bullet, the company does exist and the acts of the administrators are deemed to be acts carried out by the company. Nevertheless, this issue is not clear and there are no court precedents.

The general consensus is that the law concerns itself not with individual acts, such as drawing a cheque or paying compensation to a worker, but rather with general areas of the company's business. In carrying on business in areas indicated in the bylaws as being objects of the company, the administrators may perform any legal acts and agreements without coming under this liability, as long as those acts are not forbidden by the bylaws or the shareholders' meeting.

1.3 To whom the duties are owed

Directors' duties and obligations are owed primarily to the company itself, and only the company can determine the responsibility of an administrator for breach of those duties by means of a decision of the shareholders' meeting. Neither shareholders individually nor third parties can impose duties or obligations on the directors, or in any way require from them the fulfilment of any of their duties or reprimand them for failure to perform them.

Nevertheless, Article 266 of the Commercial Code also establishes a general obligation not to cause damage to individual shareholders or third parties by a breach of duties. Therefore, although the duties are not owed to those parties and they have no legal standing to require the performance of the duties, they do have a right to be indemnified for any damage that the faulty performance or non-performance of those duties may cause them individually. As the acts of the administrators are deemed to be those of the company, it shares this responsibility jointly and severally with them.

1.4 Common defences to and exemptions from liability

To avoid joint and several responsibility, Article 268 of the Commercial Code excludes the liability of directors in those company decisions and acts:

- that are not caused by their failure (ie, by their personal negligence, imprudence or intentionally harmful act);
- only to the extent that those decisions and acts have been opposed by the administrator explicitly in the signed minutes of a meeting of the board of

directors (which must be transcribed and signed in a special book prescribed by law); and
- only to the extent that such opposition has been notified to the comptroller.

This clearly means that directors are not relieved of their liabilities merely by not being present, abstaining from voting or voting negatively. Rather, there must be written evidence of the director's opposition.

Nevertheless, actions of the executive organs and representatives of the company that are neither decided nor known beforehand by the directors, and which could not have been opposed or overseen in the course of the diligent discharge of their functions, will probably not cause any liability for the directors. However, the burden of proving these circumstances would rest solely on the directors.

2. Who can bring claims

Claims may be brought by the corporation and by individual shareholders or third parties for damage caused by the breach of an administrator's duties.

This liability is arguably derived from tort as a breach of legal obligations and regulations, and not from any breach of contract, because the relationship between the director and the company is a matter not of individual agreement, but rather of appointment to a function.

For individual shareholders and third parties, it is immaterial whether the administrator is really an officer or some form of agent or employee, because the breach of his duties that causes damage bears no relation to any agreement between him and the director. The liability is always tortious.

The significance of this distinction between tort and contractual liability lies in the fact that in Venezuelan law, contractual liability is limited by the law in several ways, whereas tortious liability has few legal limitations.

According to the law, payment of reparation must extend to all damage caused directly by the tortious act. This includes:

- the actual value of the damage;
- reasonable expenses incurred to minimise the damage;
- loss of profits resulting directly from the act; and
- an amount set by the court to repair, compensate or mitigate 'moral damage' – that is, bodily injury or injury to the reputation or honour of the victim, or the exposure of his confidential information or violation of his domicile.

Indirect and consequential damages are not actionable.

2.1 The company (and its liquidators)

Through the shareholders' meeting, the company can at any time reprimand or dismiss the administrators, force them to produce company accounts or decide to claim from them any losses that the company may have suffered as a result of their breach of duties. The shareholders are also free to decide to take no action against the administrators.

Court action may be ordered by the shareholders' meeting for recovery of those damages, or to force the administrators to present in court accounts and explanations relating to any part of their management of company business which has not been approved by a previous shareholders' meeting.

To make this responsibility more effective, the comptroller has an obligation to investigate any notice of irregularities in the administration of the company, either at his own behest or at the request of any shareholder.

If the number of shareholders requesting his intervention represents more than 20% of the outstanding capital shares, then the comptroller must carry out a thorough investigation and present a full report to the next shareholders' meeting. This meeting must also be convened by the administrators if requested by shareholders representing at least 20% of the outstanding capital shares, and eventually by a commercial court at the request of such shareholders or the comptroller. If the number of shareholders complaining represents less than 20% of the company's capital stock, the comptroller is also bound to make a full investigation and inform the next shareholders' meeting of his findings.

If any administrator has caused damage to the company by action unrelated to a breach of his duties, but which is nevertheless the result of negligence, imprudence, intent to harm or disregard for the law, the shareholders must decide on the course of action and it is they who can order that the administrator be sued.

During liquidation, the shareholders' meeting continues to function and has the same prerogatives not only regarding former administrators, but also towards liquidators.

As administrators and comptrollers may block the convening of the shareholders' meeting, a number of shareholders representing at least 20% of the company's capital may go to court and present their suspicions relating to the duties of the administrators. The court will then order the comptroller, or appoint a special comptroller, to report on the matter and may call the shareholders' meeting to decide on it; but it is always the shareholders' meeting which will ultimately decide whether claims are to be brought against the administrators.

2.2 Minority shareholders on behalf of the company

In Venezuela, shareholders have no right to go to court to claim anything owed to the company for any reason, either as a group or as individuals.

Nevertheless, a creditor of the company, even if he is a shareholder, has a right of action against company debtors to recover the amount owed to him. In this 'oblique action', the shareholder acts as a creditor, on his own behalf and that of the company.

2.3 Minority shareholders on their own account

Any shareholder who suffers damage due to breach of the administrators' obligations may sue them jointly and severally. As the actions of the administrators are also those of the company, it is also liable, jointly and severally with its administrators. In this action the shareholder acts individually, not as part of a group, and the damage must also be individual. Therefore, damages do not include loss or diminution of share value.

Recently, the Venezuelan Supreme Court's Constitutional Chamber published a decision establishing a new mandatory interpretation of several articles of the Commercial Code with regard to the protection of minority shareholders' rights in closely held stock corporations. This interpretation can be summarised as follows:

- Minority shareholders, no matter what percentage of capital stock they represent, have the right to examine the financial information of the company. This includes all relevant information that supports the company's balance sheet and the company's accounts themselves. However, this right can be exercised only in the 15 days prior to the date of the general shareholders' meeting convened to approve the company's balance sheet.
- During a general shareholders' meeting called to approve the company's balance sheet, any shareholder has the right to interrogate the company's comptroller and the administrators.
- The duties of comptrollers have been expanded to include the assessment of the stock shares' book value. However, their valuation is not binding.
- Any shareholder, no matter what percentage of capital stock he represents, may denounce to the comptroller those actions of management he believes to be questionable. The comptroller is then under an obligation to investigate and report his findings to the next shareholders' meeting.
- If comptrollers fail to fulfil their investigation duties as outlined above, any shareholder, no matter what percentage of capital stock he represents, may request a court to appoint an *ad hoc* comptroller to perform the investigatory duties provided for in the Commercial Code.

2.4 Third parties

Directors can be held liable towards third parties. This liability arises where third parties suffer damage as a result of 'illegal' company acts that are, at the same time, a result of a breach of the directors' legal obligations. Article 266 of the Commercial Code clearly states the responsibility of the directors. The action is for damages in tort, as explained above.

Labour laws regulating the avoidance of workplace accidents also make the administrators personally liable and jointly liable with the company for harm caused to workers as a result of any breach of the company's responsibilities.

Where bankruptcy occurs, according to Article 920 in conjunction with Article 260 of the Commercial Code, if the administrators have not fulfilled their obligations towards the corporation due to negligence or voluntary bad management (by failing properly to maintain the shareholders' register, the shareholders' meeting minutes records or the board of directors' meeting records), claims may be brought against them by any creditor of the company in bankruptcy proceedings, insofar as such acts or omissions have caused him harm.

Environmental laws also make the administrators personally liable to the state for damage to the environment caused by their negligent, imprudent or wilful acts, or breach of environmental rules and regulations.

Normally, directors are not liable for the company's taxes, but the Tax Code makes administrators jointly liable together with the company for amounts of taxes and penalties resulting from breach of the company's duty to declare them. This liability according to the Tax Code is limited to the value of the goods or assets being administered.

2.5 Criminal actions

In Venezuela, the conduct of criminal cases is reserved to public prosecutors, except as regards libel actions. Victims may promote such actions in the sense of presenting to the prosecutors evidence that a crime has been committed, but may not directly start any court action.

Directors are held criminally liable for breach of their duties relating to labour safety measures, where such breaches result in personal injuries to employees. They are also held criminally liable for grave damage to the environment caused by failure to implement measures required by law or regulation.

Administrators, in general, are criminally liable for bankruptcies caused by their failures, such as:

- breaching their duties to ensure that the company accounts and all company books are properly and truthfully maintained;
- continuing business after more than two-thirds of the capital has been lost; or
- covering up the company's inability to pay its debts by ruinous borrowing or other questionable means.

3. Claims culture

3.1 Litigation

In practice, company directors are rarely, if ever, sued by third parties to recover damages arising for breach of their duties. Almost all of the rare cases of directors being taken to court derive from criminal acts and not from omissions or breaches of normal business practices.

This means that although liability may seem extensive in law, actions are very rarely brought to court. This is especially so because third parties prefer to issue claims against the company itself, as this is considered to be a more reliable source of economic compensation.

Litigation in Venezuela is expensive and time consuming, and companies and shareholders tend to avoid claims against administrators.

3.2 Ability to bring class actions

Class actions, which are known in some common law jurisdictions, do not exist in Venezuelan corporate legislation or legal practice.

A person can represent only himself and those persons who explicitly bestow upon him the power to represent them. Nevertheless, a person may represent himself and all his co-owners of a specific property or his associates in a civil partnership, or persons under his legal tutelage.

3.3 Funding of claims and whether loser pays

The losing party may be required to pay the entire costs of the winning party when the court has ruled entirely in favour of only one party. These 'costs' cover not only trial expenses, but also lawyers' fees paid by the winning party.

Costs awards may not reflect the total amount expended by the successful party, because there is an upper limit to what can be claimed as costs. This limit is set at 30% of the value of the matter on trial. This value must be set by the suing party at the beginning of the trial.

Furthermore, a losing party may be required to pay other costs, such as court-appointed experts' fees and expenses and the cost of the winning party's experts.

The lawyers of the winning party may sue the losing party for the portion of their fees which have not been paid by the winning party, within the same limits as stated above. Contingency fee agreements are considered unlawful.

3.4 Plaintiffs' bar

Venezuelan legislation requires attorneys acting in trials or otherwise to be registered in any of the bar associations of the different Venezuelan states and also in a national collegiate association called *Inpreabogado*; but no plaintiffs' bar exists.

3.5 Procedural barriers

Procedural barriers and formalities required in order to bring a claim against a director are no different from those required by procedural law for any other civil or commercial claim to be properly filed before a competent court. No prior court or shareholder approval is required in order for a claim against a director to be filed, except when the company brings such claim, since in this case the action must issue from the decision of a shareholders' meeting.

There is no specific provision in the Commercial Code as regards limitation periods relating to the liability of the administrators of a corporation. Therefore, general Article 132 of the Commercial Code applies. This article establishes that: "The ordinary prescription in mercantile matters is verified once a 10-year term has elapsed."

4. Indemnification rights

4.1 When the company can indemnify

The law does not expressly forbid the company from indemnifying directors for liabilities arising from their breach of duties or from reimbursing them for litigation costs associated with such liabilities.

However, such indemnification must be decided by the shareholders' meeting, as the directors and the administrators in general are jointly and personally responsible for such liabilities and have a clear conflict of interest in this matter.

After any such liability has arisen, the shareholders' meeting may decide on an *ad hoc* basis to waive all responsibility towards the company for damages arising from the breach of duties, and even to reimburse partially or totally the amounts paid by the director in the event of a claim by a shareholder or third party. It is not uncommon that company lawyers defend a director in these circumstances.

Nevertheless, for a company to establish in its bylaws that it has an obligation to reimburse such amounts would present commercial and legal problems. On one hand, creditors could rightly argue that the company is mandating sloppy and careless management; on the other, such a provision would indicate that the company is in fact condoning disregard of legal duties by its directors, so making the provision ineffective.

Further, to claim such indemnification, the director would have to state his own breach of duty as partial cause of his damage, and the principle in law is that '*nemo admitittur aut audiam propriam turpitudinem allegans*' - that is, no one will be heard alleging his own fault as cause of the responsibility of the other party.

A previous agreement by the company to provide such indemnification in the event of a breach or a legal obligation would probably be deemed by the courts to be against '*les bonnes meurs*', or the general ethical standards of society, or to have an illegal purpose, inasmuch as it would offer payments where the law has been broken.

In Venezuela, therefore, there is no culture of indemnification of directors.

Nevertheless, foreign companies that have subsidiaries in Venezuela may offer to indemnify their directors in Venezuela, if allowed by their own legislation.

4.2 Formalities for indemnification

Where considered, any indemnification would have to be decided on a case-by-case basis by the shareholders' meeting, as would partial indemnifications or waivers of expenses relating to the defence of the director by company lawyers.

Action by the director to claim such indemnification would also be contrary to the above-mentioned rule of *nemo admitittur aut audiam propriam turpitudinem allegans*.

4.3 How indemnification works

If agreed by the shareholders' meeting, the indemnification would require determination of the amounts to be indemnified and payment by the officer or person indicated by the shareholders. The administrators, generally, would have a conflict of interest in this matter.

Another type of action may justify indemnification. As liabilities are joint and several for administrators, a liability may arise for a director which is not his fault, but rather the result of an action of another administrator. In such cases, if the director is sued by a third party and ordered to pay damages, Article 1240 of the Civil Code gives him a claim for indemnification against the administrator who has caused his liability towards third parties.

4.4 What cannot be indemnified?

As a general rule of law, no accord may be made to reduce the liability of a person for acts committed by gross negligence or wilful misconduct. In other words, it is not possible to disregard the known harmful consequences of an act or intent to harm.

5. D&O insurance

5.1 Ability to provide D&O insurance

Venezuelan insurance companies do not offer cover indemnifying directors against claims made by the company, shareholders or third parties and, to the author's knowledge, this has not been approved by the Superintendence of Insurance.

One of the insurance rules that seem to be incompatible with D&O insurance is that upon payment, the insurer acquires a right to claim the amounts paid against the person legally liable for the act, which in the present case would be the administrators, jointly or severally.

Another rule militating against the feasibility of this kind of insurance is that the law provides that the beneficiary of the insurance must not be indemnified for the consequences of his own actions.

5.2 Local rules on cover provided under a non-domestic D&O policy

In Venezuela, insurance can be offered only by national insurance companies with a special permit to operate. Therefore, foreign insurers cannot legally offer such insurance in Venezuela.

Cover taken out abroad by a parent company with an insurer that is not authorised to insure in Venezuela will not be valid or enforceable there; but the director may then present his action in the country where the parent company has taken such insurance and will then probably receive indemnification by that means.

About the authors

Dan A Bailey
Partner, Bailey Cavalieri LLC
Dan.Bailey@BaileyCavalieri.com

Dan Bailey is a nationally recognised expert on directors' and officers' responsibilities, liabilities, indemnification, insurance and loss prevention. As chairman of the firm's D&O practice group, he represents and consults with directors and officers, corporations, insurance companies and law firms across the country. In addition to publishing dozens of articles on the subject, he is co-author of *Liability of Corporate Officers and Directors* (7th ed), which is cited as the standard treatise on the subject.

Michał Barłowski
Senior Partner, Wardyński & Partners spk
michal.barlowski@wardynski.com.pl

Michał Barłowski is a senior partner of Wardyński & Partners spk, one of Poland's largest and most respected law firms. He heads the firm's insolvency and restructuring group. His experience dates back to the dawn of economic change in Poland in the early 1990s and covers privatisation, mergers and acquisitions, initial public offerings, insolvency and restructuring work. He is a qualified legal counsel and a member of the Warsaw Bar of Legal Advisers, as well as a member of the International Bar Association, and he holds an MA from the University of Warsaw and a Bsc (Econ) from London School of Economics and Political Science. He is the author of numerous articles on insolvency, corporate law and mergers and acquisitions, and is the country correspondent editor for *International Corporate Rescue* (Chase Cambria).

Sheila Böhm
Associate, Allende & Brea Abogados
sb@allendebrea.com.ar

Sheila Böhm is an associate in Allende & Brea's corporate group. She studied at Harvard Law School (LLM, with a focus on corporate law and governance, 2003), at the Austin School of Law, University of Texas (exchange student, 2003), and at the University of Buenos Aires School of Law (2002). She has also worked for the US Securities and Exchange Commission (Boston District Office), Enforcement and Market Regulation Divisions (intern, 2006).

Virginie Bozonnet
Associate, Vovan & Associés
virginie.bozonnet@vovan-associes.com

Virginie Bozonnet was admitted to the Paris Bar in February 2001 and has been an associate with Vovan & Associés for six years. She is a member of the firm's insurance department and her practice focuses on litigation involving general liability, contract law and insurance law. Ms Bozonnet also advises clients on insurance law issues and takes part in the drafting of insurance policies and other documentation.

Robert Briant
Partner, Conyers Dill & Pearman
Robert.Briant@conyersdillandpearman.com

Robert Briant is a partner in Conyers Dill & Pearman's British Virgin Islands office, specialising in company and commercial law.

Berth Brouwer
Senior Associate, Boekel De Nerée
berth.brouwer@bdn.nl

Berth Brouwer graduated *cum laude* from Free University in Amsterdam in 1996 and obtained a corporate law specialisation diploma *cum laude* from Grotius Academie in 2002. He started his career as a lawyer at Boekel De Nerée in 1996, when he was also admitted to the Bar. He specialises in corporate law and corporate litigation.

Mr Brouwer's practice focuses on advising and litigating on corporate law matters on behalf of Dutch and foreign companies and their managing and supervisory directors. He has broad experience of shareholder disputes, directors' and supervisory directors' liability, control and decision making within companies, corporate governance, mismanagement, investor relationships, takeover disputes and joint ventures and private equity.

Mr Brouwer regularly publishes on subjects in his area of expertise and is a member of the Dutch Corporate Litigation Association. In 2005 he lectured on corporate law at the Free University. He speaks Dutch and English.

Kevin Butler
Partner, Conyers Dill & Pearman
Kevin.Butler@conyersdillandpearman.com

Kevin Butler is a partner in Conyers Dill & Pearman's Cayman Islands office, specialising in company and commercial law.

Francisco M Castillo
Partner, Hoet Peláez Castillo & Duque
fcastillo@hpcd.com

Francisco M Castillo specialises in contract law, mergers and acquisitions, foreign investment, banking, finance and international taxation. He obtained his law degree from the Universidad Católica Andrés Bello in 1972 and pursued graduate studies in group dynamics at the Universidad Central de Venezuela in 1976. Before joining Hoet Peláez Castillo & Duque in 1983, he served as director of registration and control, legal adviser and acting superintendent of foreign investment at the Ministry of Finance (1980-1983).

He has been a director of leading companies such as FNC (Lafarge), Fondo de Valores Inmobiliarios and not-for-profit association Christel House de Venezuela; and judicial representative to BOC Gases, CA Danaven, Atento Venezuela, Alstom Venezuela, EDS Venezuela and Snacks America Latina (Frito Lay).

He is a member of the Caracas Bar Association and an international associate of the American Bar Association, the Florida Bar Association and the Inter-American Bar Association.

Graham Collis
Partner, Conyers Dill & Pearman
Graham.Collis@conyersdillandpearman.com

Graham Collis is a partner in Conyers Dill & Pearman's Bermuda office, specialising in company and commercial law.

Philippe Delecluse
Associate, Vovan & Associés
philippe.delecluse@vovan-associes.com

Philippe Delecluse was admitted to the Paris Bar in March 2001 and has been an associate with Vovan & Associés for six years. A specialist in corporate law and capital market law, he mainly advises capital investment companies and public offering companies on M&A transactions and long-term financing operations. He also practises in the fields of commercial litigation and contract negotiation.

Daniel Del Rio
Managing Partner, Basham, Ringe y Correa, SC
delrio@basham.com.mx

Daniel Del Rio is the managing partner of Basham, Ringe and Correa, SC, the oldest and one of the largest full service law firms in Mexico. His areas of practice include corporate, M&A, foreign investment, international and financial transactions, joint ventures, real estate, antitrust, banking, securities and insurance.

He graduated from the Universidad La Salle and was admitted to practise in Mexico in 1980. He also holds an MBA from Tulane University, New Orleans. He has written articles for legal and business publications, and has been invited to speak on the North America Free Trade Agreement, M&A and foreign investment in Mexico.

Mr Del Rio has been recognised by *Chamber's Global* as one of the leading attorneys in Mexico for M&A for the last two years and by the *International Who's Who of Merger and Acquisition Lawyers*, 2007. He is co-chair of the Latin American Forum of the International Bar Association and has lectured at various conferences. He was also a member of the Latin America Steering Committee that organised the First Latin American Conference held in Mexico City and other events.

Norman Menachem Feder
Partner, Caspi & Co
nmf@caspilaw.com

Norman Menachem Feder is managing partner of Caspi & Co's international practice. He advises on corporate, commercial and financial matters, and his clients include international and domestic companies, financial institutions and investment funds.

Mr Feder practised law for more than six years at Cleary, Gottlieb, Steen & Hamilton in New York. Prior to that, he served as a law clerk first to Judge Roger Miner of the US Court of Appeals (Second Circuit) and then to Justice Menachem Elon of the Israeli Supreme Court. Before that, he was a Luce scholar, acting as a white-collar criminal specialist with Singapore's Ministry of Finance.

Mr Feder graduated from New York University School of Law with numerous honours. He also served as editor in chief of the university's *Journal of International Law & Politics*. Prior to his law studies, he obtained BA and MA degrees in literature from Columbia University.

Mr Feder lectures publicly and is an adjunct lecturer at the Tel Aviv University Law School.

Ignacio Figuerol
Partner, Davies Arnold Cooper
ifiguerol@dacspain.com

Ignacio Figuerol qualified in 1993 and joined Davies Arnold Cooper in 1996.

His practice is focused primarily on D&O insurance, including drafting and adapting policies into Spanish law, and advising Lloyd's syndicates and Spanish and foreign insurers and reinsurers in connection with major and complex claims.

He also has extensive experience of domestic and international insurance litigation and arbitration, and non-contentious insurance in the professional indemnity field. In particular, he has handled important cases involving auditors, insurance brokers, accountants and lawyers.

His experience additionally covers a wide range of reinsurance disputes, and he has drafted a numerous reinsurance contracts and clauses.

Fluent in English and Catalan, Mr Figuerol contributes regularly to the insurance press and has spoken on D&O and professional indemnity insurance at seminars and conferences both in Spain and in the London market. He is a member of the reinsurance group of the Spanish section of the International Association for Insurance Law.

Bruno Floriani
Partner, Lapointe Rosenstein, LLP
bruno.floriani@lapointerosenstein.com

Bruno Floriani is a partner in Lapointe Rosenstein, LLP's commercial practice group. While his practice spans numerous areas of commercial law, he specialises in the areas of mergers and acquisitions, corporate finance, licensing and technology.

Mr Floriani is a member of the American Bar Association, the Canadian Franchise Association, the Italian Chamber of Commerce and the Licensing Executives Society. He has authored and co-authored numerous publications, including an article entitled "The Continuing Impact of the Internet on International Franchising" (*Business Law International*, January 2002), and has participated in numerous conferences, most notably as a speaker in respect of international franchising, technology, internet law and mergers and acquisitions. Mr Floriani was recently recognised as one of the best lawyers in the technology law sector by *The Best Lawyers in Canada* (2008 edition). He received his civil law degree from the University of Montreal's Faculty of Law and a certificate in common law studies from Dalhousie University in Halifax. He was admitted to the Quebec Bar in 1984.

Marcelo Mansur Haddad
Partner, Mattos Filho, Veiga Filho, Marrey Jr e Quiroga Advogados
mmansur@mattosfilho.com.br

Marcelo Mansur Haddad is a partner in the insurance, reinsurance and pension fund group of Mattos Filho, Veiga Filho, Marrey Jr e Quiroga Advogados. He studied at the University of São Paulo School of Law; the University of Paris X – Nanterre (DESS, 1994); the University of Heidelberg (LLM, 1995); and the University of São Paulo (PhD, 2002). He is the author of a book on international reinsurance. He is a professor at the Getúlio Vargas Foundation School of Business Administration, and from 2002 to 2006 was postgraduate course coordinator and professor of insurance and reinsurance law at the Getúlio Vargas Foundation Law School. He is a member of the Permanent List of Arbitrators of the Conciliation and Arbitration Chamber of the Getúlio Vargas Foundation and a member of the International Association for Insurance Law.

Michael Hart
Chairman, Deneys Reitz, Inc
mjh@deneysreitz.co.za

Michael Hart is the chairman of Deneys Reitz and head of its litigation practice. He joined the firm in 1968. From inception, his practice has been focused on the insurance industry in South Africa, both as an attorney for individual insurance companies and as adviser to industry bodies and associations. He is a frequent speaker at local and international conferences.

Darius N Kandawalla
Partner, Bailey Cavalieri LLC
Darius.Kandawalla@BaileyCavalieri.com

Darius Kandawalla focuses his practice on directors' and officers' responsibilities, fiduciary, employment and professional liability issues, exposures and insurance. He has represented insurers as coverage counsel in a wide array of corporate claims, and is a frequent contributor to articles and publications addressing the responsibilities and liabilities of directors, officers, fiduciaries and other corporate insiders.

Philipp Känzig
Partner, Staiger Schwald & Partner
philipp.kaenzig@ssplaw.ch

Philipp Känzig is a partner in the dispute resolution department at Staiger, Schwald & Partner, a leading Swiss law firm with offices in Zurich and Bern. Mr Känzig graduated from the law faculty of the University of Zurich in 1986. He is a member of the Zurich Bar Association, the Swiss Bar Association, the Swiss Association for Debt Collection and Bankruptcy Law and the Swiss Arbitration Association. His practice focuses on bankruptcy-related litigation, litigation and arbitration in the financial sector, and general commercial arbitration and litigation.

Natasa Karambatsos
Attorney, formerly with Lapointe Rosenstein, LLP
general@lapointerosenstein.com

Natasa Karambatsos is a former associate in Lapointe Rosenstein, LLP's commercial practice group. She has authored several articles to date, including articles in the areas of sureties and business development. She has also participated in the preparation of several conferences relating to her practice, including a Lapointe Rosenstein, LLP-helmed conference on mutual fund governance and liability.

Ms Karambatsos graduated from the University of Ottawa's Faculty of Law where she obtained a bachelor of common law and a bachelor of civil law conferred with *magna cum laude* honours. She was admitted to the Quebec Bar in 2006 and was appointed as an ambassador of the Young Bar Association of Montreal in 2007.

Anastasiya V Khruleva
Trainee Consultant, Jurinflot
jurin@jurinflot.ru

Anastasiya Khruleva joined Jurinflot at the end of 2006 and has shown remarkable ability, adding a considerable share to work on a number of important matters connected with financing and corporate governance.

Konstantin I Krasnokutskiy
Assistant Attorney, Jurinflot
jurin@jurinflot.ru

Konstantin Krasnokutskiy is one of the firm's youngest lawyers, graduating in mid-2006 after joining the firm earlier that same year. Despite his youth, he has rapidly gained experience in maritime, corporate and intellectual property issues.

Marvin Liebman
Attorney, Lapointe Rosenstein, LLP
marvin.liebman@lapointerosenstein.com

Marvin Liebman practises law in Lapointe Rosenstein, LLP's commercial practice group. While his practice covers many areas of commercial law, he specialises in mergers and acquisitions, banking and finance, real estate and venture capital. He currently co-authors Lapointe Rosenstein, LLP's regular contributions to the International Law Office Franchising Newsletter and is co-authoring the Canadian contribution to *Franchise 2008: Getting the Deal Through*, as well as an article on Quebec's personal property security legislation for a West Publishing Co publication tentatively entitled *International Guide to Personal Property Security Interests*.

Mr Liebman graduated with great distinction from McGill University's Faculty of Law, where he received a bachelor of laws in civil law and a bachelor of laws in common law. He is also the recipient of the William Kagan Memorial Prize (Real

Estate), the Stikeman Elliott/Carswell National Tax Award and the Bennett Jones Prize in Taxation. He was admitted to the Quebec Bar in 2003.

Juan José López-de-Silanes
Partner, Basham, Ringe y Correa, SC
lopez_de_silanes@basham.com.mx

Juan José López-de-Silanes became a partner of Basham, Ringe and Correa, SC in January 2006. He specialises in international business transactions, corporate law, M&A, antitrust, franchising and corporate governance matters.

Mr López-de-Silanes studied at Universidad Iberoamericana, and obtained an LLM in mergers and acquisitions and corporate law from Boalt Hall School of Law at the University of California, Berkeley, in 1998. In 1994 he commenced his career in Basham, Ringe and Correa and in 1995 he was admitted to the Mexican Bar. He has published articles on corporate governance and mergers and acquisitions. He is also a member of the *Barra Mexicana Colegio de Abogados, Colegio Mexicano de Abogados*, the World Services Group and the International Corporate Governance Network.

Martín G Argañaraz Luque
Partner, Allende & Brea Abogados
mgal@allendebrea.com.ar

Martín G Argañaraz Luque is a partner in Allende & Brea's insurance and reinsurance group. In 1999 and 2000 he worked for London law firms in insurance and reinsurance disputes mostly relating to Latin America. He has also worked for the International Maritime Organization and Lloyd's of London.

Christian Luthi
Partner, Conyers Dill & Pearman
Christian.Luthi@conyersdillandpearman.com

Christian Luthi is a partner in Conyers Dill & Pearman's Bermuda office, specialising in commercial litigation.

Declan McDaid
Associate and Registered Foreign Lawyer, Deacons
declan.mcdaid@deacons.com.hk

Declan McDaid has over 10 years' experience with law firms in London and Hong Kong assisting Lloyds' syndicates, international insurance companies and major international brokers with regulatory issues, advice on business structure, risk management, claims handling across a number of classes of business, focusing on professional indemnity and D&O insurance.

José Francisco Mafla
Associate, Brigard & Urrutia
jmafla@bu.com.co

José Francisco Mafla is an associate at Brigard & Urrutia in Colombia. He was admitted to practise law in Colombia in 2001 and in the state of New York in 2006. He has studied at Universidad de los Andes, Bogota (JD); Universidad Externado de Colombia, Bogota (specialisation in business law); and New York University School of Law, New York (LLM). He worked for Cavelier Abogados from 2001 to 2004 and for Harkins Cunningham LLP from 2005 2006. He concentrates his practice on commercial law, international business transactions, mergers and acquisitions and banking law.

Alexander V Mednikov
Deputy Managing Partner, Jurinflot
jurin@jurinflot.ru

Alexander Mednikov graduated from the Russian People's Friendship University in 1998, was admitted to the Bar in 2002 and became partner in Jurinflot in 2003. His principal areas of expertise are project finance, tax law and mergers and acquisitions. In the last few years Mr Mednikov has been involved in a number of projects in the fields of business purchase, ship finance and the establishment of foreign investors' operations in Russia.

Richard Midgley
Partner, Moray & Agnew Solicitors
RMidgley@moray.com.au

Richard Midgley is a partner in the Melbourne office of Moray & Agnew and practises in the area of professional indemnity and D&O claims.

Mr Midgley is qualified to practise as a solicitor in both Australia and England and Wales. He obtained an LLB from Manchester University and practised in a substantial property litigation practice in the United Kingdom prior to moving to Australia.

During the past 10 years, Mr Midgley has acted for insurers in claims in the professional indemnity and D&O area. He has also obtained advanced insolvency qualifications through the Insolvency Practitioners Association of Australia. He is a member of a number of legal and insurance-related professional associations.

John Neaves
Partner, Deneys Reitz, Inc
jmn@deneysreitz.co.za

John Neaves is a senior litigation partner of Deneys Reitz. He joined the firm in 1980. Prior to joining Deneys Reitz, he worked in the insurance industry for a few years. He is an associate and fellow of the Chartered Insurance Institute. His practice is mostly insurance related, specialising in property and liability insurance, as well as financial markets and directors' and officers' insurance.

Susanna Norelid
Partner, Advokatfirman NorelidHolm
susanna.norelid@norelidholm.com

Susanna Norelid is a Swedish attorney. In 2005 she left her partnership with one of Sweden's largest law firms to set up her own legal business, Advokatfirman NorelidHolm, with a partner colleague. The firm is one of the country's top law firms in the field of insurance and reinsurance law.

Ms Norelid holds an LLM in international business law from University of London. She is a specialist in insurance law, as well as in EU competition law and marketing law. She represents a large number of international insurance companies and brokers, and provides her clients with services in relation to policy terms/interpretations, legal opinions, claims handling, litigation and arbitration. She is a regular speaker at both national and international insurance conferences.

Shigeru Ogiso
Senior Partner, Yuasa and Hara
sogiso@yuasa-hara.co.jp

Shigeru Ogiso is a lawyer in Yuasa and Hara's corporate and commercial group. The main focus of his practice is on corporate and business law, with particular expertise in mergers and acquisitions involving both Japanese and foreign companies. He also handles international commercial arbitration as arbitrator or counsel representing his clients.

Mr Ogiso is a senior partner of Yuasa and Hara. He joined the firm in 1970 when he left the judiciary, after serving for 19 years as civil judge.

Antal Pearl
Associate, Caspi & Co
apearl@caspilaw.com

Antal Pearl is an associate in the Tel Aviv law firm of Caspi & Co. She advises on international transactions and finance. Ms Pearl's practice emphasises cross-border transactions. As part of her practice, Ms Pearl advises financial institutions, multinational and other corporations, and investment funds.

Ms Pearl obtained her LLB from Tel Aviv University. During her studies, Ms Pearl was staff editor of faculty law review *Theoretical Inquiries in Law* and served as assistant to several professors in the fields of corporate and tax law.

Dezsõ Perlaki
Senior Partner, Burai-Kovács & Partners
dezso.perlaki@burai-kovacs.hu

Dezsõ Perlaki is senior partner at Burai-Kovács & Partners, a leading Hungarian law firm with strong international relations. Dr Perlaki has worked as a lawyer in international trade for almost 25 years and spent seven years in Frankfurt am Main as a legal adviser to Hungarian trading and industrial companies with operations in Germany, thus gaining specific industrial experience. He has particular expertise in large-scale cross-border M&A transactions, corporate law, project finance and litigation. He has been with Burai-Kovács & Partners since 1997.

In addition to his native Hungarian, Dr Perlaki speaks English and German.

Jodie Potts
Solicitor, Moray & Agnew Solicitors
JPotts@moray.com.au

Jodie Potts has over seven years of litigation experience in Australia as both a solicitor and a claims manager responsible for a significant volume of indemnity claims. Her work has involved acting in substantial corporate and financial services-related claims on behalf of insurers, as well as advising on a wide range of general insurance claims against professionals and others. She holds an honours degree in law.

Julia Santoro de Camargo
Associate, Mattos Filho, Veiga Filho, Marrey Jr e Quiroga Advogados
jsantoro@mattosfilho.com.br

Julia Santoro de Camargo is an associate in the insurance, reinsurance and pension fund group of Mattos Filho, Veiga Filho, Marrey Jr e Quiroga Advogados. She studied at the Catholic University of São Paulo School of Law and at the Catholic University of São Paulo (extension course in tax law, 2005). She gained professional experience as a foreign attorney with a Lisbon-based law firm in 2005 and a London-based law firm in 2006 in the field of insurance and reinsurance, mostly undertaking work relating to Latin America, Portugal and Spain. She is a member of the International Association for Insurance Law.

Anthony Scott
Partner, Moray & Agnew Solicitors
AScott@moray.com.au

Anthony Scott is a partner at Moray and Agnew, Melbourne. He practises in insurance law, with a particular emphasis on directors' and officers' liability and professional indemnity risks. He has been instructed by underwriters in relation to major litigation against company directors in Australia. He holds honours degrees in commerce and law.

Oliver Sieg
Partner, Nörr Stiefenhofer Lutz
oliver.sieg@noerr.de

Oliver Sieg was admitted to the Düsseldorf Bar in 1995. He joined Nörr Stiefenhofer Lutz, one of the leading independent German law firms, as a partner in January 2002. Mr Sieg heads the firm's insurance practice group and co-heads its dispute resolution practice group. He is specialised in insurance and liability law and litigation, and his client base includes many of the leading domestic and international primary insurance and reinsurance companies on the German market. Mr Sieg is one of eight members of the German Bar Association's Committee on Insurance Law, appointed by the association's president. Mr Sieg has published numerous papers in his fields of expertise and has spoken at many conferences and seminars. He is co-author of the *Handbook on Professional Liability* together with three judges of the German Federal Supreme Court.

Edward Smerdon
Partner, Reynolds Porter Chamberlain LLP
edward.smerdon@RPC.co.uk

Edward Smerdon is a partner in the international risks and reinsurance department at City of London law firm Reynolds Porter Chamberlain LLP. He specialises, and has 12 years' experience, in the field of directors' and officers' liability, and is currently involved in claims against directors in the United Kingdom, the European Union and the United States. As an expert on liability, he has been well placed to advise upon and develop insurance products to protect directors, and indemnification arrangements between directors and their companies. In doing so, Mr Smerdon has become a leading authority on the interrelationship between D&O insurance and indemnification, and lectures widely on the subject.

Jan ter Meer
Partner, Boekel De Nerée
jg.termeer@bdn.nl

Jan ter Meer graduated from Leiden University in 1982 and obtained a PhD, *cum laude*, from Erasmus University in Rotterdam in 1993. He started his career as a lawyer in 1983 with Boekel De Nerée, becoming partner in 1989. From 2002 to 2005 he was the firm's managing partner.

His practice includes litigation on policy disputes, recoveries and liability issues. He has obtained landmark decisions in the Dutch Supreme Court. His name appears in numerous cases reported in the law reports on transport and insurance law, and he frequently acts as an arbitrator.

Dr Ter Meer heads the firm's insurance and liability group, which provides services relating to all areas of insurance law, including marine insurance and liability insurance. The group has years of experience and significant expertise on general, product and professional liability. Clients include leading domestic and international insurance companies and intermediaries.

Gad Ticho
Partner, Caspi & Co
gticho@caspilaw.com

Gad Ticho is managing partner of Caspi & Co's civil litigation practice. His practice focuses on civil, corporate and commercial matters. Issues on which Mr Ticho litigates include administrative law, banking and finance, contracts, commercial disputes, corporate governance, directors' and officers' liability, intellectual property, insurance, insolvency, real estate, securities and torts.

Mr Ticho has handled many trials and has represented individuals, domestic and international companies and cooperative societies. He is well experienced in class action litigation, in which he often represents defendants. Mr Ticho also has conducted numerous internal corporate investigations and has assisted in the development of compliance programmes. Mr Ticho graduated from Tel Aviv University Law School.

Serena Triboldi
Partner, Pontecorvi Mannaerts & Triboldi
serena.triboldi@pmtlex.com

Serena Triboldi has extensive experience representing both international and Italian clients in corporate, capital markets, international and European law matters.

Before co-founding Pontecorvi Mannaerts & Triboldi, she worked at several international Italian firms, including Pavia e Ansaldo and Studio Legale Cieri Crocenzi in Rome and Milan.

Ms Triboldi completed a degree in international law in 1999 at the Universita Cattolica del Sacro Cuore in Milan. She also holds a master of laws in international business and trade law from Fordham University School of Law in New York City. In addition, in 2003, Ms Triboldi completed a course in EU law organised by the *Società Italiana per l'Organizzazione Internazionale* in Rome. While completing her law degree, Ms Triboldi was a student at the University of Nanterre, France, under the Erasmus scholarship programme. She is a member of the Rome Bar.

Ms Triboldi is fluent in Italian, English, French and Spanish.

Carlos Umaña
Partner, Brigard & Urrutia
cumana@bu.com.co

Carlos Umaña is a partner at Brigard & Urrutia in Colombia. He was admitted to practise law in Colombia in 1983. He studied at Universidad del Rosario, Bogota (JD); New York University School of Law, New York (MCJ); and Universidad del Rosario (taxation). Notably, he has teaching experience as a professor of public utility law at Universidad del Rosario. He worked as a foreign attorney for Burke & Burke in 1985. He has devoted his practice to public utility law, commercial law, corporate law, international business transactions and mergers and acquisitions.

Frits van der Woude
Senior Associate, Boekel De Nerée
Frits.vanderwoude@bdn.nl

Frits van der Woude has worked in the international insurance industry for almost 20 years. Before joining the legal profession he occupied several legal and management positions in the insurance sector (underwriting, claims handling and broking).

After graduating from the Higher School of Economics, Mr Van der Woude obtained qualifications in Dutch law and notarial law from the Free University. His area of practice is liability law, with an emphasis on general liability, professional liability, directors' and officers' liability, product liability and employers' liability. He is specialised in the defence and settlement of (professional) liability claims. He has specific experience in assessment and advice regarding national and international insurance contracts, (international) insurance programmes and the handling and settlement of policy disputes.

Sarah Xerri-Hanote
Partner, Vovan & Associés
sarah.xerri@vovan-associes.com

Sarah Xerri-Hanote was admitted to the Paris Bar in January 1992 and is the head of Vovan & Associés' insurance and reinsurance department. Her practice focuses on the drafting of insurance policies, advice on insurance and reinsurance law issues, claims handling of portfolios for the London market, litigation, domestic and international arbitration in insurance and reinsurance.